the bridge

Dialogues Across Cultures

Edited by: Talia Levine Bar-Yoseph

Foreword by: Mackie Blanton

Gestalt Institute Press
Metairie/New Orleans, La. USA

Editor: Talia Levine Bar-Yoseph, M.A.

Chief Editor in English: Mackie Blanton, Ph.D.

English Editor: Deirdre Givens, M.S., M.P.S.

Cover design: Tammy Malkov

Cover photographs: Avraham Hay

The descriptions of clients and situations in this book have been changed to protect their confidentiality. They no longer bear resemblance to actual people living or dead.

First Printing, September, 2005

Library of Congress catalogue card number applied for.
ISBN: 1889968-48-X

Published by
THE GESTALT INSTITUTE PRESS
THE RELATIONSHIP CENTER
1537 Metairie Road
Metairie, Louisiana 70005 USA

(504)828-2267
http://www.gestaltinstitutepress.com
Email: gestaltinstpress@aol.com

the bridge:

Dialogues Across Cultures

Contributing Authors

Editor – Talia Levine Bar-Yoseph

Nahi Alon
Arye Bursztyn
Michael C. Clemmens
Nigel Copsey
Iris Fodor
Lynne Jacobs
Vera Kishinevsky
Anna Kubesch
James Kuykendall
Philip Lichtenberg
Edna Manielevitch
Mark McConville
Dennis Palumbo
Lenny Ravich
Mario Rivas
Lolita Sapriel
Oshrat Mizrahi Shapira
Sa'ed Tali
Anne Teachworth
Holly Timberlake
Geoff Warburton
Gordon Wheeler

To my mother, Ya'el,
who swims so naturally
in the pool of difference.

Acknowledgements

The idea leading to this project was to produce the first book in our field which addressed the bridging of cultural differences. I believed that such a book ought to be created by writers from different cultures. The plan was for all chapters to be co-written so the readers would get an 'on-line' experience of the writers' bridging of their differences during the writing process for this book; hence, the personal accounts written by the writers follow each of their chapters.

I wish to thank Philip Lichtenberg who helped me see that single writers are as valuable as pairs, he challenged my fixed Gestalt and as a result, the book was enriched by a number of excellent writers. My heartfelt acknowledgments to all the writers, hand picked one by one, who put into the writing, energy, thought, heart and trust.

Gordon Wheeler identified the need for a book about the bridging of cultures and honored me by requesting that I compose it. I thank Gordon for this and for staying a colleague and a friend throughout this beautiful however complicated process.

Sonia Nevis, Joe Melnick and Lynne Jacobs for their unmediated practical and emotional support which often carried me through times of doubt and frustration.

A delightful smile to my professional god-parents, Erv and the late Miriam Polster, who introduced me to the poetic truth, an essential component of co-existing.

Many thanks to Cornelia Muth, the first to invite me to address differences in Germany, to my Slovak and Czech students who taught me humility and enhanced my ability to stay with diversity.

To Anne Teachworth, the publisher, who took 'The Bridge" under her wings, to Mackie Blanton, the chief editor in English, who cared to cross every 't' and dot every 'i' and to Dee Givens the English editor, who walked the last few miles next to me, I am deeply thankful.

Two dear friends are responsible for the book cover. Tammy Malkov who designed the cover with care and sensitivity, and Avraham Hay who contributed the meaningful as well as magnificent photograph – shirts, each representing a different tribe, arranged next to each other on a market ground in Guatemala.

Gratitude to my late grandmother, Anieta and my late grandfather, Nahum, from whom I learned tolerance, forgiveness, and love for people.

Thanks to my dear friends, many of whom were ready to be there with me, push, encourage, celebrate, and especially Malka Avitzour, Sylvie Goldman, Eitan Barzilai, Sid Wartel and Yochanan Cahan for their never ending support.

Last, but by no means least, special warmth and love to my two daughters, Neta, and Adi, for the grace, maturity and love in which they shared me with this slow-to-mature 'baby;' and their father, Benni, who wrote about cultures long before me.

Talia Levine Bar-Yoseph
Editor

Table of Contents

Section Four: *bridging in therapy*

FOREWORD

Introspection as a Bridge

It is a commonplace nowadays to note that language undoes us – that is, *recreates* us -- even as we are in the act of creating and honing it so that it may achieve for us what we desire others to know.

Toward the end of her strongly introspective Introduction in Chapter I to this anthology, Talia Levine Bar-Yoseph notes that she seems to have been responsible for "more questions than answers" regarding the enterprise she undertook of culling together the essays we find here in this collection.

As I read Talia's words below, I was reminded, as many of us would be once we thought about it, that inherent deeply in the precepts of Judaism is the principle that to question is a form of worship. I therefore doubt that Bar-Yoseph could have arrived at doing anything different, and we are all the better for it. We also know from this tradition that the most valuable questions are not ones with answers but ones that evoke responses. As Talia says:

> "As a researcher and practitioner, I am facing some painful questions: Could I decide to stop being an Israeli? I could give up my passport, I could try and lose my accent, but I shall remain an Israeli and/or a former Israeli in the cultural sense. The reader will have to take into account that being an Israeli at this point in my life is not just my civil orientation but also a question of cultural affiliation. The questions of identifying with a new citizenship have a certain influence on one's own cultural definition."

Bar-Yoseph's introspection, as well as the observations of the other authors in this collection, encourages us to notice that practically everyone of us on the face of this planet embody multiple cultural identities that some of us also express in intercultural ways.

In the following chapters, these Gestalt therapists and their research clearly reposition us in the world not only as professionals inclined toward a certain therapeutic practice – but also as citizens of the world who need to be more conscious of how our individual practices will and should influence global, social, educational, civic, and political policy.

This research also suggests that the question of Self entails the deeper question of global Citizenship. Bar-Yoseph consequently locates herself as a holistic Self in the center of the multiple identities reflected by her clients, by her colleagues worldwide, by the contributors to this anthology, and by the clients and patients of her contributors. Once in the center of these multiple identities, she gets to express her own evolving relationship with a multicultural and intercultural world.

Moreover, Bar-Yoseph's enterprise suggests a way through the terminological ambiguity lurking between the terms *multiculturalism* and *interculturalism*. This ambiguity often reflects an unconscious national perplexity and an ambivalence regarding how Self and Other wear down one another's will in societies such as the US, Africa, and China.

This struggle for terminological clarity of cultural realities that already exist is an issue of enormous social and political policy. As such, it is a challenge to establishing clear approaches to healing social and national conflict.

Multiculturalism is the reality of a single country and reflects the state of affairs of members of that country, accompanied by the privileges of citizenship therein. *Multiculturalism* is always an insider's reality wherever a country has multiple ethnicities and religions. Multiculturalism, a cultural state of affairs where we find mixed cultures coexisting, names what and who is native to a territory of ethnic and religious differences. It identifies the realities of the multiple national Self and the national Other.

While the research in this volume ostensibly constructs a multiculturalist frame for us, the discourse as a whole also recreates itself on another plane where we will surely eventually realize that we are also being invited as citizens and as new professionals. This is the plane of *interculturalism*.

Interculturalism, a cultural state of affairs where we find distinct cultures interacting, suggests the outsider Foreign Other. *Interculturalism* reflects the state of affairs of the outsider, the immigrant or emigrant, who enters or is invited to enter another's country, where one has to apply for the privileges of citizenship. The imperative of a separate, unique, different geography defines the intercultural moment.

Hence, the citizens of a multicultural United States or of Israel, and of intercultural lands such as Iraq, the African continent, of China, and of India -- are citizens of multiethnic, multireligious lands struggling daily to draw up a social contract for an evolving pluralist consciousness. Into these states of affairs – the multicultural and the intercultural one -- the Bar-Yoseph enterprise that we now hold in our hands invites us to enter both as citizens and as therapeutic professionals.

A clear voice worldwide from the field of psychotherapy on these issues had therefore been wanting. Once there is a voice to be heard, which Bar-Yoseph's (*inter alia*) clearly is, we are then pressed to wonder for whom new psychotherapy research, as well as foreign policy research, as well as diversity research, has been created?

The value in all of these essays is what they suggest not about clients or patients but about the professional therapist, because they suggest it is the therapist who needs to look inward to Self in order to be with the Other, their client. Some of these essays suggest this point theoretically, and without actual case studies; others do this pragmatically, and do so with multicultural or intercultural clients.

This appeal for therapists to be always ever ready to turn to Self and be with the Other on a multicultural or intercultural plain should not surprise us, because diversity education and initiatives were never designed for the "multicultural minority" or the "intercultural guest" in our societies.

Rather, by using the minority who inhabits a multicultural world, or the intercultural guest, as case examples, the point of view of diversity research is designed to make a person who fits the "majority culture" more aware of differences; and often this means the teacher, politician, police officer, grocery clerk or the therapist.

These essays are therefore not so much about the multicultural or intercultural minority client who has sought out a therapist as much as they are about a therapist from the mainstream culture who has to adjust to and put aside surface differences in the client in order to reach a gestalt healing relationship with that client.

Our authors openly face their own initial shortcomings and suggest, in theory and or practice, how they have surmounted them, and go on to suggest what the rest of us need to look at in ourselves in order to do likewise. With each new client they describe, we find in ourselves an order of shortcomings that we learn to step into and through.

In the West, for example, we must often balance a repositioning of the social order in order to make room for the Native Other (*multiculturalism*) as we must then turn toward developing curricula and training programs for the Foreign Other (*interculturalism*).

Either we create more programs to let in more internationals; or we create more external multinational programs abroad in order to allow ourselves to exit from internal present contexts. Sometimes we are actually more comfortable with expressing our curiosity about the Foreign Other than we are about the Native Other.

Without the perspective that a *multicultural* and an *intercultural* perspective bring to bear, some of us in the past may have needed to be convinced, for instance, that there were ultimately systemic, gestaltic differences between studies describing African American and Hispanic American clients and studies describing British Blacks and Whites, or native born Israeli Jews versus European Jews who once made their aliyah to Israel.

The principle that would have defined that kind of pre-Bar-Yoseph thinking rested on the assumption that only the personal experiences of the clients differed, but not that all clients nonetheless brought into the therapeutic room the same definable set of human pain and suffering and trauma from which they needed to be released.

It is not the ostensible treatments that we get to read here that are finally significant as much as it is the wealth of implications we need to mine here which hold enormous promise. This book is about more than culture, whether it is the culture of *multiculturalism* or the culture of *interculturalism*.

This is a book not just about culture – but also about society and individual human behavior. This will be a book for sociologists, anthropologists, historians, and philosophers. Let me explain.

Part of the problem within academia regarding the concepts of *society* and *culture* is that some universities list and treat anthropology or psychology as a social science, while others list and treat them as humanities.

Though social sciences and humanities belong to the larger category of Liberal Arts, the distinctively different listings do suggest a different treatment and receptivity. Within the halls of academe, we professors have been traditionally trained with this orientation, despite our prior or post-graduate life experiences.

The upshot of this kind of focus on psychology, and especially on anthropology, is that sociologists avoid speaking of culture, preferring instead to speak about *social structure* or *social norming*. *Culture* for them is too facile a term and they question it on the assumption that *culture* is a misnomer way of describing why people in different societies do what they do and behave how they behave.

Their point is that we occupy places in a society, not in a fiction called "culture," and we are driven to behave the way we do because of how we subconsciously tend toward certain social norms as target behaviors.

This theoretical point of view of sociologists also explains why sociologists in the room are uncomfortable with the term "multicultural." *Multiculturalism* suggests to the eye and ear how we obviously differ one from another, but it is the reality of systemically invariant social structures, the sociologist insists, that reflect multiple human complexity.

"Multiculturalism" for them suggests programming moments, such as games and dances and music or poetry recitals and therapeutic theatre, while *social structure norms* analysis explores the rules and norms, the norming and behaviors, underlying those ethnorelative moments.

Even if we attempted to be on the side of the sociologists and suggested that intercultural communication is also a part of the social sciences, sociologists would nonetheless counter that perhaps the term ought to be renamed Intersocial or Intersocietal Communication.

In his abstract to "Culture, psychology, and cognition" (2002), Matsumoto observes succinctly that "The study of culture provides three main contributions to our understanding of human behavior and mental processes."

"First, there is great knowledge to impart about cultural similarities and differences in behavior, and these form the basis for improving psychological theories.

Second, the study of culture is a prime example of critical thinking in the field, as cross-cultural research begs the question about whether our notions of truth and psychological principles are applicable to people beyond those who were studied.

Third, research on intercultural adjustment provides us with clues about possible psychological constructs that may be universally necessary for adjusting to life well in a pluralistic and diverse environment."

In conceiving the turn this anthology takes, Talia Levine Bar-Yoseph has entered this conversation and has given her contributors the opportunity to do so also. One way to resolve these theoretical differences, she obviously discerned quite some time ago, is to take up the challenge in the very way that she has encouraged this series of essays to give voice to the problem at hand. A volume like this one has to be exactly what it is: an empirical inquiry into the complex range of multicultural and intercultural behavior, cognition, society, and citizenship.

Mackie Joseph Venet Blanton, New Orleans, Louisiana USA

References

Matsumoto, D. 2002. Culture, psychology, and education. In W. J.
Lonner, D. L. Dinnel, S. A. Hayes, & D. N. Sattler (Eds.), Online Readings in Psychology and Culture (Unit 2, Chapter 5), (http://www.wwu.edu/~culture). Bellingham, Washington: Center for Cross-Cultural Research, Western Washington University. Cited on:
http://groups.yahoo.com/group/interculturalinsights   by   Madhukar   Shukla (10:53 AM), David Matsumoto (12:02 PM), Barbara Schaetti (8:46 PM), Sunday, February 13, 2005.

Section One

bridging of cultures

I. INTRODUCTION - MAKING A DIFFERENCE

By Talia Levine Bar-Yoseph, M.A.

The Gestalt Focus

Gestalt theory enables a dialogue across the divide by means of the value it gives to heritage, subjective experience, difference, and context. The bridge it builds across the divide is composed of meeting through separateness, listening, trust, interest in the other, and conviction of the other's right to exist no more or less than one's own.

At this early point I would like to share some personal information with the reader. I am an Israeli Jew, the daughter of parents who were born in what would become Israel. My grandparents immigrated to Mandatory Palestine in the 1920s from four different places in the former Soviet Union. They chose to immigrate along with many others who were striving to build a Jewish state amidst the Arab population already living there.

I grew up in a land of many languages and cultures. The grocer counted in Polish, the greengrocer in Arabic. Our neighbor did his sums in Hungarian. My grandfather shouted at my grandmother in Russian, but when things were peaceful, he insisted that we all speak only Hebrew. Our life was enriched with colors and smells from all over the world.

I learned how to differentiate between people in order to assess the best way of speaking to them and I was especially tolerant of the latest wave of immigrants, however funny they appeared to me or to my Israeli-born peers. And no doubt I was proud to be a second-generation Israeli with parents who spoke the same way I did. Many of my friends felt ashamed of their parents for not being born in the country, while the pride I felt in my parents, who were native Israelis, was existential to my upbringing. At that time, differences were so common among Israelis that they became the norm.

Throughout the early 1960s, I looked up at the magnificent walls of the Old City of Jerusalem on my way to school, not understanding why I should watch out for Jordanian soldiers aiming at me, yet very curious to see what was on the other side. Until 1967, those walls constituted the border between Israel and Jordan—the wall between me and "the enemy." What a way to grow up!

Until November 1977, when President Anwar Sadat of Egypt flew to Jerusalem, publicly embraced Prime Minister Menachem Begin, and signed a peace treaty with Israel, all Israel's borders were with enemy states. This meant that the only way out of Israel was by boat or airplane—even though Israel is not an island!

I shall never forget the day, many years later, when I was in my forties and living in Europe, when we packed our car with all we needed for a month-long trip, took our passports, and drove to another country by car! What a symbol of freedom—I can still feel the thrill in my body!

By the time Israel became a state in the mid-twentieth century, its character had been formed by the will and resolve of a people who promised themselves that never again would they plant themselves among the seeds of hatred and cruelty like those of the Nazi regime in Europe of the 1930s. Sadly, Israel found itself in the midst of a vast Muslim population.

Given the enormous differences between the Jews and Arabs living side by side, their mutually abrasive presences continue to evoke ambiguous relationships. Many personal contacts vary in intensity over time alongside growing hatred and resentment. I belong to a country that wishes to be a democratic safe haven for Jews from all around the world and for the Arabs who have always lived within its borders. Nevertheless, the history of the State of Israel has been marked by its ongoing conflict with its neighbors and its Arab citizens and the wish for it to become a safe haven has not yet come true.

It was inevitable that I would compose this book. Although raised in Israel, I have lived and worked in the United States and United Kingdom and worked in Eastern Europe for many years, so a mixture of languages in the broader sense of the word is part of my makeup. Gestalt theory further deepened my being as a person entrenched in cultural difference.

Why Make a Difference?

By definition, "making a difference" can mean both to differentiate and to make a significant contribution. To be able to make a difference means to enable and facilitate differences while respecting them. This book is about bridging the gap between those who differ from one another, about enabling the separate and the divided to converge, while preserving differences and holding on to the context from which each derives energy. It is about acknowledging the gap, living with it, and then finding a way to connect with the other in order to coexist.

In a purely rational manner, making a difference is more than differentiating between the possible and the impossible. Making a difference, means acknowledging differences, without aiming to change the parties of the interaction, yet accepting the possibility that such a change may occur. And indeed the word "sharing" comes to mind, albeit in its more traditional meaning: Sharing in this respect means a mutual field of contact where the mutuality has an existence of its own, influenced by, yet independent of, the particular entities or parties.

Sharing does not mean sharing thoughts in the very narrow sense (wide though that is) as much as letting the other know about our feelings. Sharing in this respect means being in mutual contact and bridging differences while acknowledging the unbridgeable.

The human experience on the whole is the same: we are all born to live our lives and to die. However, each individual has a specific personal way in which she/he configures this experience. Within the same general framework, each individual writes his/her own story. Members of the human race share the very mortal essence of their life; however, the process of reacting to the given, the choice of existing in it, and the development within it are all personal and differentiated.

Making a difference is a demanding task. It involves recognizing the infinity of boundaries while accepting the limitations of infinity. Human beings are mortal. This means that a line is drawn determining the end of each human being. This line is the boundary between life and death. It defines the day, albeit unforeseen, on which one will cease to exist. This boundary, which seems remote when we are young, has more presence and meaning as we grow older. It marks the fact that every moment comes to an end and prompts questions of time, output, capacity, mortality, and a demand to hang on to a deadline.

So What Exactly is "Making a Difference"?

- Is it hearing a baby cry, in any language, wishing you could take away the pain from him or her, and knowing you cannot swap pains?
- Is it looking into the eyes of a young mother giving birth to a child, hoping you can give her courage through your sympathy, knowing her hopes are beyond your reach?
- Does it means staying with someone else's joy without taking it away?
- Does it mean watching the other observe a religious feast without feeling threatened?
- Does it means looking into the fearful eyes of the dying, wishing you could comfort them somehow, wishing you could be there instead of them, and knowing you cannot?
- Is it acknowledging the different attitudes of people from different cultures and their beliefs towards life and death?
- Is it being able to sympathize with the difficulties of an immigrant trying to blend in without relinquishing his former identity?
- Is it accepting the fact that it is adversaries who make up and enemies who have to meet to negotiate in order to make peace?
- Is it talking to the other trying to find a bridge for coexistence rather than for taking over?

"Making a difference" is giving without giving up, reaching out and touching, giving without taking over, taking without devouring, giving without being devoured, changing, and agreeing to be changed.

There are some experiences that no human being can fully share with another: birth and growth, dream and fantasy, and pain and death. The definition of the inaccessible may vary according to religion and culture and be considered God's decisions, luck, destiny, or fate. Jewish thought holds that God knows everything, yet the freedom of choice remains. Though God knows what decisions will be made, man and woman are indeed free to make them. In other cultures, the consequences of our decisions may be defined as destiny, fate, stars, God, or pure luck.

We will shortly take a look into the cultural and intercultural aspects of this book, but for now let us consider a Jewish legend about creation and the Creator—a story about man's envy of what he perceives the Almighty's powers to be. This parable illustrates the dream of being someone else, the belief and the assumption that it is possible to assume another's position using any means necessary to become that person.

The legend relates the events that occurred after creation when man became envious of God and asked him to trade places just for one small moment. Good-naturedly, God agreed but after the time they had agreed upon elapsed, man would not return to his place as man, for he wished to remain God instead. The power of the Almighty was now in human hands and who would give up such an opportunity?

Since then, God has been forced to remain on earth while his human stand-in enjoys playing God. It seems that until this very day, the eternal quarrel between God and man continues, with God wanting to return to His original place and man refusing to give up the power he has acquired. One way the ancient quarrel is expressed these days is through the desperate attempt to fight back against the Taliban's assumption of its godly powers using a different version of assumed godly power. The dream contains the wish to be what one is not—to be the other. The assumption is that wanting to be another person and assuming his or her position, habits, and culture actually makes one become that person. Well, the dream also contains the false belief that being the other is better than being oneself and that it is an achievable desire. So man believes he is now God. Only what he really is believing is his God from within, what he configures to be God, losing sight of the fact he only assumed the position of God from without. Man holds on to God's seat as he feels God from within. The contact with the environment is lost and the sense of difference between the God from within and the God from without is lost.

So "making a difference" also means distinguishing between the internal, experienced sense of God and the external God. The ability to be in a relationship with one's internal being and the environment around is a fundamental requirement. The art of being is in the constant movement between the person and the environment he or she is in.

Gestalt views and observes differences, takes an interest in the way each culture configures the field, and strives to create enough common ground for bridges to be stretched across them.

When Gordon Wheeler first suggested I invite the essays for this book and edit it, I knew in my bones he was right, yet I dreaded the project. Every part of me feels the imprint of my culture, the pain of difference, and the delight in being defined. I have lived the meaning and consequence of conflict: the hope alongside the hopelessness. I know as deeply as one can possibly know the unique contribution that Gestalt thought brings to the hope of building a bridge between opposing parties.

As the year 2001 stretched into 2002, as 2003 and 2004 came and went, and as 2005 is now engulfing us, the world seems to be further than ever from resolving its differences and more preoccupied with attributing blame than with looking inward. It is harder to hold on to my utter conviction that there is a way to bridge differences. Paradoxically, this difficulty also encourages me to pursue this project and hopefully to contribute some hope in some small way. The human race needs whatever help, however small, it can get at this given moment.

This book will have earned its right to exist if the reader finds that it has contributed a fresh attitude towards better understanding and bridging of cultural differences. The structure of the book derives from its definition. Most of the chapters are co-authored. The writers are elaborating a theoretical stance, reporting about research, and/or illustrating some application of their work towards bridging diversity. Most of them have been generous enough also to share with the reader their inner process of writing.

As a book, it is unique because it includes personal accounts of the process of writing, which for me is the book's soul. It is my belief that this book has a soul of its own, expressed in the essence of the personal accounts of the writers and their interaction with the impressions of the readers. A book about culture, differences, and the art of bridging includes a myriad of viewpoints. The contributing authors are Palestinian, Israeli, Russian, American, British, Austrian and Hispanic and are Jews, Christians, Muslims and Buddhists. This mix reflects the colorful bridge they write about.

In today's world, the questions of ethnic, cultural, and other diversities appear to me to be becoming more profound and complex. The meaning and concept of the word "boundary" has gradually changed. The universe is smaller and travel has become easier, albeit more complex since 9/11. On the other hand, people have more first-hand experience of the different communities on this planet and hence are more aware of the differences. Some things have been written, a lot has been said, and more and more is being done to address the issue of cross-cultural relationships.

In this respect, this book in itself is an exercise in building bridges. Bridges are stretched between the contributors to this book as well as internally, within the contributions themselves. The contributions address cross-cultural issues and are also themselves examples of them. Most of the essays in this book are the result of therapeutic, cultural, or literary cooperation—a clear example of a bridge, if ever there was one.

Field theory stresses that all parts of the field are interconnected; hence, they affect each other whenever there is a movement in the field, however remote. At times then, when people in conflict are unable even to talk, let alone have a dialogic relationship, the support for a dialogue across the divide can come from less involved parts of the field. It is quite common for a third party to be directly involved in closing up the divide.

Countries get involved in other countries' affairs, therapists working with couples are invited to support a lost dialogue between partners, and judges bridge relationships outside of the court room in their chambers. This has all happened throughout history and continues in the present day.

The refreshing and hopeful thought following the field perspective of no vacuum between field components leads us further. Again, as we trust that any movement in the field impacts on the rest of the field, a fair measure of attention can be paid to a conflict or to difficulties. In fact, our interest and critical thought when reading or listening to the news can create a positive stance towards dialogue in order to support the divided parties so that they may attain receptivity and reciprocity through dialogue.

We are quite intentionally painting a somewhat political image of Gestalt, for if we can contribute to the political stature of Gestalt, we will have seen our role in this anthology as facilitating another new and unique way of bridging the divide and, in that respect, hopefully furthering acceptance of intercultural relations within those differences rather than seeking to diminish uniqueness.

What is a respectful process of intercultural dialogue? It is meeting without a preconceived outcome, all of the parties to a dialogue maintaining their own identity (the concept of who they are in their own eyes), while facilitating the impartial view of the other, as another legitimate self, ready to change the other and to change—in essence, enabling a better world to self-create.

Life can be more fulfilling and whole if one maintains one's identity, respects others, and, no matter how great the cultural differences, treats other people with respect, honor and dignity. It takes a dialogical meeting between two phenomenological fields to enable the process of bridging to begin and to make a difference. This book is about dialogical meetings between foreign entities, who recognize the context that each party comes from, and mutually respect the subjectivity in which each entity is viewed.

The philosopher Martin Buber (1980), suggested a way of relating through dialogue. The main requirements of a dialogic relationship in his view are that the parties to the dialogue enter into it with no preconceived outcome, that they are present and ready to include the other, and that they are open to change and to be changed.

This book contributes creative thinking about bridging cultural diversity and practical ways of addressing issues of doing so, taking history, interests, feelings, and uniqueness into account. It's about bridging diversity while maintaining respect for oneself and the other to a degree that enables all parties in the relationships to co-exist.

The grounds for a meeting include a sense of safety in the mutual interest of the contact, enlarging the field of choice, and allowing one to be what one is. A meeting, by definition, highlights the differences, creates conditions, and has the potential to bring about an inevitable change.

This book is in itself an exercise in the very same approach it addresses: staying with the other and with the differences and sharing the experience of sharing differences while being aware that the fact that one has agreed to be there together means change. The book is based on the willingness to experiment, to take a risk, and to be exposed differently. It relies on the interest in dialogue as well as on the acceptance that each partner in the dialogue holds his/her own phenomenology in his/her own heart. Each has his/her own subjective point of view on matters.

Let me give you an example:

"You don't have to be Jewish to enjoy Levi's rye bread," claimed a famous New York advertisement. I would paraphrase this ad and say: "You don't have to be a Gestaltist in order to enjoy this book, to understand it, or to find it useful." However, if you are, you will most likely find it speaking to your heart. Many examples in this book stem from different cultural worlds. Looking through the table of contents and list of contributors may give you a sense of the wide intercultural spectrum of this book, all of it linked to the Gestalt philosophy.

Let me establish some common ground here. Bear with me. The basic concept of Gestalt is holistic, or should we say polyholistic, since there is more than one entity involved in the Gestalt process. What if, for example, I brought forth at this early stage in my dialogue with you a very impersonal example of the dialogic relationship through a tabletop game?

Imagine an aquarium-like vessel with phosphorescent blue and green oily fluids gently floating in a transparent watery substance. When turned upside down, the dialogue within the vessel begins. The fluidity of the situation is evident. The fluids coexist as separate entities; each has a clear boundary, governed by its own chemical composition, instinct, or nature (and indeed by physical laws), both trying to find their peace and place within the constraints of the environment, the vessel. Between them they define the field—they *are* the field—leaving no void.

We understand the field as Kurt Lewin (1989) does: all parts of the field are interconnected; any place touched will affect the rest of the field. In the give-and-take process, the water and the oil find their ways to settle near each other, within the field—the vessel. Even in a new configuration, each is fundamentally the same, however differently shaped, while occupying a different space as they adjust to each other.

The dialogic relationship between people is very much the same. Each person taking part is regarded by the others—and regards them—as individuals setting out in a vessel on a journey. The vessel is neither an executive toy nor an ocean liner on a set course. The way that any of the partners in the voyage swings an oar will immediately affect the boat's course. Any movement in any part of the field impacts on the whole field. Understanding and cooperation will bring the vessel to a destination, albeit not necessarily the one originally intended. Upon entering the boat, or any shared vessel, the process of adjustment begins. Waves hit the vessel, and the participants row. The process of adjustment is an active flow of negotiations.

If the above is maintained, the different entities in any vessel will find their way to settle down with each other when they set out to achieve any common goal. Where intercultural contact is maintained, the possibility of peaceful co-existence is enhanced. Pulling together and giving and receiving mutual respect bring us closer to seemingly distant shores.

Culture

Speaking of intercultural contact brings up the need to define the term "culture" as used in this book. The term "culture" is most commonly used with the assumption that the meaning of the word is shared and accepted by all. A pilot once complained about a group of people at the airport, declaring that they had "no culture," meaning that they were misbehaving in public. Someone else corrected him: "It is not that they have 'no culture,' but that their 'culture' is different from yours." It may indeed be high time to look into the definitions of culture, as cultures are the bridgeable and the unbridgeable differences between human beings. So let us have a similar working definition when reading this book.

The New Columbia Encyclopedia (1975) describes culture as "the customs, ideas and attitudes shared by a group..." all of which depends on our capacity to assimilate such traditions and perhaps expound upon them over time, thus transmitting the cumulative knowledge to generations to come (New Columbia Encyclopedia, 1975: 696). This definition can work reasonably well from the core of a Gestaltist's perspective when working with people from various cultures.

Edgar H. Schein (1985) asserts that the term "culture" should be reserved for the deeper level of basic assumptions and beliefs shared by members of an organization that operate unconsciously and that define, in a basic "taken-for-granted" fashion, an organization's view of itself and its environment. These assumptions and beliefs are learned responses to a group's problems of survival in its external environment and its problems of internal integration .... "[C]ulture, in this sense, is a learned product of group experience and is, therefore, to be found only where there is a definable group with a significant history" (Schein, 1985: 6-7).

This definition encourages us to examine closely the concept that culture is a learned experience stemming from a group, where we also understand "group" to mean an entity with a clear boundary, a shared significant history, and a common set of assumptions and beliefs. In other words, a culture is a defined organism in the field and most of the time it is clear who belongs to it and evident that it has its own characteristics.

One arm of anthropological science involves the study of cultures. Cliford Geertz (1973) devotes a long chapter in *The Interpretation of Cultures* to the history of the definition of culture. He describes the ethnographer as someone who learns about a culture that he or she observes. The ethnographer, he stresses, is to be concerned not only with gathering information but also with the existence of multiple complicated conceptual structures, i.e., field conditions and phenomenology.

The ethnographer has to understand that both his/her presence and the fact he/she is there to learn about the community impact on the community and influence the results of the study. To the Gestaltist, this brings to mind Kurt Lewin's belief (1989) that any touch to the field changes it. Human cultural behavior, including, inter alia, manner of speech, gait, clothing, color used in painting, lines written, and choice of musical tonality, can be perceived as symbolic. All these qualities are symbols infused and suffused with meaning.

So questions abound: Is it enough to define or to address oneself to a particular outgoing message? Isn't it legitimate, or even necessary, to ascertain another person's intention when communicating with you? Does similarity across several communicative moments always imply a search for the same meaning? What do we mean when we speak of communicative intention? What effect do different behaviors have on a message containing the same symbolic forms, for example, when the same word is expressed in anger, irony, or in a mocking tone? How does the word "symbol" change when another word, of equal symbolic value, is attached to it? And, indeed, there is a need to be able to overcome the tricky differences of interpretation of mere words in different languages, or dialects of the same language. Evident observation also lies in the humorous way that the English and the Americans are described as two people separated by a common language.

The aforementioned questions can find at least partial answers when we encounter different existing cultural codes. The existence of these differences may be better understood by realizing there are (at least) two parties to every cultural discourse. The intent of the outgoing message is not always and not necessarily the content of the interpreted incoming message.

Cliford Geertz (1973) sees culture as a specific interpreted structure that is also identifiable and mutual. Culture is public because its meaning is public. The differences among interpreted frameworks demarcate a culture. We see culture as the difference between interpreted wholes. This principle corresponds to Martin Buber's concept that one exists only when there is another. Culture, like the self, is the in-between.

Culture, I have concluded, is a publicly shared, specific and identified framework in which the meaning of symbols is common. It has a clear boundary and is the in-between. Culture will be found where there is a definable group with common history that shares fundamental values, norms, and practices. Culture is a fixated creative adjustment to what was the given during the process of the development of a specific system.

In order to explore the configuration of a given culture, in order to understand it, we need to learn its polyholistic structure: its symbols, meanings, values, etc. Benjamin Bar-Yoseph (1996) suggests a way of understanding a culture. He illustrates culture as a tree. In order for a particular tree structure to qualify as a culture, its members should share the same fundamental values, rules, and norms and patterns of behavior. The fundamental values are the roots of the culture-tree. The basic values are interpreted as a set of norms represented by the trunk of the tree. The norms are patterns of behavior specific to the whole culture. These patterns of behavior are represented by the treetop.

The patterns are like the twigs and branches, some reaching for the sun and growing leaves, others drying and dying without affecting the tree as a whole. Still others are growing in different directions, entangled in branches of other trees (other cultures). Sometimes it is hard to tell the leaves of one from the fruits of another. High up, above the cultural roots and trunk, there is room for individual interpretations and varied practices. Still, in order to maintain the culture defined under study and exploration, we should expect to find some commonality where the branches intertwine, regardless of their original culture (roots). Furthermore, it is not uncommon to see branches of a tree disregard the fence and trespass into a neighbor's property, traverse that property to get somewhere else, or, albeit rare, to be welcomed to share land or area. Benjamin Bar-Yoseph (1996) claims that the essence of culture is in the processed interpretation of the basic values. Different encoded interpretations of the same basic values will lead to different norms that, in turn, will lead to different patterns of behavior—hence, the origin of different cultures. However, within this framework there is space for individual interpretation regarding some cultures more than others, as long as the interpretation does not betray the basic values and adheres to the norms.

The issue becomes more complex when we extend the metaphor: to whom do the cross-boundary fruits belong? The question does not remain theoretically philosophical, ethical, or moral, it has practical implications. If the fruit does not fall far from the tree, where does it belong—where it falls or where it grows?

Let me take this thinking a step further into the realm of the meeting between two cultures. I can suggest that analysis of separate cultures calls for potential meetings to discuss points of identified conflicts. For example, a meeting between a culture that believes the celebration of a religious holiday is a fundamental value and one that keeps the holiday because of tradition is fraught with potential difficulty. Another example occurs if the value of ethnic roots collides with the value of belonging to a new country, a new culture.

Recently, cross-cultural issues have become an important public issue as well as academic subject. For many decades, attention was paid to the relationship between the dominant culture of a country and the ethnic and minority groups, which were regarded as separate entities. The *bon ton* was for them to be incorporated into the predominant culture.

These days there is a change. The melting pot concept is cooling off. The new perspective is interest in intercultural relationships and in shaking off the belief that in order to belong, all people have to be the same. In other words, there has been a shift of focus and a change from the attempt to incorporate other cultures within a dominant absorbing culture into something else: a wish to meet, a search for dialogue, a quest for fruitful co-existence.

The previous paradigm that claimed at its extreme that there is one right way has hopefully given way to a new notion, fundamental to Gestalt, that any phenomenological being is to be met as is and to be dialogued with, rather than monologued against. Questions of belonging, of relationship, and of selfhood emerge between the partners to the dialogue, rather than being interjected from the outside.

In fact, what emerges is the unique as well as the valuable Gestalt contribution to the construction of a new paradigm. The way towards more acceptance and mutually respected and respectful existence leads through continued phenomenological dialogue, which takes into consideration the field conditions. Respect for who people are, where they come from, and where they wish to go clears the way for a two-way contribution and mutual benefit inherent in the meeting. In short, meeting, making contact, conducting a dialogue, and having a relationship provide the answer to the differences and the difficulties presented.

Gestalt therapy, with its emphasis on subjective experience, on contacting and withdrawing as a basis for experience, and on a field perspective of relationships offers a unique contribution to the study of interactions of people from different cultures. By paying attention to specific elements of experience, elements upon which we habitually concentrate, as well as by attending to the field condition in which they are embedded, we can understand how differences arise and probably how they can be surmounted.

A meeting is between two phenomenological experiences, between the known and the unknown. The emphasis is on the subjective experience, the personal point of view, in conjunction with the new and unfamiliar. In such a meeting, persons are to be respected for who they are and for what they believe in, while being invited and supported to establish a dialogue with the other. Fundamental to this process is the conviction that even though change is inevitable as a result of a dialogic meeting, one can still maintain what is fundamental to oneself. The starting point is that of meeting and allowing, as opposed to demanding and imposing change.

The change in the world toward greater inclusiveness is clearer nowadays as communication and transportation have become so much easier. The familiar and defined system of boundaries is in a process of massive change wherever international commerce takes place.

When we lived in Boston in the 1970s, we received a newspaper from Israel once a week—four days late. We read it, mainly to keep in touch, out of a sense of remote belonging. By the 1990s, one could buy the same Israeli newspaper all over the world, wherever there was a demand, on the day it was printed. Nowadays, you can define your own needs and get your custom-designed newspaper over the World Wide Web, wherever you are, whenever you want it. Something has happened to the mobility and immediacy of the sense of belonging.

During most of the nineties, as a family, we lived in the United Kingdom. Interestingly enough, all this change that seemed to allow a greater sense of belonging did not really meet our needs as a family. Eventually, against all odds, we ended up choosing to go back home, where we felt we truly belonged—Israel. We were lucky that we could choose. Or was it really a choice? Did we really have the internal freedom to choose otherwise? And what is the destiny of those who cannot return to their homeland, for external reasons that are beyond their control? I suspect that the value of belonging somewhere defined for us where we could feel the most comfortable.

The implications of the New Age are that nowadays one can live almost anywhere and have the technical and environmental support to feel that one still belongs, however far one is from home. Physical and emotional boundaries shift and become more flexible, less clear, or at least differently defined. The known, familiar, common definitions of self and belonging become less evident or are lost altogether. Hence, one way to survive is to search for the new comfortable "known."

It is possible that the parameters around the historical desire to seek a new identity (to become part of the American dream or to be the new Jew proud to be in Israel, etc.) have utterly changed. In the old patterns of immigration and cultural mobility, the great risk was that one would lose one's former identity. In actual fact, in general, that was the wish of the immigrant and the expectation of the absorbing society (see Kishinevsky and Fodor in this collection).

This dynamic resulted in difficulties in maintaining one's perception of self. It also led to alienating responses and the inevitable cultural generation gap within the immigrant family. The need to adapt did not prevent others mocking the immigrant's foreignness or relieve him or her of the shame of being different. Disappearing culturally for the sake of merging into that new identity resulted in moving to the extreme polarity, bringing with it the painful process and a hurt sense of cultural and personal identity.

The shift from one polarity to the other hardly gives a suitable answer to the needs of people in transition. A deep need emerges to maintain one's identity while meeting new components of one's adjusting self. The next step is to find a middle ground through a dialogue between the differences, making space for people as they are, and who they wish to be (see the contributions by Holly Timberlake, Copsey and Bar-Yoseph, and Rivas in this collection).

Ruth's Story

Ruth's story focuses on the dilemma between the wish to belong and the need to retain one's identity. Ruth immigrated to Israel from Poland with her parents in 1960. Her parents believed that the only choice they had for a relatively safe life was to live in a Jewish state. The "only choice" actually meant "no choice."

> "I was born in Poland and immigrated to Israel when I was six years old. My parents chose to live in a town where they had some relatives, assuming that it would be easier to feel connected to a place where they had family. The reason behind their decision, beyond the family ties, was that they could leave me with our relatives while they went to a residential school to learn Hebrew.
>
> I was sent to a local school where I was totally unprepared for the new child image that I was about to meet. I was dressed in a black tailored skirt, white shirt buttoned to the neck, white socks, and fancy shoes. I even wore a hat. Wonderfully dressed for the first day of school in Poland—only it wasn't Poland any longer. This land was desert hot and most of the children wore as little as possible and wandered around barefoot. I could have not looked more out of place!
>
> I was as different as different could be. They expected me to be the same as they were and apparently so did I. I did my best from that day on. I dressed like them, learned to speak like them, and I felt more and more as if I was becoming one of them. Forty years later, I can still feel the little pebbles between my toes and the ground, sizzling hot like a fiery furnace. This remained forever the symbol for the cost of that transition. The worst was yet to come.
>
> Six months later, when my parents returned, I found to my dismay that my mother had not been able to learn Hebrew properly, while she found to her dismay that I could hardly speak Polish any more. My father, who did master Hebrew, decided that we should leave the Polish behind us altogether and speak only Hebrew. I still have postcards that he sent my mother, stained with her tears. He insisted on the Hebrew and she wept with frustration at not being able to understand what he wrote."

The notion that the only way to have the right to exist is to become the other involves disowning parts of oneself, projecting them, outside of awareness onto the environment and paying the price of shedding parts of the self. Those parts could be described as belonging to the desired other. A dynamic relationship is created outside of awareness between both cultures. Both sides invest in blurring the boundaries on one hand and on trying to maintain the differences on the other. The list of examples of people who have been ready to forsake their cultural characteristics and, indeed, their cultural identity in order to belong is almost endless.

When Ruth was brought to Israel she looked Polish and she *was* Polish. She lost her support system. Her parents disappeared, her Polishness was "wrong," meaning that *she* was wrong, and her familiar environment was gone. The way she understood the field was to believe that the new environment would only be ready to consider accepting her if she was the same as it was. However, she was not the same, but she was too young and too lost to see differently.

Israel, which metaphorically, put the statement "A country for all Jews" on its flag turned into a melting pot of sameness. At that time, it seemed that the only way to create a Jewish state was for immigrants to leave behind the familiar trappings of their origins, their past, and their tradition. At that time, it may have been the best creative adjustment for this newborn nation— this new country that had to accommodate an endless stream of Holocaust refugees (see the chapters by Kubesch, Bar-Yoseph, and Alon in this collection).

Ruth and her family had no choice but, like other individuals, to go through the impossible experience demanded of them and to experience the seemingly hopeless assumption that a human being can change, as a snake sheds its skin each year.

Losing Identity

There were, of course, reasons for this apparent impossibility, which I recall each time I remember an observation my daughter once read to me, in the United Kingdom, from her school textbook assignment: "In the modern age, Jews were told, 'You cannot live amongst us!' In the Nazi era, Jews were told, 'You cannot live.'"

Such an experience often represents the essence of what we are dealing with here. In my own history, as in that of so many other people, not much attention has been paid to the possibility that there is space in the world for everybody to live among or nearby each other (see the chapters by McConville and Jacobs in this collection).

Territorial claims and ethnic priorities are still the main cause for war. Alas, Martin Buber's stance (1980), which says one exists only when there is another, has not been given enough attention in the twentieth century. Among the bloodiest examples of this are the Holocaust, as a mechanized effort to eradicate a people; the systematic reciprocal slaughter of the Hutu and Tutsi tribes in Africa; the massacre of the Armenians by the Turks; the Chinafication of Tibet; and the bloodbaths in the former Yugoslavia; not to mention the terrorist attack that shattered the world on 9/11/2001, and the ensuing, and understandable, retaliation perpetrated in Afghanistan and Iraq.

My hand trembles as it records this partial catalogue of human agony. The list places a question mark over the fundamental trust I have in the possibility of bridging the divides between us, but also, ironically, heightens my sense of the need to build the bridge. Nowadays, one can assess one's illusion of safety as a contribution to the sense of security and power that was shattered so cruelly on 9/11, when Americans were shocked by being so dramatically attacked on their own land. The extreme of losing one's identity is the very loss of one's life.

There are few far-reaching ways to let go of what one is. This universe of ours could be a place of excitement and anxiety and of anticipation and dread. The anxiety of losing one's identity could hold back the excitement associated with the newly acquired desired identity. One's anxiety over the desire to fully belong may become mixed with the excitement of the illusion that one can start afresh.

For example, is Christmas to be celebrated purely as a religious holiday or can it also be a secular one? And who should celebrate it? If it is a secular holiday, why not celebrate it anyway, whether you are Christian or not? Members of Christian denominations are increasingly expressing reservations against the growing secular and business-oriented practices of this holiday. The Church argues that the gifts have become more important than the religious content of the holiday. This may be the case, but their doubts are not the crux of my argument. Let me explain. I myself reacted negatively to my Israeli friends in the United Kingdom who joined in the Christmas cheer. The Israeli paradigm is that taking part in the religious traditions of others is absolutely wrong. There is no allowance for individual decision.

Writing those words, I feel the internal conviction that this is correct. Entering the discussion could in itself be a danger to the survival of Judaism. Will my friends really lose their Israeli or Jewish identity by being drawn into Christmas activities around them? Or will I lose mine? How will their Christian friends regard this? Is identity so fragile that the only way to maintain it is in isolation or at least behind thick barriers, rules, and regulations? My friends are over 50 years old and are as Israeli and as Jewish as they come. It is obvious to them that they recognize the non-religious aspect of Christmas and enjoy the holiday in their own way while enhancing their social relations with the British non-Jews amongst whom they live. So if I look at the situation with a more open mind, I could say that perhaps my friends have found their own way to maintain their Israeli/Jewish identity while enjoying the excitement of Christmas and the sense of belonging to the country where they have chosen to reside.

Historically, the recognition/celebration field of the merriment surrounding another's religious holy day may very well be organized as a pseudo equilibrium: members of the larger, dominating culture are comfortable in the so-called predominant one's position and, through transference, the minority members project the wish to be like the *not me* of the predominant culture. The position of the minority strengthens the strong and paradoxically creates more of a gap between the cultures. At the same time, diminished contact creates more of a wish to be like the perceived better/luckier one. This configuration of the field keeps the predominant culture safe from undesired anxieties that provoke changes, or at least maintains the illusion of safety within the known and the wished-for by others.

Members of strong cultures might realize that the idealized transference has blinded them to the fact that any meeting inflicts change all around. In fact, as a result of the attempt to become the other, members from predominant and lesser dominant cultures may together form a new culture impacted by a partnership taking place outside of their awareness: a new culture in which many members are rather uncomfortable since they are not fully conscious of what they could be and or want to be. This might be one interesting explanation of the persecution of minorities. Their wish to become the other threatens the identity of the predominant culture by their attempting to mix in, and therefore change it. This process occurs out of awareness, which makes dealing with it even more difficult. All parties to the blending of cultures tend to end up in discomfort.

The historical process creates a polarity: the given cultural affiliation at the one end, and the chosen, desired one at the other. The present world is becoming more of what has become known as a global village. More mobility and more communication mean more opportunity to group differently. The boundary of a culture moves beyond the geographical. Affiliations vary. Being either-or becomes next to impossible, as impossible as being both seems to be.

Cooperation goes beyond the physical space. Hence, the definition of dominance changes. The *I* boundary of a given culture can now include a larger population aware of its identity and, indeed, spread all over the world. While in the past this position was perceived as mostly undesirable, nowadays it is created and accepted as an aspect of the New Age. Defining who is who is not that simple any more. Indeed, who one can be, or desire to be, becomes more complex. Why not respect who we are and find ways to develop and grow within that framework? Again, in this book we try in more ways than one to suggest that the only way to be fully present is to meet through the differences, rather than through the desire to submerge oneself to become someone else.

The taken-for-granted choice (or should we say lack of aware choice) of whether to be isolated yet keep one's identity or to merge with the other at the cost of disowning one's self is not the only game in town any more. In their own way, each of the contributing authors to this book depicts a variety of dialoging choices and relinquishes isolated stances. Writing from who they are, striving to understand what is communicated to them by their clients, knowing that they might change and be changed in the process, not out of coercion or loss of boundaries, but by the sheer wish to meet and co-exist. In Gestalt terms, we are trying to create a middle ground between the polarities of isolation and confluence.

It becomes crucial, as well as interesting, to study the shift from a local village to a global village. This shift is a polarity. Currently, the world is somewhere on the global village end of the polarity. One reason for the vast interest in cultural boundaries and intercultural relationships may stem from being in the polarity of the new organization of boundaries. There is less sense of boundary as everything becomes one village. Hence, there is less sense of difference, while on the other hand, a sense of a need and the possibility to maintain one's identity remains. The field is reconfigured to hopefully allow differences and maybe begin to accept others as they are, in their own identity.

This might explain the sense of urgency and tension around these issues. Within the village, there are swift and frequent changes in boundaries, which can be rather unsettling. Moreover, the shift can be experienced as a lack of boundary, which then means a threat to identity. What previously felt simple and clearly defined is no longer so. Hence, desiring to be the other becomes more complex. It is not clear who the other is and what the difference is between the "me" and the "not-me." And again, all of this calls for a need to clearly define one's boundaries rigorously.

The wish for clear-cut definitions may miss the point, since the inherent need for meaning, as we recognize it from Gestalt theory, may take over the phenomenological process and achieve a premature and faulty sense of satisfaction, as we attempt to solve the sense of discomfort arising from the fluidity of definitions. There is a new need for definitions, and a need for new definitions that are flexible enough to handle the whole entity.

Not only is staying with the process of rigorous definitions difficult for most of us in the Western world, there is also a strong demand/introject to move/change swiftly in order to survive. So how do people remain fundamentally who they are while at the same time shifting and growing? And can they stay fundamentally who they are when they have grown? When does a culture become a new culture? And is it important, as long as its members lead a full life and are, by their definition, happy?

As long as the ability to assess one's position is sharp, the boundary is flexible, the soul is at peace, and the whole person has a sense of belonging throughout, the above questions are answered in a different way from how we usually respond to them.

The inherent need for change in some human cultures may suggest that for them the practice of tradition is tantamount to staying, or to being left behind, that slowness (i.e., a state of apparent no-change) is bad. This might be the explanation for the general buzz in the air that allows little space for slow thinking, for assessing of options, or for hesitation.

Any number of examples raise the question of whether the need for change is stronger than change itself. That is, are the expectations for change a motivating force in introducing changes? For example, a global company that has not changed its product or gone through structural change, or outsourced, or moved to a new location might be considered to be stagnating. By my larger inquiry here, I do not intend to suggest that anyone should doubt the speed by which technology introduces changes, but to suggest that one should be willing to question further the driving force behind the larger inquiry. Is change internal or external?

The basic need for change, I have found in my inquiry, has turned into the assumption that there is a need for instant change. Deconstructing the constructed has become part of the constructing process, almost as if the present has no value other than to be re-sketched. Hence, we observe that the field is in constant formation/construction and deconstruction. The known turns constantly into an unknown transforming toward a known to be observed anew. The value in experiencing the given is to notice that the present is suddenly gone – and that discomfort then may settle in.

Here is my suspicion: a process that, I believe, is an inevitable agent in growth might somehow have imperceptibly and suddenly become the objective itself. If this is indeed true, this new, imperceptible, sudden objective-in-itself has then become a new, imperceptible, sudden object of new inquiry and new study. That there is always a variable toward the new is the constant given.

At this point, it would be useful to address two points: One, that we should always want to investigate a culture as it is given as a whole, including an assessment of the so-called minority subculture amidst which the apparent predominant culture exists. We should always assume that the meeting space between or among cultures is an independent organic space that nonetheless depends on the basic phenomenological field of each of the individual cultures. If a culture is a whole, then it is more than the sum of its parts, it is its own entity. At the contact boundary, we observe a meeting between the two entities, supported by each culture/entity.

For further illustration, let's imagine a musical meeting between a classical Eastern orchestra and a classical Western one. If the two orchestras appear on the same stage on two different evenings with two different programs (each of a different cultural orientation) in front of two different audiences, the concert hall may be thought of as a space for cultural events but could hardly be described as a hall for cultural interaction or even a hall for cultural meetings, in the fullest, sense of the term. On the other hand, if the two orchestras were to perform consecutively in front of the same audience, we would have to consider what they were playing in order to ascertain whether there had been a musical meeting. But in any case, the audience would be at the focus of the cultural meeting (the contact space/boundary).

The questions would change if the orchestras were to play pieces that were not those culturally expected from them or if they were to play a specially composed intercultural piece of music together on the same stage—or even play each other's pieces. What if, to keep pushing this illustration, the concert were to feature an intercultural piece called *Mozart in Egypt*, which combined Nubian desert songs and Mozart's Fortieth Symphony?

The focal point changes naturally from event to event and we should consider the possibility of actively shifting points of view and reference. The experience changes as the field configurations change. Can we say that the meeting is the figure and the rest is the ground? Does this possible perspective change if on stage we see the famous musical meeting between Ravi Shankar and Yehudi Menuhin? Is that a meeting space of cultures? Or what about the (less famous) meeting between Sir Yehudi and Stephane Grappelli, the noted French jazz violinist.

What are the building blocks of these meetings: the personalities, the music featured, the instruments, the religious faith of the audience or musicians, the citizenships preset in the meeting space, the academic and artistic disciplines present, the sheer will to meet, the meeting itself, the audience during the very moments of experiencing and absorbing the meeting, or the recording protocols of the meeting? Do any of these have a phenomenological life of their own?

I seem to have provided more questions than answers, but at this stage of the journey along the path of intercultural coexistence, I hope to have evoked some interest in the reader to justify a further look into the fascinating accounts of the contributions to this book. As Sapriel and Palumbo point out in their essay, the individual is a culture of one. It is the internal nature and internal individuality of this one(ness) that interests me here.

Moreover, the therapist/researcher becomes an integral part of the new field created by the intercultural meeting itself. The therapist has no ability to be objective, because both she/he and the client change while interacting. We have to take into account the influence that we have on the culture when we actively study it or when we are involved in a therapeutic situation with it.

So, in fact, unless we are dealing with our own culture, we influence the culture we work with by the mere fact of being different. However minute our influence as therapists may be over the culture of the client as a whole, there is a process of change that takes place. Furthermore there is a change taking place because of the very meeting and it affects not only the client's culture, through the therapist, but also the therapist's culture through the client.

Measuring or quantifying changes can be an impossible task and a futile effort. This book is not about quantifying influence and measuring forces, but rather it is about acknowledging differences and the fact that the meeting of differences creates change. It is a ground assumption to the fascinating accounts you are about to read in this book.

As a researcher and practitioner, I am facing some painful questions: Could I decide to stop being an Israeli? I could give up my passport, I could try and lose my accent, but I shall remain an Israeli and/or a former Israeli in the cultural sense. The reader will have to take into account that being an Israeli at this point in my life is not just my civil orientation but also a question of cultural affilliation. The questions of identifying with a new citizenship have a certain influence on one's own cultural definition.

The process of creating and editing this book was exciting, painful, disheartening, and hopeful. At all times, I was clear within myself about what I was doing and why. I knew what a unique contribution Gestalt brings to the bridging of differences and had no doubt that I was failing to get this across, at least to some of my most important professional and personal friends.

Growing up in the Middle East and especially residing there in recent years—years of detrimental conflict—has taught me the depth of depletion and the pain of holding on to the trust I have in the Gestalt stance of dialogic relationship. The pages of this book contain a lot of personal and collective pain, frustration, and hope. I was determined to have space in it for difference and at times I thought that it might never be published. It has ended up being a collage of accounts that relate how, with tenacity and conviction, bridges can be stretched across the divide.

References

Bar-Yoseph, B. (1996). *Ideology, Culture Change, and Management Patterns in the Israeli Kibbutz*. London, City University, Ph.D. Thesis (not published).

Buber, M. (1980). *The Secret of Dialogue*. Jerusalem, Bialik Institute.

Geertz, C. (1973). *The Interpretation of Cultures*. London, Basic Books, Inc.

Lewin, K. (1989). *Resolving Social Conflicts*. Jerusalem, Keter Publishing House Jerusalem.

Schein, E. H. (1985). *Organizational Culture and Leadership*. San Francisco, Jossey-Bass, 6-7.

The New Columbia Encyclopedia (1975). New York and London, Columbia University Press, 696.

II. CULTURE

By Philip Lichtenberg, Ph.D.

Gestalt therapy, with its emphasis on experience and on the concepts of contact and withdrawal as the basis for experiencing human relationships, can contribute significantly to the study of interactions of people from differing cultures. Simply by exploring the elements of experience upon which we customarily concentrate, such as the nature of awareness, and the reliance upon dialogue for expanded awareness, we can show why difficulties arise and how they can most likely be surmounted. This is a preliminary effort toward such an examination.

If we take the common view that a culture exists in patterns of reflective interactions that establish shared meanings, we can see how a theory of Gestalt therapy might contribute to and enhance a theory of culture. We can suggest that culture embodies patterns of contact and withdrawal of individuals, of groups, and of larger systems; additionally, culture embodies ongoing representations of these common reflective patterns. Culture is made up of events and episodes with unique beginnings and endings and with what is allowed or disallowed in events and episodes. The structural and functional properties repetitively co-created in such events and episodes foster the unfolding of what we consider to be culture.

In the habitual structures of real-time contacting and withdrawing, we can observe special adaptations of contact functions in each culture. Furthermore, when we study touching, seeing, hearing, moving, tasting, and so on, we ourselves develop an early understanding of the particularities of a given culture. Food preferences, for example, typically help to define a culture. How people look at each other, or protect themselves from being seen, as in the use of veils; or how far apart they stand when in conversation; who may look at whom and who is to be looked at; or who may speak and who is to listen, are some of the many basic underpinnings of the function of contact within a culture.

Peculiarities of contact-function create power differentials, gender identities, conceptions of categories of individuals, and similar grounds for patterns of interaction and the development of shared meanings. By contact-function, we mean the sensory and motor functions by which persons connect with the environment. How do individuals use seeing, hearing, touching, smelling, and so forth in their everyday interactions? One component in describing a culture -- and then a difference between cultures -- is to study the contact-functions emphasized and obscured in that culture.

Moreover, we might also study how the loss of the function of ego may characterize a culture. By ego function, we mean how a person includes and excludes from the awareness of others -- or sometimes from the awareness of self -- various aspects of his or her own being and aspects of the surrounding field. A loss of ego function will inherently involve keeping unavailable the experience of one's own attributes or of one's own environment. If a person has internalized a demand from the outside world and replaced his or her own determination with that demand, we say the person is living out a faulty experience; the loss of ego function is then a result of problematic *introjection*.

Conversely, if a person experiences something of himself or herself not directly but as a characteristic of something externalized on the outside, we say the loss of ego function is a matter of faulty *projection*. If an individual turns back upon the self that is meant for some other person and is unaware that this is the case, we consider the loss of ego function to be *retroflection*. And if a person fuses with others before there is a clearly defined "I" and "You," we say that the loss of ego function is an unconscious premature demand for *confluence*. We can then ask: which *losses* are stressed: retroflections, introjections, projections or confluence?

Cultures that depend upon indoctrination – for example, cultures built around fundamentalist religions or authoritarian political regimes -- rely upon demands for confluence via introjection. The indoctrination calls for introjecting authority and diminishing one's attention to one's own preferences; and the indoctrination aims to create group cohesion by having all members of the group being too readily confluent with each other and with the authority. An individual's coherence might be sacrificed so that a draconian leadership may indoctrinate and sustain group cohesion.

Cultures that are anti-sexual demand considerable retroflection of normal sexual excitement -- this is the central argument made by Freud in his *Civilization and Its Discontents* (1930). Groupings that are constructed on the basis of uniting against enemies foster both faulty confluence and unwholesome projection. The unity of the group is not forged by independent agreements but by an insidious series of confluent emphases upon a common out-group; and the negative qualities assigned to the out-group are typically projections of what is devalued and disallowed in the in-group by in-group leadership.

Which *issues* are central to systematic loss of ego function is another focus for attention in this domain that should be examined in understanding a given culture. For instance, is aggression inhibited or exaggerated? Is the same true for sexuality? Are restrictions on casual friendships in place, as between men and women, or intimate relationships, as between men and men? Must individuals conceal or display their wealth? These and many other choices may be the basis of the loss of ego function in a given culture. If men and women are highly segregated, for example, conditions are ripe for faulty projections, as both men and women replace what they do not know intimately about one another with an imagination fueled by the forces that keep them segregated.

Furthermore, in connection with the loss of the function of ego, we may consider how *much overall loss* takes place. Cultures vary in how they promote psychological wellbeing to the degree that they are motivated by patterns of interaction that promote loss of ego function. Highly authoritarian cultures promote identification with the aggressor and projection upon out-groups, both of which are significant losses of ego function. Authoritarianism involves hierarchies in which superiors at each level dominate those below them and demand obedience to their commands: a basis for faulty introjecting. In identification with the aggressor, such faulty introjecting leads persons to dominate themselves, to self-regulate so as not to differ from, or antagonize, their superiors.

Similarly, to control the rage instigated by such self-domination, authoritarian systems promote hatred of out-groups via projections. Similarly, militaristic cultures depend upon premature demands for confluence to maintain power differentials. The requirements of unexamined obedience to military command lead to fusions of followers with each other and with leaders. These fusions are prominent losses of the ego function of choice (Kaiser, 1965). Thus, Erich Fromm's analysis in *The Sane Society* (1955) can be adapted by

Gestalt therapists who focus upon loss of ego function as critical to understanding individuals, groups, and organizations.

A third concern is tied to special attributes in contacting and withdrawing in the everyday events created in the culture. Study of typical episodes for emphases in fore-contact, contact, final contact, and withdrawal will show differences between cultures that will be useful in cross-cultural encounters. Contact and withdrawal events define the processes by which people construct the moments of their lives. From a vague, chaotic background, initial forays into connecting with other people or materials are stimulated by desires of the individual and by possibilities and demands from the environment. These as yet unsupported and undeveloped actions are instances of fore-contact.

As excitement mounts and the individual encounters others and creates his or her own uniqueness in the event, and invites or welcomes the particularity of others, contact infuses the quality of the event. At the climax of contacting (that is, at the final contact), individuals "meet" and form a unit larger than each; fusion more or less of the parties ensues.

Then the event ends as the participants withdraw from one another. In the United States, individuals tend to minimize fore-contact, as they will often more readily act as if one is already in contact without the preliminaries to be addressed. So, too, in the culture of addiction, there is a rush to final contact, to the experience of the high, with a limitation in contacting. The addict avoids particularizing self by the routines of addiction. The repetitive forms of behavior that characterize addictive life place severe restrictions on the complexity of contacting that would take place in a more fully developed personality.

The rituals of any given culture may illustrate the highest forms of contacting and withdrawing, and they can be analyzed for the strengths and limitations they carry. For example, coming together to pray several times a day, a ritual that characterizes some cultures, provides a basic sense of confluence, or togetherness, for members of that culture. A strength of this ritual is that it provides a ground of support in a community. Each person feels part of something larger than himself or herself. The humility in the prayer may help persons deal with profound feelings of uplift, or of vulnerability or helplessness, each a natural human reaction to the certainty of the face of death that gazes eventually upon each of us. The prayers may carry lessons as well as comfort. Other strengths can be noted by those most attuned to such a ritual. Limitations can be seen as well.

Confluence without the expression and resolution of difference is not only promotive of anti-democratic social practices but also limiting to the individuation of the persons in the collective. If the ritual segregates men and women, it fosters projections upon the opposite sex and probable oppression of one by the other. The strict in-group aspect of the ritual may be the basis for out-group hatred and distrust. In terms of episodes of contact and withdrawal, such a ritual favors premature confluence rather than confluence at final contact when ego functions have been prominent in the contacting process.

A fourth notion for use by Gestalt therapists in defining cultural patterns pertains to the predominant subject matters in contact and withdrawal interactions. By this we mean such matters as work, religion, recreational sports, and the like. For example, as American football takes precedence over baseball as a subject matter in the culture, the importance of aggression, of hierarchy and of group interaction increases; and with that, we observe an increase in the support of different contact functions (such as different motor patterns), different losses of ego function (such as different demands for confluence), and different patterns of contacting and withdrawing (after each play versus after each inning; and different meanings of the clock). In so far as a culture is dominated by economic concerns, losses of ego function at work will permeate lesser systems.

Thus, more democracy in the workplace results in more democracy within family life. When downsizing at work becomes common in the culture, the uncertainty and insecurity about a job causes individuals to be suspicious and raises the likelihood of faulty projecting not only at work but also at home and elsewhere. Similarly, when work is organized around an authoritarian hierarchy, identification with the aggressor becomes common and more generally affects home life, religious orientation and social life. Autocratic economic practices foster religious fundamentalism and conservative politics, because economics then controls cultural subject matters.

A fifth concern is the level of affect acceptable in alternative contexts. Every culture regulates affect: its intensity, its appropriateness to a given context, its place in the hierarchy of feelings that are promoted or tolerated (Cole, 1998). How do people typically grieve? What permission is given for anger at work? How does carnival time differ from everyday life? Self-control of anger and its cold expression helps to define who is strong or dominant in a culture, while helpless rage creates powerlessness (Lichtenberg, 1990).

In some cultures, family life is aimed at enabling the full range of feelings, while other cultures, say those cultures in which marriages are arranged, may have different purposes for the family. Different jobs foster different levels of emotion in ongoing ways, and thus promote different work cultures, as, for instance, assembly lines in automobile factories in comparison with work structures in a computer development company. Children are allowed to cry in some societies while adults, except for given rituals, must curtail weeping. Examining level of affect can be a significant contribution to the conception of a given culture.

Given our awareness that cultures vary along these dimensions, we can acknowledge why difficulties arise when individuals or whole societies meet persons or groups from a different culture. Challenges between persons or groups can be a function of characteristics intrinsic to a culture or, alternately, to the different emphases and matters that are avoided that typify separate cultures when meetings take place. With respect to intrinsic factors, a culture may demonize out-groups in general or diminish other cultures as part of its demand for in-group confluence. For example, some fundamentalist religious groups condemn all persons or groups who do not fit within their perspective. Thus, intermarriage is severely curtailed.

Holy wars may be promoted. Figures from different religions may be portrayed as evil. A society dominated by religion may cast a secular society as immoral in its nature. Projection upon an out-group becomes the glue that seals the required confluence. Similarly, some large city lesbian groups become tightly knit and members may feel threatened if one of their own begins to explore heterosexual yearnings, a reactive mirror image of homophobic society at large. Or a social system closed by its inner dynamics rather than by persecution from the outside, such as Japan was many years ago, may try to make any stranger seem dangerous and unwelcome. Whenever a social organization builds its unity by obscuring in-group difference and magnifying out-group dangers, we have in place the demand for confluence bolstered by demands for introjecting and projecting, and troubles in inter-cultural relations inevitably follow.

In addition to this more elementary constraint upon inter-cultural contact, which is the more extreme instance, as the examples show, the theory of Gestalt therapy and its focus upon interruptions of contact poses an interesting source of difficulty in what is allowed and what is disallowed in differing cultures. If making eye contact in a conversation is promoted generally in one culture and highly differentiated in another then contact is likely to be ambiguous and awkward between members of these cultures.

Suppose in one culture women are to avoid eye contact and men to look closely, but everyone is expected to use eye contact in a second culture. Anxiety and confusion are easily developed under such background orientations, and it may be difficult to communicate adequately in time for some sort of negotiation to take place. If a woman from the second culture makes eye contact in her usual manner with a man from the first culture who is unaccustomed to this, they both may become disturbed in their interaction from this basic difference that can lead to misunderstanding.

That which is disallowed in a given culture, whether in the name of morality, law, or simple social propriety, becomes a basis for the production of anxiety and discomfort. If the disallowed behavior appears in the culture being contacted, or the urge toward it begins to arise from simple biological desire while engaging the other culture, the matter is one of doing the forbidden. The behavior is both attractive and frightening in its connection to that which is commonly understood as interesting but is systematically disallowed. Conversely, if the behavior or urge is successfully suppressed, its imagined potency is dramatically increased, and its appearance in the other culture becomes magnified in its ability to arouse fear. When social forces are insufficiently attuned to personal proclivities -- as is true in all cultures created to this point in time in human history -- differing sets of social constraints pose threats to persons on either side of the divide.

Commonly in international political affairs, ignorance of the cultural specifics of established enemies prevails. Into the space of ignorance come projections, as we have learned in the study of how people construct and deal with enemies. And the more cultures are built upon self-conquest, the personal counterpart to imperialism and exploitation, the more the narratives of culture are built upon faulty projections. These projections not only reflect the anxiety of individuals and groups who cannot manage the emotions that are aroused, they also tend to foster perceptions that other peoples and other cultures are dangerous, and, consequently, they promote further anxiety.

That which is allowed or promoted in a given culture has been established as at least minimally satisfying to members of that collective. Every culture is based on meeting the needs of its members, so that every culture is in some sense "right." While every culture can be seen as limited and distorting, by the same token, no culture would survive if it did not provide in a significant degree for the gratification of its members. We know from studies of families and small groups, everyone achieves something in relationships, even the most oppressed, when a collective form is ongoing (Lichtenberg, 1988). Accordingly, any given culture will have something to offer to members of an alternative culture in the way of presenting something that is novel.

Interest in other cultures, attraction to them, has both a positive and negative basis connected to the novelty of difference that is operative. On the positive side, that which is new offers possibilities for satisfaction that are incompletely realized in one's native culture. Modesty and humility may offer a sense of privacy and separateness/autonomy to a person whose culture promotes excessive demands for transparency. Similarly, when persons move to urban cultures from villages and small towns, they find the new anonymity freeing in that they can now try out previously restricted activities. On the other side, the novelty of difference in the alternative culture may become a depository for projections of an unwholesome sort, possibly giving rise to a newly-formed disenfranchised and pathological out-group. To a small town citizen, the big city may seem to be entirely too filled with aggression and passion run amuck. We can summarize the perspective developed here with three statements:

- Insofar as a culture is tightly regulated, persons of that culture will find the novel threatening and are disposed to react to persons of another culture as if endangered.
- Different cultures allow and disallow different behaviors and experiences and, accordingly, are disposed to raise both interest and anxiety among persons meeting across cultures.
- Since it is the novel that is most nourishing, cross-cultural interaction is likely to be greatly promotive of growth when adequate supports for experience are provided and limiting of growth when such supports are absent.

     Gestalt therapy enables people to manage their own tendencies to introject, project, retroflect, or demand confluence in faulty ways. Similarly, it helps persons to deal with others who wish to force introjecting, promote projecting, require retroflecting, or insist on confluence in distorted forms. Since its early days, Gestalt therapy has provided experiments as well as theory for the undoing of distorting ways in the construction of experience (Perls, et al., 1951). These can be adapted for helping persons deal with social situations that arise in cross- or trans-cultural contacting. For example, my colleagues and I (Lichtenberg, et al., 1997) have proposed the necessary components for successfully befriending persons who make unwelcome racist, sexist, homophobic, or anti-Semitic remarks in a social gathering. We see the issue as dealing with demands for confluence in respect to projections upon members of an out-group. How we deal with projections in psychotherapy can help explain how such remarks are met socially.
     Freire's (1968) conscientization represents an attempt to undo introjects and retroflections that are a consequence of oppression, as Fanon (1963) tried to accomplish in a very different way in a different culture. While both dealt with introjects, Freire's method was educative and nonviolent while Fanon's was revolutionary and violent. Both succeeded to some degree and failed to some degree. We can enlarge upon their efforts with our theory. In psychotherapy, we are careful not to promote unhealthy introjecting, just as we are concerned to undo the influence of oppressive introjects. The many studies in this series show the fruitfulness of Gestalt therapy in cross-cultural happenings. We have much to contribute and herein resides a vital beginning.

Personal Account

Philip: When Talia and I sat down and discussed her idea about creating this book, I began to wonder about me becoming a co-writer for a contributing chapter for this book; I hesitated. I was not that distant from writing my last book and I was not yet ready to begin anew, even for a short chapter. I did not know Tali personally and I had had an unnerving experience in my last collaborative endeavor, even though I had previously done a fair amount of joint writing. Further, the task she had in mind, that is, providing a theoretical base for the book, the more general topic to precede more focused chapters, seemed like a major undertaking. The vitality of her conversation and the persistence of her asking drew from me an ambivalent agreement. Shades of that ambivalence continued to this day as I now write my personal reflections.

Talia: Those "shades" are part of Philip's make-up which he brought to our encounter, i.e., straight dialogue and simple communication even at times of potential conflict.

Philip: Having agreed to try my hand at co-writing the chapter, I set about what I considered applying the basic themes of Perls, Hefferline, and Goodman (PHG) to the theme of culture, a concern always at the forefront of their thinking as I interpreted them. Accordingly, I wrote a straightforward account, leaning on PHG as seen from my background of studying, teaching and writing in psychoanalysis for many years. The psychoanalysis I adhered to stemmed from the socially radical perspective, as did the Gestalt therapy theory posed by the founders. My chapter is the result.

I remained open -- in some degree at least -- to collaboration on a theoretical underpinning for the book. My background, both in psychoanalysis and in Gestalt therapy, in which I was heavily influenced by Isadore From, led to a slant on the theory of Gestalt therapy significantly different from that of Tali. The differences in our conceptions had much more of an effect on the limiting of a joint chapter than any cultural or gender differences between us.

Talia: Fair account, I found myself wanting to overcome the differences between Philip and myself by bridging them into creating a comprehensive and united piece of writing. In my background was my difficulty to compromise on my dream for all chapters to be co-written. To a degree, I was contemplating compromise at all cost. Thanks to Philip, (to Lynne Mark and Gordon later) I have experienced a fresh form of bridging. Philip's confrontation regarding my insistence of all chapters being co-written, opened up my ability to see otherwise. Our mutual understanding about 'not co-writing' entailed a dialogic meeting between two phenomenologies: what better example of 'Making a Difference'?

Philip Lichtenberg, Kennett Square, PA, USA
Talia Levine Bar-Yoseph, Jerusalem, Israel

References

Cole, P. H. (1998), Affective process in psychotherapy: A gestalt therapists view. *The Gestalt Journal*, XXI(1), 49-72.

Fanon, F. (1963), *The Wretched of the Earth.* New York: Grove Press.

Freire, P. (1968), *Pedagogy of the Oppressed.* New York: The Seabury Press.

Freud, S. (1930), Civilization and its Discontents. *Standard Edition,* 21:64-145. London: Hogarth Press.

Fromm, E. (1955), *The Sane Society.* New York: Rinehart & Co.

Kaiser, H. (1965), *Effective Psychotherapy: The Contribution of Hellmuth Kaiser.* Louis B. Fierman, Editor. New York: Free Press.

Lichtenberg, P. (1988), *Getting Even: The Equalizing Law of Relationship.* Lanham, MD: University Press of America. (1990), *Undoing the Clinch of Oppression.* New York: Peter Lang. Reissued as: *Community and Confluence: Undoing the Clinch of Oppression.* Cleveland, OH: GIC Press, 1994.

Lichtenberg, P., van Beusekom, J., & Gibbons, D. (1997), *Encountering Bigotry: Befriending Projecting Persons in Everyday Life.* Northvale, NJ: Jason Aronson.

Perls, F., Hefferline, R.F., & Goodman, P. (1951), *Gestalt Therapy: Excitement and Growth in the Human Personality.* New York: Julian Press.

III. CULTURE, SELF, AND FIELD

By Gordon Wheeler, Ph.D.

"Goods are often incommensurable. People come at life from different places, they understand the world in different ways, they strive for different ends. This is a fact that has proved amazingly hard to live with..."
-- Louis Menand (2001)

The Context and Ground of Culture

Culture, as a term referring not to arts and education but to some defined social entity with particular shared practices and meanings, is a relatively young usage, deriving out of the emergence of anthropology as a discipline and practice in late 19th Century Europe. These "Victorians" (especially the British, but including their Continental and transatlantic contemporaries as well) were great travelers, collectors, and cataloguers of "the exotic" (also known as "the primitive") much like the Greeks before them, only on a world scale now, and imbued like the Greeks with a vigorous sense of their own cultural identity, self-consciousness, and natural superiority.

Thus the noun culture, in the sense of a culture, itself arose at the boundary, out of multicultural contact and conquest, and in a context in which contact and conquest were overlapping, indeed nearly synonymous terms. In other words, from the beginning any discussion of culture has inherently implied a context of multiculturalism whether as a conflict between or among more than one identified group, or as an analytic activity involving a student or savant who is by definition looking on or in from outside the group studied. This inseparability of cultural from multicultural is a point which will become important for us below, as we try to articulate a distinctively Gestalt contribution to scientific discourse and practice.

It is important to note that in this 19th and early 20th Century context, this new usage of culture was also quite close, often identical, to then contemporary usages of the word "race," a broad term generally understood in those days to include not just shared practices and beliefs but more importantly, the presumed basic characteristics and capacities of members of that group. Calling a culture or ethnicity a race had the effect of lending an air of scientific, biological legitimacy to the discourse of cultures, in a time where science was rapidly replacing religion as the wellspring of authority and values.

This was the age of Darwin and of Social Darwinism, a time when biology burst free of the subservient role it had played since Aristotle's day (and even more, since Newton's), as mere taxonomer of God's creation, to become preeminent in the sciences, the arbiter of all the others, and of religion, philosophy, and social policy as well. Social Darwinism, the original ground of what we now would think of as multicultural discourse, claimed scientific status for the ideological notion that the distribution of privilege and power, within and among cultures, must reflect the distribution of innate intelligence, capacity, and worthiness, by virtue of the simple principle of survival of the fittest.

But more than worthiness was at stake here; for in the metaphysics of Social Darwinism, to tamper with the privileges of the powerful was so contrary to the supposed demands of nature that it threatened the very survival of the species. Humanity itself hung in the balance, with the scientific principle of

Natural Selection replacing the Divine Right of Kings, as the metaphysical conceit of the existing social order.

It was in this context and spirit that the statistician Sir Francis Galton (1869), for example, Darwin's cousin and a prominent Social Darwinist, made part of his reputation by scientifically demonstrating that the social (that is, financial) achievement level of sons in a cross section of Scottish families correlated closely with the innate intelligence of their fathers. Now the financial standing of sons is at least a clearly measurable variable, but how exactly did Galton undertake to measure intelligence in the fathers?

The answer, it turns out, is that he simply assumed the father's innate intelligence levels from their level of social class! (Moore, 2001; Robinson, 1986; Wheeler, 2000). The self-serving circularity of this kind of science didn't seem to disturb very many people at the time: Galton was knighted for his contributions to biology and what we now would call evolutionary psychology -- a school of inquiry which is still struggling to recover from its misuse in the hands of the early multiculturalist imperialists.

All this was culture as what psychologists call trait theory. Like all group trait theory models, this conception of culture tended strongly toward the very problematic notion of essentialism, the doctrine that some essence of the group "Englishness," "Latin temperament," "the Oriental mind," and so on. (including of course "masculinity" and "femininity") is a real thing and somehow inheres within each individual member (and possibly their descendants). Thus the world is safely pigeonholed into a manageable structure of groups—all from the point of view of a right-thinking, presumably male subculture self-consciously identified as Anglo-Saxon, whatever that is taken to mean.

But essentialism, even when it starts out according a separate but equal status to the membership, always seems to collapse rapidly into hierarchical rank generally, though of course not always, with the perceiver at the apex. The farther out one radiates from a self-perceived center of identification, the more inferior the labels then tend to become: Women are pure, if capricious; the Irish are born poets and drunks; Russians are soulful, but prone to violence; Jews are highly gifted, but clannish and avaricious; Orientals are inscrutable, and unreliable; the Colored are musically talented or athletic, but are like children; and on and on.

Thus, even the separate but equal aspect tends to collapse rapidly into a designation of unequal but divinely (or scientifically) ordained. As Galton's knighthood now plainly suggests, the effect of the application of Social Darwinism to public policy could only be to justify European imperialism, and to validate the existing social/political arrangements within the nations of Europe and the Americas as well, from the politics of race and class to the politics of gender and the family.

What all these differing schools and approaches tend to have in common is their general stance of judging a culture from the outside rather than attempting trying to understand it from the inside, as a primary goal. As always when analytic/objectivist models are applied to human affairs, the assumption is that a learned expert, sitting in his (sic) lab or armchair in some center of Western learning, just naturally is in a better position to understand what the relevant dynamics of a society, a relationship, or an individual psyche really are.

Indeed, the very fact of being involved participants in one's own culture, psyche, or relational life, with real stakes and values, and real consequences that matter, automatically disqualifies a person, in an expert model, from having a valid point of view on anything to do with her/his own process. He/she simply lacks the necessary detachment and distance, for an objective, scientific perspective. (This caveat is of course not applied to the expert him/herself).

The point of view is thus analytic/judgmental, not hermeneutic in the current sense of referring to the understanding of meanings in communication (though the term itself, much favored now in postmodernist discourse, had its own positivist roots in biblical textual studies back at a time when interpretation of texts was still understood as a process of revealing their objective, univocal meaning from Hermes, the god of secrets, divination, and fire).

The prevailing perspectives on culture by the early 20th Century were materialist/biological, Eurocentric, and somewhat generally dynamic/organic, in the sense of being powered through some sort of lifecycle by underlying forces that were generally invisible, and largely denied. Two of these dynamic stage models in particular, the Marxist/materialist (with its liberal/progressivist cognates) and the Freudian/psychosexual (together with its derivatives) then tended to dominate the field of cultural and multicultural studies at least through the first half of the century in Europe and North America.

Both these traditions appealed to materialist science as their authority source both with perhaps equal dubiousness, since two currents of thought more squarely based on untestable metaphysical assertions about reality, history, human motivations, and the like could hardly be imagined. Still, by mid-century, under the banner of scientific materialism and/or depth psychology (itself presumably based in biology), these two currents had effectively vanquished their more metaphysical rivals from the culture field (the folkloric, the fascistic, and the historicist or spirit-based) using the now-familiar Nietzschean argument that if you disagreed with their propositions, that only meant that you were either too squeamish (the Freudian variation) or too self-interested (the Marxist) to face up to the plain truth.

At the same time, challenges were being mounted to both these families of models, again on a speculative/analytic basis, from quite a different quarter. This was the new cluster of interpretive disciplines and methods generally grouped under the movement known as Structuralism, which had long roots in the philosophy of mind and epistemology, the study of how we know things, and particularly the study of language and the emerging discipline of linguistics.

Since linguistics was based in the history of languages, it naturally seemed to be largely co-extensive with the history of cultures; and since it was also concerned with communication, how languages convey meaning, it seemed to lead cultural studies back to the study of mind itself, those structures and categories of thought itself that must surely have something to do with the structures and categories of social interaction and cultural patterns since it is the mind, after all, through which we know and engage in social/cultural inter-actions in the first place.

Structuralism, through the first half of the 20th Century, was then loosely associated with a number of quite diverse movements in art, psychology, and cultural studies, including Structural Linguistics, Symbolism, Semiotics, Hermeneutics, Phenomenology, Neo-Kantianism, and Gestalt psychology itself, among others. What united these various currents was their common reaction against the limits of reductionistic, positivist materialism (whether of the Marxist, the Freudian, or the lab science variety) basically classical mechanics and Newtonian particle physics to human thought and human affairs. In psychology, this positivist line of thought was known as Associationism, the doctrine that perceptions correspond exactly to discrete physical stimuli in the environment.

Stimuli were thought to somehow be strung together by the contiguity of external stimuli, or perhaps just of like stimuli. This was a common formulation that seemed to beg the questions it was trying to answer, since what was not clearly defined was how a person recognizes likeness of stimuli in the first place, so as to sort out the like from the unlike in building up some coherent picture of things.

Having once questioned the circular argument-by-assertion inherent in the pure objectivist model ("The likeness is somehow just in the stimuli"), most of these movements then saw themselves steadily forced into more and more constructivist answers, in the way of the movement of Hermeneutics mentioned above, which evolved from revelation of the hidden meaning of a text, toward the study of how communication of meaning takes place at all, to how meaning is encoded into a verbal or other text, and then decoded by a listener or other audience (to use more contemporary post-modernist terms).

Likewise for linguistics, which moved during the century from the study of how meaning is packed into a sentence, say, to a more relational, structural, and contextual approach to the dynamics of communication processes (Deacon, 1999). Certainly, nowhere was this movement more pronounced, away from the search for the structure of reality, toward a more distributive, relational approach to understanding human process, than in Gestalt psychology and its later offspring, Gestalt therapy.

Meanwhile, Structuralism had given rise to a seemingly new approach to cultural studies, with the work of Claude Levi-Strauss (1963), work which continues to have considerable influence on cultural anthropology and popular models of cultural studies and cross-cultural work. Cultures, according to Levi-Strauss, are best understood structurally, that is, as thematic clusters of certain repeating patterns which permeate all aspects of that culture's life. These themes - broad categories like centripetal/dispersive, found/made, open/closed, horizontal/vertical, hot/cold, cooked/uncooked, and so forth - are of course largely invisible to the participants in the culture, who in any case are not likely to be individuated enough to take a decentered perspective on matters and processes they are living holistically and unreflectively.

Since both economic and psychosexual factors are rejected as causing these dominant thematic patterns, it is largely left unclear what exactly does cause them, or how they arise developmentally, so that the various primitive cultures come to differ so much from each other, or for that matter from us.

All these basic attitudes, categories, and meanings, always emerging out of scientific studies, are part of what we mean by culture. Culture is all those relatively stable features of a social group that are learned, are variable from group to group, and are in some way passed on from one generation to the next over time. Like anything in development, what is learned earliest then tends to be the most organizing for subsequent learning – and thus the most embedded, the most resistant to change later on. What is earliest (ground- and brain-structured for subsequent learning), may also be what is out of awareness, and this is often experienced not as something learned but as just "the way the world is." In other words, all those patterns in our experience that are most deeply acculturated, are also likely, as lenses that do not see themselves, to be the ones we are most unaware of.

Hence, in an encounter between any two or more members of different cultures, the greatest source of difficulty and challenge may come not from the overt clash of beliefs and isms but from a much deeper, more paradigmatic level of assumptions: things like basic attitudes of trust or mistrust, emotional response to change, attitude toward outsiders, sense of autonomy and self-determination, attitudes toward future and past, gender and other expectations, none of which may be very clearly in the participants' own self-awareness, or their awareness of the inner world of the other person.

The deepest level of culture, then, is reality itself: all those things that we take to be not cultural, but just "the way the world is." This then leaves us with a very tricky kind of problem indeed: for not only is culture itself built in to the nature of our species, but intercultural difficulty and even conflict are in a certain sense built in as well.

Today, with the multiplicity of viewpoints of a global culture in a post-modern world, it is easy to see both the arrogance and intellectual limitations of these more extreme Eurocentric approaches to understanding culture and cultures, including Levi-Strauss's. At the same time, for all its limitations and distortions, and along with the deeply embedded, implicit imperialism of the viewpoint, there are real contributions here that will serve us as we try to develop a model that is more dialogic and mutual.

Fundamental to these contributions is Levi-Strauss's firm sense of cultural holism, the way the various dynamics and thematic elements of a given culture tend to work together as a whole. This is in contrast to the more atomized tone of some interpretations of Functionalism, where each separate element or practice of a culture may be discussed for its immediate pragmatic value, without reference to how it fits into a whole picture (see for example Malinowski, 1944).

With Structuralism, growing as it does out of linguistic studies, the perspective moves in the direction of being more deeply syntactic: that is, the meaning of a given element is always contextual, in relation to its interaction with all the other elements just as the meaning of a particular symbol or sentence is understood, ultimately, not just directly in reference to the action or thing it points to, but in relation to the language system as a whole. We thus understand cultural elements – such as practices, rituals, transactions – to be understood symbolically, that is, in relation to all other symbols and signs of culture.

Beyond Structuralism

If Structuralism dominated the field of cultural and multicultural studies for a time at mid-century (in European thought often blended with psychoanalytic views and always in stiff competition with Marxist models), it has since given way to approaches known, for want of a better collective label, as poststructuralist. The shift here is generally some attempt to get beyond the assumption and imposition of the structure of a culture by an outside observer, to the more interactive perspectives of participant observers, struggling with the more complex and rewarding problems of that more engaged position. Of particular interest to us here is the work of Clifford Geertz (1973, 1988), as the line of thinking perhaps closest in many of its assumptions and approach to those of a Gestalt perspective on culture.

For Geertz, culture is to be understood first of all as a shared system of communicated meanings. A culture is therefore a particular, relatively coherent set of signs and symbols that a certain group of people are able to communicate and transact together successfully. A group is able to do this by decoding communications and signs successfully, through an appeal to a common fund of shared underlying attitudes and assumptions (Vigotsky, 1978). The definition of a given culture then becomes that group which shares a given or overlapping set of such underlying assumptions. Since many or most such assumptions will be out of awareness most or all the time, it becomes clear how and why it is that the possibilities for intercultural misunderstanding and conflict are almost limitless.

The peripheral boundaries of such a group then always have to be seen as somewhat fluid, geographically or socially, with varying degrees of centrality or marginality and thus varying degrees of capacity to communicate successfully in the culture. Does a border tribe or border province group, such as for instance the Tex-Mex region of the Rio Grande valley in the southwestern United States, belong to US culture, to Mexican culture, or to its "own" culture? The answer would have to be all three of these, in varying ways, depending on the particular issue invoked and the communication being transacted. The resonance here with a Gestalt model of field organization in terms of shifting experiential boundaries is immediately clear.

Conflict, both within and across various cultural boundaries, is then understood not just as a clash of interests (though it may or may not be that, of course), but as a clash of meanings. Meanings in this sense are close to values - the valences we attach to particular actions or principles, which are always in relation to other values. To try to solve a conflict across a cultural boundary then becomes misguided or counterproductive, unless and until one has engaged in some understanding of the dynamic, interactive place of that issue and its meaning, in the shared subjective context of the culture of each party.

Such engagement is necessarily dialogic in the sense of the Gestalt model's use of the term (meaning the attempt to enter into the other person's or group's experience and worldview, from the inside), and clearly dependent on the establishment of safe and supportive conditions for such an engagement. Again, since many of those meanings are held out of awareness at a deep level, the wonder is not that cross-cultural contact and communication are so often problematic and conflictual, but that they are possible at all.

Plainly, Geertz's world, of the inherent challenge and difficulty of intercultural contact, is our world, the world we see everywhere around us today, in the workplace, on the multinational stage, between and among the generations or genders, and the religions of the world. This is namely a world rife with the possibility and propensity for intercultural misunderstanding and cross-cultural conflict, often tragic in nature. In this world, alas, safe and supportive conditions are most often exactly what are missing, in cases of multicultural contact, conflict, frustration, or breakdown.

To deal with this challenge, what is needed is a new model of cultural and multicultural studies, one that can synthesize all that is usefully true out of these cacophonous and conflicting traditions, and provide the outlines and the foundations, at least, of a clearer methodology for approaching and transforming destructive multicultural contact and conflict. And to do all that, we need a new and clearer anthropology, in the sense of an understanding of human nature and its dynamics in relationship and culture. Hence, we need to begin to articulate a specifically Gestalt approach to understanding and intervening in multi-cultural issues.

A Gestalt Multicultural Model of Culture, Contact, and Conflict

We are now herein suggesting an approach to cultural studies and multicultural contact that emerges from, and is informed by, a Gestalt, that is, a whole-field, evolutionary approach. We take as a point of departure our most basic, creative problem-solving/gestalt-forming nature, our hallmark adaptation for flexibility and problem-solving, as a species that is necessarily low-instinct, high-learning, and the most complexly, flexibly social of all the animals.

This combination of conditions and evolutionary responses, taken together, led us to the observation that culture is our basic species adaptation. Culture, that is, is not an overlay on our biological nature, something "added on" to "who we really are" (or even counter to who we really are, as both the traditional Freudian and early Gestalt models sometimes tended to conceive it). Rather, culture is the completion of our biological development, which is left incomplete at birth to allow for that maximum adaptability to different environmental conditions which is the fundamental human survival strategy, human nature itself. Nature, in other words, is not separable from nurture, at least in the human case.

Our gestalt-formation process, the active rendering of the chaotic world of stimuli into usable, organized wholes or meaningful units, is likewise part of our evolutionary nature, our underlying process/structure which yields our flexible problem-solving strategy for dealing with a range of different physical and social environments. That is, we must scan/select and form whole pictures, compare them with our accumulated learning, run scenarios in imagination, estimate the outcomes, and sort out those predictions into emotional/valuative terms.

This is what flexible problem solving is, and how it works (see also Wheeler, 2000, 2003b). Relying and building on this basic process is how modern humans have become, in the winkingly brief span of around a hundred thousand years, the dominant (large) species on the globe.

Part of this process is what in the Gestalt model is called figure formation, the selection and organization of features of the environment into coherent wholes in relation to our felt needs and concerns. But figure formation by itself is meaningless without ground, which is the Gestalt term for the organized structure and process for retaining and evaluating these mental, felt pictures, or learning. We may metaphorically liken the distributive nature of the human brain to a set of concentric rings, whose active center constantly invests attention and memory with evaluative, emotional responses. Based on that energetic charge, our attention and memory may become discarded as neutral information we needed only for a moment. Or they may become linked into a network of associated imagery in the surrounding rings of progressively more remote background circles or layers. Linked attention and memory will require progressively less attention and energy to run.

Thus new learning is constantly being converted and relegated to automatism, with new, short sequences of attention steadily integrated into longer, smoother sequences of more or less automatic behavior giving us a steadily richer repertoire of learned capacity to draw on, and at the same time available attentional energy to devote to the new problem, the new "figure," as we deal with ever newer situations and demands. This is what learning is: the conversion of figure to ground.

In problem solving, this sequence is then reversed. The new problem is generally addressed (at least in imagery or mental rehearsal) with the automatic response which is closest to the center, and takes the least time and energy to summon up. Only when this leads to a bad outcome (again, in real action or in imagination) do we need to reach further, stopping and devoting the time and space and effort to sort through a range of possible scenarios and responses, activating more and different associations and response networks. In extreme cases we may even take apart, deconstruct, tightly integrated response sequences, so as to color their parts with different emotional charge, enabling them to integrate anew, and differently.

This is deep relearning; of the kind that goes on in therapy whether it be physical or psychological. The deconstructive process of relocating and attending to the parts that went into integrated wholes of learning, and then experimenting with them in order to change their therapy, is the cognitive/emotional/physical sequence and meaning.   Integration itself, the move from separate intentions to automated sequence, is a spontaneous process that we don't have to will: it is the deconstruction of prior assumptions, previous patterns, that has to be willed, and takes extra support and energy.

All this is directly relevant to our consideration of culture and multicultural contact. Indeed, the earliest, deepest level of tightly integrated, automatized, long-sequence learning what in learning models is sometimes called basic assumptive set, is culture itself. As observed earlier, culture, at this deepest level, is everything we assume about the way the world "just is". Paradoxically the most basic level of acculturation is that which does not strike us as cultural, but universal. This is why inter-cultural contact and experience can sometimes feel disorienting, giving us a sense of losing our bearings. Such contact may threaten our firm grip on reality since, to repeat, reality itself is our particular cultural ground.

Hence, a Gestalt perspective leads us straight to the dual propositions that not only culture itself, but the potential difficulty of intercultural contact as well, belongs inherently to our nature. Our natural first response to threat at this level will always tend to be to strengthen and rigidify the automated sequences and assumptions already in place.   The more demanding and conflictual the conditions and the stakes of the encounter, the more rigid we are likely to become because deconstruction requires time and energy, which means safety from the pressure of emergency.

In other words (and this is the first corollary of the dual proposition above), productive, creative intercultural contact requires particular conditions of safety and support conditions and support which are most often lacking, in the real intercultural conflicts and emergencies of the real world. We can never be sure that we have come to the end of the questioning and deconstruction of our own culture, our own acculturated assumptions about the world and the people in it.

Rather, what we can do, in the light of these Gestalt insights, is to adopt a metacultural perspective on our own assumptions and beliefs. This means that rather than getting over our cultural limitations (or claiming/imagining that we are ever able, finally to put them aside), we hold our own culture and assumptions differently, more lightly, using them as the basis of a dialogic inquiry about the other's culture and using that dialogue as the necessary means, for learning about our own.

With these Gestalt perspectives in mind, what are we then to make of the past century and a half or so of cultural studies in our own Western culture? What parts of that heritage are useful to us now, as we move to explore a specifically Gestalt approach to culture and multicultural studies bearing in mind the tangled web of cultural blinders and self-justifying assumptions that permeated that legacy, parts of which must still be with us today?   What specific insights and tools of the Gestalt model can serve us in our approach to this difficult field now, as we articulate our model?

What is needed now, since we can never finally free ourselves from our own acculturation, is a model that is not just deconstructive/dialogic, but includes as well the tools for its own deconstruction, for questioning itself and us, as we employ it.   In what follows, we will present eight propositions from the Gestalt perspective we have been developing here, on human nature, the human learning process, and their implications for cultural studies and work. Each of them has direct applications to multicultural work, either changing the approach somewhat or clarifying some practical principle already known in the field.

Fittingly for a holistic model like Gestalt, each of the propositions also tends to contain, imply, and/or follow from all the others.   Taken together, they give us the beginnings at least of a coherent Gestalt stance toward this difficult, urgent work.   Such a model then changes our understanding of culture and its dynamic role in our lives, and changes our approach and our interventions in this complex, challenging field.

Eight Propositions

1)   All contact is cultural contact: This follows from our discussion above, about culture as human nature, and Gestalt process as the fundamental structure of human functioning.   For any perception to be meaningful and usable to us, it must be related to a network of previous perceptions and learnings what in Gestalt is called ground.   At the deepest level, those ground assumptions - basic, long ago learning about the world and our place in it - do not feel like learnings at all (because they are largely preverbal, relational, and embodied).   Rather, they strike us, if we lift them up at all, as reality, the way the world is.   And these deepest, out-of-awareness assumptions are not only culturally determined and culturally variable: they are culture itself.

It is important to note that this idea goes sharply against the grain of liberal, Western, assimilationist assumptions and social norms.   In our individualistic society, it is common (and even considered progressive) to think of people as individuals first, and thus of culture as a sort of limiting bias, something that educated people get over.   The implication is that once we attain some ideal developmental level of individuation, we are beyond cultural limitations, and ready to have culture-free (read real) transactions and communications. This idea is then both dangerous and counter-productive to successful multicultural work, in ways that we will be developing below.

The complementary concern of the liberal attitude is the quite reasonable fear that relating to people in terms of their cultural background or memberships may seem to play into stereotypes and prejudices as indeed it may, and inevitably will, as long as we assume we know the meaning and relevancy of some particular membership or heritage from the outside, without inquiry of the person or persons involved. The answer to this dilemma involves a shift to a more complex way of thinking and holding awareness.

Meanwhile, doubtless no two people in the world can ever have exactly the same background assumptions in this sense; even within the apparent same culture, differences of subculture, ethnic group or region, gender culture, religion, class and family culture, and so forth will mean that fundamental, integrated conclusions or schemas about the nature of the world and ourselves will differ from person to person and group to group. Still, as long as the cultural overlap is similar enough, then people may generally get away with ignoring or deferring the differences. However, even within what appears (for the moment at least) to be the same culture, the contact that occurs is still a cultural experience. It is still filtered through a particular cultural lens even if that lens for the moment is (or seems) unproblematic because there is no other kind of contact.

Indeed, our greatest and most dangerous blind spots may often arise precisely when we are speaking with people from the same culture as ourselves because those are the times we may feel least challenged to lift up our own unexamined assumptions for new awareness. And this may tend to happen precisely at moments of intercultural pressure or perceived threat just at the very times when we need a broader perspective most! Under a felt threat, instinctively people will often "reach for" points of assumed cultural similarity with those around them, to strengthen relationships and solidarity, glossing over differences (sometimes with unexpected consequences, as when they wrongly assume that some shared membership will yield a shared prejudice or particular view of the world or that the shared solidarity will outlive the emergency).

2) The encounter between consultant (counselor/therapist/coach) and client is itself an intercultural exchange: This follows of course from Proposition 1, but it is important to state it directly for emphasis. It is easy for us to see that the client or clients, or the various parties to some intercultural difficulty, have a culturally biased point of view: much harder, oftentimes, to remember that our own point of view, ultimately, is also biased because there is no such thing as an extra cultural point of view. Again in Gestalt terms, outlined above in developmental and evolutionary perspective, this would be a figure without a ground, by definition something completely meaningless.

This in turn means that in any meaningful encounter, culture can never be "off the table." That is, whenever a client (again, whether in consulting or therapy) is not supported to question the cultural perspective of any other party (including especially the consultant or therapist), then the effectiveness of any intervention will be diminished because the client will necessarily discount the intervention for its unknown or potential cultural bias. The working rule of thumb is always: whatever is out of bounds is potentially controlling the conversation. If it's not on the table (at least potentially), it's under the table. If you can't talk about it, then you have to project: that is, to imagine the meanings behind the behavior, so as to know how to interpret the person and deal with his/her behavior at all.

There is no prior, categorical solution to this inherent, dynamic dilemma of all human contact, no way to solve this problem for once and for all, or even to hold it constant, while other things vary. Culture, and the necessity of each party to take relevant perceived/imagined membership into account, as she/he interprets and evaluates the other's communications, are always dynamically present. The only remedy lies in a change in process. To prepare the ground for understanding the nature and importance of that change, we need to understand something about cultural membership itself, and how it is that we know what culture we belong to and identify with.

3) All culture is multiculture: This proposition is true in two senses. First, as the pioneering African American author W. E. B. DuBois (1986) insisted with regard to race, there is the fact that culture does not come up as an

awareness or an issue, until we are in the presence of an activated cultural boundary. That is, culture is an idea that arises in the encounter with another culture. Until that time, we do not experience ourselves as living in a culture, or even in culture; we are just living. This point has profound implications for Gestalt work with cultural issues.

Secondly, every person belongs to multiple cultural groupings, each with its own boundaries, interests, criteria, and meanings. This notion builds first on the observations of Bentley (1908) and others more than a century ago. It was Bentley's insight that cultures, particularly large national cultures, are never by any means so monolithic as outsiders imagine them to be -- and particularly as outsiders may perceive them during times of intercultural stress or conflict.

Rather, a culture is made up of many distinct interest groups, such as class or religious/ethnic group, which may be at odds with each other in various ways. These groups may fulfill all the criteria of cultures, having identified membership and boundaries, traditions and rituals of their own, and particular meanings and relationships of terms and concepts that are different from those held by other groups in the same (national) culture.

This is of course a central idea of the liberal/pluralist tradition: the unifying theme and insight, for example, of the great leftist film director Jean Renoir (generally regarded as the the most influential artist in the dominant Western medium of the 20th Century), whose work constitutes a sustained lament that the social units that have armies and weapons (that is, nation states) are, tragically, not natural social groupings at all. To Renoir, the natural affinities between people and among peoples are along lines of class, not nation, with wars often serving the real purpose of reestablishing the hegemony of the privileged classes.

In his films members of the working class of different nations, even nations at war who do not even speak the same language, still recognize each other instinctively and communicate easily. Likewise the aristocrats and plutocrats of the nations of Europe have an instinctive affinity and speak the same symbolic discourse (and sometimes, literally, the same language, as in pre-Bolshevik Russia, whose upper class, like those of other Western nations of the day, all spoke learned French in society. French, indeed, was actually the first and sometimes the only language of Russian aristocrats).

But Bentley tended to regard such identifications as fairly static, or at least arranged in some stable hierarchy (as in U.S. politics, where religiously affiliated politicians often take pains to assert that they are "Americans first," and religious congregants second). In fact, each of us belongs, potentially and in various circumstances, not just to class and religious/ethnic identity groups, but to many other groupings as well, with varying levels of depth of influence on our perceptions of the world, both in and out of awareness. Some of these, like age group and (especially in post-industrial societies) profession, may change over time; others, such as ethnicity or gender, now seen as a powerful codeterminant of one's perceptions and outlook, are (almost always) stable.

Still others, such as primary sexual orientation/identity, are relatively stable and powerfully organizing, but may sometimes change in the course of a lifetime. Moreover, where earlier thinkers and artists often thought in Marxist derived terms of conscious self-interest, a Gestalt perspective points us more broadly to issues of belonging and identification, of which immediate self-interest may be a part, as organizing dynamics of the experiential field.

This multiplicity of group identification and membership may be most evident in modern pluralist societies, but it applies to traditional or holistic societies as well (that is, to those cultures which used to be known as primitive, largely for their presumed failure to emphasize individual over collective identity). Such cultures may look consistent or monolithic from the outside, but inside them people are quite expressive and aware about the importance of their multiple memberships in various clans, totem groups, families, regions, professional, and especially gender groupings, each of which may have its own calls for allegiance, interests, and ways of looking at the world and communicating with each other (and with outsiders).

The Gestalt perspective tells us that we have to organize our perceptual world, to render it into a world of experience, dynamically structured perceptions which we can invest with intention and emotion, on the way to coping and experimenting and problem solving in the real worlds of our lives. Culture theory points out that this dynamic organizing process is heavily prestructured and codetermined by our felt experience of belonging and identity, which enters into our interpretive process, bending and coloring it toward structures and concepts that are intelligible to our fellow group members in a shared way. All that is part of our natural equipment, naturally developed through nurture (which is always acculturated). Our being, that is, is a being-in-culture; nature and nurture.

To this picture we now add a sometimes dizzying plethora of potential cultural memberships: it is in this sense that each of us is inherently multicultural group identities which may of course conflict, between members of "the same" group, or even within one person. Moreover, plainly some or all of these significant memberships may be in play at the same time, or in rapid succession. And yet people have to act, to make choices and at times to take sides. How do we know which one of these potentially conflicting identifications counts, which one trumps the others, at a given moment? Here too the Gestalt perspective can shed some light, in a way that is both commonsensical and theoretical clarifying as should always be true of a model that prides itself on being experience near.

4) Boundary depends on context: The short answer to the question above is simply, it all depends. What it depends on is the shifting organization of the experiential field at the moment. That organization, our sense of felt reality, what the world "looks like" at the moment, depends on which membership or identification (which cultural ground) is salient to us at the moment: that is, which is most relevant as a dynamic context for our felt concerns, needs, and intentions at the time (including our need for belonging, which implies the welfare of our identified group or groups).

These identifications need not be in conscious awareness to have organizing power, though they will tend to come into awareness at times of conflict, particularly internal conflict (as when I am torn between loyalties, or conflicted about my identity). These conflicts can be particularly anguishing, at a conscious level and particularly disorienting, when they take place at a level out of awareness. An acute example of inner/outer struggle of this type would be the poignant case of patriotic Italian Jews, with the coming of Fascism in the 1920's.

Italian Fascism was officially (yet not for the most part violently) anti-Semitic, and at the founding of the Party, Jews were not allowed to join. Some liberalization took place during the 20's but after the Nazis came to power in Germany in 1933, restrictions on the civil rights of Jews in Italy progressively increased (open violence and deportations became common only once the Gestapo moved in, after the fall of Mussolini in 1943). For almost the first time since the Middle Ages in Italy, deep cultural habits, assumptions, rituals, and relational gestures that a person might express as a Jew came into direct conflict with those that the same person might experience and exhibit as an Italian. This conflict was all the more excruciating in that Italy as a national identity was quite a recent cultural innovation: the creation of the unified Italian state was still within living memory at the time; and Jews had generally been among the strongest supporters of the union.

Ethnic/political conflicts like this and they are only all too common through history, and today are often tragic; but parallel examples on a less dire level abound. I have written elsewhere (Wheeler, 1997) about the experience of arriving in Africa for the first time, and inquiring of an African psychiatrist colleague how much he had tipped a young man in a restaurant, whom he had sent out on a small errand. His response was to correct me earnestly, saying that it was not at all a tip, that the young man owed us the service just by virtue of our being older, and that in the village he would know that, reciprocally, we would take care of him and his family in case of need. Since we were not in the village, he had given the young man money for food, to indicate the caretaking, and compensate for the fact that in a city of over a million people, he had no village elders of his own.

On the one hand, this vignette illustrates Geertz's (1973) point which also derives from the terms of the Gestalt model as we are outlining it here: namely that the same gesture (giving a small coin on the occasion of a personal service) is not really the same at all, in the context of a different cultural ground.

In the conscience of my own American culture, an economic exchange of labor and money has integrity, and satisfies the demands of my own internalized cultural standards and belonging, when it is characterized by fair pay for fair work. In my host's culture, the same gesture was in satisfaction of the membership values and meaningful criteria of a village culture of mutual caretaking. But at the same time, the example also serves to illustrate my colleague's attempt to reconcile his own felt internal multicultural tension, as he enacted a small echo of the meaningful gestures of his culture of origin, in the quite different context of an urban, Westernized professional world, with a money economy and literally tens of thousands of young men in the city with no supportive social connections and no particular occupation, eager to perform odd jobs in the expectation of monetary reward.

Thus my colleague, who told me he often felt quite overwhelmed by the sheer numbers of homeless and rootless youth, and who was already supporting perhaps twenty dependents on a small University medical salary, was attempting as best he could to enact both cultures at once in a single gesture, which had at least somewhat compatible meanings in two quite different cultural systems (in either understanding, the boy did at least get something to eat).

In a greater or lesser degree, each of us experiences inner multicultural tensions of this sort, in which various loyalties and cultural instincts may be activated, some of which may conflict with others. As always in our cognitive/emotional life, our natural response is to try to achieve an integration that transcends the apparent conflict, a whole picture which is well enough structured and articulated to serve as a reliable base for action; this process, which itself transcends culture (and indeed gives rise to our experience of it) is what the Gestalt model is all about. Where we cannot achieve this, and have to choose between different cultural imperatives and meanings which are both activated and important, we feel significant tension, in proportion to the importance of those identifications, and the felt threat to our membership.

In my own case, I am readily aware of the felt pressures and pulls of my memberships/identifications as a member of Western/rationalist culture (with its steady pressure for consistency of ideas), as an American and specifically a Southerner (and more particularly, as an American with progressive political identity, and a Southern liberal/dissident, both quite self-conscious sub-cultures with meanings, traditions, and demands of their own), as a man in the gendered sense (with a tendency to assume certain commonalities of meaning and experience with other males, certain shared pressures and responsibilities again in the more specific context of an identified sub-group of "non-macho" or in a sense dissident-identified males), and also a member of a particular professional culture (one which is quite self-conscious about its own cultural demands).

All of these are deeply organizing to various degrees, and exert powerful pulls in particular situations, sometimes in contradictory ways. In addition, a later identity (yet one that builds clearly on family / sub-cultural traditions of political dissidence) is as a member of an emergent world culture, with accompanying feelings of responsibility (and often helplessness) with regard to global problems.

Which of these cultural memberships (and others) is up at a given moment? This is an important thing to know, both to understand oneself and make decisions more successfully and especially to know of other people. After all, if we do not understand the context and meaning of particular gestures to that given person in that given situation (in other words, the relevant cultural boundaries being evoked), then it quickly becomes impossible to predict, understand, or negotiate the person's behavior. Communication, teamwork, management, and personal relationship alike then suffer, or even become impossible.

Plainly, knowing the relevant cultural ground at a given time is no easy matter especially given, as we have already said, that this is something we are by no means always aware of ourselves. Simple asking may well not suffice, if the person does not have a clear cultural perspective on him/herself (as in the case of all those cultural beliefs and assumptions that just feel like givens, the "way the world is"). Our answer is dialogue, in a special sense which lies at the heart of all inter- and intrapersonal work that is informed by a Gestalt perspective. And dialogue is a term that is important enough in our perspective here to stand as a proposition in its own right.

5) Dialogue as the fundamental intervention of a Gestalt approach to culture issues: We come here to a familiar term which has a particular use and meaning in Gestalt work, one which is directly relevant to our concerns here. Dialogue, as we use the term here, means a particular kind of conversation in which the goal is not limited to expressing your perception or position, but rather focuses on clarifying the sources and meanings of the various points being expressed: not just what you want or believe, but why that particular thing is important to you.

The intention that organizes the activity and experience is not prevailing, but deep understanding. In Gestalt terms, this means a shift in focus from figure to ground. Not your position itself, that is, but where you are coming from, what the meaning of the figure is to you, in relation to your own ground of beliefs, values, goals, expectations, and loyalties. These are things, as we keep saying, that we may not immediately know ourselves, or know fully; thus the conversation requires active listening, or listening coupled with a particular kind of open inquiry, aimed at making sure we understand and have been understood.

The significant position held is not one of not being agreed with: that would be in the nature of a conventional debate. Rather, the stance in dialogue is one of exploration and discovery, not right and wrong – but understanding how the perspective of the other person coheres and relates to her/his actions (and making one's own understood), as distinct from winning or losing a point.

The applications to communication across a cultural boundary are immediate and evident. If culture is in the ground of the perception or position and if that ground, again, is often unexamined or taken as obviously given, then trying to come to some kind of understanding or agreement at the level of figure (behavior, perception, the position you take or the goal you seek) may often be hopelessly off the point. The terms of the discussions, and the values attached to them, may simply be different, even incommensurate, across a significant cultural boundary. If we cannot find a way to stop and shift the discussion to those meanings and values, and how they connect with other meanings and values in that subjective, felt world, then oftentimes the parties will just be "talking past each other" -- as indeed we see every day in the world around us, and often in our own contact and communication efforts as well.

It is here that we can draw on the insights and implications of "poststructuralist" (or "postmodernist") approaches to cultural issues, particularly with regard to the work of Geertz (1988) and others who share his views. If culture is a shared system of symbols and meanings (a definition that is completely in harmony with the Gestalt perspective being developed here even as the Gestalt model adds an emphasis on emotion and belonging), then we understand intercultural conflict and misunderstanding as not so much a matter of conflicting goals or desires, but more as a clash of meaning systems.

To be sure, individuals or groups (across cultures or within an identified culture) will often compete for dominance or access to some limited resource, and that competition may or may not be amenable to negotiation, compromise, or some kind of non-zero-sum partnership solution. Such conflicts are difficult enough at times. Indeed, they are the whole reason for government, under classical "social contract" theory, which essentially is simply the insight that we may all be better off (the strong as well as the less strong) if we agree to subscribe jointly to some superior authority, rather than each of us spending most of our separate resources guarding against unexpected aggression from all the others (Wright, 1999).

Intercultural conflict typically adds a whole other layer of complexity and challenge to these difficulties. Intercultural, by definition, means reflective of different grounds of belief and value, different systems of meaning and belonging. Indeed, it is the underestimation of the basic human need for belonging which lies at the heart of much of the Western difficulty with intercultural communication (other cultures bring other difficulties to the table). Much of Western individualist/ liberal ideology, after all, is based on the abstract notion of the *homo economicus*, the free individual who always acts in his own rational best self-interest (Wheeler, 2000). But rational is a culturally relative term, in that actions which flow from an invisible cultural ground may look irrational, or without defensible meaning, to outsiders when insiders could explain them perfectly rationally and well. Likewise, self is a culturally variable concept: is the honor of my ancestors part of my self system or of the economic attainment of my children? Again, it all depends.

And again, this points to the dialogic intervention. It is no use to argue about whether a given action is or is not justifiable. Rather, the working assumption of a dialogic perspective and intervention is that everyone's actions make sense -- to him/her! This is why the emphasis is on dialogic inquiry, as both a means of knowing the other better, and also the beginnings of a shared perspective and even joint action.

6) The intentional focus is on supports: The intention organizing the activity of dialogue, we have said above, is not prevailing but deep understanding. Well and good, but people and groups still desire to prevail. Even if the cultural aspect of an intergroup conflict has to do with different systems of meaning and belonging, the conflict almost always has simple competitive dimensions as well, for control of some resource that is felt to be scarce, fragile, or under threat.

This is the complexity of intercultural conflict that makes this type of clash so resistant to solution and difficult to work with. The competitive aspect of the conflict itself might well be successfully addressed by creative, non-zero-sum solutions of the type that have defined the expansion of civilization since at least the time of our primate ancestors and characterized evolution in general, but it never gets addressed, since the participants are talking past each other in cultural-meaning terms. And yet those cultural meanings also never get addressed, because of the stakes and pressure of the competition or threat itself! How can we ever break this kind of dynamic lock, and get to that ideal intercultural dialogue in the first place?

The answer has to be: by the provision of additional supports. In a Gestalt field model that captures human behavior and experience, all events are understood in relation to their supportive conditions in the field. This is axiomatic in the system: what happens is what the relevant field, the source of events and energy favors, with field understood as comprising everything dynamically relevant, including the inner experiential worlds and intentions of all its subjective members (Wheeler, 2000). To change or add any behavior (including the behavior of focusing on ground beliefs and belongings) requires a change in the system of supports in the whole field.

This additional support may come in any dynamically relevant area, ranging from physical boundaries to felt intentions and meanings. An example comes from the acute political/cultural conflict between Israel and Palestine, in which both these conflictual dimensions competition for resources and clash of meaning/belonging systems -- are vividly displayed. A famous intervention in this case began in 1993 (after long preparation, of course) with transporting the principal representatives of the conflict, Yitzchak Rabin and Yasser Arafat, to a private estate in Norway, where they lived for the duration of the negotiations, taking their meals in the intimate personal atmosphere of their host's family.

This move to change the physical setting of the principals of a conflict to someplace apart and well-bounded off from the location of the conflict itself, is a common one in negotiations large and small (even including the "neutral turf" of a therapist's or mediator's office), and serves to support the refocusing of attention, for the duration of the negotiations at least, on questions of meaning as opposed to urgent practical issues and the pressure of other members of each group.

To be sure, selling any resulting agreement to one's own side afterwards can then be a new challenge, as the negotiating team may be perceived (rightly) by people back home as having begun to constitute a special cultural setting of its own, distinct from that of either home party to the conflict. Union/management negotiations are often plagued with this problem, and end up walking a delicate line between the necessary privacy to engage in horse trading, and a degree of ongoing transparency of process which may block any movement at all. In this case, this issue was illustrated tragically by the assassination of Prime Minister Rabin of Israel two years later, by a member of his own culture, thereby illustrating Proposition 3 above as well, that no culture is monolithic.

Another dimension of support for resolution of this complex conflict at the level of meaning systems and belonging was provided by Rabin himself, both before and after the Oslo Accords. Long known as a "hawk" in Israel, upon becoming Prime Minister in his later years, Rabin began speaking of the future, reframing the issues of the conflict in terms of the world the participants were going to leave to their grandchildren.

This, too, is a classic intervention sometimes known as invocation of a supra-ordinate goal -- that is, a goal both parties can share, which transcends and trumps the immediate issues of the conflict (Sharif, Asch & Milgram, 1969: 91-128). In effect, what Sharif's study demonstrates is that working with teams (as, for example, at a boys' camp) can create artificially two different cultures, each with its own defining criteria and membership (though the assignment to one team or the other was arbitrary), and then turn them loose at some point. The results were so quickly and powerfully conflictual that in the end the experimenters had to manufacture a shared emergency (they purposely broke the camp's water system) to overcome the intensity of the cultures that had taken hold.

Thus a certain fund of applied knowledge has grown up about the supports required for dealing with this difficult area, deriving from negotiation theory and practice in general, and the especially thorny area of intergroup and multicultural negotiation in particular. Much of the contribution of the Gestalt model here, as in some other areas, is to insist on a primary focus on the dynamic issue of supports itself, and to systematize the informal body of wisdom and practice in the area.

7) Experimentalism as an organizing attitude: Experiment, in Gestalt, is understood in two senses. One is the more formal sense of the term: the explicit enactment of a trial case or scenario, to get feedback (from the environment or other people), evaluate, and decide on a course of action. We do this all the time, of course, in cases large and small, from tasting a bit of something to see if it is good all the way to scouting something out, spending time with someone to see if our interests coincide, trying a new strategy in any area of life, casting a vote in a particular way to try to influence an outcome. In this sense experiment is part of our evolutionary heritage, a direct implication of the learning style and strategy described above, which make up our inherent Gestalt nature and process.

The experimental method, in the scientific sense, is then really just another level of formalization of this necessary, natural process, which is key to our species survival. The particular hallmarks of scientific method are the attempt to be explicit about the hypothesis being tested, and the formal effort to control all the relevant factors. Of course, we never can know that we have controlled all the possibly relevant variables. You cannot prove an open-ended negative with logical tools. In this sense even hard science remains always a culturally influenced construct, not objective reality itself, since deep cultural assumptions will always permeate our decisions about the boundaries of inquiry about relevant factors.

But these same principles of knowing what prediction we are testing out and attempting to see the relevant causal factors, are always involved, in a rough and ready way at least, in the ongoing learning experiments of life. It is in this everyday sense that experiment is implied by constructivism itself, the fundamental Gestalt insight and proposition that we are not the passive receivers of our experiential world, in the way 19th Century psychology imagined, but rather active agents and co-constructors of that experience. All intentional action has an experimental aspect, as long as we are at least open to considering the results of the action as a test case which is to say, as a basis for useful learning and prediction. In the human case, predicated on flexible adaptation to novel circumstances, experiment and learning are inseparable.

This then leads us to a second sense of experiment, one which is directly applicable to our consideration of cultural and multicultural issues here. This is the idea of experimentalism not just as a strategy but as an attitude, an organizing stance, in a particular situation or in life in general. Intention, as we keep emphasizing in this discussion, organizes our experiential field by selecting/directing attention; this is a fundamental precept and corollary of the basic Gestalt proposition of our co-construction of experience itself. When we shift our intention in any given situation from outcome to learning, our attention necessarily shifts as well. But this is then the same as the shift we were discussing in the previous section, from espousing or defending a position, to inquiring about what is behind that position, for oneself as well as for the other person or group.

In this way experiment as an attitude or stance is intimately linked with dialogue: dialogue, in the special sense we are giving the term here, is the experimental method of cultural studies and multicultural intervention. Our dialogue is based on an authentic inquiry, that is one in which I genuinely want to know the other person's answer, and his/her world. Inquiry, in turn, is necessarily based on some hypothesis, however informal or implicit. The result is then to confirm or disconfirm that previous notion or wondering: in other words, to learn something.

This in turn leads us to our final proposition, for a Gestalt-based approach to this field: the necessity of intercultural encounter for self-knowledge and growth, both as an individual and as a community or culture.

8) Multiculturalism as a value—intercultural contact as a condition of personal growth: as Gregory Bateson (1972) observed, it takes two to know one. Culture, as we have developed and defined the concept here, is something that in a very real sense only arises in multicultural contact. That is, we enact our culture and know it as well, to a degree, in that we know how to enact it. But much of that knowing is implicit, performative or automatic, and largely out of awareness. This follows from the understanding of the term as we have outlined it here, in Gestalt perspective: culture, ultimately, is that which we take for granted, and hold to be stable, so that our attention can be free for all those variable interests and urgencies of life that have to be lived and dealt with. But taking it for granted means we do not know it very well ourselves, or at least not in an articulated way.

As with the individual's interior world, which is revealed (to her/himself as well as to the other person) in the intimate encounter with another

(Wheeler, 1994), so with our cultural worlds: we get to know our own culture, in the encounter with another culture.

Conclusion

In the end, we would argue here, this encounter is more than a value: it is a necessity. It is at this level that we see a justification and a rationale for those much beleaguered cultural values, cultural pluralism, tolerance, and the liberal tradition. At least, since the time of the Enlightenment period in 18th Century Europe, the idea of cultural pluralism as a positive value has emerged as an integral consequence of the rise of the movements known as Western liberal humanism. This marked the beginning of when Western culture valued tradition. This was also in the West over the past three centuries, a period marked by genocides of the Jews, the Gypsies, the Armenians, the Amerindians, and many other groups in the world at EuroAmerican hands, as well as by mass enslavement and deportation of Africans, religious and ethnic and gender persecutions and countless other unspeakable violations and contradictions. Then, it also became the first successful movements to ban slavery in the history of humankind, the founding of the United Nations, and the Declaration of Human Rights, including the growth of women's and other civil rights movements for cultural groupings at every level of definition.

But is this evolution and conditional spread of these values a case of cultural domination or of the emergence of something new in the world, multiculturalism as a metacultural value? That is, is Western humanism itself just one more cultural value like others, imposed in the end like some forms of globalization, which can amount at times to no more than Western economic imperialism under a new name at the point of a gun? Or is it something more, a value with cultural roots (in many cultures) to be sure, like all values, but ultimately one of those evolutionary steps, a new level of feedback and complexity which contains the power to deconstruct and transcend itself?

In other words, is liberalism itself the metacultural proposition that people and groups have certain rights which trump the local values of any particular culture? If, for example, we actively oppose ourselves to the tradition of genital mutilation of certain groups, are we merely espousing the domination of our culture over another culture or are we (also?) participating in a metacultural stance, which claims some metacultural ethical basis? And what, for another example, of the multitude of fundamentalisms burgeoning today defined as claims for the revealed status of some particular text, and for the particular interpretation of those texts being espoused at the moment, as lying beyond the reach of further interpretation or doubt and their claims of divine sanction (usually, ultimately and inherently, of the sword, as we would argue here)? How do we adjudicate the conflicting cultural claims of such groups and practices other than by the sword?

The Gestalt evolutionary perspective we have taken on culture and multiculturalism can help us here toward resolving this old dilemma, which lies at the heart of humanistic toleration, and is nothing less than the most urgent issue of our times (equaling, perhaps surpassing, the desperate claims of global environmentalism). By appealing to our basic Gestalt-forming, field-resolving nature as a species and by grounding that process description firmly in both hard research and evolutionary theory we arrive at a new basis for justifying both multicultural toleration and the deconstruction of certain cultural claims alike (which in the end are the same thing).

Our basis and our claim here, growing out of this model, are this: cultural pluralism and liberal tolerance (and certain intercultural interventions) are based on and justified by the proposition that multiculturalism and its corollary, cultural relativism, constitute an advantageous way of gathering and processing/interpreting information, a superior learning stance over monoculturalism as a value, a stance more in harmony with our basic human nature as constructivist learning animals in a shifting field, and more supportive of the direction of human evolution, toward greater levels of complexity, greater articulation of human experience.

By appealing to the terms and conditions of our basic species nature, we seek and begin to find the outlines of the values of an emergent world culture, one that will necessarily in some way hold and contextualize local cultures, and place them in some (hopefully) viable, creative relationship among themselves. Will that holding context be one in which the whole tends to homogenize and obliterate the parts, in the way of the nation-state in relation to its subsidiary factions (Wheeler, 2003a)? Or will it be more along the lines of the classic cultural/political metaphor of the human body, where the hand, say, becomes most vibrantly alive, its best and fullest self, by concentrating on its unique hand-nature and by harmonizing dynamically with the whole body.

To separate and then oppose these two dialectic ideas to/from each other, i.e. self-definition and belonging, is to condemn both to loss or destruction, either by atrophy (losing the unique functions of that limb or organ or subculture), or by invasion and domination of the whole by the part (unrestrained imperialistic dominance, or the body metaphor, cancer).

This means that our next step in cultural evolution now, out of this perspective on experiment and dialogue as fundamentals of a Gestalt understanding of the field, must be in the direction of greater complexity of vision, a new level of articulation of our shared human experience, one that holds the other and the self. In the end this is experimentalism as a stance and a value, the logical fruits of the application of a Gestalt perspective to the field.

Personal Account

My own views on questions of culture and multi-culture, as I can see more and more clearly as I grow older, were very much shaped by my early experiences growing up in the American apartheid South in the latter half of the last century. I'm sure, coming out of that time and place, that I've never gotten over my early conviction that "culture," "people like us," indeed the use of "us" and "them" at all, were all just code-words and -phrases, in the end, for racism and oppression. When White politicians of that era spoke of cultural "essence" or "our Southern way of life," what they really meant, I soon realized, was keeping the Blacks down.

Since that time I've come to have a deeper appreciation, to be sure, of the riches and resources of culture -- in the sense of *cultures*, particular social identity groups with their own systems of meaning, symbols, and tradition. One of the great joys of living in today's complex, multi-cultural world, after all, is the access we have, physically and spiritually, to all the cultures of the past and present, all the myriad variations on the human spirit, speaking to us from every conceivable way of life and point of view, each in a unique and revelatory voice.

But note that we *do* have that access, they *do* speak to us meaningfully -- differently maybe from how they spoke to their own original audience, yet still recognizably, still meaningfully. This has to mean that somehow, beneath or through the filter of culture, there is still something that might be called our common humanity -- even if that humanity is always, everywhere expressed through some cultural lens and language.

Another thing I realized early on was how cultural boundaries shift. As a student activist in the late sixties, in youth programs in the northern urban ghettos, I found I could bond with Black parents of my young tutees through the medium of a shared Southern culinary heritage. It was their great joy to be able to host their child's volunteer tutor at a Sunday dinner table of home cooked cornbread, collards, fried green tomatoes and smoked ham and sweet potato pie -- the cuisine that was just then becoming self-conscious as "soul food," but which to me was just Southern country cooking, the same kind of cooking my grandmother learned on the farm just after the Civil War, and later served to me as a boy -- as my old aunt still did in her late nineties, just half a dozen years ago.

This was culture, to be sure, in the form of a high popular art. But note how the location and meaning of the cultural *boundary* shifted, depending on the setting and moment. In the region my hosts and I both came from, in those days we were positioned as adversaries in a feudal system of stratified classes and castes; a few states away, in the same country, and we were fellow expats, with a common enthusiasm for the okra pods the grandfather of one of my students' families grew in tubs on the back porch, because you "can't get it around here."

In other words, the central fact of culture is, like any living thing, *it all depends*. We all belong to multiple cultures at the same time -- potentially as many as there are possible situations, where common or conflicting identities and loyalties may be forged or elicited. Boundaries that seem sacred and absolute in one time or place, may suddenly vanish or reconfigure, given different exigencies, different supports. Take religious community boundaries, sometimes claimed to be among the most intractable: when I was a boy, again in the American Old South, virulent anti-Semitism was taken for granted among

White evangelical Christians; nothing could be more startling to people of my age and background than to turn on the tv in the US and find the same group preaching Israeli expansionism (for quite devious motives, to be sure, with regard to the survival of Jews, and Judaism as a culture).

Indeed, we might define "fundamentalism" as a cultural boundary that doesn't shift -- i.e., one which is dead, defending against some powerful felt threat but no longer serving the growth of the whole living field, or of its members. Fundamentalism (of whatever stripe) always insists that only one dimension of our complex living selves matters, and that the relationship between our group and all the rest of the field is fixed and inflexible, not a living dynamic. And yet in all the most intense, most formative experiences of life -- childbirth, the nurturing of children, illness and dying, war and other great dangers, erotic love, or any other kind of spiritual intensity, people always seem to find that these apparent divisions melt away, leaving our shared humanity at the fore.

Unlike finches, or cyclostomata, or mites, humans are a single breeding pool, one common genome, with a common evolutionary history, a common spiritual and bodily nature -- and a common future. Let us work and pray for a world in which all the unique parts are celebrated, yes -- but always in a way that emphasizes their shared heritage, their mutual contribution and enrichment, and their interdependence on each other and the whole cultural field.

Gordon Wheeler, Big Sur, CA, USA

References

Bateson, G. (1972). *Steps to an Ecology of Mind*. NY: Ballantine Books.

Bentley, A. (1908). *The Process of Government: A Study in Social Pressures.* Chicago: University of Chicago Press.

Boas, F. (1912). *Changes in Bodily Form in Descendants of Immigrants. American Anthropologist*, 14, pp. 530-62.

Chomsky, N. (1972). *Language and Mind*. NY: Harcourt Brace Jovanovich.

Deacon, T. (1997). *The Symbolic Species*. NY: Norton.

deWaal, F. (1996). *Good Natured: The Origins of Right and Wrong in Humans and Other Animals*. Cambridge MA: Harvard University Press.

Dewey, J. (1967). *The Early Works 1882-97*. (Ed. J. Robinson). Carbondale: Southern Illinois University Press.

DuBois, W. (1986). *Writings*. NY: Library of America.

Ehrlich, P. (2000). *Human Natures*. Washington D.C: Island Press.

Erikson, E. (1950) *Childhood and Society*. NY: Norton.

Fogel, A. (1993). *Developing Through Relationships*. Chicago: University of Chicago Press.

Galton, F. (1869). *Hereditary Intelligence*. London: Macmillan.

Geertz, C. (1973). *The Interpretation of Cultures*. NY: Basic Books.

Geertz, C. (1988). *Works and Lives: the Anthropologist as Author*. Palo Alto: Stanford University Press.

Hamilton, A, Madison, J & Jay, J (2003). *The Federalist Papers*. (Ed. T. Ball). Cambridge: Cambridge University Press.

Hegel, G. (1828/1931). *The Phenomenon of Mind*. London: Macmillan.

Levi-Strauss, C. (1963) *Structural Anthropology*. NY: Penguin.

Levi-Strauss, C. (1975) *Tristes Tropiques*. NY: Modern Library.

Macchiavelli, N. (1531/1988). *The Prince*. Cambridge: Cambridge University Press.

Malinowski, B. (1944). *A Scientific Theory of Culture*. Chapel Hill NC:

University of North Carolina Press.

Menand, L. (2001). *The Metaphysical Club*. NY: Farrar Straus Giroux.

Moore, D. (2001*). The Dependent Gene*. NY: Holt/Times Books

Nietzsche, F. (1884/1956*). The Birth of Tragedy & A Geneology of Morals*. Garden City NY: Doubleday.

Perls, F, Heferline, R. & Goodman, P. (1951). *Gestalt Therapy*. NY: Julian Press.

Robinson, D. (1986). *An Intellectual History of Psychology*. Madison: The University of Wisconsin.

Rorty, R. (1999). *Philosophy & Social Hope*. NY: Penguin.

Sharif, M, Asch, S., & Milgram, S. (1969). Group Conflict. *Gestalt Review* (9.1), 91-128

Spengler, O. (1926). *The Decline of the West* (transl. C. Atkinson). London: George Allen & Unwin.

Sullivan, H. (1953). *Interpersonal Theory of Psychiatry*. NY: Norton.

Vigotsky, L. (1978). *Mind in Society*. Cambridge MA: Harvard University Press.

Wheeler, G. (2005). Culture, Self and Field: A Gestalt Guide to the Age of Complexity. *Gestalt Review,* Volume 9, No. 1.

Wheeler, G. (1994). The Tasks of Intimacy. in G. Wheeler & S. Backman, eds. On Intimate Ground. San Francisco: Jossey-Bass.

Wheeler, G. (1997). Sex, Truths, and Gestalt. *Australian Gestalt Journal*, II: 1, pp. 24-31.

Wheeler, G. (2000). *Beyond Individualism: Toward a New Understanding of Self, Relationship, & Experience*. Hillsdale, NJ: The Analytic Press/GestaltPress.

Wheeler, G. (2003a). Shakespeare's Dream: Gestalt, Politics & Human Nature. *Australian Gestalt Journal*, VI:1, pp. 75-86.

Wheeler, G. (2003b). Contact and Creativity: the Gestalt Cycle in Context. in M. Spagnuolo-Lobb & N. Ament-Lyon, eds, Creative License: the Art of Gestalt Therapy. NY: Springer.

Wordsworth, W. (1800/1962). *The Prelude and Selected Poems*. NY: Henry Holt.

Section Two

bridging of
social phenomena

IV. IN THE SHADOW OF THE HOLOCAUST

By Anna Kubesch, DSA

We cannot speak of the disorder of Shoa (Holocaust) survivors and their children. Likewise, we cannot speak of the defense mechanism or the symptoms of these survivors or of their descendants. No, we are dealing with people who, in most cases, appear to lead a normal life, who are capable of achievements, success, and love and who suffer from different anxieties, just as a large percentage of the population of any city or country.

Why does it make sense, nevertheless, to put survivors and their children at our centre of attention? I do not have a pathological interest in this question but rather a wish to create an understanding of the psycho-dynamics of survivors as well as of their children down through generations in Austria, a country that participated federally in the Shoa (Holocaust). We psychotherapists must develop sensitivity to seeing disorders not only as the manifestation of an individual's strategy to survive but also as a manifestation emerging from a historical, cultural, and political context.

My approach and my motivation to deal with this topic are not only personal but also political. Some members of my family are survivors of the Shoa; others were murdered. There are no other members of the family -- not any more -- they are dead or were not even born, as a precaution -- after the Shoa.

I was born after the Shoa -- the only child in a formerly large Viennese family. I thus represent the Second Generation, the child of survivors of the Shoa. I live in Vienna, in Austria -- after the Shoa. I know the atmosphere of silence, obscurity, mortal fear, renunciation, repression. I know bewilderment. I know what it means to be on the run; always to have a valid passport, to have money for a ticket and to have a solid suitcase. I know how it feels to be homeless and the desire to belong. I know these symptoms from my own experience. I feel and understand myself to be of the Second Generation of Shoa survivors. The Second Generation is at the same time the first generation after the Shoa, who live facing the ground of non-connection, of non-relation, who have children and look towards the future.

My long, often painful, training in analysis that has time and again confronted me with this subject has helped me not only to come up with individual solutions and recognition -- and has cured parts of my own self -- but has also made it possible for me to see and understand myself as part of a whole. I have been made to understand disorder patterns in a social context, to notice rage and grief about political and social monstrosities, to verbalize and thus to start a dialogue.

The benchmark term of this essay is *SHTIKA* which is Hebrew for silence. Silence is of central significance for the Second Generation after the Shoa. For me, it has become important to break the taboo of silence. This is why I am writing this article, as a Jewish Gestalt therapist and colleague, about a subject that is central to me: to establish contact with colleagues and interested readers; and -- in establishing a dialogue -- in order not to remain silent even among colleagues, with clients, within the family; in order to make clear how important it is not only to talk to each other but also to pose questions and to bear the answers.

To pose questions and to continue doing so is part of the Jewish culture of those who have survived the Shoa. To open one's heart and, at the same time, to pose questions make contact and relations possible. A vivid dialogue here and now is one of the basic principles of gestalt therapy, and I would like to invite and encourage you to enter into this with me.

On one hand, it is impossible for therapists to completely understand the events and experiences of concentration camp survivors; on the other hand, the survivors themselves are unable to put their experiences into words. Also, the children of the survivors live without words, are therefore speechless, and have to make do with gaps in their parents' stories and memories. But they do have atmosphere at their disposal. Hence, Gestalt therapists can and must offer to develop a specific language of personal expression, particularly by working creatively with mood swings, smells or temperatures, family photos, music, language melody -- so that clients may develop a language that expresses their feelings accordingly.

The aim is, as expressed by Fritz Perls (1993), "...to further the process of growth and to develop the human potential .... We also have to fill in the gap in the personality, to complement what is missing and to make a whole and complete human being" (Perls, 1993: 11). In Gestalt therapy, we establish a dialogue with our clients. I think that this dialogue is especially important in our work with the Second Generation. The therapist, of course, must know his/her own sentiments, anxieties, insecurities and his/her own approach towards Jewish people as well as towards the Shoa. If the therapist does not have a clear position as regards the history of his/her own parents during National Socialism's anti-Semitism, its guilt and shame, and of the silence now, after Auschwitz, when National Socialism is not so long gone but still present in various disguises, then a part of the historical self of a therapist is missing, which is then also not available to his/her clients.

The experiences in one's own training analysis are probably also of great importance. Were National Socialism and its effects on the individual and collective psyche a topic in one's own training group, in the training analysis or in the theoretical discussion? Do we know what our trainer analysts did during the time of National Socialism, how and where they were positioned politically? Do we know to what extent they kept silent during the Shoa, assuming that either nobody was personally affected or that everybody was horrified to the same extent about what had happened? Under what circumstances was there no need for a discussion for them?

In his article, *Der ges(ch)ichtslose Psychoanalytiker - die ges(ch)ichtslose Psychoanalyse* (The psychoanalyst without history or face - psychoanalysis without history or face), Sammy Speier expounds on the idea that extreme abstemiousness in psychoanalysis is not caused so much by the fear of opening "the door to the parent's bedroom, but rather by the fear of opening the door to the gas chambers" (Speier, 1988 in Heimannsberg & Schmidt: 17). I think it is necessary that we continuously ask ourselves the following questions: Where do we stand in this context personally and professionally? What language is at our disposal in this silence? How can we do an anamnesis or reach a diagnosis so that the basic knowledge and understanding of the parent's experiences during National Socialism can be applied?

But let us return to the therapy: How can a therapeutic dialogue be beneficial? One of the central symptoms of clients in psychotherapy is the feeling of emptiness, often because of lack of information, speechlessness, and repression in the family. This void also appears in therapy and in transference.

A Gestalt therapist can make concrete therapeutic offers of relations here and now. In the frame of the therapeutic setting and with the help of the therapist, the client is invited to become aware of how the experience with the family disrupts the life he/she is leading. In addition, the personal and political position the client takes against the background of his/her biography coupled with the way he/she identifies either with the parents' experiences or the way he/she denies their special history and its effect on him/her as a child. When the client better understands his/her own life, takes responsibility for his/her own life and maintains a balance between the bonds to the parents' experiences -- autonomy develops.

As a result of this process, therapy has succeeded to a large extent with a therapist who, together with the client, is not afraid to face the experiences of the parents, grand parents, possibly other relatives, and who is not afraid to ask questions and help the client to ask questions; and lastly, who helps to bear a limited scope for grief, annoyance and acceptance.

Also, the concept of the here-and-now can become a trap, if one gets stuck in the here and now, which is one way to avoid abiding trauma. Let me explain. When a Gestalt therapist working in the here and now expresses a void in the transference back to the client in an attempt to reflect reality, the client will develop voids outside of therapy. He/she is thus confronted with silence and uncertainty, just like in the family and in a broader social reality. Thus, the client is still too weak and not encouraged to further develop his/her identity. An insistence on the here and now in this situation is possibly a home-made trap that prevents the therapist from confronting alone and, also in the discussion with the client, the causes of, in this case the mass extermination of the Jews.

It is always important to recall Erving and Miriam Polster, who say: "First of all, gestalt therapy sees the processes of remembering and planning as present functions, although they relate to the past and future. Secondly, we also deal with questions that go beyond the direct interpersonal confrontation and that refer to many important themes, such as for instance Vietnam, city planning, friendship, government, racism, etc" (Polster, 1985: 21).

One can say realistically that therapy always leaves something open but this should not be seen negatively. The question of identity, in this case of self-defined Jewish identity, before the background of mass extermination, is so central that it is not one of the open topics of ongoing therapy for survivors or their children but the centerpiece itself of therapy. Furthermore, many additional symptoms such as sleeping disorders, nightmares, vegetative disorders, are closely connected and cannot be treated isolated from identity formation. As long as the client as well as the therapist remain silent, the client sees this silence and the feeling of emptiness connected with it as something normal, self-understood, trivial and not as a social consequence that might save one's life and at the same time make one sick.

A Client

Let's consider a client of mine. She is 28 years old when she starts her therapy and her problem seems to be an eating disorder. Already in the first session, when I asked about her family, I found out that she comes from a Jewish family that has become very small and that, apart from her old father who lives in Vienna, she has an uncle and an aunt in Israel. She says, however, that none of this is relevant to her being Jewish. She rather wants to be seen as a radical feminist and animal lover (i.e. Animals must be liberated from their prisons!).

The topics mostly discussed in the first four months of the therapy were her depressions and her problem with eating. She tries to stick to the symptoms and only hesitatingly talks about her mother who died a year earlier from intestinal cancer. Her mother had not really treated her kindly and had always competed with her. She had always dressed her unbecomingly and disparaged her as a girl. The client's father is already in his 80s and lives alone after the death of his wife.

The client told me that she had been very much overweight (during her puberty), had suffered from this fact and had only reduced her weight after many crash diets. At the time of the therapy, she was not overweight any longer but still felt that she was too heavy and was very much concerned about food and about her looks. Food meant a lot to her. Safety, security, emotion were important for her. When I asked her how she would feel if she did not have anything to eat one day, she first started to cry and then she became aggressive and threatened to break off the therapy if I were to continue to bother her with such questions. I took this situation as a possible sign that the loss of food would be a trauma, but did not have any idea yet about the kind of trauma.

When I asked about the eating habits in the family, who cooked, if they ate together, about possible family rituals, the client was very reluctant, froze outwardly and thought my questions "silly, not to the point." After some silence, she told me that her mother had insisted that she eat up everything, that she should take some more and that the mother often weighed her when she was a child to check that she weighed enough. While relating all of this, the client became angry and perplexed. She could not understand why the mother had checked her eating so much but otherwise quite neglected her.

Later on in the therapy, I asked about the mother's life, about her childhood. In the first session the client had said that her parents had emigrated from Israel in the 50s, and that was all she knew. I suggested she ask her father. In the beginning, she objected, as the father was already too old and should be spared.

After a dream in which her mother had ordered her to ask her father about her life, she asked her father whether he could tell her something about her mother's life. Then she learned for the first time that her mother had been in Auschwitz as a young Polish girl and that all her family had been murdered. The mother survived by chance (her name was already on a list to be gassed), and nobody knows why. Another woman in the camp took care of her mother and hid her in the women's barracks. She could organize clandestinely bread for her, but all the same she was almost starved when Auschwitz was freed.

When the client came to the therapy with this completely new knowledge, she was shocked and dumbfounded. She had not known that her mother had been in Auschwitz. The father explained that already in Israel the mother had decided only to move to Austria if nobody there would ever learn about her youth, not even her daughter. This secret was kept consistently.

A new phase of the therapy began. The client became more depressive, she neglected her appearance, she lost weight and started to isolate herself. She considered breaking off the therapy and spoke of nightmares, but not about their content. At that time I had a cat in my practice that for various reasons had it had lost its home and could not stay at my house because of problems between it and my own cat. The cat had never been present at the therapy sessions until then, but one day it scratched at the door and meowed miserably, and the client decided that she wanted the cat to be in the room.

Five minutes later, the cat sat on her lap and purred; the client revealed that she had had a cat until it died recently and that she loved cats very much. From that moment on, my cat was always present at these therapy sessions and played an important role in them. The client told the cat what she could not tell me, and had the cat "reply" to questions by speaking through or with the cat in front of me. The client became softer and easier to reach. She identified with the cat that had lost its home (the client thought that her mother as well as herself had lost their childhood) and for the first time something like a relationship came about between her and myself.

My client now put her problems with food and her experience as a child in relation to her mother's experiences, and started to understand, and later to mourn. She had taken over the real survival anxieties of her mother that she might starve, although she did not know her mother's experiences.

Every mother worries about her baby's food. For parents who have survived hunger, food for their children is a question of life and death. They are disproportionately concerned with eating behaviors of their children, check and thus restrict them. The result is a difficult and disturbed communication between mother and child in the oral phase. Children get the feeling that it is their task to solve the conflict that their mother -- as in this case -- has with hunger and food.

For my client, it was more difficult for her to relate her mother's over-consideration with food to her mother's rejection and refusal of her in other respects. She asked the cat for explanations, the cat should identify with the mother, and the client, who used the cat as a medium for the mother, replied back to her. It was this way that she recognized that her mother possibly could not help what she had been doing. Nonetheless, my client did not want to accept this explanation. A mother, after all, has to love her child.

Survivors and Their Lives

In order to examine the subject of the Second Generation of survivors of the Shoa, it is necessary to look first at the nature of survival itself and at the life of the so called First Generation, of survivors. If we want to understand how the Second Generation manages their lives and comes to terms with life psychologically, or how certain disorders originate, we have to see them relating to their parents and grandparents and to their specific history of persecution.

Only when we have comprehended and perceived the survival strategies of the parents and grandparents will we have a basis to understand and treat the special structures and defense mechanisms of the Second Generation.

But it is not only the Second Generation that has to be seen in the light of German National Socialism; it is also us therapists. Therefore, we always have to consider also our own approach, our own biography, and our own defense mechanisms.

The Second Generation was born into this world and guided and influenced in their development by parents and grandparents (if alive) from within their own surviving possibilities. The early childhood, for example, the formative years, can only be understood therapeutically if we are to remain aware of this connection and if we do not try -- in order to avoid our own anxiety -- to immerse the life of people into a leaden historic vacuum. Otherwise, an unholy alliance between silent therapists, or therapists in denial, and silent clients will result.

The term survivor is essentially far-reaching; it is used for refugees, emigrants, so called submarines, as well as for people who survived in concentration and extermination camps or who were hiding under constant mortal fear and those who have suffered the loss of many members of their family. American Holocaust research discusses the extent to which these terms, *survival* and *survivor*, should be used when trying to understand the psychological context in a differentiated way.

I personally think that it makes sense to delimit the sense of the phrase *survivor of the Shoa* if we want to acquire a greater understanding of the psychological dispositions of a segment of people who have survived the concentration or extermination camps or who, at some point in their life, were in hiding under constant mortal fear. Our aim is not to introduce different classes of people or categories or to mitigate contexts of suffering, but to facilitate understanding. It is equally important to understand the specific situation of emigrants and refugees and to pay proper attention to their fates. However, this essays deals now mainly with people who have survived concentration and extermination camps or who were hidden, and perhaps hidden with their children of the Second Generation.

What was the situation like for Jewish people in the extermination camps? What was the situation of those few who survived National Socialist extermination camps afterwards? Surely, we already know more than we care to know about the unimaginable atrocities committed in concentration and extermination camps of the Third Reich with the aim of the "final solution of the Jewish question." Nonetheless, we still need, even more so today, to enumerate some of the horrors.

People were transported across Europe for days in dark, locked cattle wagons, without water or food; upon arrival in the extermination camps, they were either herded directly into the gas chambers and then burned in the crematories, or pushed and shoved into camp confinement for an undetermined period. Women and men were separated, families divided, acquaintances and friends who had arrived together were separated. The old and the young and the children were torn apart. Children were separated from their mothers and immediately murdered.

People were shaved, and, a number tattooed into their arm, they were left without a name; but they had a number and prison garments with a yellow star. People were herded into shacks; four or more to one-plank beds, they were always at the mercy of the guards. In constant mortal fear, they were seriously ill, and, starving, suffered from plagues, and were tortured, beaten, humiliated, violated, shot, slaughtered, immersed in mud, mutilated, and maimed and killed by medical experiments.

Many lost their will to live, did not have any energy left, died in order for their children to survive, became psychotic, apathetic, witnessed every day how those they knew were killed and expected their own death any moment. The objective of this industrial extermination was not only the physical eradication of Jewish people but, before that, the breaking of their identity. This is an important point to understand because it helps us to interpret the sadistic tortures. The prisoners were forced to become aware of their unworthiness and of their worthlessness: to become aware that they were of no value and were not worth living. They had suddenly and irrevocably lost their names, their families, and language; and their cultural behavioral patterns, such as hygiene, ritual meals; religion, ritual study habits, ritual human relations -- nothing that constituted a human life was any longer possible.

Only very few persons survived this long-lasting chaos in the extermination camps. Officially, the war was over in May of 1945, when the Allies liberated the camps. A sense of a new suddenness overwhelmed them: they were free, suddenly -- whatever freedom might have meant in a situation like that.

Almost all witnesses now speak of a sudden unimaginable silence, which I do not think of as atmospherically silent, as an ambient silence, but rather as a perplexed emptiness, without warning and orientation. And still many of the prisoners, though now liberated, continued to die from exhaustion, hunger, or out of simple resignation. How could life go on? How could life be possible at all?

Anja Lundholm Morgengrauen (1992), a Swedish writer who survived Ravensbrück, describes herself and other women after the camps as walking corpses, as people without any identity, without direction, without sex, as ghosts haunting Europe.

Austria

An abiding sense of insecurity in Austria, of not being sure how the population or the government will behave in situations similar to past situations, conditions one to feel a lack of security always everywhere. Is Austria home to returnees or just a transition? But where can there be a home in this century? Moreover, for European Jews, Israel is not necessarily home; the absence of anti-Semitism alone does not give an identity. There is also the potential of anti-Semitic statements in the air; especially because Jewish culture, religion, and tradition are little represented beyond the oleaginous philo-Semitic transfiguration of language in such formulations as "*liebe jüdische Mitbürgerinnen und Mitbürger*" (Dear Jewish Compatriots).

As post-Shoa survivors and descendants, one belongs in the world to a minority that is not talked about and that does not talk itself, where there are few social patterns and fitting ideals. The experiences of one's parents as Jews cannot be a model and no other models yet exist, or no longer do. At the same time, the Second Generation is obliged to create a normal life for their own children, even if their own life had been or still is abnormal

Let me explain further: Second Generation children were born between 1945/1946 and approximately the late 60s. When we closely examine the individual background in these families, as well as their new political situation, we realize that the close proximity of the individual and the political dimension is very significant. The political climate of the post-war period strongly influenced the individual's experience and behavior.

The time I am speaking of is mainly the 50s and 60s. Austria was busy with the State Treaty, with reconstruction, with creating an economic miracle. The manifestation of the idea of Austria as having been the first victim of National Socialism has today provided an important school-book pretext for Austrians to start from zero, to look forward, to orient themselves toward the future and to repress, deny, and ignore what had happened the years before. The memory of the murder of Jews and other victims of National Socialism, as well as a memory of their own former actions and ideas, was repressed.

I think that this attempt to discontinue one's own past historical development and identity, whatever the habits of that development and identity, will cost them dearly all their life. Not to confront the past, all the while blatantly constructing the future without the past, will be a very costly denial, indeed.

At the same time, nobody took notice that a few Jews had re-settled after the war years in Vienna. There was never a confrontation, however, between two peoples, one now without a concrete national history, the other now with a concretely denied history. But the ideas, the attitudes, the remorse, remained and manifested themselves in silence. Nothing was said, nothing was done, nothing was heard, and nothing was seen. Dull silence covered the country and its inhabitants.

In 1938, the Jewish community of Austria had grown to approximately 180,000 to 200,000 registered members. In 1945, there had been only 3,955 left. Jews were not sure whether they should stay. They began passing through, looking for relatives who might have survived, or they began to bide their time until they could travel to Israel or the United States. They were partly without orientation, without plan, waiting, exhausted, chronically empty or aggressive. Immediately after the war, nobody believed that the Jewish community would continue to exist in Austria.

William G. Niederland, a psychiatrist treating survivors in the United States, described the psychological situation of the survivors as follows: "*They suffer all their life from a sorrow which stems from National Socialist persecution within and outside the concentration camps, as well as from emotional atrophy"* (Neiderland, 1989 in Herbst & Goschler: 37f).

Niederland (1989) found typical psychological reactions and after-effects in former concentration camp inmates, which he termed *survival-syndrome.* *"The syndrome,"* he went on to say, *"appears to be characterised by the persistence of multiple symptoms among which chronic depressive and anxiety reactions, insomnia, nightmares, personality changes, and far-reaching somatization prevail"* (Neiderland, 1989 in Herbst & Goschler: 37f). Feelings of guilt towards dead family members, friends, and acquaintances constitute important elements of this condition of the survivors. These elements, of course, vary according to the individual.

Our questions abound. How did the people who returned or emerged from hiding cope with their experience, knowledge and emotions? Was there any place, any community, where they felt at home and well, given their traumatic experience? How did they get along with their former neighbors, colleagues at work, clients? How did they cope with being left alone or being part of a much reduced family?

Dreams about reunions with family and friends who had not lost their will to survive in the concentration camps were often unfulfilled. Furthermore, who was there who could give professional support?

Europe a shambles, six million dead Jews: back in a country of silence, where nobody was responsible, because Austria was the first country to be occupied and nobody knew what had happened; back in a country that was surprised to see real Jews alive who had not been gassed; back in a country where people were busy looking into the future, spreading a cloak of silence over the past, where de-Nazification happened fast, but restitution took more than fifty years -- this was the atmosphere, the climate into which the survivors of the Shoa entered to re-live. The questions of the children and grandchildren as to why they had returned here of all places can only be understood emotionally. What were their elemental experiences but for language, culture, memory, a vague feeling of home, and the hope that further members of the family might have survived, and the desire to participate in the reconstruction out of no other desire except that of simply not seeing any alternative than to go back to where one had lived before the war.

"The victims, not the perpetrators felt guilty of having survived, of having dared to remain in their home country -- this is one of the absurdities of the survivor-syndrome, this collection of depression and mistrust, regression, self-denial and fearful assimilation. By returning to the place of the crime, the country of the Shoa, the victims stigmatized involuntarily the life of their children: they were again selected from the offspring of the perpetrators" (Rheinz, 1998: 76).

Inconspicuousness was their motto, in order to survive and to live, including assuaging their anxiety and desperate attempts to leave the traumatic past behind and just to continue to live. Though grateful to have survived, they felt guilty for having survived and for still maintaining the will to live and for having children, in spite of their experiences in the extermination camps.

Children satisfied an inner desire to feel alive, to give life to life, and to observe life all around them. Living children also became a compensation for the many dead children of the camps, and a possibility to fill an inner void, as well as being a testimony of still being alive. Children of the Second Generation have a special significance. The birth of each child born into the Second Generation is accompanied by special emotions.

Various Holocaust researchers have emphasized that the war of the National Socialists against the Jewish people was aimed mainly against their physical continuity, that is, against their possibility of reproducing as a people.

Many women were afraid that because of their experiences in the camps, they would not be able to give birth to children and to educate them. But not to have a child was seen as final defeat.

A child was the proof and the expression not only of one's own survival but also of the survival of the Jewish people and was thus also very precious at that level. For many Jewish parents to have a child after 1945 meant a definite victory over the National Socialists.   A new life was created in spite of insurmountable obstacles.

For other families, the birth of a child had a religious significance, especially the children born immediately after 1945, who had to fulfill a very special task.   Already in the 1960s, Canadian psychoanalysts (Sigal, Silver, Radkoff and Ellin) wrote about the special significance of these children: "They should fill their empty life and serve as compensation and substitute for the dead family members, extinguished communities and even for their own life earlier on. Had they not been able to see their new-born children as a continuation of the lost loved ones, their whole life and all their efforts to survive would have seemed a futile sacrifice" (in Wardi, 1998: 58).

Surviving parents tried to re-establish their feeling for identity through their children. The children were seen as an extension of oneself and thus they satisfied the needs for identity and identification of their parents, thereby being prevented from possessing an individuation and formation of their very own identity.

In the post-war years, parents had high hopes for their children. At the same time, they had an ambivalent feeling towards them. They had experienced the world as a dangerous place for Jewish children (after all 1.5 million Jewish children were murdered) and they put all their energy and power into the individual fight for the survival of their children.

In Jewish tradition, the family is highly valued. The development of the children and the passing-on of traditions and values have a special significance within the family and, especially for the mother, values have a strong connection to the development of ego structure and ego strength. But if the mother's or father's ego has been damaged just as much as that of survivors of the Shoa in general, post-Shoa parents often then reacted inappropriately to the developing needs of their children. They had difficulties setting limits for their children, their limits being either too narrow or too wide; so that their children might go on to develop trust in the world outside the family.

The inhumane camp experiences of eventual post-Shoa parents often made them dwell upon their children through cautionary gaze imbued with their own past confrontation with death and destruction.   Children, having the experiences their parents lacked, were therefore overprotected. Children of the Second Generation are influenced to a large extent by unexpressed desires and demands of their parents and they often cannot differentiate between their own or their parent's wishes.

Another reaction survivor parents exhibit is not being able to love their children demonstrably, nor to invest any emotions in them. They are so preoccupied with their own experiences and losses and with their repressed attempts at mourning that they have no emotions left for others.   This phenomenon has been observed among members of families who have suffered eventual pain and loss or other types of traumatic experiences in their new lives, such as the result of murder or divorce or loss of family income. Or perhaps as children of survivors themselves, long before becoming parents, they had had no enduring happy childhood, lacking strength and support from their survivor families and thus were unable later in life to pass on to their own children a fit sense of self. Hence, children of the Second Generation see family and education as either very disciplined or without limit, and as chaotic, non-committal and without familial orientation.

The unadmitted expectation of children today is that it is often at least a certain child, in families with more than one, who should fill the family's emotional void by establishing and keeping contact with the family's history. It is this child's task to establish a connection to the family members that were murdered. Dina Wardi describes these children as "commemorative candles":

"Before the Holocaust the core family of the future survivors was bound to the community, the environment and the Jewish people by their social attachment and identification in the larger family - and at the same time with the generations of the parents and children. The Holocaust broke the elements of these chains and destroyed its connections. The part of the "commemorative candle" relates therefore to the personal history of the parents in the Holocaust, on the one hand, and to the attempt to reconstruct the broken ties between the parents, the relatives and the community where they lived before the Holocaust, on the other hand. Survivors usually tell their children very little about their past, because this is very painful for them. They confer this task to the "commemorative candle" to fill the void in their hearts and to assemble the broken and hidden mosaic stones" (Wardi, 1997: 62).

In her therapeutic group of members of the Second Generation, Wardi diagnosed anxiety and deep mistrust towards other people. Many suffered from rigidity towards themselves, rigid emotions in general, identity disorders, constant preoccupation with the parents, and re-occurring dreams of death. The parents, often the only survivors of their own first families, suppressed their memories of death and dead ones. This was their only way to come to terms with the horrors they had experienced. But they passed the dread on to their children wordlessly.

One memory that Wardi (1997) excavated was that of a death march experience. During a death march in a camp, a woman, when she was still a child, had experienced the execution of her mother behind her. She saved her own life by marching on, without looking back. When, as a parent herself, her own daughter was but a few weeks old, she taught her not to cry. Another survivor's daughter told how her mother often sat in a dark room, holding her little sister for hours and sighing. The sheer misery of many parents was simply too deep to pass on emotional security to their children.

Children were also often confronted with a wish that could not be fulfilled. It seemed as if they were also expected to heal the trauma of a rift in the continuity between the generations. Therefore, many were named after murdered relatives. They were expected to be a reminder of the dead ones without knowing the personal history of those who had suffered horrible deaths.

Such children often filled the voids with fantasies. Fantasies might fill a central role regarding a parent's sexuality, according to Wardi; as, for example, when a child assumed that the mother had only survived the camp because of her prostitution.

A fantasy of this sort helped to escape from an emotional rigidity, when a client shared such a secret with the therapy group, by allowing the fantasizer to confront her own pain and grief. An internal analysis of the real facts, of course, was also necessary for the healing process to reach closure. Wardi (1997) points out as soon as "commemorative candles" are able "to confront the experiences of their parents, their ability to come to terms with the real problems of their emotional and sexual life grows" (Wardi, 1997: 136).

Children of survivors resent -- quite rightly -- that all their actions and behavior may be defined symptomatically and pathologically; but on the other hand, they do have a lot in common with one another. I think it is therefore important to understand emotions or feelings of theirs that can lead to the re-establishment of relative normality. Hence, we must pay considerable vigilant attention to:

- *Anxiety*, because of something terrible that happened might happen again.
- *Uprootedness or Rootlessness*, from former generations and future ones
- *Homelessness* in these centuries, for Israel is not necessarily *home*; the absence of anti-Semitism alone does not give an identity
- *Not belonging*, especially against the backdrop of potential anti-Semitic statements and cloying philo-Semitic rhetoric
- *Make-believe*, that is, the lack of having a choice to make-believe, as if personal or collective de-rooting had never happened, and therefore to learn through it
- *Loss*, of grandparents and other elderly relatives and symbols of security, continuity and rootedness

"Today we miss the elders and the contemporaries. The old sages who we love and venerate; to learn from them must have been one of the nicest experiences - in a time when they still lived. They were taken away from us, we had to grow up without them. But we also miss our contemporaries. So few are still here today. And often we stick to each other because it is much more complicated with the 'others'" (Wardi, 1997: 136).

- *Abnormality*, because one belongs in the world to a minority that is not talked about and that does not talk itself
- *Shame*, of being different, of having been stripped of family value during the Shoa; shame instead aggression because of the way history is dealt with officially; shame to ask for restitution
- *Reduced identity*, an identity reduced by a history of persecution, reduced by the diminishing of a Jewish identity, based on 5765 years of continuous tradition, where experience with persecution only once played a minor role
- *Repressed rage and aggression*, affecting ethnic individuation

According to Jewish tradition, many children were named after dead relatives in order for these relatives to be remembered. This tradition became especially significant after the Shoa, because most family members had not died a natural death but had been murdered. Consequently, many children tried to take over the identity of dead objects in order to solve the insoluble conflict of their parents. Heller (1982) states that "commemorative candles" develop a higher sensitivity for social problems (Heller, 1982: 249). This is possibly an explanation of why children of survivors to a large degree choose professions in social, care giving, and artistic areas. These children not only live their own existence but also that of their dead brothers and sisters, whom they never knew, or that of other members of the family.

This is the fate of children who could not and were not allowed to find their own individuality. They became symbols for the loss of their parents. They were loaded with names which they had to embody. The children were hearses or urns for the ashes of the dead of human tissue, to fill the "immense void" (Moser, 1997).

The Transmission of Trauma to the Children

Various psychotherapists, American analysts (Judith Kestenberg, 1995) as well as Israeli colleagues (Dina Wardi, 1997 and Yolanda Gampel, 1995), describe the interrelations between the age in which the parents were traumatized and the "disorders" seen in the children of survivors. The intensity of the trauma and the time when it occurred strongly influences the behavior of the surviving parents towards their children. A conflict that is found in many survivors and their children is to find a substitute for those loved persons that were killed in the Shoa. This desire can be a conscious or subconscious motto of life. This desire, when it is still subconscious, may manifest itself in often changing friends and partners, in feeling a chronic void, urge, constant search. In this group of clients, depressive moods are not a reaction to a certain event but rather an atmosphere of absence and loss.

Special attention is often paid to anniversaries of the family as well as to historical-political events. The memory of certain important events in the parent's life naturally influences their behavior towards their children. As a consequence, children take over their parent's history and its significance for their parents into their own relevance. To become aware, see and understand, is an important aspect of therapy.

For example: Children of survivors often have a big crisis that can even lead to hospitalization, at the same age that their parents had lost their home. The life of a survivor's child that reaches the age of a family member murdered in the Shoa can also become critical. A further reaction of parents may be an inadequate care or even negligence of children at a certain age (the age, when other children in the family had been murdered or they themselves had lost part of their childhood), without them being aware of this death wish.

Here I would like to give an example about the atmospheric transmission of horror from parents to their children. The case in point is described by Yolanda Gampel in *A Daughter of Silence* in Bergman, Jucovy, Kestenberg (1995). A mother takes her seven-year old girl to see a psychoanalyst because of sudden absences and paramnesia. At the end of the first session, the girl - out of context of the previous game/theme -- tells the analyst that "she does not want to be an electric fence in the Warsaw Ghetto." The analyst asked the mother and the father (who did not oblige) to come to the next session and there, she asked about the possible meaning of the daughter's image. The mother said that the Shoa had never been discussed; official family history only stated that the father had come to Israel as a child. When questioned further, the mother related that the father had been in the Warsaw Ghetto and afterwards in Auschwitz. But they had never talked about it. The daughter could not know it (Gampel, 1995 in Bergman *et al*: 103).

In the following sessions, the analyst, the daughter, and the mother worked on the connection between the father's absences and the father's history. The father did not want to be present and to talk about any of it, but he permitted his wife to tell everything that she knew about his history to the analyst and the daughter. Afterwards, the daughter's symptoms vanished.

Later on, Gampel describes psychotic disturbances in children as an "echo of the parent's conversation." If parents behave as if everything in their life had been normal, it may happen that their seeming health may remain, "but the children will decompensate due to their mechanisms of identification and projected identification, which the parents attach to their offspring in the course of their children's development. The children show symptoms which, at first sight, do not have any connection to their family history" (Gampel, 1995: 149).

Whether parents have spoken with their children about the persecution or not makes a great difference in coming to terms with the traumata. That does not mean that children of talking survivors are less traumatized, but rather that they come to terms differently with the experience of the survival of their parents.

Anne Karpf is the daughter of two survivors, Joseph and Natalia. She had reported that for decades all of her energy was used to escape death, thus leaving no strength for her life (Paraphrased) (Karp, A.) Josef Karpf, a Polish

Jew, escaped to Russia. His wife-to-be, Natalia, was a concert pianist and survived the concentration camp by playing Chopin to the camp commander, Amon Goeth, in the Plaszów camp. Steven Spielberg used this episode in his movie, *Schindler's List* (Universal Studios, 1994, a Steven Spielberg Production). When Anne Karpf was born in 1950, her parents lived in safety and liberty in London. Apparently, in reality, their battle continued and even haunted the life of their children. They continuously faced an event that was not their own and which was almost obsessively avoided by the adults, although it hung over them like the sword of Damocles every day.

Anne Karpf developed an anxiety neurosis, became depressive, and suffered from a psychologically caused neuro-dermatitis. At the same time, she worked successfully as a journalist in London and nobody noticed that she could master her daily professional life only by using her utmost willpower because within Anne's subjective experience, her innermost self was a "concentration camp" where she played two roles simultaneously – one being "the guard" and the other "the inmate." Only after a long period of psychotherapy and after long talks with her parents could she finally grasp the connection with the Holocaust and see that she was continuing her parents' struggle for survival.

The psychodynamics between mother and daughter, sometimes even grandmother and mother, and later on mother and daughter, exhibits deep trauma. Dina Wardi's research gives an impressive description of the parent's trauma on the children's emotional life. There is a basic difference if the parents survived the traumata as children in the period of latency or as adults. I think that it is also necessary to consider the sex of the survivor in view of the psychosexual development, especially in women. Dina Wardi (1997) differentiates surviving women "according to the emotional developing phase at the beginning of the Holocaust, how much their identity as a woman and mother had developed and which situation they were in immediately after the Holocaust" (Wardi, 1997: 103).

The first group consists of women who, at the time of the Holocaust, were still girls in the period of latency or adolescence. They had just started to develop their female identity. To the second group belonged women who were just about to terminate their adolescence or had already terminated it when the Holocaust started and whose feminine identity had been partly or fully consolidated. Women who were already adults belong to the third group. Some of them were already married and had given birth to children, i.e. not only their female identity but also their identity as mothers had already been developed.

Survivors who survived as small children (up to the age of three) showed the most serious psychological trauma, according to an Israeli research. As grown-ups - as far as one can generalize - they passed on the atrocities which they had suffered from their parents and brothers and sisters and repeated the brutal treatment they had received from their persecutors, an image they held as "the punishing and protecting father" (Paraphrased) (Wardi, 1997).

Dina Wardi (1997) reports that the little girls who had lost the protection of the nearest persons of reference matured earlier and in many cases they experienced sexual violence themselves. As a result, their sense of self-worth and their body images were "bruised" (Paraphrased) (Wardi, 1997). Immediately after the end of the war, girls/women pushed their anger aside and made room for loneliness, guilt, because they had survived, endless grief and the feeling of loss, so that no room was left for other emotions. They idealized their idea of being a mother, yet they were unable to develop their own identity as a mother (Wardi, 1997). But for some women, even this was impossible. They could not identify and when they became mothers themselves, it was extremely difficult for them to fulfill this role.

Their own children, the Second Generation, were confronted with their mothers' void, depression and exhaustion. Already, when children, they knew that they were not supposed to talk about it. They developed a refined sensorial system of communication with their mothers; they could read their facial expression and could adapt in order not to increase their mothers' grief. These children learned early to suppress their rage and aggression because they felt that their mothers would not be able to bear them (just as their mothers had to suppress their own aggressions) and later on became also sad and depressive. In this mother/daughter relationship tremendous non-verbal, but very subtle, aggressions exist. Because of the lack of rage and aggression the separation from the family can only take place with difficulty. The children are afraid to leave their parents because they grew up being the only thing that was left their parents after the Holocaust and because they had not developed their own identity yet, independent of their parents. Thus the dependence remains for a long time. People belonging to this group often come into childhood, adulthood, and motherhood with depressions and with questions about the meaning of life and complicated relationships based on very dependent relations and feelings of anxiety.

The women who were adolescents during the Holocaust were in a different situation. They had children very soon after the war and worried during pregnancy as well as after the birth of the child that they would pass on to their children the injuries they themselves had suffered or that something would happen to their children. Many women belonging to this group of survivors often had very complicated pregnancies and often miscarried. Therefore, many families had only one child, who was considered a miracle and something special because all other children had been either stillbirths or miscarriages.

Especially immediately after the Holocaust, mothers felt the void and the loneliness, sometimes also towards their partners, who often remained alien to them. In spite of this void, a difference can be noted as regards women who were still children during the Holocaust. The young women had already before the Holocaust somewhat separated from their parents/mothers and thus had a potential for coming to terms with issues of depression and trauma. Two different problems become apparent when dealing with their children. Some live in their depression, withdraw and delegate the children's care to others because they feel too weak, although often the joy of living returns when giving birth. Others plunge into activities as compensation; they do not develop strong ties to their small children and seem restless and hectic. "Their problems to dedicate themselves....to the child's care might be explained by an inner restlessness, based on unsolved conflicts and on the constant endeavor to escape the conflicts and to repress them" (Wardi, 1997: 100).

For the survivors who were already adults before the start of the Holocaust, the situation after the war is as follows: "[T]hey already had a determined and defined identity and had already had experiences with pregnancy, birth and the life together with a partner. They had had the opportunity to come to terms with their identity as a mother in an intimate secure environment, surrounded by the family" (Wardi, 1997: 104). But the women could not overcome the loss of their own children who had been murdered.

Even if the women married again and had children, they and their "new" children and often also new partners lived with the feeling of loss and incompleteness. They often could not derive strength from giving birth, sank into chronic grief, and often did not have a clear-cut relation to their children. "Because such a relation would have revived the strong feeling they had for their first, lost children and would have imbalanced their fragile psyche. A direct confrontation with the loss would have deepened their sorrow and in order to protect their ego from an overflow of emotions they had to keep an emotional distance to the nightmares of the past and detach themselves" (Wardi, 1997: 104).

Parents indirectly expected their children to live on behalf of those killed in the Holocaust. Children were not seen as individuals but rather as objects that should give meaning to the empty life of the parents, to remind them of the past, of former children and relatives. The mothers were in a chronic state of undigested grief and had little resources for their new children because they were still busy with their own feelings of loss.

Some people got married rather quickly after the war, without the partners knowing each other very well. The choice of partner seemed arbitrary but they shared many experiences and losses and they transmitted part of their feelings for their parents and other relatives to the spouse. A pattern prevalent in partnerships that were embarked upon immediately after the war is mutual or one-sided dependency. Intimacy did not seem possible in view of the many slain family members and the thrust of the resulting feeling of guilt and numb grief. Numb emotions really prevent love, intimacy or safety and security. Children from such relationships feel lost, lonely, not loved for their own sake, like a substitute for their mother's dead children.

Concluding Remarks

All such notes, reports, studies, and research as these show clearly and distinctly the effects the Holocaust had on the survivors and the consequences of these effects on the children of the survivors. Gestalt therapy is being called upon not only to lift the veil of forgetting but also to raise the cover of silence because of its approach and its history: it can express itself in all forms and facets.

A central theme of Jewish people is the development of their own identity, Jewish identity based on a tradition of 5765 years of history, culture, and religion, as well as a collective family experience of persecution. Especially at the end of the millennium, at a time when borders are being opened but other borders remain closed, the definition of one's own identity, beyond external attributes, folkloristic blurs and philosemitic efforts is an eternal theme where psychotherapists guide their clients by reflecting and listening. Psychotherapists do not have to know everything, but we have the possibility of starting a dialogue to broaden our emotions and our knowledge and to face problems beyond our imagination with a certain humility.

The Shoa (Holocaust) is not only part of Jewish history but also of Austrian and European history - thus it concerns everybody.

Personal Account

I first thought that my topic - therapeutic work with the Second Generation (Holocaust survivors) - may not relate directly to this project .On second thought however, I felt that there is indeed a connection, a very special and personal one.

I am Jewish and was born in Austria after the Shoa (Holocaust). Am I a Jewish Austrian or an Austrian Jew? I cannot give a clear answer, my focus changes all the time. It is one of the themes of my life to keep up the dialogue of the various cultures not only on the outside, but also within myself. I often feel like a stranger and not belonging in my own country, not knowing where I could build a bridge or if I even want to build a bridge. In Austria, I belong to a minority, my Jewishness is something special for me, but it has no real contemporary place in the official Austrian culture. In my country, I perceive the cultural "ditches" more than the "bridges" that span them.

In Israel or New York where so many Jews live, it seems so commonplace to be Jewish that I find myself a stranger and an unknown, because I ignore much of the normal, everyday, unbroken Jewish life. It makes me melancholic and nostalgic. And I miss my Austrian part, which should give me security .Therefore, I feel that I must work on building my "inner bridges", in order to be able to contribute to the building of external ones.

Nowadays, email is my bridge to Tali and Mackie, with whom I interact. I am very touched by the closeness and mutual appreciation made possible in this way between people living in quite different parts of the world. Tali, with whom I have a heartfelt relationship, and Mackie, whom I don't know personally, have still worked with so much sensibility and empathy on our common text. Many thanks for that.

My heartfelt thanks to all the translators, i.e., builders of verbal bridges, who let me write in my own language but made this chapter appear in English.

Anna Kubesch, Vienna, Austria

References

Bergman, M., Jucovy, M., & Kestenberg, J. (1995). *Kinder der Tater, Psychoanalyse und Holocaust,* Yolanda Gampel: *A Daughter of Silence (p. 103).* Frankfurt/Main.

Heller, D. (1982). Themes of culture and ancestry, *Psychiatry*, 45, 249.

Heimannsberg, B., & Schmidt, Ch.J. (1988). *Das kollekive Schweigen. Nazivergangenheit und gebrochene Identitat in der Psychotherapie*, Speier: Des ges(ch)ichtslose Psychoanalytiker die ges(ch)ichtslose Psychoanalyse (p. 17), Heidelberg.

Herbst, L. & Goschler, C. (1989). *Wiedergutmachung in der Bundesrepublik*, William Niederland: Deutschland, Munchen.

Jureit, U. & Keine, H. (1997). *Verzweiflung und Selbstzweifel in den Erinnerungen weiblicher KZ-Uberlebender; in*: Heinson, Vogel, Weckle (Hg) Zwischen Karriere und Verfolgung: Frankfurt/Main.

Karpf, A. (1998). *Der Krieg danach*, Berlin.

Lundholm, A. Morgen-Grauen. (1997). *Verzweiflung und selbstzweifel in den Erinnerungen weiblicher KZ Uberlebender;* in: Heinson, Vogel, Weckle (Hg) Zwischen Karriere und Verfolgung. Hamberg.

Parlett, M. (1994). *Wir erschaffen unsere Systeme, unsere Systeme Erschaffen uns. Feldtheorie fur Gestalttherapeuten., in:* Freiler, Ventouratou-Schmetterer, Reiner-Lawugger, Bosel 100 Jahre Fritz Perls Wien.

Perls, F. (1993). (1993) *Gestalttherapie in Aktion*, Stuttgard.

Perls, F. (1980). *Gestalt, Wachstum, Integration*, Paderborn.

Polster, E. & M. (1985). *Theorie und Praxis der Integrativen Gestalttherapie*, Frankfurt/Main.

Rheinz, H. (1998). *Die judische Frau. Auf der Suche nach einer moderner* Identitat, Gutersloh.

Spielberg, S. (March 15, 1994). *Schindler's List*. An Amblin Entertainment Production. Released by Universal Studios. CA: USA.

Wardi, D. (1997). *Siegel der Erinnerung. Das Trauma der Holocaust* Psychotherapie mit den Kindern der Uberlebenden. Sigal, Silver, Radkoff & Ellin: Stuttgart.

V. HIV AND CULTURE

By Geoff Warburton, M.Sc. and James Kuykendall

Introduction
HIV does not belong to a culture. HIV is a virus that attacks the immune system regardless of cultural identity. HIV has no belief system about diversity and so does not divide or discriminate. It is our contention, paradoxically, that each culture gives diverse meaning and definition to HIV and that each culture configures the meaning depending on its beliefs, its traditions, and its stories. This meaning will determine what is allowed within the field and so determine discriminatory action that hurts and divides its members. In this discussion we will look at how such configuration of meaning has shaped the treatment of people with HIV.

We will use the story of AIDS in the UK to demonstrate prevalent discriminatory attitudes towards people with HIV and to reveal clues to a way forward that will enable the healing of the hurt and division. We suggest that this way forward involves a shift from an individual paradigm[1] to one that embraces our relationship as humans to a greater force beyond our individual will.

Stories, Beliefs, Traditions — The Culture Responds
The dictionary defines culture sociologically as "the sum total of a way of a living built up by a group of human beings and passed from generation to generation." The way of living becomes realized as certain stories, beliefs, and traditions interweave and coalesce into a fabric called culture that suggests meaning for a specific set of individuals. There are stories around religion, gender, sex, politics, education, money, emotions, other people, other places, cleanliness, health, sexual orientation, class, just to name but a few of the fabric's threads. The stories, beliefs, and traditions will determine what is allowed within the field.

For example, western relief organizations working with Sub-Saharan communities, where more than 20% of all sexually active adults are HIV positive, encourage dialogue about HIV within the extended family in the belief that HIV infected individuals will be better supported.

While true for some, unfortunately HIV positive Africans are shunned within and excluded from their communities. One case in point, as we entered the 21st century of the new millennium: when an African woman with possible HIV related tuberculosis presented herself to a London Hospital, the staff at this teaching hospital was shocked, as they had forgotten the gauntness rarely now associated with HIV in the UK. The woman said that she kept out of sight from her community and therefore did not receive the urgent medical care that she required. In the secrecy of the night, a black HIV AIDS organization consequently transported her to another hospital.

A second example can be seen within Hispanic cultures, where there is usually an emphasis on male machismo. Hispanic men may acknowledge the risk of HIV transmission but nonetheless do not wear condoms, as they are felt to block virility and hence machismo. We can see then that cultures configure not only the beliefs surrounding HIV but the social behaviors that result from such held beliefs. These beliefs dictate what is allowed within the culture. What is not allowed within the culture is projected on to others.

When we broaden the field, we observe further that not only do subculture beliefs, as exemplified above, create tensions within their own communities but often superimposed is the macroculture's belief pressuring subcultures into possible behavioral responses that increase vulnerability to HIV. For example, a story/belief held within the British culture is that Injecting Users (IJUs) are a detriment to legitimate society and should therefore be excluded from it.

The response to exclusion invites the HIV community to bond even closer as they live out the habit of sharing their needles with each other. It also seems to be the case that because of their degree of awareness of the hostility in the field, IJUs will frequent a highly effective HIV transmission route, resulting in further exclusion and vulnerability to the virus and the larger field. This is how HIV has been seen to belong to minority cultures, through an act of projection. An attempt to keep out something too threatening within the wider culture -- and the culture has made it happen.

The Communicable Diseases Centre on Jan 13th of 2000 stated that minorities in the US now epidemiologically represent 52% (up from 31% in 1989) of the gay and bisexual men diagnosed with AIDS in 1998. Dr. Helen Gayle, Director of the National Centre for the prevention of sexually transmitted diseases & TB stated "that fear continues to drive too many black and Latino men to die alone, rather than face the risk of being shunned by family and friends." The article suggests that shame within certain communities about homosexuality is standing in the way of AIDS prevention in the very communities where the population of people with AIDS was increasing most rapidly. The stories and the beliefs that make up a culture are determining the spread of HIV.

When HIV appeared in the early 1980s, it threatened, and in some instances did, to tear lives apart with its perceived and very real potential to kill and to dehumanize. Early victims infected died relatively rapidly without the benefit of either HAART (combination therapies) or effective treatments for opportunistic infections. It dehumanized in a kaleidoscope of ways. It could render intimacy dangerous. It allowed infections to physically devastate the body, producing, for example, pigmented skin lesions, or acute lung destruction leading to fatal pneumonia. It could inhibit the body from taking in the essentials of food and water, leaving it starved and dehydrated. In some, the virus affected the brain, causing dementia. In others, it enabled the CMV Virus to lead to blindness. And in others it allowed Cryptosporidium to cause abdominal cramps, fever, nausea, vomiting, and profuse diarrhea. Many victims had multiple presentations. Truly dehumanizing, HIV could also dehumanize through association with certain behaviors.

In summary, transmission of HIV in the U.K has happened primarily through unprotected gay sex and intravenous drug use. These behaviors are typically condemned as" abnormal", "bad" or "anti-social" in most Westernized cultures. Because of these cultural prejudices, infected/affected individuals are excluded or harassed and subjected to heightening dehumanization and depersonalization. Landlords, for example, have been seen to be extremely intolerant. In one situation we know of personally, a dying man and his lover were given a fortnight to vacate their premises.

In circumstances where landlords are sympathetic, neighbors can make life unpleasant with several instances of letter bombs, as reported by the authors' clients. Some employers have fired those identified with HIV and in supposedly safe havens health care workers regularly refuse to care. This mayhem underlines not only the moral tone that the culture ascribes to HIV, that is, HIV = a bad person but also the intense fear of the reality of death that it engenders in all those surrounded by HIV; that is, HIV=AIDS=DEATH. Initially, the mortality rate from AIDS appeared to be at 100%. The creator of the first major care centre for people with HIV in the UK, Christopher Spence, recognized that the fear of dying from HIV rendered our culture helpless to respond humanely to the crisis.

The heavy conditioning to deny the centrality of death in the cycle of life is a pervasive hurt on the whole of society, installing and reinforcing powerlessness at every turn. It causes us to live in the shadow of unresolved fears, of our own and one another's death: it keeps us trapped in the painful legacy of yesterday's losses; it estranges us from our fellow human beings, it renders us helpless at the very moments when life calls us to step out of our timidity and act" (Spence, 1986: 13).

The archaic religious concept of a tainted people being judged by God was revived as a kind of denial in order to explain away this horrendous disease, thereby perpetuating cultural blame. The popular press in the early 1980s labeled HIIV "the gay plague" or stated that black Africans had caused HIV. The focus of the media coverage was on the innocence of white heterosexual people who got this virus from "guilty black prostitutes" or "evil bisexuals." The beliefs and the cultural stories served to heighten the suspicion. HIV profoundly highlighted the processes within our culture that divide and hurt and the need for healing and unity was not answered. How could this happen?

Jung referred to community in relation to the archetype of conformity. He noted the value and worth of conformity as it supports socialization and community: logically then a most needed and welcomed creative adjustment. Sometimes even the best creative adjustments can turn against the organism when it becomes fixed -- too rigid for exploration and review.

Rather than maintaining and enhancing organismic growth, division and hurt arise as a polarity is created, with conformity representing everything that is good at one end and diversity representing everything evil at the other. Conformity becomes something to strive for to the exclusion of diversity and is used to push out anything that threatens the prevailing status quo. It incorporates and uses all the internalized cultural, social, political, and religious beliefs to maintain itself. The pall of HIV and AIDS threatens the cultural homeostasis and because it touches on so many beliefs, it receives many responses.

The Story Unfolding

Having introduced some of the general cultural dynamics that came into play upon the arrival of HIV, we will now look at the story of HIV and the characters involved within the UK. The story began what seems a very long time ago, although in fact the story of HIV in the UK started in December of 1981. At this time only a minority was infected, while those surrounding them constituted a larger affected group of partners, friends, relatives, and healthcare professionals (a few among whom were also infected or belonged to an affected minority group). The overwhelming majority believed that they were neither infected nor affected and everyone responded accordingly.

People were certainly motivated to acknowledge HIV at this time, even if it was only to categorically state that it was something that affected other people. Where there were large numbers of people affected within a community or subculture, political action to lobbyists agitated for support and healthcare. These people were profoundly affected and interwove HIV relationally into other struggles. Many of these same people were already engaged in a political struggle recognized as also worthy within their society. HIV became the prominent content of their experience with which this battle was focused. The result of this struggle was to secure money and resources from the majority who still refused to own HIV as their issue.

The story unfolded dramatically within the process of denial. Denial is a creative adjustment designed to support an individual when something is or is perceived to be too threatening or too provocative. In the early days of the epidemic, denial was played out through disowning HIV and projecting it elsewhere; for example, Western Europe saw this as a problem of the United States; the United States saw it as Africa's issue. Within the United Kingdom the majority of individuals labeled it a gay issue, and/or an injecting user issue, or a transfusion recipient issue.

The majority of people had no awareness of it affecting them. This appeared to be substantiated as early predictions of HIV infection of the general population did not materialize, allowing much of the public to feel complacent and justified with the result. Meanwhile, those who were living with HIV or supporting HIV-infected individuals became overwhelmed and stuck, and retroflected all the horrors of HIV and what it symbolized to them awashed in their denial. The retroflection often took the form of self-destructive behaviors, such as unprotected sex (bare backing) and even suicide.

Beneath the denial lay anger and fear ("It might affect me and I'll do everything possible not to own it!"). Before the general population responded to HIV, a taste of what was to come could be seen with healthcare workers. The first person with AIDS in the United Kingdom died a lonely death in one of the London teaching hospitals in December 1981.

Over the next few years, nurses would refuse to care, porters would refuse to bring in food trays, and technicians would refuse to carry out tests. Whipped up by media hysteria, the fear permeated the general population. Individuals lost their employment and homes of infected individuals were firebombed. This violent acting out served no healthy purpose other than making us aware of how deep the cultural divisions were.

The tabloid press, supported by their readers, developed the idea that "as it is only a minority issue, if you avoided and or castigated the minority, then there would cease to be a problem." However, the problem worsened. As condemnation of the infected increased it distanced the majority from the virus and the infected individuals. Although resources for HIV became ring-fenced, so did the client groups. A meaningful cultural response diminished further and general apathy deepened.

Minorities Take Action

In direct response to the general apathy ensuing, the subcultures most affected, for example, Black Africans, gay men, and injecting drug users began to take action. Unfortunately, their energies did not coalesce into a unified strategy but rather played out in two dramatically different ways. One way was to lobby by attempting to transfer the introjected shame and blame onto the majority ("We, the minority cultures infected and affected, are hurting so much that we will shame you into action!"). The initial result of this coercion was successful. It heightened awareness of the suffering of those with HIV, leading to the funding of support services.

However, the lobbying did not succeed in fostering the acceptance of HIV as an issue for everyone. Any chance for dialogue throughout the wider culture was drowned out by archaic beliefs that black is less, gay is bad, prostitutes unworthy, and that drug users don't belong, and so on. These issues became so deep and frightening to address that it became easier to cover over the pain and the distress of the disease with well-meaning resources; yet the social rift was maintained nonetheless.

The second way of responding was to set up services addressing the psychosocial needs of people with HIV. Without statutory services to back them up, however, many of those who staffed these organizations became overburdened and succumbed to stress. In ways they could not imagine, these workers became overwhelmed with multiple bereavement, clinical depression, and stress-related illness. This was further exacerbated by Western cultural introjects that prevented the expression of feelings and vulnerability, such as "Big boys don't cry" and "Pull yourself together." Self and environmental support was not realized or even understood as being essential under such stressful conditions. And to add to this unfolding tragedy, many of these pioneers were infected with HIV themselves and died. As the pandemic evolved, statutory involvement with HIV increased. By the late 1980s, health authorities, particularly in London, provided excellent medical care. Both Council and Health Office authorities began funding local and national community support services. It appeared as if the statutory sector had fully signed up to fight the war against HIV. However, our culture did not live happily ever after. Without the realization that HIV was an issue for the culture at large, a true dialogue had still never taken place. Without dialogue, the intolerance of what was still believed a minority disease became more entrenched. The result was backlash.

By the mid 1990s, funding to community services was systematically withdrawn. In 1995, the health authorities in London (where 80% of infected people in the UK live) funded approximately 84 agencies that provided counseling to people affected by HIV. By 1998, they funded approximately five agencies. In the year 2000, they funded only one central agency. Although there had been financial mismanagement of HIV funds, and although streamlining of services has been needed, the enormity of the disappointment and outrage suggests that the backlash as the key to more favorable outcomes will come from a much deeper cultural place.

Some community services have survived by relying on large donations from rich and famous people who identify with the affected culture; the popular musician Elton John, for example. Unfortunately, for black communities, particularly black African communities, there is not such organized or wealthy backing, resulting in further divisions within the wider culture.

At this very moment, the numbers of people in the UK being infected with HIV has not diminished. In fact, 50% of the total number of newly acquired HIV infections within the year 1998 was in the age group below 21. It seems that health education aimed at preventing the risk of HIV transmission has not been internalized by our youth. Understandably, part of this is a reflection of the fact that young people apparently behave as if they are immortal. Also, this fact hasn't personally affected their generation until now and has been a tool to foster denial and complacency. But it is not just the young that did not internalize a life-affirming education program to prevent HIV transmission. There has been an increase among gay men in general of unprotected (bare back) sex. We can see then that an entire new generation may have to deal with the ravages of HIV, unless an effective education strategy is instigated. This may be a difficult concept to grasp, for as we began the twenty-first century, HIV has actually appeared to be less of an issue.

The media has talked of the new treatments that seem to turn HIV into a manageable chronic disease, creating a perception that it is no longer a killer. In truth, some individuals with HIV are experiencing improved quality of life. Many are returning to work and giving up disability benefits that they had believed would be with them until their not too distant death. Unfortunately, however, not everyone responds to these much specialized combination therapies.

Some, although they are responding, are having side effects that seriously affect their quality of life. Others are building up resistance to drugs, creating effectively more difficult strains of HIV that one hopes can be presently treated. Whilst the majority of infections caused by HIV can be treated with sophisticated regimes, there are also new syndromes developing, such as, that is, an increase in cancers associated with HIV. It is frightening to put this into a global context with the very sobering statistic that over 90% of people with HIV live in developing countries where the benefits gleaned through such treatments are unavailable due to finance.

The End Not Yet in Sight

Even during the first waves of HIV that were met with the initial energy that produced such innovative services to people with HIV, the work was not integrated into the fabric of the culture. Part of this was that the archaic and ingrained cultural beliefs, including those on diversity, did not change substantially. Dialogue, as we see it through Gestalt lenses, is based on openness, understanding and respect of difference rather than the transfer of shame onto the difference. Health promotion tactics that simply mandate safer sex were/are doomed to failure unless the message is coupled with the curiosity to find out about cultural difference.

For example, what does it mean to be masculine? Earlier, we noted that a Hispanic man's cultural belief was that if he was to be masculine, he must ejaculate inside his partner. To wear a condom was a barrier to being masculine. Hence, to arrive at clear distinctions, the sharpest question to pose to a gay male is: What does it mean to have HIV in your culture? For one black African man, this meant coming out as gay, which could have meant ostracism from his community. However, his small black community was essential to him in a country where the majority was white; he therefore became confluent with the cultural introjects and denied both his gayness and his HIV status.

From Therapy to the Wider World

There is a lot we can do in a therapeutic one-to-one setting. We can start by creating a stance of openness that contradicts the cultural introjects. We can model the curiosity that invites a dialogue and create the conditions of safety for it. We can model that there is no taboo here and address what is culturally unspeakable (Death, Sexuality, HIV, injecting drug use). We can say YES. To quote Buber: "Surrounded by the air of chaos which came into being with him, secretly and bashfully he watches for a YES which allows him to be and which can come to him only from another" (in Hycner & Jacobs, 1995: 22). With many of our HIV clients, one of our tasks no doubt would be "an active effort of turning toward and affirming the separate existence of the other person -- his otherness -- his uniqueness and his common human bond with me and with others" (Hycner, 1995: 24).

If we look at the totality of our clients' lives on a social scale beyond the realm of the therapeutic relationship, then we will see that they live in a hostile environment -- sometimes overt; more often, subtle. It is important to hold this view on a social level of a client's life and move beyond the life of the therapy room. The task for us is to assist clients in translating the work of the therapy room to this different environment. But how do we tackle the wider field? Perhaps the work that we do on an individual basis can suggest a resolution.

Our field perspective gives us the knowledge that working with the individual has an effect on the wider field. As Gestalt practitioners, we never really work with "just only an individual" because human beings always exist within systems of relationship. They identify with families, communities, occupational groups, and nationalities. Such affiliations, roots, and historical continuities serve as important human stabilizers and contribute significantly to a sense of identity. Lives and collective systems intertwine and need to be considered as a unified field, the Gestalt term for the web of interconnection between person and situation, self and others, organism and environment, the individual and the communal (Parlett, 1991).   From this perspective the therapeutic relationship begins to tackle the wider world. We begin to engage with the structures of the field that shape the fabric of culture: its rituals and beliefs, its stability and tradition.

In acknowledging and addressing the structures owned by the collective, we contribute to both the individual client and the larger social field. We go beyond our personal space and time. This necessitates, at the baseline at least, respect if not a labor of love for humanity as a whole, and means somehow applying the concept of creative indifference[2] on a social and cultural scale -- all the while holding the paradoxical needs of desiring a culture that respects diversity and not being invested in changing the world to this belief.

Can we still love others who deny essential aspects of ourselves, of our blackness, our gayness, our using of needles, shared or otherwise? If we take the stance that cultural beliefs are a set of introjects that create and bind a community, such introjects are seen as the very creative adjustment for survival. Our introjects are where our resistance and power live. To attack something at this core level of being is doomed to fail. Added to this is that we are all relationally part of this cultural system that defines, for example, blackness and gayness as bad. We are therefore all engaged in the definition.

We need to understand how being so represented through the maintenance of a belief supports either the individual or the community, and to understand what function and dysfunction the belief creates in here-and-now time. For example, Ken Livingstone, Mayor of London, observed: *Homophobic legislation such as Section 28 and, until now, the unequal age of consent, harm the health of gay people and it's vital that this outdated and unjust legislation be repealed (paraphrased, U.K. television interview).* Whether the health he referred to be emotional, physical or psychological vulnerability to HIV and or suicide, we need to discern what prevents his message from being heard.

What support do we need in order to maintain the energy to find more healthy ways to maintain the definition of ourselves as part of community and culture? How do we address the fears that block us, without blame or shame, in order to be able to extend the present parameters?   We confess our own difficulty with this task. Our readers may detect a tinge of blame and anger in our questions posed as responses to the question we inferred from Livingstone's observation -- "What prevents this message from being heard?" This is certainly not even a position of creative indifference on our part.

To say that we are talking about enormous dynamics is an understatement. We are talking about structures that have been developed over centuries, structures that so far, according to our present knowledge in the field of psychology, are beyond our individual capacity to significantly change. This work, then, that we suggest here involves a labor of love, love of humanity beyond our individual lifetimes. There is no immediate gratification or narcissistic thrill from doing this work. To some extent this means facing our powerlessness.

At one level of our research when looking for responses, we take heart and comfort in an observation of Yalom's:

"The sentiment that one should have done something more reflects, it seems to me, an underlying wish to control the uncontrollable. After all, if one is guilty about not having done something that one should have done, then it follows that there is something that could have been done -- a comforting thought that decoys us from our pathetic helplessness in the face of death. Encased in an elaborate illusion of unlimited power and progress, each of us subscribes, at least until one's mid-life crisis, to the belief that existence consists of an eternal, upward spiral of achievement, dependent on will alone" (Yalom, 1991: 139).

So being limited with our power, how can we raise awareness within the cultural field to support dialogue and integration of gay, black, and the fierce reality of HIV into our culture? The ways of activist groups such as Outrage do not seem to have supported dialogue, though their feelings of outrage may be understood.[3] Can we deduce then that no matter how understandable feelings of outrage are, the shaming others does not seem to be a viable approach to dialogue? Is there something we know as Gestalt therapists that could enhance the conditions for dialogue? Lynne Jacobs (this volume) writes about the importance of acknowledging our own shame in order to support a healing dialogue. Others have also: "Such acknowledgement is usually the first step in resolving a disruption or impasse and ultimately enriches the therapeutic dialogue as a whole" (Lee & Wheeler, 1998: 302).

We can recount an example of such an acknowledgement that occurred for a colleague as he lectured on racism. In two separate incidents, he was reprimanded by a black audience member for excluding the slave trade from both Black and European history. On the first occasion, he felt immobilized and unable to enter into a dialogue with the other person. He realized in retrospect that the challenge had triggered a feeling of shame. With this awareness in mind, when challenged the second lime, he allowed himself the experience of his shame and consequently felt free to apologize for his omission. Through the owning of his shame, he was able to remain open to dialogue without retaliation and aggression. He also came to realize that his dignity as well as that of the challenger remained intact. Both parties concerned continued their dialogue after the lecture and both realized that they had been enriched by their encounter. This suggests that we may need to start with the acknowledgement of our own shame as we make the move towards a meaningful dialogue that supports cultural integration.

In South Africa, to dialogue about past oppressive attitudes has been an essential part of the process of coming together. This has brought about the understanding that oppressive behaviors begin with introjects that hurt our being and divide our common human bond. This not only supports us to confront how introjects have operated but also to discern how we continue to manifest them in the here and now. We, of course, recognize that this process of genuine and unreserved, supportive, healing communication comprises one-to-one therapy. Also, on the other hand, "Gestalt therapy expects that by being present, and by communicating genuinely, the therapist will influence the patient.... [Being present in the here and now] is also crucial in a meeting that heals in a genuine dialogic manner" (Jacobs, 1995: 67).

With our knowledge of healing processes, as can be witnessed in South Africa and from the extensive clinical knowledge from one to one therapy, we see that the stance of being genuine and unreserved are part of the conditions for dialogue to take place. We would be entering new and experimental ground to take these principles out of the therapy room and into a cultural arena, but it wouldn't be the first time that Gestalt therapy challenged and transcended previously respected boundaries.

Blame vs. Guilt[4]

HIV is not our fault. This is a powerful statement that speaks to the heart of suffering that surrounds HIV and AIDS – namely, the suffering caused by blaming and, consequentially, the exclusion of others. Blaming emerging from HIV challenges our paradigm that we are independent individuals in relation to the environment. "How can this be?" we ask ourselves, and think: "Someone must be responsible and blamable for this terrible disease, for these terrible feelings that I have." Blaming can achieve a sense of control over the disease. The actions resulting from blaming are usually ignoring, segregating, and, in extreme cases, violently attacking those with HIV.

Even those who care for people with HIV can feel the urge to blame in an attempt to control the situation. Their blame, however, has a different target. They blame institutions for not doing enough for people with HIV, often blaming the very institution they are working for.

At the other side of the polarity to blaming lies guilt. Guilt is not always obvious in the therapy room as it is often held out of awareness by clients and defended by rage and blame. We are talking here about guilt as distinct from shame. Although shame is the resulting experience of the relationship between those who blame and those who feel guilty, it is a particular type of guilt that perpetuates shame. This guilt is experienced as a feeling of being responsible, of having caused something through being a certain way, be that way black, gay or HIV positive, and so forth. In this case, persons with HIV feel that they have foisted an affliction on themselves and society. The archaic concept of a tainted community bringing plague on themselves and others is revived.

Feeling guilty or blamable around HIV are both narcissistic positions. They are narcissistic in that they are based on a self-image of having power and influence over others that is an illusion. The illusion is constituted of the image of ourselves as individuals with the power to control HIV and its social ramifications. The unbearable truth that fractures this illusion is that we are powerless as individuals when it comes to dealing with the enormous destruction of HIV. Not only are we powerless to stop the death and loss caused by HIV, we are powerless to alter the cultural systems that hurt and divide in response to HIV.

These systems, in Gestalt terms, are what we could call organizing structures of the ground on a collective level. They are structures that organize our collective ways of being and through which we relate to each other. They are systems that have been passed on through generations and owned by the collective. It follows then that to change the way these systems operate requires a "We", not an "I and them." I as an individual am powerless; we as a community may have a chance.

Although we have seen in Gestalt therapy that we can help clients to disentangle the internalization of cultural beliefs and introjects, we are powerless as individuals to change relational issues of the culture at large. No matter how good and sensitive we may be as therapists, our clients may continue to suffer psychologically because they as relational beings participate in cultural relationships. As relational beings, we are dependent on our field, a field that, in the matter of HIV, can be and often is hostile. This field, the culture at large, is not in therapy. It is not usually committed to raising awareness of itself or open to a dialogue that includes difference.

Culture itself is never the client in the room as an individuated entity. The culture at large is a living legacy of the archaic resonances of the internalized belief systems of others. This is a very different condition to the healing condition we hope to create as therapists in the therapy room.

Into the Abyss

Our power as individuals is challenged if we look at the situation from a point of view that includes our membership in the culture at large. We experience our insignificant power as individuals to change the situation. And when the situation involves death and social cruelty, as we have seen with HIV, we naturally feel dread and terror. An abyss appears before us. We see the terrible truth of mass death or our own death and the truth that the dying are abandoned and rejected by the community at large.

In the face of this abyss, we may be tempted to readily employ our knowledge and our skills to find solutions. We may wish to draw up treatment plans for our clients; to do anything to escape this abyss. We the authors were tempted to devise treatment suggestions for this chapter until we caught ourselves avoiding the question of the abyss. We were becoming anxious about painting so hopeless a picture that we would leave no significant options for therapeutic intervention.

As we inquired into our own personal experience, we realized that through our narcissism we were reluctant to surrender our illusion of power. Looking for solutions was partly a vain attempt to keep control. However, much of our own and others' energy is sapped when we react this way in an attempt to be powerful against HIV. We need only listen to the stories of the many caretakers who reached burnout quickly when working with HIV to see how this happens. Not only do we drain our energy if we react in this way, but we may also inadvertently leapfrog over a healing opportunity. The healing opportunity we refer to is the void itself. It is the ability to stay with this void, *this terrible truth* that is crucial in therapeutic healing.

The experience of this void for many brings feelings of hopelessness, deep pain, and terror. Tracking a client's phenomenology of this void consistently reveals an experience of dying on an emotional level accompanied by depression. What we believe is happening on a phenomenological level is *the death of an identity with individualism*. The part of us that is identified with the illusion of individual power feels hopeless because we are confronted with a truth that denies this kind of power; specifically, the truth that there are powers that affect our being in the world that cannot be controlled by us as individuals. The truth is we are relational beings.

Where many caretakers and people with HIV have become exhausted and depressed in relation to AIDS is that they have not been able to move from a fixed Gestalt or confluent position with individualism. It is as if they sit on the edge of the void looking into the abyss, terrified that if they fall into the abyss, they will lose something essential to their life. What we are proposing, however, is that what is dying is a fixed concept of ourselves and not our being.

Conclusion

Our observations have revealed that accepting the death of the paradigm of individualism is easier for those who have come to accept their mortality. For those whose bodies have been invaded by a life-threatening virus, such as HIV, death rushes forward from some vague point in future time to quite possibly tomorrow. This dramatic confrontation with death has led for some to an acceptance of its inevitability: a surrendering to what is.

There has been a psychological shift from hopelessness in the face of death to a place that the Buddhist traditions call *the place of no hope*. This place of no hope is what we Gestalt therapists understand as a place of creative indifference. Once we have faced our deaths in this way, it appears that facing the death of the individualistic paradigm can follow. However, both processes are not necessarily so clearly defined. Facing the death of individualism can feel as if the self is really dying, making the leap into this void excruciatingly frightening.

As we have been insisting, identifying with the paradigm of individualism has led us to believe that we can change the unchangeable or that we are responsible for the unchangeable. Many therapists burn out from working with HIV because they attempt to save the world from the ravages of HIV or at least save their clients from despair. They attempt the impossible; likewise, many clients suffer terrible depression, self-harm, and even suicide because they feel responsible for having arrived in their situation. They feel that on some level they deserve the derisive and divisive treatment they receive from others.

If we can see that there are systemic forces at work here, field dynamics that go beyond our personal selves to our collective responsibility, we may be able to realize that it's not our fault (or within our power) as therapists that our clients with HIV do not heal psychologically. Furthermore, we can only hope that our clients may realize that it is not their fault that people around them act unloving towards them. It is not because they are flawed that their environment does not support them fully.

The notion that fault does not lie with the individual can be a very profound realization. Many of our clients will have been coming to therapy to work out what is wrong with them, how they can change to make things better. Here is an example from one woman with HIV. She had been working within an organization that had suggested that it was not possible for her to continue working with them because she was HIV positive. The organization suggested that it was not fair for their clients as they could not guarantee that this worker would not get ill or die and therefore leave clients in the lurch. This woman resigned from the organization and yet remained attached for several years to it through her hatred. Her continual attachment to the organization kept her locked in a cycle of thinking she was defective in some way.

By facilitating the awareness that all parties were part of a cultural system of oppressive introjects, she was able to dis-identify from the system. As she did this, she was able to see herself and the people who rejected her in a compassionate light. She was able to see that she was not at fault, that she could not have done or been something better and have stopped the treatment she received. She then wept with the hurt from the separation from her organization, thus completing the Gestalt.

If we are encouraging clients to dis-identify with cultural introjects, as in the case study above, might we not be subtly encouraging rebellion and isolation? If we say the "Yes!" to Martin Buber's I/Thou relationship, are we not supporting the rejection of the more mainstream culture at large?

Let us go back to our case example to examine this further. The healing did not take place from simply rejecting the oppressive system. The healing came about for the client when she could connect with her fellow humanness. She not only saw how introjects made her feel at fault, she saw that it was introjects that caused others to reject her. She saw that no individual was to blame and that systemic forces affected everyone. The shaming force of the system was recognized, thereby allowing a shift away from the individualistic paradigm.

The healing opportunity for dialogue that we offer in one-to-one therapy may become a sanctuary from a hostile world. We can support diversity and teach our clients about finding people who support them and their difference. It is important though not to create from subtlety the promise of a utopian world separate from the wider culture. "The goal of therapy, we may say, is the transformation of the experience of shame into the experience of connection in the field" (Wheeler, 1996: 55). Separation from the wider culture does not transform the fundamental shame caused by the rejection of difference (a break in the relational field). Separation from the wider culture also denies that we are relational beings, all part of the field, beyond the realm of individuality.

Our humble goal in the face of such overwhelming forces at play with HIV could be to raise awareness of this field perspective; that HIV and its ramifications are no one's fault. From this perspective, we can possibly look friendly towards ourselves and others either as people with HIV in need of love or as people unaware, insensitive, and unsustained in the arena of HIV care. This would surely be a good place to attempt a healing dialogue.

Notes

[1]The term 'individualistic paradigm' in this context refers to a perspective that views the individual as a powerful entity separate from the field at large. We will not concern ourselves in this essay with a full exploration of this paradigm; Gordon Wheeler has explored the phenomenon comprehensively in "The Voice of Shame" (Lee & Wheeler, 1996) and we are indebted to his thinking in this essay. As a brief definition, we will use the words of Wheeler: "individualism — the habit of thinking that starts with the (mostly unexamined) assumption that the separateness, the isolation even, of our own awareness and consciousness is the basis and bedrock of reality and human experience, whereas connection and community, however important they may be, are somehow only instrumental and secondary to individual integration and individual satisfaction."

[2]Proposed by Pens, Hefferline, and Goodman (1994), "creative indifference" is a position to be adopted by the therapist. It is a position whereby the therapist is open to, and interested in, the client's world without investment in outcome or success of intervention.

[3]The House of Lords in the UK a few years ago blocked government legislation that would have allowed gay people the same sexual rights as their l6 to 18 year old heterosexual peers. Additional legislation prevents teachers from having open dialogues about gay sexual practices with 16 to 18 year olds at the very time that 50% of all newly diagnosed HIV infections are occurring in the young. Although not tested in the courts, it is practically illegal to have these discussions that could save their lives.

[4]There is another kind of guilt that people who are healthy can feel. This is guilt about being well in the face of others who are dying around them. Health and vitality are not celebrated for fear of being disloyal by the act of leaving the dying to their fate without joining them. Bert Hellinger (1998), a systemic family therapist, has discovered a methodology for investigating this kind of guilt.

Personal Account

When we first started to write this chapter, we discussed whether or not Jim should reveal his HIV status. Jim had been rejected from several organizations because of his status and was concerned that publicly declaring his status through this chapter might result in further rejection. Previously Jim had been pressured by colleagues to reveal his status to his clients, with the notion that as the diagnosis was in the field this justified the sharing of it. Geoff was aware that he might exert a similar pressure with the notion that being open about HIV would make a better chapter, in that it modeled a rejection of cultural beliefs that push HIV underground.

What we were paralleling was a cultural norm of focusing on people with HIV doing something to better a situation, to help the community, in our case the gestalt community, with HIV. This is not the flavor we wanted to convey in our chapter. We were both clear that a foundational stance of this chapter was that HIV is an issue for everyone and requires a community responsibility rather than someone or some minority being forced to take responsibility. In the event Jim has shared his status, hopefully in service of highlighting a dynamic that divides our culture.

Both of us in our different ways have been fighting for the rights of people with HIV since 1984. What we did not foresee when we began this work was that we were standing against very powerful cultural forces. We have learned the humbling and exhausting lesson that an increased ability to self-support does not necessarily alleviate psychological suffering around HIV.

Many people living with and affected by HIV continue to suffer debilitating depression and shame despite their abilities to self-support. Essentially we have observed how we as individuals are inescapably part of systems, social organizing structures of the ground and that our lives are shaped by these systems. The suffering for many people with HIV has its roots in these systems. This sort of suffering is not due to a psychological deficit, and not healed through individual will alone. To heal this suffering requires a shift on a cultural level, beyond the realm of individualism and beyond the realm of one to one therapies.

In our years of this work and including the writing of this chapter, we have found ourselves staring death in the face. This was the death of our friends and colleagues, the possible imminent death of ourselves, and the death of our attachment to individual power. At times we have both fallen into depressions and wondered how we could possibly live well in the midst of this devastation. We have both wondered about the possibility of living well in the face of this devastation. It was through the dialogue between us in writing this chapter that we realized that when we looked hopelessly at life, our hearts were closed. We feared reaching out with our hearts in case we suffered more hurt, more loss. But to live hopelessly with our hearts closed would make the tragedy worse. We honor the dead more if we learn from their experience and live well. In this way the dead live through us and do not die in vain.

Like with all systemic issues, HIV affects the entire global community. As co-authors, we have made it clear in this chapter that we believe we are all responsible when it comes to dealing with HIV. We believe it is in the best interest of community if we acknowledge this responsibility so that the few who do care enough to respond do not carry the burden alone. We have learned that the dead and dying have much to contribute to community if we are willing to honor their presence and their diversity.

Geoff Warburton, London, UK
James Kuykendall, London, UK

References

Buber, M., in Hycner, R. & Jacobs, L. (1995). *The Healing Relationship in Gestalt Therapy*. New York : TGJP.

Gayle, H. Personal Communication.

Hellinger, B. (1998). *Love's Hidden Symmetry*. Zeig, Phoenix, AZ: Tucker & Co.

Hycner, R., & Jacobs, L. (1995). *The Healing Relationship in Gestalt Therapy*. New York: TGJP.

Jacobs, L. (1996). *Shame in the Therapeutic Dialogue*, Lee, R. & Wheeler, G. (Eds.), *The Voice of Shame*. San Francisco, CA: Jossey-Bass.

Lee, K., & Wheeler, G. (1996). *The Voice of Shame*, San Francisco. CA: Jossey-Bass.

Parlett, M. (1991). Reflections on Field Theory. *British Gestalt Journal*. (1), 2, August.

Perls, F., Hefferline, K., & Goodman, P. (1994). *Gestalt Therapy: Excitement and Growth in the Human Personality*. Gestalt Journal Press, New York.

Spence, C. (1986). *AIDS, Time to Reclaim Our Power*. Lifestory, London.

Wheeler, G. (1996). *Self and Shame: A New Paradigm for Psychotherapy*, Lee. R & Wheeler, G. (Eds.), *The Voice of Shame*, San Francisco , Jossey-Bass.

Yalom, I. (1991). *Love's Executioner and Other tales of Psychotherapy*. London, Penguin Books.

VI. Russian Mothers and Daughters

By *Vera Kishinevsky, Ph.D. and Iris Fodor, Ph.D.*

"There is increasing evidence that ethnic values and identification are retained for many generations after immigration and play a significant role in family life and personal development throughout the life cycle."

---M. McGoldrick, J.K. Pearce, and J. Giordano (1982)

VERA [Opening Comment]:
Iris was my first year professor at New York University. I came to her class rather late in life, at forty-one, so Iris and I were closer in age than most of her other students. My course project was based on work with Marisol, an overweight girl from the Dominican Republic, and Iris's supervision sessions were the beginning of our dialogue on women's issues, especially on body image. Marisol's drawings were rich in meaning; they attracted Iris's attention by their expressive power. The major themes of these drawings were emigration and comparison of two cultures, Dominican and American.

Actually, it was not the mainstream American culture, but, rather, the culture of Dominican enclaves in New York City where people felt the changes as well as were changing the city they moved to. Work with Marisol opened up for me a new area of interest – mutual influence of two cultures at the points of contact. In fact, Iris's guidance led me to returning to my own roots – my Russian/Soviet/Jewish identity. While our work progressed, we made discoveries about our common personal background. We both had Russian-born mothers and adult daughters living on their own. Sharing personal memories, worries, and concerns evoked so many similar feelings in Iris and in me that we came to appreciate the extent of our mothers' influence on us and on our daughters.

By the time I started my studies at NYU, I had lived in the USA for seventeen years and had taught English for seven years. I experienced myself as thoroughly acculturated and fully bilingual, so I felt no significant linguistic or cultural barriers between Iris and me. At that time, I viewed culture as an ethnographic unity of looks, clothes, food and other visible and easily identifiable attributes. Iris's interest in researching her own Russian/Jewish roots gave me an impetus for looking deeper at our shared background. She suggested working together on a pilot project researching the immigrant experience of immigrant women from the former Soviet Union.

Iris was my guide and mentor in conducting qualitative research. What I did not know was that I was studying myself along with my participants. Trying to understand their emigration and acculturation experience, I was able to rethink my life and to uncover many themes close to Iris's heart and to her past. Our joint presentation at the Gestalt conference in New York in May of 1999 brought us together as explorers of women's and cultural issues and as two mothers with so much in common.

Two women, one raised in the US, and the other in the former Soviet Union, we will highlight the role of culture in the development of women's acceptance of their bodies. We will highlight the interplay between socio-cultural gender messages and the internalization process, which fosters the development of our self-image. We will also present a Gestalt model for understanding and working with body image and self-acceptance of immigrant women who are trying to negotiate the values of the old and new cultures.

By the time I was completing my doctoral studies at midlife I, as an immigrant mother, was interested in the stories of women who came to the United States from the former Soviet Union. Having a difficult time controlling my own weight and watching my daughter growing into a slim young woman, I wanted to learn how other mother-daughter dyads dealt with body image issues and how acculturation influenced this process. When I turned to the literature, I was surprised to find, given the size of the community, almost a total absence of studies examining the subjective experience of female immigrants from the former Soviet Union.

As I realized that the literature would not provide me with the information I needed, I decided to turn to former Soviet women for the answers. I wanted to know how beauty standards changed along the acculturation line and what cultural attitudes were carried over from the old country and passed to the next generation. I also wondered about the daughters' attitudes toward these issues and toward their mothers. I also wanted to research the influence of cultural experience on eating habits and attitudes of immigrant mothers and daughters. This study would be impossible only 20 or 25 years ago, when Soviet citizens were afraid of being interviewed, especially being taped. At that time, fear permeated the whole Soviet society, and no representative of the establishment was to be trusted. Any potential participant would refuse to have her conversation recorded as it could be used against her and lead to a disaster.

At the present time, the field is reconfigured in the former Soviet Union because drastic political and technological changes opened its population to a much stronger Western cultural influence. For the first time in seventy years, former Soviets were allowed to travel abroad, to obtain Western information, and to conduct business with Westerners.

Naturally, Western cultural values invaded Russia and influenced the attitudes and aspirations of former Soviets, especially the younger generation. Barbie dolls are now sold in all major Russian cities, and ultra-thin images of models and movie stars flood Russian media of all kinds. The "new Russians" amassed huge fortunes and want to emulate and to beat their Western counterparts to luxury and elegance. They buy Western beauty ideals wholesale and let the drops of their feasts dribble down to their less lucky compatriots, who, in their turn, struggle to look "like an American" and to buy a Barbie doll for their growing daughters: a cultural change resulting from the shift to the American phenomenological field.

Anybody who visits the Brighton Beach area of Brooklyn, NY, can attest to the drastic changes that have occurred to this neighborhood within the last twenty years. The influx of over forty thousand former Soviets have revived the dying neighborhood and infused it with new colors, smells, and sounds. But "Russians are coming" to other areas as well, bringing with them their rich culture and their desire to "fit in" the American society.

The influence of mainstream American culture is clearly visible on the younger generation – teenagers born in immigrant families rapidly acculturate because of their schooling and peers. They also influence all members of their families, including their grandparents' generations, to accept or, at least to open up to mainstream American values. Eating habits, body attitudes, dating, and a myriad of other cultural underpinnings of the former Soviet society are modified or discarded as the immigrants acculturate in the United States.

IRIS [Personal Observations]:
Vera and I have a shared interest in body image and in immigration-acculturation issues that lead to our collaboration. I am a third generation American, raised in New York City.   My grandparents on both sides were immigrants from Eastern Europe (Poland and Russia).   My young mother, reared by her Russian-born mother, still adhered to many Russian cultural traditions, but considered herself a modern American woman.   She tried to base my upbringing on many mainstream values.   My mother and my aunts struggled with their weight; so dieting and food restrictions were frequent topics of discussion at the dinner table.
During my childhood and adolescence, I was very thin, and my mother took pride in my slenderness. My first professional degree was from the Barbizon School of Modeling. My thin attractiveness was to be my route to rising in the world, not intelligence or education. Luckily, I did not make it as a fashion model, and became a psychologist. I did not remain thin with age, either. However, I have been a long-time student of women's body image issues and, as a clinician, have worked with and written about women's struggles with weight and body image and acceptance of aging (Fodor, 1998). I am interested in these issues because they connect me to my own roots.   In reviewing the transcripts of Vera's interviews, I recognized many of my own family values, even though I had never tapped my Russian heritage.   I am also a mother of an adult daughter, who is a dancer and choreographer.

Immigrants to the United States
The United States for the most part is a country of immigrants and refugees. Except for the era of forced immigration of enslaved Africans, from postcolonial days to the present, people from all over the world have immigrated to the United States and, until recently, their children and grandchildren have become Americans.   That is, they chose to adopt the cultural values and language of mainstream Anglo-Americans.
At the present time, immigration is accelerating. "One out of every five children under the age of 18 in the United States – 14 million altogether – is an immigrant or has immigrant parents" (Hernandez, 1999: 19).   In New York City, one of the major points of entry for US immigrants, a recent survey indicated that only 35 percent of the city's population is white, and the rest are the representatives of a multitude of national and ethnic groups. Multiculturalism has been, by default, a fact of life in New York with its countless social groups, that enrich its fabric with their cultural contributions from bagels to jazz. At the present time, multiculturalism is slowly becoming a way of life in other parts of the United States, introducing new intercultural values to the mainstream society.   Hence, as one soon notes, native-born Americans to the US have never been only white.
With multicultural presences emerging from more diverse cultures than ever before, and with a shift from the melting pot mentality to a multicultural mosaic, the pressure to follow the mainstream values of Anglo-Saxon society is diminishing.
However, the beauty ideal still remains unchanged and is probably the last bastion of legitimized discrimination.   Negative attitude toward full-bodied women is a norm in the United States. It is not as yet unanimously clear how multicultural bodies and looks will achieve unquestioned acceptance. In world societies we often think of as multicultural, influence means that beauty can come in packages other than a very tall reed-thin blond with blue eyes, long legs, narrow hips, and large breasts. Introducing this concept into mainstream American society would therefore mean introducing a variety of beauty ideals.

A multicultural dimension would usher in a variety of simultaneous cultural differences, not found isolated only in nightclubs and restaurants or on university campuses. What we have then is a field that is growing within the mainstream American cultural reality, acquiring strength and replacing the melting pot reality with its one language and one set of cultural norms and values. What one says or imagines about the Anglo-American female body image is so particularly true. The out-of-awareness inculcation of many American root values, including notions of beauty and aspirations to body ideal, are based on British Protestant socio-ethical behavior that values discipline and self-restraint.

Developing a Gestalt Perspective of Acculturation
Upon their arrival in the United States, immigrants need to learn new cultural repertoires and competencies of an unfamiliar culture. The adaptation process is often quite stressful and usually leads to culture shock and acculturation stress. Acculturation occurs on both the individual and group levels, and to understand this process one needs to examine the cultural values of the society of origin and of settlement.

Gestalt therapy espouses a field theory orientation that recognizes that our ground of self-experience is cultural. For humans beings, the boundaries between ourselves and others are fluid, and culture is the very air we breathe and the water we drink. Furthermore, we live, grow up, and grow old in families that are also experiencing the shifting of cultures. Moving from one culture to another becomes a "disruption of magnitude" (Parlett, 1997: 26) for each member of a refugee or émigré family, as it "disrupts the habitual configurations of the field as a whole." New cultural norms and values invade the new immigrant's self-systems and create the tension between conflicting forces, leading to the adjustment of existing systems and to the creation of new ones.

Historical events, technological progress, and small, everyday changes influence and reconfigure our experience, including that of refugees and émigrés. For example, twenty years ago, a Soviet citizen, leaving the country, had little hope to visit it again or to see those who chose to stay or were unable to leave. After the fall of the Soviet system, the finality of the emigration became a non-issue. During the Soviet regime, almost all mail coming from the West was censored and most of it was delayed if it was delivered at all. Electronic mail enabled instant communication between family members and friends living in distant corners of the world. The possibility to return or to be in contact with the country of origin has led to significant changes in émigré attitudes, interests, and psychological problems. As parts of a unified field, acculturating émigrés influence the culture of their adopted country as well.

Acculturation has been defined in psychological literature as a process of change, experienced by an individual exposed to a new cultural context. Psychological acculturation usually occurs along two dimensions as a group level and an individual level phenomenon with a wide variety of changes, determined by the specific characteristics of the group and the individual (Berry, Trimble, & Olmeda, 1986). Upon arrival, émigrés need to learn a new cultural repertoire, necessary for successful functioning within the new culture. Adopting the unknown as the known, acquiring and adapting to new competencies and values, inhabiting a new repertoire of values and vocabularies, they either completely shed their old cultural values or try to readjust them to the requirements of the new society.

As human beings, we simultaneously function within the variety of groups and social systems, thereby complicating the internalization of new norms and values and their incorporation into the existing field of experience. Émigré families have to negotiate the new sets of norms and requirements, presented by school, workplace, and social support systems. Strong intergenerational ties, usually in many émigré communities, may influence members of all generations and become a source of both support and conflict. For example, a grandmother who continues the tradition of taking care of her grandchildren may benefit from their rapid second language acquisition, but she may be offended by their newly established sense of privacy.

Every generation's experience of the acculturation process differs according to the age, social position, and immediacy of the needs. While members of the older generation, grandmothers, for example, view change mostly as outsiders, most granddaughters embrace change and shed an old cultural repertoire with relative ease. The middle generation, mothers, attempt to balance and negotiate conflicting requirements of the traditional culture and the culture of the adopted country.

Three generations of grandmas and granddaughters form these polarities. Mother is the middle ground. Polarities pull towards extremes. Mother looks for compromise. Another field is thereby reconfigured. Each holds a piece of the reconfiguring field. One reflects the need to maintain the past. The other reflects the push for confluence. The third reflects a wish for integration. Each holds a piece of the widening reconfiguration. Hence, observing this cross-generational transformation, we wonder whether there is a way in which, or a ground on which, all needs may inhabit the center and not the periphery until the collective need is organismically satisfied.

Self Experience/Schema Theory

Former Soviet women appear to be confluent with cultural messages about female body ideal. They do not discriminate between the societal messages and their own self-felt experience. They also do not question the new culture's values. Rather deeply embedded in their desire for self-acceptance, they tend to shed the old and introject the new too quickly. In the process, their own family values, conflicting with newly acquired ones, get discounted. For adolescents, there is an accelerated desire to embrace the new culture and to leave the old culture and their family at the same time. Thus, adolescents are highly prone to embracing the negative views of womanhood with resulting feelings of self-hate and shame about their bodies if they cannot look like Americans wish to look, that is, to become thin.

Our small sample of such young girls maturing into womanhood whom we observed appeared to include very thin girls and a girl with the beginning symptoms of eating disorders. It occurred to us at some point that Gestalt therapy combined with a schematic social constructivist view of field could be relevant to how we might observe members of our sample as a way of suggesting a Gestalt concept for learning and growth.

The importance of a Schema Process model is its emphasis on internalization. Extending the traditional gestalt view of introjection into a specific concept of internationalization has allowed us to enter a dynamic schema process model to understand the phenomenon of how women may evaluate self. Schemas are dynamic phenomena, created by our interactions with our environment; and they are constantly changing. Whatever elements we take in from our environment, such as socio-cultural messages, parental evaluations and introjects such as shoulds or should-nots, these elements are assimilated into our ongoing reconfigured internalized schemata. Our own cognitive, experiencing organizing structure is constantly being re-formatted as a shifting lens or template for interpreting new experiences. Even if the origin of a message is from the family or the culture, the woman, or the young girl maturing into adulthood, has adopted these messages as her own. Hence, in the shedding of the old cultural values, she takes in the new culture's messages and values.

In the case of body image, these new societal messages for women appear to be contaminants that women use as the building blocks for their own self-schema. They create a new, distorted lens in the field. Furthermore, the girl or the woman is continually taking in new information through this lens that will allow her to create ever-changing templates until she reaches satisfaction or self-acceptance, or not. The longer she lives in the new culture that conforms to her self-schema, the more she reconstructs her view of self and others on the basis of such information (Fodor, 1995). When a woman experiences approval for the way she looks, she feels pride, wants to dress up and show off. When she feels fat, disapproved of, she wants to hide and will experience self-loathing and will possibly beat up on herself for her lack of control, adding another layer of shame to her already damaged self-concept.

Following our model of study as an ongoing process, one can view up front and close another's introjections. Too often, for women, the boundary emphasis is on the others' expectations, rather than on their own felt self-needs. Often, two different basic need systems are in competition or are nested together. The need for connectedness, the need to be desirable in the eyes of the other, and the need for self-regulation will organize experiences around her own felt self-needs. When connection is perceived as an aspect of self-regulation, the boundary between self and other is blurred. Needs to connect in a new culture, to form new relationships, and to be accepted all become motivators for acquiring an American look. Clearly, schema theory, which views cultural beliefs as those assimilated by the organism into its own ongoing cognitive/affective/motor framework field, serves as a rich theoretical framework for understanding the acculturation process.

The Home-of-Origin Experiences of Russian Women Immigrants

A majority of immigrants move to America as family groups. What happens when family members, functioning at different points in their life cycle, move from one culture to another? Each member of the family will experience new values, meanings, and beliefs differently – depending on how much each developed and shaped one's own life in the old culture and how open each becomes to the new culture. In addition, when values and beliefs clash, a possibility for splits within each person, and conflicts between family members of different ages and different generations, increases significantly. Grandmothers and mothers traditionally are the agents for family acculturation. In particular, the socialization experience of the mother/daughter bond is particularly salient for passing along cultural values from one generation to the next.

As therapists working with immigrants, we need to look beyond the individuals and their symptoms and problems. Too often we are focused on the individual, leaving the family context unexplored and excluding its influence from the conceptualization of the problem. We need to address the issues and conflicts arising from the shift from one culture to the other and research their meaning for the individual and the family. Hence, focusing on issues and conflicts emerging from within the shift, we may form several aspects of a mainstream culture impinging on that shift. We focus here on particular aspects of American mainstream culture: body image, self-esteem, and the development of eating disorders.

We therefore examine how women immigrants moving from their culture of origin to the US might displace their very views of themselves, of their bodies, and of their self-perception as desirable women. We see that these views may differ in the culture of origin and in the culture of displacement, the United States. In examining this process, we highlight the experiences of three generations of Russian women, who moved in family groups to the United States.

Given the numbers of immigrants from the former Soviet Union, it is surprising to find an almost total absence of research studies of this population. Chiswick (1991), quoting from the U.S. Department of Justice, Immigration and Naturalization Service 1990 unpublished tables, estimated that "over one quarter of a million persons living in the United States... can be described as Soviet Jews, that is, individuals born in the former USSR (or their U.S.-born children) who consider themselves Jewish by religion or ethnicity and who immigrated to the United States from the Soviet Union since the mid 1960s" (260). According to Cass (1997), the largest Russian émigré population in the United States is concentrated in Brooklyn, New York: "Brighton Beach is currently home to about 30,000 Russian émigrés" (181).

To examine the acculturation process, we will present a series of interviews, reflecting the experience of female Russian immigrants, mid-life mothers and adolescent daughters, who have moved to New York City from the former Soviet Union. We will examine particular aspects of culture-gender messages, such as feelings of attractiveness, attitude toward food and eating habits, dress, and the interrelationships of women in immigrant families. We will also describe relevant aspects of the mainstream American culture-gender messages about attractiveness, family relationships, and attitudes toward food and eating that new immigrants face.

We will conclude with a discussion of a Gestalt model for understanding the schematic process of cognitive cultural shifts. This process, the underlying concept of acculturation, has been little explored from the perspectives of gender, life cycle, and family dynamics.

The similarity or dissimilarity between two cultures, commonly referred to as cultural distance, may influence the process of acculturation. While on the surface mainstream US and Russian cultures appear similar, they have deep underlying differences, reflected in cultural practices, attitudes, and traditions.

The conceptual difference between these two cultures becomes apparent when one compares the two most popular dolls that are important socialization agents for girls. The American Barbie and the Russian nested dolls known as Matryoshka symbolize the cultural views on female body image and roles of women in their respective societies.

A Barbie doll is an embodiment of a perfect young American female that has never been. She is a cheerful blonde with an unattainably slim body, full breasts, and unnaturally long limbs. Actually, the Barbie doll is all limbs, action, and glamour. Her core woman's body is diminished, overshadowed by her moving arms and legs; her aim is exercise and mobility. If a real woman, by an inhuman effort of permanent dieting and exercise, were able to achieve Barbie's proportions, she would probably be physiologically unable to have children. Barbie would also be so self-absorbed that nothing would be left for nurturing others since all her energy is invested in looking good and keeping her good looks as long as possible. Barbie comes with numerous outfits, and young American girls are encouraged to purchase and dress Barbie up for her numerous activities. Barbie's body is a commodity; she is the embodiment of the American pursuit of personal attractiveness and consumerism.

The Matryoshka, a rounded, egg-shaped nest of dolls embedded within dolls – each one giving birth to another one, so to speak, as you lift one out of the other one -- is as blond, blue-eyed, and creamy-skinned as Barbie is, but this is where their similarity ends. Matryoshka, carved out of natural wood, not plastic, represents a rounded body that can belong to a woman of any race or culture.

The Martyoshka also symbolizes a nurturing woman, a vital member of any traditional culture all over the globe. Matryoshka is all about survival, having children, nurturing and protecting them. Not that she does not need her painted-on arms and legs – probably her activity level is no lower than Barbie's, but the stress here is on her body – round, fertile, and grounded. In her full belly, several generations of women are nested comfortably and safely. Matryoshka's existence is not individual, it is part of the matrilineal family line, the strongest connection and the basis of the Russian and many other traditional cultures. Matryoshka wants to be pretty, too – her hair is neatly combed and parted, her head kerchief matches her ornate dress, and her blue eyes radiate warmth. Nevertheless, her body, suggesting beauty standards unacceptable to Barbie, is functional on a level embracing femininity and motherhood dictated solely by a need for survival.

Russian women have traditionally been the backbone of their nation (Binyon, 1983). The Russian family structure was and still is strongly matrilineal. According to duPlessix Gray (1990), the core of the Russian family is the married or unmarried daughter, her children, and her mother, married or widowed by the Second World War. Russian women pay great attention to outward appearance and spend significant amounts of their income and energy trying to "look decent." Paris has always been and still is the source of fashion and beauty standards for Russian women and French women symbolize the ideal of beauty and elegance. Russian women's femininity follows the French pattern of enjoyment of sex, cooking, and dressing up, which does not diminish with an increase in weight.

The Communist Revolution of 1917 introduced Russians to permanent food shortages. Soviet citizens have always had to struggle to obtain most primitive staples, such as bread, sugar, meat, or potatoes. As a result, the Soviet citizen's diet consisted mainly of starches, with a small percentage of meat and milk. Because of housing shortages, many married children shared apartments with their parents. In such families, the grandmother did almost all food hunting and cooking. If a family had its own apartment, it was not unusual for a grandmother to visit with dinners in tow or to have grandchildren come to dinner on a regular basis. As a result, grandmother's attitudes and habits were influential in families.

Grandmothers, women born in the 1920s and the 1930s, belong to the generation that suffered the most from several famines and constant food shortages. They grew up valuing every scrap of food and going out of their way to feed their children to save their lives. A thin child was viewed as sickly, and every effort was made to make children eat. In this situation, home cooking and baking was crucial for health and survival and, therefore, was highly valued.

The Russian Traditional Female Body Image

A traditional populist beauty ideal in Russia, as noted by many authors, was a full-bodied, strong woman with rosy cheeks and a round face of the Matryoshka doll type. "Throughout Russian history, the mother has been the focus of the Russian family, and her image is that of a large, warm, strong woman, almost enveloping her family in her ample bosom" (Binyon, 1983: 34). Thinness was considered aristocratic, and the thin-beauty ideal was a class issue before the revolution. After the revolution, health and strength necessary for the fulfillment of a double role of a mother and a productive worker were promoted by the government and glorified in the mass media dominated by the artistic imagery of social realism.

Festive Eating in Russian Society

It is hard to overestimate the role of lavish festive eating in the Russian society. "There is nothing a Russian likes better than getting together with friends and relatives for a good meal. The Russians organize lavish parties….the table groans with whatever food the enterprising host or hostess can procure. The reasons for such attitude are numerous: home life has always been the only island of warmth and happiness in the ocean of Soviet misery and bleakness" (Binyon, 1983: 70).

Having a circle of friends has a crucial survival value – the warmth of each other's company gives people reassurance of future support in times of need. A lavish table has been a rare treat in the culture of constant shortages, a compensation for scanty, monotonous daily meals. The Russian festive dinner, as a rule, contains a rich variety of rather fatty culinary creations, a necessary accompaniment to the copious amounts of vodka consumed by each guest.

Anglo-American Pursuit of Attractiveness and Youth

"Some ladies smoke too much and some ladies drink too much and some ladies pray too much. But all ladies think they weigh too much" (Ogden Nash, 1962).

All cultures that have reported numbers of eating disorders have a thin ideal. Cultures that do not have the thin ideal have few reported cases of anorexia and bulimia. Thus, these disorders, are in part an over commitment or over adaptation to the cultural ideal that is in vogue nowadays (Fallon, 1990, 102).

Mainstream white America has a culturally induced system that perpetuates women's dissatisfactions with their body. Ironically, as women in our culture have become more autonomous in the past decade, their concern with weight and appearance seems to be on the rise from adolescence throughout the life cycle. There is an emphasis on equating attractiveness with thinness, with restrained eating as a moral imperative. American women are on perpetual diets, and women are major participants in dieting and weight loss programs. Eating disorders, predominantly women's problem, are on the rise.

Every point in a woman's life cycle is shaped by societal gender role messages and expectations. Also, most of us live in families where the mutual influence of different life cycle concerns affects familial interactions. The most striking aspect in clinical work with American women is the extent to which they have a love/hate relationship with their bodies.

The reiteration of body pride and shame in a modern woman's life are related to her life cycle. The first struggle begins during the shift from the pre-pubescent body to that of a woman. In adolescence and beyond we see a lack of acceptance of the developing body in women and the beginning of eating disorders, like anorexia and bulimia.

Later in adulthood, women struggle with normal weight gains that come with age, being on a continuous string of weight reduction programs, feeling pride when they are thin, hating themselves and their bodies when they are heavier, and fearing growing older. Many mid-life women, mothers of adolescent daughters, struggle with another aspect of the culturally induced message of the ageist society – the double standard of aging. At midlife, they begin their never-ending struggle to freeze in time their youthful looks.

The Social Construction of Body Image

One of the paradoxes of the women's movement of the 20th century is that after American women freed themselves from restrictive roles and clothing, they became enslaved by a newly developed fashion industry. The development of photography and the 20th century aesthetic ideal of equating a female body with both thinness and beauty was inspired by the flapper era. Since clothes drape better on tall lean models, fashion photography and film industry has become dominated by the images of thin attractive women. Rapidly developing media bombards women with messages about only one – thin – beauty standard.

According to Gerbner's (1973) cultivation theory, the effect of heavy use of television, magazines, and other mass media gradually establishes and reinforces a preference for certain beliefs about the nature of reality. Television in particular is the source of the most broadly shared images and messages in history. Adolescent girls therefore, as they gain weight developing hips and breasts, and women, as they grow older, adapt a socially constructed view that the way their body is naturally changing is not acceptable. They learn to desire a leaner, more slender body and to fight to stay young.

Researchers overall suggest that media images of slenderness have the greatest effect on those adolescent girls whose personalities predispose them to make social comparisons and to look for guidance about conforming to dominant societal perceptions. Adolescents in general tend to look outside the family for the information necessary to "fit in" with peers. For example, in a recent study, US adolescent girls, in spite of the diversity of North American culture, described the ideal girl as follows: 5 ft. 7 in. tall, 100 pounds, size 5, with long blond hair and blue eyes. Girls formed this ideal on the models they found in fashion magazines and expressed a strong desire to be like them.

Adolescent girls construct and attempt to act out their self-image around a thinness schema (Striegel-Moore and Smolak, 1996). This thinness schema suggests experiences organized around the following aspects: acute sensitivity to societal cues; a need for social approval; and the integration of attractiveness into the self-schema, including information about the importance of thinness to attractiveness, importance of attractiveness for social and career success, the dangers of fat, methods of becoming thin, and the relevance of attractiveness for self esteem formation (Smolak and Levine, 1994). With the development of their internalized thinness schema, adolescent girls run a high risk for eating disorders. Furthermore, since adolescent girls are relatively silenced in other ways, many may find that attractiveness is one of the few available paths to success.

At the same time when girls enter adolescence, their mothers are struggling with their own body issues, such as aging, gaining weight, and struggling to hold on to their youthful look. Many adolescent girls look at their mothers, see them struggling with their own weight and body acceptance, and vow to resist the extra pounds that constitute a normal weight gain for this life stage. The greater is the mother's lack of acceptance of her own body, the higher is the likelihood that her daughter will have a body image problem.

However, not all Americans buy into the thinness schema. Black women in general feel better about their bodies (Striegel-Moore and Smolak, 1996). While black women also endorse the thin ideal and are found to be heavier than white women, they report less parental criticism of weight, fewer incidences of weight-related discrimination, and less social pressure to lose extra weight. Only when black girls experience family or environmental social pressure to become thinner does one see the same patterns of body dissatisfaction and eating disorders.

The United States of America is considered the land of plenty. Surrounded by abundant and attractive food, women get barraged by contradicting messages coming from different sides. They are both encouraged on every page of glossy print to enjoy food and to practice self-restraint. Every cover of women's magazines features delicious recipes and photographs of rich festive meals. The inside of the magazine makes the same or stronger emphasis on diets and exercise regiments. Most American women do not live with their mothers, and contact with them is not a daily part of their life. Furthermore, as American women become more invested in work and careers, they become less invested in food preparation. Affordable and widely available take-out meals, prepared supermarket dinners, and eating out take away the pressure and the need to cook from scratch.

Ever-Present Western Influence and Russian Culture
Today, immigration is going both ways. US culture is now found to be more penetrating than ever before by the former Soviet Union. Even those Russians remaining in their culture also experience, like their immigrant counterparts, the influence of the same imported Western cultural attitudes. Furthermore, the process of adapting these attitudes is happening all over the world. The disintegration of the Soviet Union has brought tremendous changes into Russian life. During the last 10 years, Russia has undergone significant changes in all aspects of social and private life. The Russian market became flooded with Western goods – food, clothing, appliances, and automobiles. Western media – French, German, Italian, and American TV shows, music, art, fashion magazines, and catalogues – introduce new standards of beauty and new portrayals of the good life.

Nouveau Rich "New Russians" turn to the West for inspiration and start imitating the styles and looks of their Western brethren. Russian youth follow the lead. By trying to look like a picture from a French or American fashion magazine many Russian girls turn to dieting and disordered eating. All these changes have created a new atmosphere of confusion and flux in lives of average Russians.

Of interest is that the rest of the world is also assimilating the same cultural messages. Recent articles on Fiji and China point to a growing epidemic of body dissatisfaction and eating disorders among adolescents and young women exposed to Western media. Prior to such exposure, eating disorders have never been observed in these cultures. American cultural messages and beliefs are cast far and wide, and we can conclude that some of them function as pollutants dominating and overriding indigenous cultural values. How come this is the process? Is it body size? Is it money? What might we believe is this power that brings so many to wish confluence with the US?

This process of cultural contamination is probably a part of the overall massive invasion of the West's worldwide lifestyle sales campaign. Wealth and the technological power of postindustrial Western societies prepare the field for the wholesale acceptance of their global superiority in all aspects of living. Shiny pictures of glamorous people enjoying carefree life have a strong appeal for the populations of less affluent or downright poor countries around the globe. The participants in our investigations who volunteered to talk about their experiences are immigrant women and their teenage daughters, who arrived in the USA from the former Soviet Union. Twelve mothers and five daughters participated in the study. Their stay in the USA spans from 4 months to 18 years. The focus of the interviews was on the experience of immigrating, adjustments to differing cultures, and, in particular, on their attitude toward their bodies and attractiveness. We also explored the change in their attitudes toward food and eating. The interviews were conducted in English or Russian, depending on the participants' preference.

Theme I: The importance of Women's Intergenerational Ties

Talking about food, one daughter recalled, "I loved grandma's soups, cakes, pastries; my mom never had the time, she was always at work. On weekends, I used to go there, especially to eat grandma's cooking, on a regular basis." Another daughter talked about her grandmother's attempts to stuff her with food: "Now I just understand that this was a grandmother's role, because everyone's grandmother tries to make you eat this and this, and this." More than once, food becomes a link between generations, and five out of seven women talked about it. Grandmothers, women who survived several famines, valued food very highly and considered feeding their grandchildren a life-saving feat. Even if they were of average weight themselves, they considered a thin child sickly.

In the United States, strong matrilineal ties in Soviet émigré families survived the stresses of emigration. One participant remembered that she "practically lived" with her grandmother who took care of her while her mother was studying English and working long hours. Her grandmother's legacy made an impact on this girl's life: on the one hand, she complained that she "was fighting with my weight all my life"; but on the other hand, she indicated that she would "definitely become the same kind of grandmother."

Theme II: Food and Attitudes toward Food

As expected, the women's stories about their life in Russia are full of descriptions of their struggles to obtain basic staples and to prepare nutritious meals against the background of permanent food shortages. All the participants reported difficulties much the same way: "In 1992, there was a rationing system in Russia, and many kinds of food stuffs were distributed by coupons. We used to wait in terribly long food lines; it was a hungry time, all food stores were absolutely empty."

Love for home cooking and tremendous enjoyment of food in general are constant themes of almost all mothers' stories. One mother recalled tasting rich fatty delicacies with gusto. She proceeded to make broader generalizations about the two political systems:

"When I first came to the United States, I opened my eyes to small details, like ice cream. In Moscow, there was a huge banner, SOVIET ICE CREAM IS THE BEST IN THE WORLD and when I was offered ice cream here, I thought, 'What's the big deal? After the Moscow ice cream I can't be impressed!' And then, I tasted it, my G-d! So with such details, like ice cream, everything was forming one chain, and after two weeks here I realized that I wanted to live here.'"

After emigrating, several participants created a psychological comfort zone for themselves by throwing old-style lavish dinner parties. All the mothers talked about tasting new food and enjoying it during the first year in the United States. "Everything I ate was new to me, even bacon. Whatever was on the supermarket shelf was interesting to me."

Theme III: Grandmothers and Mothers

Most grandmothers and other women belonging to the same generation were described by their daughters and granddaughters as overweight or as significantly overweight. "My mother-in-law was extremely fat. Both my mother and she used to say that they had to starve during bad times, so when food became available, they ate a lot and gained a lot of weight." Their beauty standards reflected fear of malnutrition and preference for roundness: "My mother thought that I was very skinny. When I used to gain weight, she said, 'How good you look!' " Another mother, mentioning her mother-in-law, who was trying to adapt to new standards, but who followed the traditional attitude toward feeding children, observed, "At that time the slimming fashion has already begun. She kept talking about the need to lose weight and at the same time she kept stuffing her son with food."

Upon their arrival in the USA, grandmothers enjoy eating new delicacies without much concern about their body size. "By the way," one woman offered, "I know many adults, even seniors in their fifties and sixties, who have been here for six-seven years, rather long periods of time. They eat huge quantities of ice cream, by the box. My mother-in-law, she suffers from ice cream obsession."

Mothers' attitudes to their bodies bear the residue of their own mother's upbringing, mixed with the new aspirations for a slimmer silhouette. On the surface, several mothers expressed the desire to look thinner, but we noted that their thinness ideal is at least two sizes larger than the Western one. One mother was happily describing how she achieved the desired weight loss to be able to wear a size 16 dress. Even the thinnest woman in our group expressed ambivalence toward her thinness. On the one hand, she was proud of her slim body, and on the other, she wished she were endowed with more curves. "It is not Russian style," she insisted. "Russian women were mainly plump, this is some foreign influence, it may end later." Out of seven mothers, three are significantly overweight, and four are of average weight. All seven women tried to lose weight, and their stories contain referrals to exercise and dieting as part of their struggle.

Clothing seems to play a significant role in all the mothers' lives, and their reaction to weight gain was triggered by tightening seams rather than by measuring body size.

Among their adolescent daughters, out of five teenagers, two are overweight, one shows signs of disordered eating, and the other one mentions her friend, also a Russian immigrant, who practices vomiting on a regular basis as a weight control measure. Both overweight teenagers have heavy mothers and are dissatisfied with their bodies. A girl with signs of disordered eating is a daughter of a woman who "always tried to be thin" and whose husband used to proclaim, "Fat women don't deserve to live." It seems that the mother's self-acceptance has a more significant influence on the daughter than her weight.

All the daughters talked about behaviors that reflected the Americanization of attitudes toward food and body issues. For example, no matter how much a mother weighs, she talks about food with gusto, describing rich ethnic dishes and full festive tables, while her daughter uses negative terms describing food and eating. Loss of enjoyment of eating is easily noted when we compare this mother-daughter dyad. The mother said, "I like tasty food. In Italy, I ate lasagna. It was of some unbelievably miraculous taste. Never and in no place have I eaten anything similar. Since I am a good cook myself, I enjoy cooking tasty food." Her daughter, reporting to us on her school lunch choices, recalled, "I used to eat pizza all the time, but they have such disgusting pizza that I stopped eating it. Now I eat bagels with cream cheese and Dorritos -- together, just not to be hungry."

Two more recent immigrant daughters were very thin, even by American standards. "Now everybody looks at me and says, 'Look how skinny she is,'" one observed.

Theme IV: Disordered Eating

Out of five daughters, one (four years in the USA) demonstrated signs of disordered eating that appeared after her emigration. She mentioned starvation and self-induced vomiting as ways of weight control and talked about feeling sick after eating. "I didn't eat anything, just drank coffee, because I wanted to lose weight. I made myself throw up. I can't eat anything sweet for breakfast, like doughnuts and I feel nauseated afterwards." There is no mention of disordered eating in any participant's description of her life in the former Soviet Union.

Theme V: Exercise and Sports
When one respondent was describing her initial weight gain in the United States, she mentioned exercise as a cure. "I gained 10 pounds.... I started working out on it [the exercise machine]. I was involved in the sports all my life, in Russia, too." As immigrant families became more financially comfortable in the United States, mothers and daughters turned to sports and exercise to lose weight and to tone their bodies.

Findings
The findings of this study of twelve Russian immigrant mothers and daughters include the following:
1. For most of the women, female intergenerational ties are very strong, often stronger than marital ones. Grandmothers are a source of emotional support and are providers of significant assistance in child rearing and housekeeping. Grandmothers also carry cultural messages about feeding children and eating well to be healthy.
2. Food and enjoyment of eating play a significant role in Russian immigrant families' lives. Festive eating at large dinner parties is a significant source of emotional support for recent immigrants. Russian immigrant women take pride in their housekeeping abilities.
3. As families get acculturated, enjoyment of eating diminishes for the next generation.
4. The teenagers in the sample tend to be thinner than their mothers. This finding coincides with conclusions of many studies demonstrating that rates of obesity decline with acculturation into Western societies.
5. Statistics on eating disorders in the former Soviet Union is not available, but our study gives us a reason to believe that Russian immigrant girls turn to disordered eating as they get acculturated in the United States.
6. Upon their arrival to the United States, the women in this sample tended to overeat without paying attention to the nutritional value of the food consumed and to gain significant amounts of weight. Subsequently, they experienced significant difficulties controlling their weight.
7. Sports and physical exercise play an important role in Russian women's lives. Upon their arrival to the United States, their involvement in sports decreases because of financial difficulties. As they get more comfortable financially, they turn to sports for weight control.

Implications for Further Work and Research
1. Helping professionals need to address the needs of entire families. Since most American therapists would not include grandmothers, they lose both a significant source of information and a strong ally in therapeutic work. It is essential that therapists include the grandmother in family work or explore the reasons for her absence.

2. Immigrant girls need extra help in integrating new experiences with messages they receive at home and in the media.
3. Prevention of disordered eating needs to include an acculturation component. Schools need to be made aware of the family structure in working with students from various immigrant groups.
4. The Therapeutic Process needs to address the acculturation process and its stresses. Differing cultural messages and values need to be spelled out and addressed in the therapeutic process.

Underlying Themes

Our analysis of these interviews identified themes relating to the women's reflections on their past and current experiences. The different stories they told expressed a similar central plot: a family arrives from the former Soviet Union. The mother and the grandmother, overweight to some degree, value food very highly, enjoy eating and home cooking, and consider feeding children a priority. A man is less important for family survival than a mother. Upon the arrival to the United States, the mother gains more weight, tasting new delicacies and enjoying new ways of eating. She feels bad about being overweight and tries sports and dieting to lose weight. The daughter develops a less enthusiastic, more guilt-ridden attitude toward food and grows up slimmer than the mother, but prone to eating disorders.

Personal Account

Iris was my first year professor at New York University. I came to her class rather late in life, at forty-one, so Iris and I were closer in age than most of her other students. My course project was based on work with Marisol, an overweight girl from the Dominican Republic, and Iris's supervision sessions were the beginning of our dialogue on women's issues, especially on body image. Marisol's drawings were rich in meaning; they attracted Iris's attention by their expressive power. The major themes of these drawings were emigration and comparison of two cultures, Dominican and American. Actually, it was not the mainstream American culture, but, rather, the culture of Dominican enclaves in New York City where people felt the changes as well as were changing the city they moved to. Work with Marisol opened up for me a new area of interest – mutual influence of two cultures at the points of contact; Iris's guidance led me to returning to my own roots – my Russian/Soviet/Jewish identity. While our work progressed, we made discoveries about our common personal background. We both had Russian-born mothers and adult daughters living on their own. Sharing personal memories, worries, and concerns evoked so many similar feelings in Iris and in me that we came to appreciate the extent of our mothers' influence on us and on our daughters.

By the time I started my studies at NYU, I had lived in the USA for seventeen years and had taught English for seven years. I experienced myself as thoroughly acculturated and fully bilingual, so I felt no significant linguistic or cultural barriers between Iris and me. At that time, I viewed culture as an ethnographic unity of looks, clothes, food and other visible and easily identifiable attributes. Iris's interest in researching her own Russian/Jewish roots gave me an impetus for looking deeper at out shared background. She suggested that we work together on a pilot project researching the immigrant experience of immigrant women from the former Soviet Union.

Iris was my guide and mentor in conducting qualitative research. What I did not know was that I was studying myself along with my participants. Trying to understand their emigration and acculturation experience, I was able to rethink my life and to uncover many themes close to Iris's heart and to her past. Our joint presentation at the Gestalt conference in New York in May of 1999 brought us together as explorers of women's and cultural issues and as two mothers with so much in common.

Vera Kishinevsky, Leonia, NJ, USA

References

Binyon, M. (1983). *Life in Russia*. NY: Random House.

Berry, J. W. Trimble, J. & Olmeada, E. (1986). Assessment of acculturation. In. W. J. Lonner & J. W. Berry (Eds.). *Field Methods in Cross-Cultural Research.* London: Sage.

Cass, F. (1997). *Russian organized crime: Russian Émigré Crime in the United States.* CA: Redwood Books.

Chiswick, B. (1991). Soviet Jews in the United States: An analysis of their Linguistic and economic adjustment. *International Migration Review, XXVI,* 2, 260-285.

du Plessix Gray, F. (1990). *Soviet women: Walking the tightrope.* New York: Doubleday. Herandez, D. (1999). *Children of Immigrants, one-fifth of America's children and growing: Their circumstances, prospects, and welfare reform.* Master lecture, Society for Research in Child Development, Albuquerque, New Mexico.

Gerbner, George, Gross, Larry, P., Melody, Wm. H. (1973). *CommunicationsTechnology and Social Policy: Understanding the New "Cultural Revolution."* New York: John Wiley Publishers.

Gerbner, George, Mowlana, Hamid, Schiller, Herbert I. (1996). *Invisible Crises: What Conglomerate Control of Media Means or America and the World.* Boulder, Co.: Westview Press.

McGoldrick, M., Pearce, J. K., & Glordana, J. (1982). *Ethnicity and Family Therapy.* NY: The Guilford Press.

Parlett, M. (1997). The unified field in practice. *Gestalt Review,* 1(1), 16-33.

Smolak, L. & Levine, M. P. (1994). Critical issues in the developmental Psychology of eating disorders. In L. Alexander & D. B. Lumsden (Eds), *Understanding Eating Disorders,* Washington, DC: Taylor & Francis, 37-60.

Striegel-Moore, R. & Smolak, L. (1996). The role of race in the development Eating disorders. In L. Smolak, M. P. Levine & R. Striegel-Moore (Eds). *The Developmental Psychopathology of Eating Disorders: Implications For Research, Prevention, and Treatment.* Mahwah, NJ: Lawrence Erlbaum, Ass, Inc.

VII. AN EXPERIMENT IN COMMUNITY

By Nigel Copsey, M.Sc., D. Psyc. and
Talia Levine Bar-Yoseph, M.A.

Introduction
    The setting is the East End of London. This inner city area is the most deprived in the United Kingdom. In addition to the problems facing a community with very high levels of unemployment, poor housing, and high levels of crime, every major report published in the last year has drawn attention to the crisis facing community mental health services: the community services simply cannot cope with the problems they are facing.
    In addition to these issues, East London has undergone a major transformation over the past twenty years. The traditional East End was a very settled community, centered around the docks that provided employment for the whole area from the city of London downstream. It has always been the most deprived area of London; however, the East End was once also a tightly knit community with the majority of the population intermarried and living within small communities. With the death of the docks and the introduction of "slum clearance" programs, the whole area began to change.
    In the post-war years, large sections of the population moved out of inner London while many of those remaining were re-housed in tower blocks. At the same time, large numbers of people drawn from overseas communities began to move into London to make it their home. In the mid 1950s and 1960s, the new population mainly came from the West Indies, while in the 1970s and 1980s, large numbers of Asians and African moved into East London. It is estimated that in the East London Borough of Newham, the non-white population now represents over 50% of the population. The new communities have brought a rich diversity of life to inner London. They have also settled in defined areas with the result that the traditional white population has either moved out of these areas or has itself moved into a number of more clearly delineated neighborhoods. The whole map is changing.
    One major result of this new population mix is the establishment of a strong Asian culture within many parts of East London. It is now possible to walk for two miles in one particular area of the London Borough of Newham and pass fifteen mosques and five temples. In addition, there are as many Africans and Afro-Caribbean congregations as there are church buildings: indeed, some traditional church buildings are host to three different Black-led congregations. It is this change in patterns of religion that has been both the most unacknowledged and also the most significant in recent years. In this one London borough, the combined congregations of Christians, Muslims, Hindus, Sikhs, Buddhists, and other Asian faiths now represent at least forty percent of the population. This means that within the space of twenty years, this inner city borough has undergone a major transformation from being a largely agnostic, even atheistic, culture into one in which nearly half the population live according to a particular theistic belief system.
    There has been a great deal written concerning multi-ethnic diversity and the importance of culture, but it would appear that there is little willingness to recognize the importance of religious belief as the determining factor of culture. For instance, the most recent report on the mental health services in

inner London (King's Fund, 1997) recognized that the leaders of religious groups needed to be involved in the provision of community mental health services. However, there was no attempt to provide any rationale as to how this might take place. While there was recognition that the faith communities are important, it needs to be understood that within many inner areas of the UK the faith communities provide the cultural identity as well as a focus for belonging to those who are struggling to find a home. Populations have gravitated to those areas where the focus of each religious community is located. It is the faith of these different communities that provides the foundation for both their culture and values.

In particular, it is significant that the providers of mental health services fail to recognize the importance of belief systems within the mental health of an individual. Not only does the psychiatric and psychotherapeutic community fail to work with the many belief systems, but it expects users to conform to what is essentially a Western model of health care. It is not surprising that the most recent report on mental health care in inner London highlights the failure of mental health providers to have any impact upon the new communities.

Gestalt Theory and Phenomenology

When I was given the opportunity to research the role of faith communities within a community mental health context in the inner city, it was like a dream come true! I was commissioned by the Sainsbury Centre for Mental Health to undertake a two-year project exploring the mental health needs of the faith communities in East London. Adopting a qualitative method of research, I visited twenty-seven traditional Christian groups, ten African/Afro-Caribbean Christian churches, two Asian Christian churches, four charismatic Christian churches, four mosques, five Hindu temples, two Sikh temples, one Buddhist group, and three other Asian groups.

In addition, I visited all groups working in mental health in the voluntary sector. My aim was to listen to their understandings of the problems facing those with severe mental health problems within their community. All welcomed me, and there was a willingness to talk freely and to be very open.

My passion for East London began when I was a student at London University studying theology. I lived in East London and began to see at first hand the poverty of the inner city. I lived through the "slum clearance" programs that contributed to the destruction of a clearly identifiable culture; namely the traditional East London Cockney. Many families were forcibly moved to outer London whilst others were re-housed in tower blocks. What is now acknowledged as a planning disaster resulted in the destruction of a community that had a very strong sense of identity and history. Cockney London was a tough place in which to live but there was a deeply rooted commitment by the community to the community itself. This identity is retained in the popular media through television soaps like *Eastenders*.

While I was training as a Christian minister, I knew that this was the place where I should live and work. Even at that stage in my journey, I felt very strongly that there should not be such inequality: the City of London is one of the wealthiest areas in the UK within walking distance of Hackney and Tower Hamlets, the most deprived areas in the UK. My strongly held belief as a Christian is that such polarities are not part of God's plan.

Once I was ordained, I went to live in the Docklands area of East London. My job was to establish a non-denominational Christian community. At that time, the population in that area was almost totally white and attendance at anything remotely religious was restricted to about 0.5% of the population. This is in stark contrast to the new communities of East London (West Indian,

African, and Asian) where religious belief is part of life. Not only was my initial task to discover ways in which it might be possible to encourage a spiritual view of life, but also to respond to the setting in which we lived. It is important to note that most professionals lived outside the area, which remains the case. The result is a co-created field in which the resident population lives out a position of being powerless and those with the power retain a clear role with control. There is very little attempt by either side to change this: hence, the polarity that exists between the City of London (extreme wealth) and Hackney (extreme poverty).

It was this polarization that challenged me when I first began to live in the area as part of the field. I could not drive away to the safety of outer London. I was faced with nails in my car tires, with fifty windows being smashed in our church facility by young children. I, too, faced the daily anxiety of wondering if our house would be burgled or vandalized. I joined with a community that was facing a slow death. The loss of jobs combined with slum clearance.

I remember well my first week on the eighteenth floor of a tower block visiting a young mother with a seven-year-old child. There was still a waiting list of 2000 to be re-housed. The lifts were broken and she lived in daily fear for her child's safety. She was suicidal because she was living in such appalling conditions with few resources. These very tower blocks were destroyed ten years later because of structural faults. But from that very day of my first week, a passion burned in me to respond to this situation.

I very quickly got married and our children grew up in the area. This was our home. The longer I lived in the area, the more I came into contact with the high level of mental health problems within the community. I gradually moved into the work of community mental health while retaining my commitment to the spiritual.

During this period, the first group of Asians began to move into the area. They were so gentle and genuine. Mr. Singh, a nurse at the local hospital, came with his extended family. Night after night, his windows were smashed by teenagers. He would call for help from the police, who never responded. He ended up by making a citizen's arrest on a twelve year old. Another man, whose only crime was to wear a turban, was beaten up by youths. Out of fear, he kept his door barricaded from that time on. Maybe the Asians represented a polarity of gentleness and dignity that could not be tolerated. They were passive, which was in stark contrast to the ethos of the dominant culture.

With the rise of the National Front, a complete reorganization of the field took place. Those in the White population who could afford to moved to outer London. Those who remained moved to defined areas. The new communities, for their own safety, also moved to clearly defined districts. It is the case today that certain districts have a population that is 80% non-White. Currently, there are very clear boundaries between the different communities. Each community has created its own culture that is clearly different from the adjoining culture.

Central to the culture of the new communities is the extended family, the faith system, and a clear cultural identity. English is not the first language of the communities. Indeed, for many, English is a poor second language. The mosques and temples dominate the skyline of the East End streets. Daily, devotees of all ages attend the many places of worship. The customs of the communities have become the norm: the norms of dress are Asian. The restaurants and shops are completely Asian. I often eat in an Asian restaurant where I am the only white person. The food is wonderful! The shared symbols of religious meaning, dress, language, and custom provide a very public display of a shared meaning.

Definable groups with a history from Asia and Africa have established themselves. A strong link is maintained nowadays with one's homeland because of easy communication access. This is illustrated by the numerous telephone shops offering cheap international calls, and by the rich and diverse range of Asian shops. The spiritual focus of each community is often linked to geographical areas in the home country, with imams and priests traveling between the country of origin and England.

The following properties form part of the environment that is East London today:

- The predominant agnosticism of mental health services in contrast to the spiritual world-view held by half the population.
- The entrenched belief system of some faith communities in contrast to those willing to be more flexible.
- The acceptance of crime and petty theft in contrast to a strongly held belief about the sanctity of personal possession.
- The long tradition of tough survival in contrast to softness and passivity.
- The prevalence of drug addiction and alcohol abuse in contrast to the moral values held by faith communities.
- The freedom of sexual expression and individualism in contrast to honor in sexuality and community as held by faith communities.

Recognizing these polarities is an important first step in providing an environment where dialogue can begin. As long as the polarities are exaggerated, little change can take place. The newly formed Department of Spirituality in Newhman is one initiative that seeks to facilitate this process. I have not referred to the African and Afro Caribbean communities. These also exist in this area of East London. Their cultural identity has been identified with their strongly held religious beliefs that are expressed openly in the many communities drawn together around cultural norms. These communities do not seem to have reproduced their own culture as explicitly as the Asian communities, although the Black-led Christian communities are the fastest-growing religious faith groups in East London.

I was part of this rapidly moving field while it was happening. I experienced firsthand the evolution of many different cultures within a very small geographical area. Each of these communities is very public, and each has personal, clearly-held beliefs. But, in fact, it has never been politically correct, so to speak, to acknowledge differences, particularly in terms of religion. No one likes talking about faith publicly, nor, sometimes, privately, to someone outside the community in question. Furthermore, attention to matters of faith, or to the faith of others, is simply not understood by a white community that is predominantly atheistic in its focus. The result has been a complete failure of any attempt at dialogue.

When a dialogue is attempted, it is based on the false assumption that differences can be ignored. An example of this is an advertisement for a public employee that stated that the post was open to gays and lesbians. The result was that no Muslim applied. Another example is that no attempt is made in community mental health centers to recognize that at certain times of the day certain religious practices are seen to be essential. No facilities are provided and the environment is not conducive to any form of religious practice.

When I was given the opportunity to research the role of faith communities within community mental health, it was like a dream come true. For fifteen years, I had been searching for a psychological system that incorporated the *whole* of a person's life. It was only now in the researching and writing of a report exploring the mental health needs of different faith communities that such a framework began to emerge.

My early training in psychological thought was psychodynamic. However, I was always searching for something further. Somehow, the predominant focus on insight left me feeling incomplete. This approach was too individualistic and I seemed cut off from the wider context that was the world in which I lived. At the same time, I was also seeking to hold together both my psychological journey and the importance of the faith community to which I belonged. The very rigid boundaries of the psychodynamic system seemed to isolate me from that reality. It was too intra-psychic and bound by a worldview that assumed that therapy took place with very tight boundaries.

Such a system seemed to be the exact opposite of all the different communities in East London who have a shared belief in communal support and shared identity. The isolation of psychoanalytical theory results in the therapist being seen as an expert who always keeps his or her distance from the client. He or she becomes a scientific expert who provides a cure. In such a model, there is no true dialogue of intimacy. I could not see any hope of change unless the therapist was willing fully to join the field. When I discovered a theory (field theory) that took the whole of a person's life seriously it was a revelation to me, and it was also very risky!

A combination of a *phenomenological approach*, a *dialogic relationship*, and *field theory* challenged me to re-examine the assumptions underlying the therapies to which I had been hitherto exposed.   Even the majority of humanistic therapies have been practiced around the introjected norms of the context in which they have emerged. Hence, the practice is heavily bounded by those norms.

A simple example of this would be the use of language and the accepted norm of the therapeutic hour. How many humanistic therapists start from the assumption that the culture is the field that might teach them how to form a dialogic relationship? The language of therapy, for example, counseling, therapy, awareness, and client -- all contain many assumptions. In many cases, humanistic introjects have replaced psychoanalytical ones. I was not (and never have been) working with people in a one-to-one individual and private setting. My work has always led me to be with people suffering from mental health problems in their own context. This was the challenge to me as I embarked on this research. Here I was, a white Christian minister, committed to psychological and spiritual change, seeking to learn from the many diverse faith communities in inner London.

I learned that the *phenomenological approach* stressed the importance of my learning to bracket off my own assumptions as I sought to understand how people from other backgrounds saw and understood their world. I very quickly realized how difficult this was. Especially with faith communities that were predominantly White, I realized that the assumptions I internalized were often far removed from their reality. One very good example came when I was approached by a White Christian religious group in the docklands area to provide a support group for those who needed help with the many mental health problems in their lives. This was a group that was very different from the traditional church. They met in a house. Each person had lived in that area of East London all his or her life.

This group had a large number of men, which is unusual for this area. The area has an unemployment rate of twenty-two percent and has one of the highest levels of deprivation and crime in London. Alcohol and drug abuse are a way of life to many who live in this area. Adopting a phenomenological perspective, I quickly realized that I had assumed and knew what it was like to live in such an environment (after all, I had lived in the area for fifteen years!). However, the reality was that I had no understanding of what it was like for some of the group members to live in that context. I had projected onto them my understanding of their context. Eventually, in supervision with Talia Levine Bar-Yoseph, I was able to see my process. Enlightened by this supervision, I returned to this community with a renewed desire to listen and to learn.

My subsequent renewed phenomenological investigations enabled me, and do enable me now, to discover what was needed by this particular group. One introject I carried was the size of the group. After all, four was not a group! Another was a belief that everyone should attend every time. I had to discover that what was required was a much less rigid system. I had to keep on asking lots of questions in order to be able to engage in a true dialogue with the members of this community concerning their experiences.

Whereas with the White religious group I had begun with an assumption (albeit wrongly!) that I fully understood the culture, when I now began to approach the Asian, African, and Afro-Caribbean communities, I realized at the outset that I had to adopt a phenomenological approach. I quickly realized that Western interventions use a language containing many assumptions. For example, the very notion of counseling has little or no meaning to an Asian elder. In the first place, there is no equivalent word in their language. My Asian colleague and I spent a morning seeking to draw up a list of words that we use as psychologists but which have no equivalent in the language of the Asian communities.

In addition, there is often an association that is unhelpful. For example, the terms *counseling* and *client* have associations with the science of the mind, which in turn is associated with madness and being cut off. The implication is that everyone has given up on you. Even the word *helper* implies that persons are unable to help themselves. If a professional from the statutory services is involved with a family, then there is a deep sense of shame, as it is perceived that such a person will only be involved when there is a failure in the family.

The structure of the family is very important to an Asian family. This very simple example illustrates how anyone seeking to intervene needs first of all to discover (by joining the field and enquiring) how he or she will be perceived. Even the use of introjected language could prevent true contact. I approached one Hindu group to ask them what problems they faced only to be told they don't have problems. This very obvious word immediately met with resistance, as it did not communicate what I was attempting to convey. In a subsequent meeting, I was able to reframe my question. I asked what it was like living in London. The response was immediate. Underpinning all these examples is the assumption that at the contact boundary there is difference.

For me to be able to discover meaning for these different communities, I needed to adopt a *dialogic approach*. This was very important because the traditional method of working has been to approach the new communities with a set of Western assumptions and assume that those communities will adapt to a Western model. This is true of both psychiatric and therapeutic services. A dialogic method assumes equality and a willingness to come alongside others and learn together. I was surprised to discover how many people from the Muslim and Hindu communities were visibly moved by the fact that I was visiting them in their own setting (whether it was the mosque or the temple), and was prepared to join with them in their time of worship and then learn from them by respecting their faith and culture. As a result of this approach, there are now a number of key people keen to share with me in the next stage of the journey.

The Gestalt emphasis on *field theory* provided me with the necessary framework to evolve a radical approach to mental health provision for members of the new communities. It is my contention that such an approach is needed in order to have any impact on the effectiveness of mental health provision for members of the new communities. The first step is to recognize that religious belief systems are part of the field. Instead of ignoring what is a crucial area of life for a large proportion of the population, there is a need not only to recognize it, but also to integrate it holistically with its mental health needs. It is often this area that is mostly *figure* or foreground for large sections of the population. Failure to recognize this means that anyone attempting a therapeutic intervention will *fail* to be sensitive to how the field is organized.

The belief system of the faith community is inextricably connected with both the culture and the extended family. This is very important as most therapeutic interventions (with the notable exception of systemic theory) take place with an *individual* and exclude the family. While in recent years there has been a focus on the importance of the cultures of the new communities, there has been a failure to recognize that the traditional White East End population similarly has its own culture and very clear identity and, together with the new cultures, is a part of the richness of the inner city. In many respects, individual therapeutic work is just as alien to this culture as it is to Asian and Afro-Caribbean culture.

Traditional East End culture has always placed a heavy emphasis on the mutual support of the extended family. The very notion of confidential professional help has all the associations connected with dependence and failure to cope with life. Individual therapy by its very nature is experienced as a sign of weakness and of being cut off from the reality of life as it exists. The reason for this is that the majority of those working in therapeutic roles come from a different social background from that of the community within which they are working.

There is an implicit assumption that by working with intra-psychic processes, an individual will cope better. The reality is far more complicated. Within the field, social and political forces are often far more powerful than any intra-psychic resolution. In many cases, there needs to be a recreating of support systems. Any therapy that fails to recognize the importance of support within the community will have little or no effect. Hence, therapists are perceived as professionals along with social workers and other statutory agents who are separate from the world in which the client lives and struggles. There is a danger within such a system that both clients and therapists co-create a dependent culture of powerlessness.

Emerging from the points noted above is a clear sense that East London presents a highly complex picture in which a whole range of different influences form the field.

An Experiment in Community Psychotherapy

I set out first to find a trained Gestaltist living and working in this area of London. I was also looking for someone who was working within community rather than operating in a counseling centre *per se*. In addition, I was looking for someone who came from one of the new communities and saw his or her religious belief as a part of his or her life. I wanted to work with a Gestalt-trained therapist because I needed someone who shared my commitment to moving into the field, and who was flexible enough to work with the phenomenological data. I also needed a colleague who could quickly gain the confidence of those communities with whom I had only limited contact. This is particularly important when considering the issue of language and the willingness of Asian women to relate to another woman from their own cultural background. The importance of their faith impinging on every aspect of their lives needed also to be both understood and fully empathized with. I knew that it was simply not possible for me to become part of this section of the community.

I was unable to find a fully trained Asian female Gestaltist! The reason for this is that therapeutic training is very expensive and focused primarily within Western middle class culture: a culture that ignores the values of the new communities. Such trainings expect trainees to conform to the values of the Western world-view. It can therefore be seen that for someone for whom spirituality is a part of life, such a value system is experienced as alien. After much searching, I found a co-worker from within one of the Asian voluntary organizations who was in the process of completing her Master's Degree in Counseling Psychology.

In order to discover how to proceed, I moved into the field. In one mosque, both the President and the Imam said that they were willing to engage with me in discovering how the mental health services and their religious organization could explore ways of working together. A Sai Baba group invited me to their worship as an honored guest and was willing to explore future partnerships. In both cases, I did not stipulate what the content of the dialogue should be. Instead, I was willing to engage in a process in which we joined together in discovering a relationship of trust. My willingness to join with what was already in the field enabled us to embark on a dialogue. In both cases I started from the assumption of difference. I had also established a working relationship with an Asian mental health charity as a result of adopting the same approach.

In addition to the group already referred to above (the White, East End, Christian group), the most exciting development has been the establishment of a women's Muslim group. In my two years' of research, I discovered a very special Muslim lady who had herself experienced severe mental health problems, directly related to a number of factors linked to living in East London. In our discussion, she realized that there were many Muslim women who actively sought her out for help -- she is a natural listener and, because of her own journey of both suffering and survival, does not preach to those who come to her.

I should add that in my many discussions with faith community leaders, I was repeatedly told that Asian men and women would not come together in a large group and openly talk about difficulties. They would seek help by using existing networks that were informal, normally in dyads. From these discussions was born an idea. I asked this wonderful lady if she would meet my co-worker with a view to establishing a small group of those with whom she has contact. She was very enthusiastic about this suggestion and has herself become the co-worker.

My colleague and her new co-worker are now in the process of establishing a small group in her home where those who come can meet and share. Using the principle of avoiding all language that could be misunderstood, they are simply establishing a morning together. The aim is very simple: to encourage those who come to decide together how to proceed and to create a place of safety where they can explore new possibilities. It is possible that what will emerge as safe for them could be a time to chat. For many Asian women there is a deep fear about discussing anything to do with their faith in case they are told how to behave. It also seems to be a fact that because many Asian women retroflect their pain, the mental health services only ever see anyone when all other methods of coping fail.

This is also true for others from the new communities. One example is a group of African men who told me that they would never refer to anything religious within earshot of any mental health worker for fear of either being sent into hospital or having an increase in medication prescribed!

Although this experiment is at an early stage, I do believe that the outcome will have important implications in how to engage in community psychotherapy. I imagine that what can become figure can be something very different from what we have hitherto defined as psychotherapy scope and focus.

Supervision

I would like to pause at this point and refer to the role of supervision in this process. My supervisor joined me in this venture as I was bringing together many of the findings from my research. It is very significant that she comes from a different culture from mine -- she's Israeli and I am English -- and from a different spiritual background (Judaism and Christianity). From the ground of our relationship has emerged a mutual respect that is held together by differences. It is as if we mirror the process that I am undertaking with my Asian colleagues. I hope that my Asian colleagues and I will also be able to model this. They are Asian, Muslim, and Hindu. I am English and Christian. Both in my supervision and in the work setting, true dialogue is only possible by recognizing the differences. This is also a basic assumption in Gestalt theory.

Tali Levine Bar-Yoseph's role for me has been similar to that of a consultant. I have been able to ask lots of questions and be clear about what I need from her. In turn, she has challenged me in many areas, not least about my own introjected assumptions. She has also enabled me to keep a very clear focus on the phenomenology emerging as figure and ground within the field. I see such a role as crucial, for she is separate enough from the situation to be able to avoid fusion. I would sum up her role as providing me with the challenge to remain focused on what is figure in the field, and to concentrate on the phenomenological data rather than on interpreting the content.

The group that has now been established the longest has been the one linked to a White Christian group. It is not the policy of the group to be totally white, but because it meets in the white area of the district, it draws solely from that community. As I indicated earlier, this group consists of a small mixed gender group, all of whom are living with major social problems as well as mental health problems. I soon discovered that the members of this group had adopted the introject of the wider community, which resulted in their believing that they could not influence the structures of society. The structures do, in fact, reinforce this perception. The co-created reality is one of powerlessness. The main task has been to help them to draw on the very strong resources of their faith to begin the process of creating a different environment for them.

My goal has been to encourage them to co-create an environment of mutual support in order to empower one another to effect change in their daily living. Although my work has been to support the system to affect change, I am willing if necessary to become part of the wider field in order to enable this to happen. In this setting, the field involves major inequalities that are both social and political.

I am convinced from the early experience of these two groups that working in groups is the only way. People need the support of a family-sized group. Again, I have been willing to adjust the size of the group according to the needs of the participants. It seems that a total of five is an ideal number. This fits with the cultural norm where people only share personal details with a chosen few.

I also realize that small groups have an important place in all faith communities in this area of London. These groups come from a tradition that is not based on individualism. The extended family is essential as a way of life for them. This is in stark contrast to suburban London, where there are high levels of mobility and where people live in very unsupported environments. However, a further common denominator of the groups is that there is a shame connected with the sharing of mental health problems. By their forming an alliance with the supportive structure of a faith community, we all hope that we will be able to evolve a safe group to explore such problems. It is early days but the signs are encouraging.

Conclusion

Based upon the work achieved so far, I am confident that a new paradigm is emerging. It is grounded in a belief that every cultural group has its own very clear history and culture. In the case of inner London, that history includes the spiritual beliefs of those communities. Spirituality is part of the field. Ignoring this results in a failure of a clear figure emerging. As Gestaltists, we claim to be able to respond to the whole field. My argument has been that in these highly complex settings, we have failed to be true to this important belief. We have not been truly phenomenological but have been driven by our own therapeutic introjects that have their context within white, middle class, Western psychotherapy.

However, I am optimistic, because I believe that Gestalt theory has at its core a willingness to abide patiently focused with the field in order to discover what emerges from the field and to join with what emerges to co-create something new. It is the beginning of this journey that I have sought to convey in this chapter. In ten years' time, I hope to be able to record the next stage. What is exciting is that I do not know how it will emerge. As I write, the National Health Service in East London has just released funding for a new Department of Spirituality, Religious and Cultural Care, which will seek to respond to the observations I have made in this essay. My hope is that a new paradigm of therapeutic work will emerge that has its roots in both Gestalt theory and in inner London. The richness of the diversity of the different cultures combined with a dialogue that respects those differences will form the foundation of that journey.

Personal Account

The writing of this article has challenged us both to examine the meaning of co-writing. You will see that the article is written out of Nigel's personal experience and in the first person. However, it came to be created by both of us sharing a journey together whereby each one of us was bouncing ideas off of one another. It was because Nigel was in the actual setting that the story reads as his experience. His experience was shared by me, Talia, both as a supervisor and as a consultant, away from East London in the safe environment of supervision. The content of the article was jointly created as a result of mutual discussion and dialogue. Co-writing in this case has really meant co-creating as the actual writing was done by Nigel.

Nigel Copsey, Oxted, UK
Talia Levine Bar-Yoseph, Jerusalem, Israel

References

Bhopal, R. (1965). The interrelationship of folk, traditional and western medicine within an Asian community in Britain. *Social Science and Medicine*, 22 (1), 99 – 105.

Bhui, K. et al (1965). The essentials elements of culturally sensitive psychiatric services. *International Journal of Social Psychiatry*. 41, 342 – 356.

Copsey, Nigel, Bar-Yoseph, T. L. (1999). An Experiment in Community Psychotherapy. London: The Gestalt Review, Analytic Press, Vol. 3, 285-300.

Copsey, Nigel (1997). *Keeping Faith: The Provision of Community Mental Health Services within a Multi-faith Context*. London: The Sainsbury Centre for Mental Health.

Helman, C. (1994). (3rd Edition) *Culture, Health and Illness*. Butterworth/Heineman.

Hycner, Richard & Lynne Jacobs (1995) *The Healing Relationship in Gestalt Therapy: A Dialogic/Self Psychology Approach*. New York: The Gestalt Journal Press.

Lee, Robert G. & Wheeler, G. (1996). *The Voice of Shame: Silence and Connection in Psychotherapy*. San Francisco: Jossey-Bass.

Parlett, Malcolm (1997) The Unified Field in Practice. *Gestalt Review* 1 (1).

VIII. GESTALT EDUCATIONAL COUNSELING

By Mario Rivas, Ph.D.

Many traditionally underrepresented ethnic minority students -- African American, Native American, and Mexican American/Latino students -- enter community college with a lack of trust in self and a sense of shame and doubt with regard to being successful learners and college students.

For such students, this lack of trust often translates into personally limiting thoughts and statements such as the following: 'I'll never make it....I'll never be successful....Science is so difficult....I'll never be able to do it....It's hopeless....I don't like writing....It makes me feel hopeless....Why can't I understand it?....Will I ever be good at it?....I want to be sure of myself....I can't stand that part of me that feels weak....I hate it! I hate being scared when I go to class! I want to be relaxed and confident.'

Of critical importance, these statements reflect a challenge to counselors in higher education to learn and become proficient in how to assist traditionally underrepresented ethnic minority students to understand the origin and impact of thoughts and expressions that undermine their efforts to succeed in college.

Furthermore, these possible self-expressions signal on the part of many traditionally underrepresented ethnic minority students a split in their thoughts, feelings, and behaviors regarding their ability to face and effectively manage the difficulties of college. The split is between a positive and negative experience of the self – a struggle of "can" versus "can't," of "strong" versus "weak," of "hope" versus "hopelessness," and of "ease of doing" versus "too difficult to do."

On one side of the split, students from family and social backgrounds with little experience with college fervently hold within themselves a strong desire to face the challenges of college related to a need for growth and development. On the other side of the split, these students hold such a lack of belief and confidence that "parts" of themselves make them less capable of facing the many challenges that college invariably presents.

Counseling the students I work with at the community college level evokes the emotional experience and challenges faced by many ethnically diverse community college students. Often under-prepared academically and psychologically, these students understandably doubt themselves and can be hesitant when faced with learning situations that signal a threat to their sense of confidence and self-worth, especially when this threat resulted from repressed hurtful early childhood experiences when the individual did not have the psychological maturity to work through painful interpersonal experiences.

Laura Rendon (1994), a well-known researcher of this student population, has written of the experiences of many community college students from under-prepared backgrounds and has defined this population of students as having low confidence, low trust of self and others, and high need for validation. She characterizes these students as individuals who have been treated as so stupid or incompetent that they yearn for acceptance and validation.

Among the students she researched, Rendon has observed that "many non-traditional students talked about wanting their doubts about being capable of learning erased" and that this was "especially true for community college students, first-generation students, Hispanic, and African American students." Rendon also has noted that these students continued to be at risk when, faced with challenges to their emotionally tentative stance, they eventually abandon their studies.   It is evident in Rendon's ideas that many underrepresented ethnic minority students face some very difficult emotional challenges when they attend college.

Bernard Weiner (1985) has hypothesized that an individual's negative self-perceptions of low ability and high task difficulty lead to specific negative emotions. Weiner determined that self-perceptions (attributions) of low ability lead to feelings of shame and doubt.   Similarly, self-perceptions of high task difficulty lead to feelings of helplessness and hopelessness.   Needless to say, negative feelings, especially when experienced in difficult learning situations can tax the confidence of under-prepared students, overwhelm them and make them want to avoid, put off, or leave such circumstances.

John Nicholls (1984) also developed a social psychological interpretation of what students experience in difficult achievement situations. Specifically, Nicholls hypothesized that an ego-involved student focuses on a negative comparison of self with others, often perceiving others as more competent. Similar to Weiner's ideas, an ego-involved orientation in achievement situations often results in negative emotions such as low self-confidence, frustration, shame, fear, etc.   A well-known Gestalt phrase "Compare and despair!" pointedly identifies the negative emotional effect of a person who compares self to others in a negative self-defeating way.

All three of these researchers have suggestions for how to help at-risk students entering college to persist in the face of emotional difficulties. Weiner proffers that the best way to assist such students is to change the students' perceptions about their abilities and task difficulty during college study (1) by breaking the tasks of college up into doable components and (2) by reinforcing effort attributions.

Students' negative feelings would hypothetically change from shame and doubt about low ability to confidence that achievement tasks that are broken up into feasible components can be learned and mastered piece by piece. Similarly, students' perceptions about facing a much too difficult task can be changed from helplessness and hopelessness to hope by reinforcing in the students the belief that they can achieve their goals little by little through constant effort and perseverance.

Nicholls also offers that the negative emotions of ego-involvement can be changed to positive emotions by shifting the students' orientation away from a stance of comparing self to other to a focused position on mastering a given task little by little. Again, negative feelings of students are changed from fear, frustration, and shame resulting from comparing self to others to positive feelings of hope that come from focusing in a task-involved way on the step-by-step requirements that students need to complete in order to achieve success.

In addition to what we note in the research of Weiner and Nicholls, we also note that Rendon suggests how we should assist at-risk students to learn to have more confidence and faith in their ability to succeed in college. In this regard, she suggests that colleges should create social and learning environments where students feel support, acceptance, and belief in their ability to succeed.   Doing so, according to Rendon, will result in students learning to be more powerful, active, and involved learners.

The Gestalt Way

While the above directions for how to assist at-risk college students to achieve success have merit, what must be added to them is an orientation of empowering students to address directly how emotions affect their persistence in college. Gestalt concepts, in contrast, promise a different gift to students – namely, that they can learn how to empower themselves to persist in difficult achievement situations by learning to understand how they need to grow cognitively, behaviorally, and emotionally. Gestalt personal development work, in turn, supports students to directly experience and to work through challenging emotional blocks that result from negative past learning experiences that have resulted in ineffective cognitive and behavior habits that inhibit, make more difficult, or undermine effective learning.

The apparent inability on the part of underrepresented students of color faced with the challenging emotional experiences of college to resolve this split from self often results, in turn, in a crippling inability to support self. If addressed properly, however, through counseling and support by counselors, faculty, and staff in the college environment, a resolution to this split can lead to students becoming more effective and successful in pursuit and realization of their goals. Gestalt Educational Counseling (GEC) promises this. I will therefore address how Gestalt Educational Counseling (GEC), an offshoot of Gestalt counseling that I have developed, can be used to support traditionally underrepresented ethnic minority students and students from similar backgrounds to better handle the emotional challenges of community college.

Statistics show that a great number of underrepresented students begin their studies in higher education within the community college system. Statistics also bear out that many of these students do not succeed in community colleges and too often leave higher education dejected and filled with greater doubt and insecurity than when they began their studies. And even though many of these students do, indeed, make it through their community college studies, too many do so with only average grades and with only limited increases in their level of personal confidence. Added to this, not enough of these students transfer to four-year colleges; and even when they do transfer, it's only with minimal increases in their levels of confidence and belief in their ability to take on challenging majors in upper division institutions.

From a Gestalt counseling perspective, these observations prompt us to address the plight of underrepresented -- often first-generation university-educated -- ethnically diverse students and to address how to help them resolve confusing and personally non self-supporting splits or polarities in their thoughts, feelings, and behavior toward college. The Gestalt counseling perspective is one of empowering an individual to learn how to integrate conflicting parts of the self so as to become a more integrated and complete person. (A popular Gestalt aphorism related to this is that "It is our birthright to achieve completeness!")

With regard to supporting students to be more integrated in their thoughts, feelings, and behavior in college, Gestalt counseling can guide them to learn how they separate or split themselves off from developing and actualizing a unified and more effective self. In achieving this, students would no longer be overcome by conflicting positive and negative thoughts and feelings about the ability to be a successful learner; instead, students would become knowledgeable about how to support self to be more effective students who can more skillfully learn and work toward mastering difficult coursework (English, math, physics, engineering, and so on) and one who can take the actions necessary to ensure greater confidence and success in college and beyond.

Gestalt counseling techniques are recognized to be effective in helping persons to understand and resolve emotional, cognitive, and behavior problems (Seligman, 2001). Nevertheless, these techniques have yet to be applied in a comprehensive manner to assist the success of community college students, in general, or first-generation underrepresented community college students in particular. So we need to address how Gestalt counseling strategies can be an effective way to assist underrepresented ethnic minority community college students to handle the psychological/emotional difficulties that they undergo when attempting to face the challenges of colleges. This is especially true for those difficulties that challenge the individual student to learn about parts or aspects of themselves they are not confident about and have rejected, split off from, or think of as being weak, unacceptable, and non-effective.

Gestalt Educational Counseling (GEC)

Gestalt Educational Counseling (GEC) is a method of Gestalt counseling that combines teaching the principles of Gestalt personal development to first-generation underrepresented students so they may learn how to self-initiate Gestalt counseling interventions. At the center, this approach assumes that learning the ideas and concepts of Gestalt is an important prerequisite for underrepresented ethnically diverse community college students to eventually master Gestalt personal development work that, in turn, will lead to more effectiveness and success as a student.

Another important aspect of GEC, directly in line with the idea of teaching students how to benefit from Gestalt counseling work, is the notion of the counselor modeling openness to students about his or her growth challenges. This approach is in line with Jourard's 1964 conception of counselors facilitating growth in clients by presenting "a transparent self" who supports others to open up and share themselves as part of the process of growing and becoming more effective persons.

This approach is also important because it recognizes that students of color often enter community college having had many negative experiences in education that have resulted in a damaging lack of trust about how sincere and committed counselors and teachers are regarding supporting the success of these students. In short, a counselor who shares him or herself with students of color supports and encourages these students to trust the counselor, thereby increasing the students' willingness to open up and share their personal doubts and insecurities about being able to succeed in college. As such, the students can then do the difficult personal development work needed to become self-aware in ways that they need to develop themselves in order to be more effective in college.

I will present here a variety of examples of GEC interventions that will show how this counseling approach can be used with students who come from backgrounds that subject them to more difficult challenges of adjustment in college in comparison to students who enter college with a greater amount of knowledge and readiness for college. Beyond addressing the internal split that often exists within students of color regarding belief in their ability to succeed in college, an important point that I will make through some of the counseling examples is that the split within the personality of students of color often results from specific negative experiences that these students have had in their educational histories. The negative experiences of these students often centered around instances of when teachers, counselors, and others in the school system were not supportive, and were negating or overly critical.

In the California community colleges, counselors are given the charge of responding to the educational and personal development needs of students in order to support academic success (Academic Senate for California

Community Colleges, 1995). This charge has been translated into a plethora of diverse counseling interventions that, from my perspective, are a result of the diverse theoretical and practical orientations of counseling training programs that feed counselors into the community college system. Of significance, the diverse counseling approaches often used in community colleges can lead to a lack of focus in developing and identifying particularly effective counseling interventions. Also, diverse counseling approaches can confuse students regarding the meaning of counseling and how counseling can be helpful to them.

Gestalt Educational Counseling (GEC) will therefore be a powerful intervention maximizing what counselors are able to accomplish at the community college level, especially with underrepresented student populations. In turn, GEC is very much in line with the uniqueness of the mission of a community college counselor as it regards work with students from academic and social backgrounds that make college a more challenging experience.

Specifically, GEC is an aggregated form of counseling that has four component parts. First, the counselor introduces different examples of the intellectual, emotional, and behavior challenges that students will face in their college career. At the same time, the counselor addresses how counseling in general can help students to face the difficult personal development challenges of college. One example of a challenge that will be faced in college is that students will have to learn how to face self-doubt in the face of needing to master learning tasks that initially or periodically seem impossible to learn.

The second step of GEC involves the counselor sharing personal experiences of growth that he or she has experienced in difficult life or college circumstances as well as how counseling has been beneficial with regard to facing difficult challenges. For example, I once shared with students that at one point in my doctoral study, I became very anxious with fear of failure so much that I was unable to focus on writing my dissertation.

Third, the counselor introduces Gestalt counseling and specific Gestalt counseling concepts pertaining to what students need to develop in themselves in order to face the emotional challenges of college. By way of example, students are told that Gestalt counseling is a way of learning how to be an effective learner in life, one who "can identify what [he or she] wants and how to go about getting it" (Nevis, 1987).

The fourth step in GEC is when the counselor conducts individual or group sessions that are a combination of counseling and teaching so students experience the power of Gestalt counseling methods and at the same time learn through instruction from the counselor how Gestalt counseling methods directly result in personal growth and increased effectiveness in college.

Levine and Padilla (1987) observe that Latino populations (and by extension many other students from social and academic life experiences similar to that of Latinos) need education and counseling much more than they need therapy. In this regard, I have witnessed how educating underrepresented ethnically diverse students about psychological growth, especially Gestalt personal development concepts, when coupled with sound counseling interventions, can be effective in helping students to develop the psychological insights and strengths needed to face the many emotional challenges of college. As such, I began to initiate the practice of GEC as a combination of education and Gestalt counseling.

The Gestalt counseling approach emphasizes helping individuals mature and become more emotionally, cognitively, and behaviorally effective in life by increasing personal awareness of feelings and associated thoughts and behaviors related to how an individual generally handles/mishandles life's challenges. As an individual becomes more and more aware of his/her unique way of facing life's challenges, the counselor helps the person experience how ineffective ways of facing emotionally difficult challenges are often based in negative habitual patterns of feeling, thinking, and behaving.

These habits are left over from past emotional trials (usually from childhood) that were not resolved or satisfactorily completed. In Gestalt this is euphemistically known as "unfinished business." Importantly, the emotional trials within college that often lead to doubt and lack of belief in self are instances of life experiences that signal one's need to grow beyond previously learned ineffective habits that were often learned either within the family-of-origin or – and of particular importance to our discussion here -- during the educational history of the student, when the individual was not affirmed or supported by family members, teachers, counselors, etc. to develop the psychological strengths necessary to persevere through difficult life situations.

The result of past negative learning, according to Gestalt concepts, is a split self wherein a person battles between a past learned self who doubts his or her ability to be effective as a person with a part of self that truly desires to learn and act in a competent, confident, and successful manner. Gestalt counseling methods support a person to expand his or her awareness to include emotions, thoughts, and behaviors that heretofore have been blocked from the person's experience and understanding.

As such, Gestalt counseling methods assist persons to integrate or own more and more of their emotional self, especially those emotions that because of past negative learning experiences are most difficult to accept. In doing so, a person being helped by Gestalt methods becomes more integrated and complete with regard to the amount and breadth of thoughts, feelings, and behaviors available as options with which to handle life. Consequently, rather than being confused, disunited, or de-energized by conflicting, unacceptable emotions, thoughts, and behaviors, individuals become more capable of responding to challenges in life with a greater focused or more integrated self because they have learned to handle and incorporate into their being a fuller range of emotions, thoughts, and behaviors.

Beyond increasing in an individual a habitual awareness of how to face the trials in life that are often not supportive to learning and growth, an important factor of Gestalt counseling is to support persons to experiment or creatively reframe one's spirit to fit life's challenges by learning new ways to handle difficult emotions, thoughts, and behaviors. As such, Gestalt counseling methods assist individuals to become more adaptable, flexible, and creative in meeting the exigencies of day-to-day living. Finally, as a person develops or grows in the ability to experience life's challenges in ways that support personal expression and effectiveness, persons are supported to continually work at accepting and supporting the expression of their unique way of facing life (A well known Gestalt expression related to this process is "Feel self, express self, be seen, and take up space!")

It is important to note here once again that a great deal of the lack of success of ethnically diverse students relates to their inability to psychologically support themselves to work through emotional impasses that block them from successfully facing the challenges of college.

Case Overview

Currently, as part of my duties as an upper-level administrator in the California Community College system, I counsel students who are subject to dismissal from college. I use Gestalt counseling methods as part of my consulting work along with special well established and tested support programs in higher education, such as EOPS, Puente, MESA, and the San

Francisco State University's National Institute of Health Program, "Bridges to the Baccalaureate."

The settings of the Gestalt Educational Counseling interventions have varied but have generally been day-long group meetings for first-generation underrepresented students enrolled in a variety of community college academic success and leadership programs. In these workshops, the majority of the participants have been first-generation-to-college, low income, underrepresented ethnic minority students. The primary goal of the workshops are to support the students to be better prepared intellectually, emotionally, and behaviorally in order to support themselves to handle challenging academic majors, including Engineering, Chemistry, Physics, and pre-health preparation. Some of the examples here come from individual or group work that I have conducted with ethnically diverse students either in the college where I work or in various community settings. As a general overview of GEC, the format followed in workshops, though abbreviated here, will be used as a means of describing how GEC is conducted.

In the initial part of GEC workshops, students are introduced to the notion that every individual has the potential to meet the diverse challenges of college. To achieve this end, I narrate the experience of a 12-month old child learning to walk. In this regard, students are asked the following question: "How many times does a 12-month old child fall down when learning to walk before he or she gives up learning how to walk?" The answer, of course, is that the child -- in a very natural way -- never gives up. The students understand this instantly, because they observe without being prompted that "It's part of our nature to walk." In addition, "The child has something inside that keeps trying" and "It's exciting to keep trying to walk until you achieve your goal."

Other anecdotes are shared of young people learning, including the following scenarios, initially framed in the form of a question. "If you went into a kindergarten classroom and asked for all those students who could sing to raise their hands, how many hands would go up?" The answer given by students generally is that almost all the hands in the class would be raised. I then follow this with a similar question about how many high school seniors would raise their hand to the same question. Students answer that only a few seniors would raise their hands to such a question.

A discussion then follows regarding the belief that some people in our society think that our schools are fear factories, wherein students learn to "compare and despair" about their ability to be skillful. Going back to the infant learning to walk, I make the point that a child learning to walk does not stop herself from continuing to try by saying negative statements to self when making mistakes. For example, the infant does not think, "I sure look stupid falling down!" or "I must really be dumb falling down!" or "I'll never be able to learn how to walk!" "No", I insist to them, "these statements are learned in the process of growing up, from feedback that is given to individuals by misguided family members, peers, counselors, or teachers who incorrectly criticize a child's mistakes, which often leads to internalizing a negative, criticizing self whenever mistakes are made."

At this point in the workshop, a discussion ensues with students emphasizing that each of them has between themselves the drive to move forward in powerful ways toward cherished goals, much like the child learning to walk. Along with this, a discussion addresses motivational observations, such as 'Everybody is born unique, but most of us die copies'; and, 'Get better not bitter'; and, 'It is our birthright to achieve completeness.' The discussion then centers on how to recapture the strength and drive to learn possessed by the growing child and "how to support self to keep going when things get tough."

I then share personal experiences from my own life regarding challenges to my growth. In this instance, I share having come from a broken home with a very negative and frightening father and having been separated from my mother for two years at the age of seven, after my mother had divorced my father. Along with this, I share my fearful learning history stemming from coming from a welfare family where my mother only had a sixth grade education. This early life experience translated into diffidence about myself as a learner because I compared myself to others in society whom I felt came from better families or who were more skillful or smarter. As a final part of this time of personal sharing, I also share some of my more significant later challenges in college, wherein I often became really scared and felt that I could not continue toward my goal of achieving a doctorate.

I then conclude this portion of my communication to students by sharing with them how Gestalt counseling methods helped me to be effective in facing the learning challenges and how Gestalt practice itself helped me to learn to breathe and not tense up and trust myself in difficult learning situations.

In the next part of doing GEC in the group workshop, students are introduced to key Gestalt concepts, an understanding of which will benefit them as they experience Gestalt counseling. Specifically, students learn about Joseph Zinker's Cycle of Experience (1977), which outlines a process individuals can learn to successfully experience or face emotionally challenging life events. The process proceeds from (1) the experience of sensations to (2) awareness that sensations signal a state of dissatisfaction to (3) mobilization of energy to do something about the dissatisfaction to (4) taking action to (5) "contacting" or experiencing meeting one's needs to (6) integrating or assimilating the learning experience itself into one's overall being, and, finally, to (7) withdrawal from the experience of a specific life event because it is completed. According to Gestalt theory and Zinker's Awareness Cycle (1977), following withdrawal from individual events, individuals move on to other cycles of experiences associated with whatever life circumstance emerges as most important.

In our workshops, students are further informed that individuals stop themselves from going through the Cycle of Experience because they don't have enough inner self-support to work through difficult emotions experienced in each phase in the cycle. This lack of personal support is generally learned by individuals as a result of childhood experiences, wherein students were not supported by family members, teachers, counselors, and didn't learn how to support themselves in difficult circumstances.

Students learn about specific Gestalt concepts in order to be able to understand and do their own personal development work. The concept of self-regulation, for example, when introduced as the inborn ability of each person to be able to maintain a balanced self in the midst of difficult life circumstances, suggests a healthy individual who can move forward and constantly learn more ways of supporting self through difficult emotional trials. Similarly, the importance of learning to breathe rather than tightening and not breathing deeply in difficult situations introduces how to support difficult situations.

Finally, an extremely helpful teaching is the principle of polarity that introduces the primary notion that individuals split themselves into a warring *top dog versus underdog* self that leads to becoming *stuck* in difficult life situations, because the individual can not resolve the inner war between a supporting self and a doubting self and, therefore, finds it difficult to move in a unified and energized way toward a desired goal.

At this point in the workshop, I introduce students to the Gestalt experimental concept of doing empty chair work. Here, students put one of the warring aspects of themselves in one chair and the contradicting or non-supportive aspect of self in the other chair. I then assist them in having a dialogue with the conflicting parts within themselves by shuttling back and forth within the two chairs. This counseling method, of course, helps clarify at what point within that dialogue or conflict exists the point of being stuck. Students soon learn that this method generally uncovers long held unfinished business, so often related to negative experiences with significant people in their development, which has been built in to the personality as non-supportive emotions and beliefs within the self. They consequently learn that becoming more aware of these internal conflicts, in turn, will allow them to (1) resolve and let go of these conflicts and (2) learn to make more effective choices when trying to resolve present-day conflicts.

The key always, of course, is for me to discuss how I learned to work through difficult challenges by learning to use Gestalt methods to free myself from habits of fear, shame, and doubt that I had learned as a small child. As I have said, I share concrete examples of how my past negative learning within my family of origin and from some of my childhood school experiences resulted in my initial inability to support myself through difficult challenges in college.

After the short discussion of the Cycle of Experience and related concepts, I then ask for volunteers to do Gestalt work on issues related to their inability to face academic challenges.

Case Scenarios

Let me recall some salient moments of past workshops. One setting I would like to relate included a particular student who was part of a diverse group in which students were asked to share challenges that they were experiencing to ways that they wanted to improve the level of success in their studies. As the students took turns speaking about difficulties with their studies, I would invite an individual student to do some individual Gestalt work in front of the group members.

Sereta: The first student to speak up was Sereta, an African American female of approximately 21 years of age, who complained of not doing as well in her science coursework as she would like. After some questioning, I determined Sereta had gotten a D grade in a Chemistry course, and, consequently, was feeling diffident toward pursuing her science-related major. Also, Sereta complained of "not being able to support" herself enough to stick with very challenging science course work. To myself, I noted she was not breathing very deeply and was holding herself in a very tense and tight manner.

At this point, because I wanted to assist her to work through the split or polarity in her approach to handling her problem, I asked Sereta if she would be willing to try the empty chair technique. A polarity-causing split in one's personality happens when a person is at odds within herself as to how to respond to a personal concern, with one end of the polarity usually being disparaging and the other end of the polarity usually being more constructive, yet negating of the other end. My wish for Sereta was that the empty chair technique in her case would allow her to shuttle back and forth between the two chairs while acting out the two sides of her psychological split. In this case, the split was between Sereta's need to support herself and her equal inability to support herself to stick with her demanding science studies.

After Sereta agreed to participate in this Gestalt counseling strategy, I asked Sereta to sit in one of the two chairs where she would act out that part of herself that needed support in order to face up in an effective way to the challenging task of studying Chemistry. In the other chair, Sereta would act out that part of her self that was unable to be supportive of that part of her self that needed support. The following is part of the dialogue that took place:

Need for support: "I can't do this without your support; it's too scary. I need your help."

At this point, I asked Sereta to change the word "it's" to "I" in order to more directly experience the feeling (scary) to which Sereta was alluding, e.g., "I am too scary." I then asked her to switch from the "need for support chair" to the "inability to support chair." In this new position, she was to respond to the request for help.

Unable to Support: In this chair, Sereta looked down and could not respond to the request for support that she had just made from the other chair.

I waited quietly for Sereta to say or do something, noting that she seemed unable to look up or to take any action. I then asked her whether she had heard the request for support.

Unable to Support: Sereta answered "yes."

"Do you think you can try to respond to the request for support?" At this point, Sereta looked up, and, in a tired manner said the following:

Unable to Support: "No, I can't support you."

At this point, I suggested she switch back to Need for Support chair.

"How did you feel when you heard the rejection to your request for support? What was your feeling then?"

Sereta said she felt confused and hurt, and then she began to tear up and then to cry. I moved closer to her and placed my hand on her shoulder while she cried. I then asked her to switch to the Unable to Support chair.

After she switched, I asked how she felt watching Sereta cry in the Need for Support chair.

Unable to Support: "I feel tense."

"As you sit there in this chair, describe this feeling of tension to me."

Unable to Support: "I don't know. I guess I feel some tension in my shoulders and in my arms, like I want to stop myself from going forward."

Asking her now to move back to the Need for Support chair, I then wondered aloud to her what she felt while listening to the Sereta in the Unable to Support chair. Sereta answered that she felt frustrated. At this point, I noted that Sereta was holding her breath and not breathing very deeply. I wondered aloud whether this feeling of frustration and interaction reminded her of any similar interactions that she had experienced in her life.

At this point, Sereta began to cry in a very strong way. I asked her if she could share with me what this situation reminded her of from her past life. Sereta answered that she could. She then recounted a story of a time in her life when she was twelve and when her father had died suddenly. Sereta also told of how her mother had been unable to offer care and support to her at that time and, in fact, had talked very little to Sereta about her father's death.

I asked her if she had wanted support from her mother at that time and, also, what she had felt during that experience. Sereta answered that she very much wanted to talk to her mother about her father's death and had equally needed her mother to care for her because Sereta was very sad and hurt following her father's death. I then went on to ask Sereta if her relationship with her mother had improved since the death of her father. Sereta answered it is pretty much the same.

At this point, I inquired of the group members whether someone from the group would come up and sit in the Unable to Support chair and offer Sereta the support she needed. A Caucasian woman was the first to volunteer, although an African American man and a Latina young woman also volunteered. Though strongly inclined to choose the African American male, I chose the Caucasian woman because she had jumped out of her chair and had expressed a strong willingness to offer support to Sereta. So I asked the volunteer student to offer her support to Sereta, almost as if she was Sereta's mother.

Volunteer in the Unable to Support Chair: "I know that I have not given you the support that you need, but I want you to know that I love you very much and that I very much want to support your hurt and confusion."

The volunteer then embraced Sereta, and both of the students cried. I allowed this encounter to continue for a minute or two. After a moment or two, I then asked, "Sereta, what are you now feeling?" Sereta responded by saying that she felt more calm and peaceful. I also noted that Sereta was breathing in a more relaxed and deep manner.

Next, I began soliciting from Sereta what insights she had gained from this Gestalt counseling session. Sereta said that she had not known how much her mother's lack of support had affected her. Also, she said that she needed to learn how to better support herself when she became confused or hurt during her studies. Then I invited Sereta to walk around the group and choose students to look in the eye and say, "I need to learn to support myself better when I get confused or hurt regarding my studies." Sereta did this, and two of the students she chose were the African American man and the Latina who had initially volunteered to play the role of the caring mother. As for the African American man, he told Sereta that she could always count on him to support her whenever she doubted herself. He also told Sereta that he thought she was a strong woman who would succeed in achieving her goals in college.

As part of the teaching part of Gestalt Educational Counseling, I at some point introduced important Gestalt concepts, such as the observation that barely breathing can indicate not supporting self; or that splits in one's personality may lead to moments of impasse, to being stuck in a position of inaction or inability to act in an effective manner. Also, I shared with students that often the inability to resolve our present-day challenges often relates to past life traumas, many from childhood, wherein we learned non-supportive ways of facing difficult feelings, thoughts, and behaviors.

This example of Gestalt counseling with multicultural community college students exemplifies how Gestalt methods can be used in a practical way to help students understand the "psychology of attending college." Specifically, in the case of Sereta, we find a student who because of a significant past experience with her mother did not learn how to support herself in a situation where confusion, doubt, and fear combined to lessen her ability to support herself in the face of a difficult challenge. Sereta and her group mates saw the counselor use a Gestalt strategy of allowing Sereta to dialogue with different parts of herself that were in conflict regarding whether or not she could support herself to face a confusing and fearful situation in her college experience.

Carmen: The second example of Gestalt counseling applied to community college students of color is with a student named Carmen. Participating in a different group from Sereta's, Carmen, a 20 year-old Latina, complained of feeling discouraged in school because of her poor grades. I inquired about Carmen's performance and was informed that Carmen had earned a B in Chemistry, but had failed her first course in Physics. This grade of F weighed heavily on Carmen and made her feel discouraged about continuing her studies in Engineering.

I asked Carmen if she would be willing to do some work regarding her poor Physics grade. Carmen accepted, and I set up two chairs, one for Carmen to act out her discouraging thoughts, feelings, and behaviors related to earning an F in Physics and the other for Carmen to speak to her discouraged self as if she were the Physics course. The following is an excerpt from the Gestalt counseling work that was conducted with Carmen.

I first asked Carmen to sit in the Poor Physics Grade Chair and to share with me what she felt in that chair. Carmen said that she felt hopeless and discouraged. I then asked Carmen to say this to the Physics Course Chair.

Discouraged Poor Physics Grade Chair (to Physics): "I feel hopeless and discouraged." Carmen added, "And, I can't understand you."

I then encouraged her to switch chairs and to speak to the Discouraged Carmen from the Physics Course Chair.

Physics Course Chair (to Discouraged Carmen): "I am too complex, and you'll never understand me, especially because you're too stubborn."

At this point Carmen began to tear up. I then suggested she move to the Discouraged Poor Physics Grade chair. After doing this, Carmen became very emotional, so much so that she could not look up as she heaved and cried very strongly. I quietly watched over her and allowed her to experience her emotions. After about thirty seconds, I asked her if her interaction with Physics reminded her of any interactions with key people in her life. To this question, Carmen's crying became more intense.

I waited patiently for Carmen to feel her way into and through the painful emotions that she was at once remembering and experiencing at the same time. After a short time, I wondered aloud whether she would be willing to share who was coming to her mind in this present situation.

Carmen softly revealed, "My aunt." I followed Carmen's disclosure by asking her if she was willing to put her aunt in the Physics chair. She agreed. I then asked her to speak to the chair designated as her aunt.

Carmen: "You never support me; you always treat me like I am not important. All I ever want is your help, but you always turn your back on me."

Then, I once again encouraged her to switch to the aunt chair and to then respond to Carmen as if she were the aunt.

Aunt: "I know that you don't like me. You're always so stubborn and you never listen to me. You'll never be successful because you always want to do everything your way."

At this point, I spoke to the group about what I thought might be happening in Carmen's present life. Specifically, I hypothesized – and admitted that this was only a hypothesis -- that Carmen had possibly learned from her experience with her aunt that some situations could not be figured out because the situation came down to Carmen holding her position of being stubborn versus giving in to another situation that was not supportive.

I then asked the group members if any one saw the connection between Carmen's past and present experience with Physics. One member suggested that perhaps Carmen was being too stubborn in her approach to Physics and maybe she needed to be more flexible. I asked Carmen if this feedback made sense to her. Carmen answered, "Yes." I, in turn, asked Carmen to elaborate. Carmen answered that she really tried hard to do well in Physics, but that she had used the approach that had been effective for her in Chemistry -- intensive memorization. At this point, another group member asked Carmen if she had tried reading more basic Physics books or using tutors to help her understand Physics. Carmen said that she had not tried either of these alternatives.

At the end of this session, I asked Carmen what insights she had gleaned from the experience. Carmen acknowledged that she was possibly being inflexible in her way of approaching what she perceived as a very tough subject that was hard to understand. She vowed to try the course again, but this time to reach out for help from those around her, including her professor, other students, and tutors. Carmen also volunteered that she clearly saw that she carried with her some intense unfinished feelings from her interaction with her aunt, whom Carmen felt had been hurtful and non-supportive to her during a very difficult time in her life.

Carlos: The third example of Gestalt counseling recounts an individual counseling interaction with a 22 year-old Latino student who was completing his first year of community college study. The difficulty that this student was facing was a real deep hurt and shame regarding his current efforts in college. Specifically, the student, named Carlos, was considering pursuing a different major than he had been studying in his first year of college. The problem was that this indecision about his major came on the heels of four to five years of abusing drugs as well as of not advancing in college or a job. After one year of college, Carlos felt shame that he was possibly not going to follow through on a promise that he had made to his single-parent mother who was funding Carlos' education.

I began our contact by asking Carlos to describe the feelings that he was experiencing. Carlos said that on top of the shame, he was also experiencing a lot of anxiety regarding his present circumstance and toward his future. I asked him if he would like to try some Gestalt counseling in order to clarify his situation. Carlos accepted. I had previously shared with Carlos some background information on Gestalt counseling, including the end goal of Gestalt work, to help persons to be more aware of how their habitual thinking, feeling, and behaving negatively affects their ability to live fulfilling lives.

I began this counseling work with Carlos by asking him to play two roles, one being the anxious and shamed part of Carlos and the other that part of Carlos that was contemplating changing majors. I told Carlos that the way he would play the two parts of himself was to alternate between two chairs, one which would be the ashamed-anxious part of Carlos and the other the part of Carlos that wanted to change majors. I asked Carlos to sit in one chair and first speak of being anxious and ashamed and share his feelings.

Anxious-Ashamed: "Here I go again, messing up my life by not doing what I need to be doing!"

"What are you feeling at this very moment," I asked?

Carlos answered, "It's the same old thing; I'm no good and am just proving that I'm worthless."

I then asked Carlos to switch chairs and be or act that part of his self who was considering changing majors. Once Carlos switched chairs, I wondered how he felt in the Changing Majors chair. Carlos said he felt frustrated and scared. I then asked Carlos to speak to the Anxious-Ashamed chair.

Changing Majors: "I'm scared about you messing up my life again; scared about you taking me under again."

I had Carlos switch to the Shame-Anxious chair, and to share what he was experiencing listening to the Changing Major chair. Carlos said that he felt lost and confused. I then asked him to speak from this feeling.

Anxious-Shame: "I need your support; I'm scared and anxious and I don't know what to do."

Switching back to the Changing Major chair, he answered.

Changing Major: "I don't want you in my life. I don't like you. I don't want to feel like you."

Sensing that we might be nearing some sort of closure, I had Carlos review the dialogue that he had just carried out between two aspects of himself. I also prompted him to try changing the "you" statements in his dialogue to "I" or "me" statements. The following is an example.

Changing Major to Anxious-Shame: "I don't want you (me) in my life. I don't like you (me). I don't want to feel like you (me)."

When Carlos did this, he began to tear up. I then put my hand on Carlos' shoulder and asked him what he was thinking and feeling. Carlos told me that he could clearly see how bad he was treating himself and how much he was turning his back on that part of himself that really needed his support.

Classrooms of Shame and Seats of Doubt

There are, of course, other examples of where I as counselor worked with students specifically addressing unfinished business related to school experiences. In one situation, I was lecturing to a large group of ethnically diverse persons on how Gestalt counseling works to help one overcome fears that were developed in childhood. One of the persons in the audience was an African American woman who said that she wanted to do some Gestalt work related to being more confident in school. During the work with this woman, she became tearful when she recounted her experiences in elementary school where she often "felt like I didn't belong."

After a short discussion of this woman's experience, wherein it was evident that the woman held many strong emotions related to her early school experiences, I arranged three chairs in a row, simulating a row of chairs in a classroom. I invited her to take a seat and to close her eyes and remember herself as a little girl in her classroom. The woman closed her eyes and immediately bent forward, grimacing slightly and beginning to show strong emotion. I asked her what she was experiencing, and she replied that she felt a pain in her stomach. I then invited her to stay with her pain and to share what the pain was like. She said the "pain was like an intense burning that wouldn't stop." When I subsequently asked her to speak in the present tense as if she was that pain, the woman bent more forward and whispered something that I could not hear. I softly touched the woman on the shoulder and asked her to give more strength to this voice. The woman hesitated for a good minute, obviously struggling to allow her voice to come forward. I again softly spoke to her, saying that I believed in her right to speak and supported her to give voice to what she was feeling. To this, she blurted out in a loud voice, "I can think! I can learn!"

Following a short pause, I shared with the group what she had learned in this exercise. She shared how painful it had been for her experiencing the many, many hours that she spent in school wanting to speak up about her belief in her ability to learn. She told the group and they, in turn, verbalized support for her that she could indeed go to college and use her mind to learn and to achieve.

In another situation in a group of Latina women where I had introduced the participants to GEC, one of the women asked to work on her lack of confidence in her ability to learn to write well. Seeing obvious signs of tension in the woman, I asked her to describe how she felt whenever she thought about writing or actually sat down to write. The woman then described feeling "scared and doubtful" that she was smart enough to learn to read and write. I asked the woman to describe more in depth what she felt in her body when she thought about writing. The woman said that she felt a tension in her legs, as if she wanted to run away. I asked her if this reminded her of any situations in her early school experiences. With a surprised look, she answered that yes she could remember a time when she was in an English class and she was very frightened that a substitute teacher would find out that she was "dumb and couldn't do English." The woman recounted the many times that she slipped out of the class before the teacher came in to avoid being "found out" by the teacher.

I therefore decided to arrange a classroom-like situation to in essence role play what the woman had experienced as a child in school. To this end, I had the group arrange chairs in rows and asked everyone to take a seat. The woman said that she didn't want to re-experience this part of her past. And to this, I said, "Maybe we'll do something different." Once the chairs were arranged in rows, I asked the woman to sit in the chair closest to the door. When she was seated, I inquired after her feelings. She said that she felt "like running out the door." To this, I asked her to speak as if she was the door. Speaking as the door, the woman said, "I'm going to shut you in so everybody sees how dumb you are." When I then asked her how she felt as the door, the woman responded that she felt "mean and angry."

At this point, I shared with the group that I was going to experiment and play a supportive and caring teacher who wanted all the children to feel good about themselves as learners. So I requested all the women to pretend they were students in the class. I then surveyed the room to determine whether anyone had any questions about learning English that they wanted to ask. I asked all of the women present to pretend to be very inquisitive students who were really excited about learning English.

Most of the women raised their hands with enthusiasm to role play as if they were excited and had questions to ask about writing. The woman with the issue about writing seemed hesitant to participate. I therefore supported the woman to raise her hand and ask a question. The woman tentatively looked at her group companions, but finally raised her hand as if she had a question. To this I called out her name and said with enthusiasm, "Let's see what question (the woman's name) has!" The woman hesitantly asked, "How do you use a comma?" To this question, I enthusiastically responded with, "What a great question!" and I then also asked the other would-be students, "Isn't that a great question!" The other participants enthusiastically chimed in. They also wanted to know how to use a comma.

I asked the woman who had asked the question if she knew some rules for using a comma. The woman looked around at her would-be classmates and hesitatingly said, "Yes, I think I do." As the would-be teacher, I answered with "Great. Let's hear what you have to say!" The woman then hesitantly shared a rule that she thought related to the use of commas, and the counselor/teacher with enthusiasm congratulated the woman on providing useful information to the class. At the same time, I asked the role-playing group members if they appreciated the ideas shared by their classmate. The group members in chorus said, "Oh yes, she's really great and helpful!"

At this point, the Latina with the concern about her writing became visibly emotional, and I then stepped closer to the woman and held her hand. This lasted for a couple of minutes, after which the woman shared how aware she had become through this role play about the level of hurt and shame that she had carried within herself as a result of her early experiences in school. She vowed to the group that she "would make a serious effort to start believing in" her ability to learn to write well and that she would begin to work more seriously on developing her writing skills.

As a postscript to this group role play, a couple of other group participants shared that while taking part in the above dramatization, they got in touch with some strong feelings related to shaming and demeaning experiences that they had experienced in their early schooling. One woman, in particular, mentioned how she had been filled with terror about the possibility of going up to the front of the class to do work on the chalk board. This led me to have the woman have a dialogue with the chalkboard, wherein the woman took the role of the chalkboard. The outcome of this work was that the woman became aware of how behind this fear of the chalkboard lay hurt feelings that she had long harbored toward a very close relative who constantly criticized the woman as a young girl for not being as smart as her cousins.

The Relationship of Gestalt Concepts to Student Achievement

Zinker's Cycle of Experience (1977), as has been noted earlier, is an effective way to clearly tie Gestalt psychological concepts to the experience of ethnically diverse students in difficult achievement situations in community college, especially as addressed by Rendon, Weiner, and Nicholls. A simple example of the cycle as applied to a basic achievement situation wherein a student successfully negotiates the cycle can be used as a means of tying this concept to the general experience of our student population.

Imagine a student experiencing stress because of an upcoming test. In the first phase of the cycle, a student might feel tension (*sensation* in her neck, shoulders or stomach...). Being *aware* of this sensation, the student *starts to mobilize her energy* to study in order to *take action* related to handling the sensation of stress associated with the upcoming test. The studying or *action* would result in learning the material in such a way as to satisfy the need to learn in order to prepare for the test. The experience of effective learning would be an example of *contact* in the cycle because the act of studying is satisfying the need associated with the sensation of tension related to mastering the upcoming test.

Following the contact phase of the cycle, the student would *assimilate* her experience into an effective way of behaving that would be turned to in future achievement situations involving preparing for tests. The specific learning material would also be assimilated by the individual to provide a greater reservoir of knowledge for future learning. The final phase of the cycle would be *withdrawal*, wherein a student lets go of studying for a particular test, ideally at the point of fulfillment of the need to learn and prepare for the test. The student would then move on to a new situation and renew the Cycle of Experience as a way of creatively adjusting to a new learning situation.

Taking a look at an ineffective negotiation of the Cycle of Experience, we see that the challenges to students that Gestalt concepts address involve when students get stuck moving through the cycle. For example, in the situation above, a student could get stuck in the *sensation* part of the Cycle, wherein he might be totally overwhelmed by the sensation of stress related to the need to study. In such a case, he would be at an impasse and might then procrastinate or do other non-study activities as a way of avoiding the sensations associated with feeling apprehensive or fearful toward an upcoming test.

To extend this example further, another example of impasse in the cycle might be that even though a student might become *aware* of the *sensation* and see the clear relationship to the need for study, she might not be able to *mobilize her energy* to study. This might translate into a constant attempt to read the assigned text, review class notes, or attempt to memorize course material with no success in being able to focus on the task at hand.

Another extension of this example might involve a student experiencing the cycle all the way through to the *action* of studying but nevertheless not be able to really have *contact* with the material so as to experience successful learning. In this case, the material would not be actively broken down, digested, and understood by the student.

Gestalt concepts diagnostically define how an individual doesn't progress through the cycle by revealing that the person is unable to support self to work through the feelings associated with each phase in the cycle. For example, a student who gets stuck in the sensation part of the Cycle of Experience might be unable to support himself to feel and work through the stress *sensations* associated with the upcoming test.

Similarly, a student who is unable to learn in a complete way from his action of studying (*contact*), barring a learning disability, might be explained from a Gestalt perspective as having an inability to support self to hold on to feelings associated with a concept of self as a confident and successful learner.

But what concepts does Gestalt use to explain (1) why a student might not be able to handle various phases of the Cycle of Experience and (2) how a student might successfully support self to work through an impasse or resolve being stuck in some particular phase of the Cycle? First, it is important to introduce the concept of *organismic self-regulation*. This Gestalt concept describes an inherent characteristic of being human -- namely, the ability to work through difficult life experiences and their associated emotional trials if one simply trusts one's natural ability to experience, make sense of, understand, and support self to work through challenging learning experiences.

The Gestalt approach, proffered by Perls (1969), says that because of negative developmental experiences of lack of support, individuals lose sight of and trust in their in-born ability to regulate themselves. This happens, for example, when parents or significant others, e.g., teachers, overly control or direct a child to face life in the adult's way or manner, rather than supporting the growing child to develop a sense of being that trusts self to learn and creatively handle difficult situations.

Conclusion

From a Gestalt perspective, students' inability to work through the Cycle of Experience of preparing for a test possibly resulted from past learning experiences wherein they learned to doubt, avoid, or reject feelings similar to the ones being experienced in the present test situation. For example, with regard to not being able to support self to feel the sensation of fear or doubt related to an upcoming test, a student may have had in her childhood an experience with a parent or significant adult where the adult punished or belittled the very personhood of the child in an achievement situation. This, in turn, led to the inner child of the individual to shut down feelings associated with the general threat of being tested because as a child the person did not have the *maturity* to handle the difficult emotions that the person had to face as a child.

In essence, *maturity*, according to Perls (1969), involves being able to experience frustration, which implies staying present with and experiencing difficult feelings. This, in turn, introduces the Gestalt concept of *self-support,* wherein an individual is able to maintain contact with self as difficult emotions are experienced and worked through. In short, the individual who shuts down emotions in the present does so because present feelings recall feelings that were never fully experienced, understood, and resolved in childhood. This occurred essentially because the child did not have the ability to experience and remain present with difficult emotions or the ability to understand the emotions. That is, the individual could not support self.

Furthermore, according to Gestalt principles, adult individuals are unable to handle the emotions of the present because similar emotions and related thoughts and behaviors were never experienced and handled in the past, especially in childhood. This brings up the concept of *unfinished business,* wherein Gestalt reveals that most of the emotional difficulties individuals experience in the present are a result of past experiences that were never fully experienced or resolved to completion. Consequently, what the individual does in response to present emotional trials is dictated by the emotional habits that the individual developed in the past handling similar difficult emotions.

The counseling examples of the negative experiences of students of color in school settings are also worthy of note because they clearly show how the unfinished business of negative early learning can stay with a person into her adult life. Both the African American woman who hid in her school chairs for years, and the fearful Latina who wanted to run away from her English class because of the threat to her self-worth, clearly show how long held negative emotions of childhood affect day-to-day learning experiences.

Gestalt personal development concepts, especially as used in Gestalt Educational Counseling, go beyond the powerful suggestions of researchers of achievement motivation in that GEC allows counselors to make real in a direct experiential way both what the challenges are to students' success as well as how to begin changing oneself in order to address in a more effective way the emotional challenges of college. With respect to ethnically diverse students, GEC promises this student more than insights about why college can be overwhelming, for GEC offers students of color a powerful tool to grow through difficult emotions that undermine effective learning.

Specifically, in Gestalt Educational Counseling, the counselor focuses on educating students about developmental challenges and ways of facing these challenges through direct experience. In doing so, the counselor would emphasize the importance of developing increasing awareness on the part of students for how they generally stop themselves or don't support themselves to grow when faced with difficult emotional challenges. Also, the counselor would emphasize helping students to understand or learn about how their present difficulties related to facing difficult emotional challenges in college are examples of ineffective learning in similar personal trials from the past.

A final comment is warranted regarding the important challenge that face community colleges with regard to helping underrepresented ethnic minority students to succeed in college. For over forty years many, many efforts have been initiated to assist this student population to more effectively face the challenges of college. In this regard, I observed the following in my 1988 doctoral dissertation, *An Exploratory Study of a Group Intervention for Underprepared Minority University Students*: In 1967, Daniel Katz wrote about the crisis facing psychology because of the poor performance of ethnic minority persons in the American educational system. Since that time, the Commission on the Higher Education of Minorities (1981) and higher education researchers (Astin, 1982; Cross, 1974; Nieves, 1978; Tinto & Sherman, 1974) have echoed Katz (1967)'s call for a serious and concerted effort by professionals to resolve this problem.

In 2004, the current lack of significant improvement in the success of students of color in higher education in no way signals a time to stop experimenting with new and more powerful ways to help underrepresented ethnically diverse students to better handle the challenges of college.

One of the powerful benefits of Gestalt counseling is that persons are gradually assisted to experience deeper and deeper levels of difficult emotions over time. Moreover, coupled with Gestalt Therapy, Gestalt Educational Counseling promises to be a powerful tool to make achievement, success, and leadership a true reality in the lives of more and more of the ethnic minority students who are currently enrolled and will continue to be in our community colleges. Importantly, GEC also promises to be a powerful tool to help the achievement of other students, including the new ethnically diverse populations now attending higher education in ever increasing numbers.

Personal Account

I have very much been influenced by the work of Erik Erikson, and, especially, with his conceptualization of persons as developing from trust and mistrust to integrity versus despair. In "Dialogues with Erik Erikson," by Richard Evans, Erikson talked about "hope as the basic ingredient of all strength...a basic human strength without which we couldn't stay alive." Erikson talked about hope as a human virtue that does or does not develop in the life of every person because of the experience of trust and/or mistrust of self and others in the world.

Erikson went on to say that in man, because of his lifelong struggles between trust and mistrust in changing states and conditions, it (hope) has to be developed firmly, and then be confirmed and reaffirmed throughout life." My life journey as a person and professional of color in this society has been one of learning to trust, accept, and support myself to develop as the unique person I am. Personally, acknowledging and accepting my uniqueness has not always been easy because my experience is that this society does not readily value me "feeling myself, expressing myself, being seen, and taking up space."

In the study of counseling, and, more recently in the experience of my personal development work at the San Francisco Gestalt Institute, I have become aware of the power that the social environment has with regard to supporting the development of acceptance and trust of self. However, as in this society, I have found that too often persons of color do not benefit from the powerful growth experience that comes from counseling, and, more specifically, Gestalt personal development work. This chapter reflects a place of development in my personal growth and professional work with persons of color. First, I have learned at the core of my being of the importance of persons of color experiencing an environment of trust and support in order to grow and develop our personal potential. In this regard, I write about the necessity for counselors to open and share their personal life's struggle with persons of color in order to build and environment of trust so that trust *a la* Erikson can be "confirmed and reaffirmed."

Secondly, this chapter reflects the importance of supporting persons of color to become aware of how we often develop in this society a basic sense of mistrust, both of ourselves and towards others. This mistrust too often leads us down a road of self-rejection and despair. I have seen, however, that through the power of self-awareness that Gestalt personal development work affords, we can begin to re-own aspects of ourselves that we lose hope for and trust in. This experience, both for myself and in my work with others, gives me hope that I may be able to make a difference toward developing greater trust, hope, and love in this world.

Mario Rivas, San Francisco, Ca., USA

References

Astin, A.W. (1982). *Minorities in American higher education*. San
    Francisco: Jossey-Bass.

Commission on the Higher Education of Minorities. (1981). (ED 214475),
    Higher Education Research Institute Inc., Los Angeles, CA.

Cross, K.P. (1974). *Beyond the Open Door.* San Francisco: Jossey-Bass.

Jourard, S.M. (1964). *The Transparent Self.* Princeton, N.J.; Nostrum, Co. Inc.

Katz, D. (1967). *Socialization of academic motivation in minority children.* Nebraska Symposium on Achievement Motivation.

Levine, E.S., & Padilla, A.M. (1980). *Crossing Cultures in Therapy: Pluralistic Counseling for the Hispanic.* Monterey, CA: Brooks/Cole Publishing Co.

Nevis, E.C. (1987). *Organizational Consulting: A Gestalt Approach.* Hillsdale, N.J.: The Analytic Press, Inc.

Nicholls, J.G. (1984). Achievement motivation: Conceptions of personality, subjective experience, task choice, and performance. *Psychological Review*, 91, 328-349.

Nieves, L. (1978). *The minority college experience: A case for use of self-control systems.* Office of Minority Education. Educational Testing Service, Princeton, NJ.

Perls, F. S. (1969). *Gestalt Therapy Verbatim.* Lafayette, CA.: Real People Press.

Rendon, L. (1994). Validating culturally diverse students: Toward a new model of Learning and student development. *Innovative Higher Education*. Vol. 19, No. 1, fall, 1994.

Rivas, A.M. (1988). *An Exploratory Study of a Group Intervention for Underprepared Minority University Students.* Doctoral Thesis, University of Minnesota, Minneapolis, Minnesota.

Seligman, L (2001). *Gestalt Therapy. In Systems, Strategies, and Skills of Counseling and Psychotherapy* (pp. 256-281). NJ: Prentice-Hall, Inc.

The Academic Senate for the California Community Colleges (1995). The role of the counseling faculty in CA: Community Colleges.

Tinto, V. & Sherman, R. (1974) *The effectiveness of secondary and higher education intervention programs*: A critical review. Eric, Document: 1974.

Weiner, B. (1985). Attributional Theory of Achievement and Emotion. *Psychological Review*, 92, 548-573.

Zinker, J. (1977). *Creative Process in Gestalt Therapy.* NY: Vintage Books.

IX. COEXISTENCE IN THE HOLY LAND

By Sa'ed Tali, M.A. and Oshrat Mizrahi Shapira, M.A.

Introduction

Tense and frightening are the streets outside; while inside there is turbulence, even though the sky is clear. We know not if this is the right time for dialogue. Perhaps dialoguing is not a luxury at a time like this, but it's certainly a necessity. There are people who need to talk when in conflict and especially when there are others who believe that they need to fight. Conflicts, we must stress, are not an invention of the Jews nor the Palestinians. They have accompanied humankind since Genesis. Cain's murdering Abel was a sign of the beginning of humanity's inhumanity, when one has become overwhelmed with conflict. Two are enough, at times even one, for a struggle to erupt. Cain and Abel had the entire globe, yet the end of their story was tragic.

We claim that there is a deep layer that creates conflict beyond and above the political, sociological, geographic levels that connect one's personal identity to more identities. Thus the motives that mold conflicts between groups and the identities themselves have to be explored not only through an external, political field, but also an intra-psychic field.

In recent years, there have been a number of attempts to map Arab-Jewish relationship groups struggling to relate to one another (Cahanov & Katz, 1990; Steinberg, 2002). Aiming to categorize how personal relationships between group participants form, Steinberg bases his attempts mainly on recent human contact theory (Allport, 1954; Pettigrew, 1998), noting that once members of opposing groups establish personal acquaintances, inclinations in stereotypical perception, stance, and relations will shift. The weakness of opposing groups emerges when they avoid the realistic politics of the power relations outside the groups, in the field. Though dialogue at a meeting place can change viewpoint and stance, it does not always take into account the field perspective as a whole.

One also notes that in groups where there is a collective identity, the collective identity, underlain initially by an asymmetric power relation, evolves to give weight to the entire field experience itself, based on trust and friendship between participants, in order to mitigate opposing power struggles between two phenomenological fields, and to create more optimal social relationships.

A third type of group is the story-telling group in which participants share personal stories with one another. The personal story evokes personal histories, including the collective history that groups with initial asymmetric power should want to arrive at eventually, and at the same time creates personal relationships. In this group, it is possible to explore the stereotypes in each member in relation to the other members. This group is a culmination of the field context and the personal history/story, enabling in the end a dialogic relationship while taking into account the total holistic experience residing internally in each member. Cahanov and Katz (1990), observing groups as workshop participants, sub-divide groups in light of their conflicts:

Human relations workshops: focusing on heightening individual awareness of feelings about members of other groups, of one's behavior when with them, and the impact of this behavior on the other group members (Back, 1972; Benne, Bradford, Gibb, and Lippitt, 1975).

Intercultural study workshops: focusing on understanding the influences their culture has on oneself and on one's other, and on the perception of the self and the possible mutuality that might emerge among people in conflict (Triandis, 1983).

Conflict resolution and negotiation workshops: creating dialogue around the working assumption that there is a real conflict of interests between the two sides. Techniques that are more suitable for decision makers and less for educators interested in personal growth are preferable (Burton, 1969; Kelman, 1979).

How we approach our group work is always evolving and hasn't reached its final form. Our approach is influenced more from the standpoint of human-relations workshops and aims to heighten awareness on the behavioral and emotional realm.

Our Own Initial Meeting

Our meeting one another happened as a coincidence -- or maybe not. Community theatre director Oshrat, a Jew from the Middle East, who perceives herself as a Jewish Arab, approached a group facilitator, Sa'ad, an Arab who defines himself as a Palestinian Israeli citizen, and suggested that they establish and co-facilitate a dialogue group in the Theatre Department of the Hebrew University of Jerusalem. Oshrat had three years of experience at that time facilitating an Arab-Jewish theatre group in a mixed town, Ramle, in Israel. She felt that leading such a group is charged and complex, when mixed. It was essential to her to bring in a professional group facilitator psychologist.

We decided to work together, even though at face value we had nothing in common: a man and a woman, an Arab Muslim and an Arab Jew, from different professional fields. In time, we discovered we also have fundamental personal differences. "Oshrat is a spontaneous extrovert actively facing outward," as Sa'ad muses, while he sees himself to be "a held-back/contained introvert, who mainly observes." Oshrat believes more in indirect work through theatre while Sa'ad prefers direct and unmediated communication through the group dynamics."

In spite of these starting positions, something pushed us to start the journey. At this initial stage we couldn't imagine how long and winding the road to integration between our own intricate parts would be. Later on, we reached the insight that in differences between us lies the secret of the power of co-facilitation, and on this point rests the uniqueness of our work.

At first, though, the difference between us was the threatening factor that highlighted the conflict. At a later stage, parallel to the group work we conducted alternately, we came upon a struggle and a dialogue at the end of which we acquired security in the uniqueness of each one of us and in our ability to accept the other. This recognition of security and acceptance enables us to produce a more harmonious conduct and a richer facilitation that we both utilize. Constantly, we re-drafted the advantages and qualities we both possess, thereby creating a whole experience. There are parallel vectors between the process we went through as a facilitation unit and the process we are trying to lead in our groups. As a pair we had to bridge differences, accept the other as is, including the right to exist in order to find mutual interest, as we maintained the wish to work as a unit, and as a whole, with our groups in conflict. Wholeness derives from a meeting between two separate entities.

The Group Framework

The group is a part of an academic workshop in the Department of Theatre at the Hebrew University in Jerusalem. In practice, the workshop is conducted in a theatre situated on the line separating Eastern (Arab) and Western (Jewish) Jerusalem.

The Rationale

The aim of the groups that we facilitate is to help the participants to observe and to explore through a theatrical vehicle the motives and the psychological aspects of life in the shadow of the Jewish-Arab conflict. The emphasis is mainly on the interpersonal functioning of the group and the raw material entails the here and now of personal experiences, feelings, and thoughts that the participants bring up. Our interventions, including the theatrical experiments, are on the level of group processes, created to facilitate communication and relations between people. We encourage free expression of feeling and personal exposure, in the wish to create trust relationships across the original groups. We evoke stories that will later be the basis for the final theatrical event.

The final event is supposed to reflect and expose the meaningful processes that happened in the group both on the personal and on the group level. The performance is an invitation to the life of the group up to the time of the event: the conflicts and the tensions, the hopes and the peace-making. The performance describes a meeting between Arabs and Jews through milestones symbolizing the nature of the relationship and the dynamics that a meeting like this entails.

The Target Population

Our target population comprises students from universities in Jerusalem and Jewish and Palestinian citizens of the city. Typical characteristics of the Jewish Israeli population is that they are twenty-two to thirty year-old Ashkenazi left-wingers, including one 50 year-old gentleman. The typical characteristic of the Palestinian participants is that most of them are students between nineteen to twenty-two years of age, both Muslim and Christian, from Arab villages in the north of Israel.

The Group

Running successfully for approximately six years now, our workshop meets its participants once a week for a three-hour session that is dedicated to personal and team work revolving around the conflict and working through conversation and theatrical exercises. It is in this arena of the work that the materials of the performance crystallize and in which the members develop acting skills. This is the most central of the three stages/phases and lasts approximately 4 months (16 sessions).

The Rehearsals

The participants meet twice a week for the duration of three hours in preparation for putting up the show. The rehearsals are not disconnected from the group process and they include within them discussions and reflections on the process on the personal level, the interpersonal level, and the group level. The main tool in this reflective process is that of acting and working through of the dynamics that evolve through group work.

The Performance

Taking place in the village of Neve Shalom (Oasis of Peace) or at The Khun (The Lodge) in Jerusalem, the final show is the culmination of the process in that it is a meeting point between performers and audience. This performance marks the joint effort of Arabs and Jews to achieve a common goal and to accomplish a personal and communal success. The show acts as the closing of a cycle, but it is differentiated from the beginning of the process in that here is a real togetherness based on a true and authentic knowing of each other. The group process draws a line between two poles – that of the starting point of conflict and the other of the ensuing polarity, the performance itself, which is the articulation of the bridging of the divides. The rehearsals are the route, the journey from one polarity to the other.

Beyond the gain to the group members, the performance evokes thought in the viewer, and takes the audience on a journey similar to the one undertaken by the team members. The viewer, through the performance, is opened to introspection about his or her place in society and about his or her feelings in the current reality of the conflict.

At the end of the show, there is an interactive session led by the group facilitators and its aim is to allow both audience and participants to share their feelings and reactions to the performance.

Workshop Objective
Our objective of the workshop is as follows:

1. The sessions will guide the participants into a journey toward their chosen personal identity, including their self-declared national identity. This journey will lead their soul through a meeting process in which their representative self also meets their other. Our goal is that by the end of the journey, they will re-own at least some of the projections they stored internally toward the other.
2. The group itself will enable the participants to enter a state of introspection so that they may confront the consequences of dealing with the Jewish-Palestinian conflict.
3. Over time, the participants will create a theatrical performance that reflects and exposes meaningful events and processes that happened in the group on the personal and group level. This performance event is kind of a window into the life of the group, into its journey of conflicts, tensions, excitements, and peace-making. The play will evoke thought and stimulate the observers to conduct similar meetings in which the main characteristic is acceptance of the other and mutual respect.
4. The theatrical event is to be aesthetic and highly professional.

The Group Structure
The group is in session for six months and is constructed of three elements: the group itself, rehearsals based on the group's dynamics, and the final performance. Fifteen people participate in the team, two thirds of whom are Jews and one third of whom are Palestinians. The women in the group outnumber the men.

A meeting between Jews and Arabs at this time and age entails high potential for explosion. Hence, the level of anxiety is very high. Defense mechanisms are in full bloom at the service of the ego, with the ego often impacting the defenses at play. These meetings quickly become a battlefield of blaming and attacks heightening the conflict that is already inherent to the group by definition. Below are a few of the common mechanisms across the different groups we have facilitated:

1. **Splitting and Projection**: experiencing aggression as if it resides within the field, a participant will excuse him/herself from the aggressive feelings emerging from within the group ("My sub-group is ideal; the other is inferior!").

2. **Projective Identification**: each member has a role in relation to another member. It's therefore possible to observe certain processes of intellectual, cultural, or sexual seduction intended to entice another to become part of the group.
3. **Generalization and Stereotypes**.
4. **Denial.**
5. **Scapegoating**: each sub-group searches for a scapegoat to pile on its own sins. "The goat" often is a participant who behaves in a fashion that contradicts one's sense of group rules as a whole and at times bluntly expresses feelings and values directly. At the first phase, the scapegoat that the Jews and Palestinians unite to kill is the facilitators; to be precise: Sa'ad, the one responsible at this time for the group dynamic underway. During this phase, Sa'ad is pushing towards the direction of a dialogue about the conflict in progress; hence, he is perceived as threatening to shake the fragile, cold peace between the two groups.

The Stages of Constructing the Group

We assume that there are a number of reasons for the fact that more Jews than Arabs come to the gatherings:

1. The lack of trust the Arab has in the ability of these groups to offer real change in the socio-political situation.
2. The Arabs' distrust and suspicion concerning any event related to the Israeli/Jewish establishment. Any activity involving Jews is perceived as related to the establishment.
3. Any dialogue with Jews against the ground of the escalation in the relationship between the Arabs and the Jews is perceived as collaboration with the Jews.
4. The theatre as a foreign and a threatening tool for the Arab society.

The theatre has an element of externalizing and of exposure, which makes it, in the eye of the Arab society, indecent, especially if women are involved.

On top of these four factors, some of the Arab participants are suspicious about the Arab facilitator and perceive him as a collaborator and as weak in relation to the Jewish female facilitator, who is anyway more active on the theatrical front. On the other hand, as facilitators, we highlight the protective elements of the theatre and, as well, an equal presence and functioning between the Arab and the Jewish facilitator.

The fashion in which we choose our participants impacts the process of the work. We are aware of the difference between the different needs and expectations of the Jews and the Arabs as well as their needs and expectations as individuals, once we come to know them well. We try to create a spirit and sense of an organized unity, allowing differences as well as drawing clear boundaries. The field (the external reality) takes over and intervenes in every stage in the life of the group.

From the start, we understand that the textbook way of facilitation cannot be followed. For example, even at the preliminary stage of creating the group, we courted the Arabs and invited them to join in any way, while with the Jews we were strict to a degree of giving them screening exams. We accept this situation as given even as we move away from a place of potential discrimination. The Jewish participants collaborate with the facilitators and make allowance to the Arabs because they too want them to stay. In time, they allow themselves to express anger and frustration about this self-imposed initial equality, which later on proves to be a developmental evolutionary aspect of the group.

Getting Started

Group had twelve Jewish members, eight Arabs. The opening phase was short, one to two meetings. It was characterized on the one end of the polarity with which we started by optimism and euphoria and on the other by anxiety and suspicion. The participants, as if briefly reborn, are delighted to belong to a special group that has chosen life as a reason for being together. The facilitators were delighted to have brought another child to the world. Group members felt that they had entered an island of peace and sanity situated in a field of insanity and a hopeless war.

They expressed wishes and hope to know one another and to make peace amongst themselves. Membership in the group is initiated by an invitation or suggestion to feel joy to be participating in a circle where something producing euphoria might get done. However, typically, joy is quickly delayed, and euphoria quickly held back, by paranoia and by dependency on the facilitators.

We begin every session with a circle of associations and monologues. Touching upon the phenomenology of each member allows an authentic meeting between individual participants. The members of the two teams are invited to share with the group their feeling, thoughts and personal stories. This part of the session lasts approximately fifteen minutes and its aim is to create a "soft landing" from the exterior reality into the group circle and to provide a personal arena to each member to share personal issues with the group, and for the group to get to know each of its members on a personal level.

After this, we begin preparing for the theatrical work; our preparation is made up of warming-up exercises and exercises whose aim is to teach acting skills in addition to the work on the personal and communal materials. All the dramatic exercises are made to fit the pace of developmental work, both from the material point of view, the dynamic point of view, and from the point of view of arriving at the creation of the final dramatic performance. The theatrical work lasts for about an hour and a half. After a break, we reconvene to another open group discussion in circle form that lasts about an hour.

So we began this phase with what we call an identity experiment. Group members were asked to wander around the room and tell their identity to a member they meet and then, in turn, to listen to the rendition of the person whom they have just met.

As they move on to encounter another new person, each member is asked to adopt the identity of the person they had just met. And thus the journey of meetings in the room continued, every meeting containing a swapping of identity. "The experiment ends," we pointed out, "when you wind up meeting the person who carries your very own identity." We distinctly remember the sensation of freedom when all identities are mixed in the room; for this brought about a recognition of similarity following upon when each person had first lost his or her identity and had come to feel a loss of personal meaning. Hence, an evolving communal identity seemed stronger than an initiating personal identity and, of course, a loss of personal identity.

At the next stage, participants were divided into to two groups according to nationality, Palestinian and Israeli. Each group was then requested to design three kinetic sculptures relating to their given perceived situation, to their desired situation and to the perceived possible. The room filled with objections and fierce looks of "Don't spoil the joy!" We discovered the difficulty in containing the stormy tempers and anxiety of the group. On one hand, we were to be empathic and containers for projections (transference); on the other, we were to be managers and function to maintain holding the group together -- all the while remember our own task of bringing together a presentation at the end of the path of this dialogic, multiple-voiced journey.

Creative Spontaneity

Initiating a session, preparing for further sessions, rehearsing experiential scripts, and bridging sessions, to say the least, can result in gruesome and awesome self-reflection. At times, such descending self-reflection produces unrehearsed creative spontaneity. We believe that it is times like these when a participant is trying to break through feeling hypocritical. We have two such examples of creative spontaneity; one involving a poem; the other, a silver ribbon.

A Poem

Social Ice Cream is a social protest poem, it reflects a rising awareness of a wish to move from pseudo-togetherness to a relationship. *Social Ice Cream* is a brave attempt to break the ice through 'sweet talk' which both covers the horror of conflict and expresses the painful wish for closeness.

"Social Ice Cream"

I want to eat something.
I want sweetness, like an ice cream sandwich.
Yes, sit on the soft sand on the beach and lick ice cream.
Politically correct flavored ice cream.
To taste the white part,
And the black,
The strength of the biscuit,
The softness of the cream,
To eat it all in gentle pluralistic movement of the tongue,
And spread on top some humane sweet whipped cream.
Without talking.
Sprinkle some rice puffs on the poor,
So I will not be able to see.
And stuff glazed cherries in my ears,
So I won't be able to hear.
Fraternity ice cream, peace ice cream, justice ice cream
Oh boy, I'm melting!

Noa's (female Jew) muffled sobbing merged with the silence of the group. Slowly members focused on her. Fidgeting, embarrassed looks slowly fill and overwhelm the room until Noa's tears occupied the entire group's attention and magnetized it. When we say *group*, we mean the entire field – chairs, participants and facilitators, gazes, postures, movement of the air and the light in the room.

All the eyes and minds turned to the facilitators: on one hand, blaming; on the other, anticipating their actions, hoping they would release the group from the sadness and discomfort that took over the room. The facilitators invite Noa to speak the tears and share what she feels with the group. Noa doesn't co-operate, as if saying, "Leave me alone, I can't!" and leaves the room. Long silence preceded a phase of objections and rejections. We understand the silence as an expression of difficulty, paralysis, often overtaking the group. The paralysis and silence, frustration and anger, created difficulties that got expressed more at the dialogic moment between the two groups. Later on, we would see that at the theatrical part where this moment was to be scripted, the anxiety and the difficulties were expressed in the content of the rehearsal of the performance and the performance itself.

Both in the theatre performance and during the dialogic layers beforehand, the two teams objected through expressions of polarized national identity. And any mention of national identity evoked discomfort. The facilitators, at this stage, drew most of the negative feeling, as they were the ones that divided the group into Jews and Arabs, were meticulous about time boundaries, and tried to shed light on places the group was invested in to keep in the dark. The members, all entrenched in suffering and overwhelmed by anxiety of events in the external field, were concerned that the meeting between the national identities inside the group as well as outside would create a painful struggle. Hence, they expressed joint preference for a meeting clear of any national identity in order to prevent pain, scare, and anxiety.

This incident of the poem was a much needed creative adjustment so that they would strengthen enough and develop enough self-support to hold them through *their moments of meeting with difference and the different.* The negative energy was aimed at the facilitators; there was almost no expression of hostility to the members. The facilitators were the object of all projections that demanded a huge amount of strength from facilitators and participants and endless attempts to understand why during dialogue and growth. They also required responses from one another on questions such as, *What were we supposed to do? Were we on the right path?*

After a considerable effort, the group was composed. Then off it went through dialogue on a mutual journey, the end of which no participant or trainer knew beforehand. A Palestinian-Israeli dialogic group currently is like a long period of treatment after having given birth to a damaged baby. The two facilitators are the parents of a sick child.

A Silver Ribbon

Another intriguing moment involved the incident of a silver ribbon. The spontaneity did not involve the perpetrator of the event as much as it did the other participants and the facilitators. The group had just started, a minute had passed, and one of the facilitators invited the entire group to open with a personal dialogue. Another minute or two of silence passed. Suddenly, Shaul got up, pulled a silver ribbon out of his pocket, and stood staring at the facilitators.

The silence continued. Shaul started to surround his fellow participants and threaded the ribbon between the group members and the facilitators, and then around them, creating a web of ribbon between everyone in the room. The sensation was of being trapped in a web, tied to a chair, tied to the group, and tied to its phenomenology. Giggling started and then reactions of surprise.

The group members encouraged Shaul with no objection. Shaul, once he finished his mission, exclaimed, "I'm not pleased with what's happening in this group. There are too many divisions, alienation and negative feeling that I feel. I would have liked people to come closer to one another. We are all human beings. I am pessimistic about this group and have even considered leaving. I debated seriously whether to arrive here today or not."

A Greek chorus was spontaneously created, expressing, even singing, its discontentment and disappointment with how the content of the day's group was developing: as if to say, "This is not the meeting we anticipated!" as they pointed a finger at the facilitators.

The following meeting started again with an open invitation to personal dialogue. We were wondering whether some of the participants would recapture the experience of the last meeting and share their feelings about it. But that was not to be. Their feelings deflected into other directions, but eventually, even so, a group resolution was reached, resulting in greater, memorable cohesion. That encounter went something like this:

Shalom (male Jew): "I left the previous meeting disappointed and frustrated. I came here with a lot of good intentions to meet Arab friends, learn and hear what they are saying. I think that I, myself, and the rest of the Jewish group members show empathy and understanding to the Arab side, even though they speak about tough things and they express difficult things that are hard for me to understand, like an empathy with terror. But we don't hear any understanding or get any listening or empathy from the Arab group towards our story."

Fadia (female Arab): "You will never understand what we are talking about! The Arab situation is much more difficult. Do you have any idea what it is like to arrive here, to the Hebrew University, from Ramallah, a Palestinian city, or not to sleep at night because of bombs? What the hell are you talking about?!"

Umayma (female Arab): "Enough! This discussion will take us nowhere. From meeting to meeting I feel we miss the point. I came in order to make theatre and to meet people, and we are not doing it."

The feeling in the room was generally that there was wall-to-wall agreement with what Umayma had said, and there was general desperation on the facilitators' side. But then:

Shalom (male Jew): "Let's do something else; let's take responsibility for what's happening here."

Dina (female Jew): "Maybe every meeting somebody will take responsibility to lead an activity."

Galit (female Jew): "We need to ask the facilitators, maybe it's impossible"

Shalom (male Jew): "There is no reason for the facilitators to object, we have the right to do it."

Irit (female Jew): "I suggest meditation"

Dina (female Jew): "Cool."

All group members agreed with the direction the conversation was now going and seemed enthusiastic. A spirit of elation took over from the gloom. They discussed whether their facilitators would agree to their plan or not. We joined in on this pacified moment, enabling this spirit of the meeting, and became part of it through allowing the group to experiment with a different experience of crowning a new leader, so to speak, for they accepted Ella's recommendation that we meditate.

The group meditated in silence for a few minuets, and was rather satisfied with itself. Then silence descended once again. Stuckness, as we say, seemed to be where we were now. There seemed to be no new suggestions forthcoming. Confusion seeped in. Eyes once again turned towards the facilitators. Even though the open declarations were about the wish to create theatre and to speak through it, in reality objections appeared also during the theatrical activity later on. There was a gap between fantasy and reality.

However, objections here weren't that primal and fundamental, but suggested a difficulty to connect to the language in the room that was beginning to expose their feelings about the content of the theatrical mission, as their sense of an emerging script was connected to the Palestinian-Israeli conflict. There was no getting around the conflict they brought with them on the first day.

The emerging script provided every Jew and Arab in the group a setting to present and to expose their feelings, values, and ways of coping. It was possible to witness the theatre as a road bypassing dangerous areas and direct conflict, enabling us to continue a less dangerous journey.

A less dangerous journey, of course, was an objective of ours, but one built on communal spiritedness, not communal avoidance. The following is an example for an interpersonal meeting between two individuals from the two different subgroups. It is a part of a theatrical presentation by a Jewish and an Arab female participant.

Dialogue between Identities

Suddenly out of the darkness of the room, an Arab participant comes on stage. She was a slim woman, who hardly ever talked before, and did not appear to be very eloquent at first. She presented to us a girl memorizing the multiplication table: "Eight times one is eight, eight times two is sixteen, eight times three is twenty four, eight times four thirty two, eight times five forty, eight times six -- eight times six …. My father cannot tolerate or hear the number forty-eight. Do you know why?" she asks us in anguish. ("1948 is the year of the war of independence in Israel," a translator comments).

"Mum once said to Dad," she continues: 'Abu Ali, I got you trousers, size 48. Do they suit you?' Do you know what happened? He grabbed the pants and threw them out the window! I cannot forget that day! I ran to the window looked down and saw someone taking the pants. Ever since that time, my dad lies in bed without pants, naked. It is forbidden to wear pants size 48. Forbidden to wear shoes size 48. Forbidden to celebrate his 48th birthday, this year! Le ' esh ("why" in Arabic, translator?) 'Why does Dad behave like this?' I asked the doctors. One day I looked and found his diary."

She Read From the Diary:

"'The year 1948, the place Dir Yassin. The time – a disaster. That day mama was hugging me and the hug started to move away from me. Mama, Mama, what are you holding in your hand? Mama, who are the strangers? Why are there dead bodies, what are you holding? You are hugging a pillow instead of me! I started to cry, my tears rose from one Arab village, which was damaged by the Israelis, to the next.'" (He enumerated the names of the villages in his diary, the translator explained to us through her narrative.) "Since then my father sleeps without pants and without a pillow."

Overwhelming clapping and excitement broke out when she ended her monolog. It was a surprising and astonishing event. This almost muted young woman finally felt able to talk in the group. We witnessed that day that a sensation of understanding was created even for an Arab girl who talked haltingly in her language about the Palestinian villages that they were destroyed.

Another meeting between differences happened when a religious Jewish woman wearing a white dress, her head covered with a scarf, came onto the stage: yet again a very quiet participant, we observed.

She started to sing the Anthem of the State of Israel. Her face expressed the endless journey of the Jews as she sang the pain and the Jewish distress, for *Hatikva* (The Hope), the Anthem, contains more helplessness and pain than hope.

From the point of view of masculine conflict itself, these two feminist expressions would always seem weak and childlike; and soft rather than attacking, spiteful, and rigid. Yet these two women possessed for us the power to expose and to present the height of the conflict from personal, different experiences.

Emerging Cohesion

These two feminist pieces managed to penetrate the walls separating the two subgroups, and to land us safely in the enemy territory. The Arab participants testified that this was for them the first time ever that they could listen to the Jewish State Anthem and let go of their anger, hatred, and hurt because it was so Jewish, and did not therefore include them. For the first time they were able to connect and to understand, and not be bothered that were not included. They were open enough to understand the pain and distress of their other – the Jew.

The Jewish participants expressed the same sprit and sentiment after the Arab woman had narrated her father's entry in his diary about the Arab villages.

For us, the facilitators, this is the meaning of a dialogic relationship that we seek to instill in our group clients. There and then we felt as well as they, and understood, that a dialogue was born. The road to collaboration between the subgroups was paved. The rehearsals for the final presentation could commence. And we could now take our show on the road -- to Neve Shalom.

An Oasis of Peace

Neve Shalom (Oasis of Peace) is a village of both Jews and Arabs in the center of Israel. It is a place dedicated to the enhancement of peace and to proving that co-existence is both fertile and possible. In Neve Shalom, there is The School for Peace that is founded on the assumption that the conflict between Arabs and Jews is a conflict between two peoples of two national identities, and not between two individuals. We accept this assumption, although we claim that it doesn't provide a holistic enough explanation of the process leading to this conflict. Hence, those whose work for peace is based systematically on this assumption are conducting only a partial task of connecting the Israeli-Palestinian conflict to the concept of national identities.

We ourselves attempt to expand on this concept of national identities by suggesting that the motive behind inter-group conflict and national identity is connected to differing ethos, in each case, tied to psychological identities inherent in the different groups that, in turn, create a different group dynamic. Different psychological forces of identity impact the emergence of a differing dynamic. One of these different forces is national identity, but by it is by no means the only one. More forces exist in the Palestinian-Israeli etiology of conflict.

At the end of the day, all possible psychological forces together override mere national identity, generating either war or peace between geo-political national identities. We can see that this hypothesis accounts more forcefully for conflicts in the region when we broaden the field of observation to include groups of people of the region, or finer distinctions among groups, that we are not here concentrating on at this time, such as the Druze, Christians (Orthodox, Catholics, Protestants, Armenians), Jews (Orthodox, non-Orthodox, Sephardic, Ashkenazi), and Muslims (Shi'a, Sunni, Sufi).

At this stage of our group's journey, some of the participants *got off the bus*, so to speak, demurring, having chosen to stay behind; some, speaking metaphorically and psychologically, sat next to the door, and some found a seat way at the back. This is how *the bus of their attitude* left the station. Sometimes not very united, or much less jolly than at the beginning and therefore more apprehensive, our group was nonetheless going on a journey. They were now a lot more sober and realistic; the optimistic part stemmed from the fact that at the end of the day they did choose to travel. By now the contact among participants in the group was a bit closer to each individual's awareness. They had, after all, decided on a common activity of their own choosing.

Our fellow travelers on the bus included Arabs communally preoccupied with thinking about their home, or that of their neighbors or other family members, that had been demolished; missing it, longing for it, and being very angry at the Jews whom they saw as responsible for the destruction. Our fellow travelers also included a few Jews, Ashkenazi Jews, individualistic in their turmoil about their own personal, psychological issues.

At this, our eighth session of the group workshop, in Neve Shalom it was possible for us to observe the beginnings of a connection within the group as a whole to their multiple identities through the psychological dynamic of the Arab sub-group. When we observed this connection taking shape, we started the theatre exercises with relaxation exercises and guided imagery about *one's home*. The relaxation guided us towards objects, smells, colors, and other content of one's house called home. Every participant was requested to choose one object from the house that would tell its own story. Afterwards, Arabs and Jews created a mutual scene under the inspiration of the objects.

The Arabs connected to their nationality, while the Jews spoke as individuals. The Jewish group had a house and it was busy exploring feelings inside the home: frustration, restlessness, and interpersonal matters. The Arab group chose one story expressing longing for *house* and *home*. For the Arabs, *house* and *home* were conflated as a single concept and principle.

The theatrical presentation of the Jews was what we would call a host's show presented for a guest audience in mind, and included personal interviews of the participants in it. For example, we learned that *A's* home evoked the presence of people within it, and she searched for the people she loved. Four physical walls of a dwelling were not significant to her, she insisted. *S*, interested in ecology, narrated his story through the eyes of a plant in the garden outside of the house. *M* dealt with personal difficulties by narrating the life of a lawn surrounding a house, as it were the lawn that experiences difficulties when being stepped on. For Jews, *house* and *home* reflected clear, separate realities.

The Arab participants debated for the first time whether to present their performance in Hebrew or in Arabic and settled on Arabic. Keep in mind that the Jewish group on the whole didn't have a grasp of Arabic. In Arabic, they crystallized their narrative, all participating in the presentation of a single story. They narrated the history of a demolished village, as told by a picture of a grandfather, a candle, a cactus plant, and a sewing machine. At the end of this narrated meeting field, the Jews were empathic, struggling to ask for forgiveness. This was the point at which the Jewish participants became interested in their own identity both as Jews and as Israelis.

Dialogue on Common Ground

As facilitators, we aimed to assist both subgroups to swap their polarities so that Self and Other could become one, or at least find common ground. We encouraged the Israelis to connect to the components of their national identity, while the Arabs were supported to connect to each individual identity. We believed that to reach a dialogic relationship, the two subgroups had to travel through the experiences of each participant in order to visit the other's polarity, the less visited one. Awareness of the whole spectrum would allow for a fuller, more complete self definition, which, in turn, would enable a meeting on common ground -- a dialogue.

These polar starting positions between the Arabs and the Jews can be understood through a sociological lens focused on a major difference between a Western sensibility and an Eastern one. The Western orientation (which includes Ashkenazi Jews) encourages the individual to demand personal freedom and a personal identity, while the Eastern one (which includes Arabs,

Sephardic Jews, and religious Ashkenazi Jews) is still heavily encoded on the collective, tribal way of existing in the world.

The workshop attempt at a common dialogue started with a negotiation, when the participants turned to the facilitators, inquiring, *what shall we talk about?* The group as a whole struggled through *how shall we talk?* as a way of resisting responding themselves to their own first question. Then, finally, they arrived where they had begun: *What shall we talk about?*

An essential part of the negotiation was whether to address the personal or the national in relation to the Jewish/Israeli – Arab/Palestinian conflict and its history. At this stage the struggle was settled by the facilitators, because we pushed at this stage towards a national dialogue between the two subgroups, trusting that it would enable a more open and authentic interpersonal one on their psychological differences.

Facing One Another's Polarity

"If this is what you want," the Jews threw at the group and the facilitators, "this is what you'll get!" They then put openly on the table the terrorist actions, the violence, and the suicide bombers.

The group, finally, had arrived at the phenomenology of two camps facing one another. The Jews accepted the direction they were being drawn toward, and looked squarely at the history of injustice felt by the Arabs. The militant leader of the Arab subgroup, who was waiting for this opportunity to present oneself, railed on about the military occupation, the blocked villages, and the road blockades.

At the height of the argument, one of the Arabs pulled a rabbit out of his hat: "You – you had Holocaust done to you, and now you are doing a Holocaust to us!" This was a common, repeated argument in every group we have run, always evoked by the Holocaust Memorial Day in Israel. This common retort entails the thrust of a jest about the national conflict. It provokes rage in Jews staggered by this jest, who perceive this comparison as unacceptable.

This process repeats itself in every group. Finally, some one member of each subgroup will lead the group into a conversation. At the end of this painful, heated, rough meeting, the Jewish group turns into a nationalistic group with a sense of unity – the common denominator being Judaism, external threat, feelings of terror, hopelessness, and then the hope of finding rest as Jews in a country safe to them. The Arabs move in the other direction. Their group, which starts out as united and nationalistic, comes to understand that entrenched difference is not always the right way.

As a result of the strengthening of the Jews who are now closer to one another because of the retort of the Arabs, the Arabs now experience a sense that their original stance will only evoke violence. The Arabs start to feel some guilt. No one denies at some point during a dialogue that it is fascinating to witness the experience of what happens when they take upon themselves each other's stance/polarity.

At this stage the participants who stressed their Jewish and Israeli identity get more power and space. They now feel freed-up and more committed to presenting on stage short pieces that express who they are where they are.

The Arabs/Palestinians lose some of the empathy and the compromise offered earlier by the Jews, their sense of being right now somewhat shaken. Pacified voices that were earlier muted are now coming alive. The militant expression among them and those who hang on to it are now left aside. A space for left wing, liberal leaders from both subgroups opens up. For the first time there is a dialogue in the room about compromise.

The danger, at this stage, is that the Israeli group will continue to move in the direction of rightwing nationality and become stronger as a group to a degree in which it will close down to the option of a dialogic relationship with the Palestinians. The danger on the Arab side is that they will give up totally on their inner-group alliance and surrender to the Jews, in attempt to be 'good and exemplary Arabs' and keep away from trouble.

In spite of the negative experience they went through, their test here is to be able to continue to hold on to their individual, group, and sub-group rights and to talk about their pain, while being able also to hold the personhood of the other in view and to give space to their difference. The demands on the Jewish side is that even though they are compared to the Nazis at this moment, and hear explanations of the Muslim Shahids (the suicide bombers), they will remain open to a dialogue between their and the Arabs' identities.

Conclusion

In a country where real buses often explode and don't arrive to their peaceful destination, the ultimate test for our journeying, conflictual sub-groups is whether they can avoid expected violent outcomes and collaborate to create a show to be presented to an audience.

The show is the last stop of the group's journey. At the last stop, we examine who stayed -- How many Arabs? How many Jews? – and, Who left? Did the Jews and Arabs get off the bus of their newly emerging psychology from the same door and go together onto the stage?

At the end of each show, there is a dialogue between the audience and the actors. As during the process of group work, the audience's reactions vary.

Some condemn the group as a whole by highlighting the Palestinian narrative. All in all, however, we end up with an authentic show. The actors have had a chance to share their intimacy with the audience. Hence, they have become ambassadors of their belief in the bridging of difference through dialogue.

In our experience, the unique contribution of the mix between theatre performance and group facilitation allows introspection and the development of the awareness and insight of the question of "Why do I act like I act?" Performance and facilitation also function as a tool for deep personal and group work, including personal and group expression, release and empowerment – all forming a gestalt in group and certainly during the time spent standing on stage in front of an audience. Furthermore, we think that the mix and the integration between the interior monologue and the exterior dialogue, along with the examination and acknowledgement of the internal parts and the external expression, create a more whole and complete experience that establishes change and strengthens it.

The schools of psychology in general, and the dynamic and psychoanalytic ones in particular, send the person inward into the labyrinth of his or her soul and try to assist the client in cracking the neurotic code of actions and experiences. We think that this is a complicated task (some would say impossible) and unnatural. Through theatre and role play, however, we return to the natural and basic means of human expression in which a person puts on a variety of masks and plays and acts out self. The personal and group expression through sound, movement, and imagery expands one's ability to observe and allows one to bypass the walls of defense, objection, and deflection. Likewise, it allows the expression of areas that are unconscious and not readily available, all the while working through them in the group constellation. The option open to the members both to act and to watch their friends act, enables the experience of catharsis.

Personal Account

During the years we worked together as an Arab and a Jew, and as co-facilitators of cross-cultural groups it was clear to us that we developed a specific model of working as we moved along. In coming to write this chapter we had to articulate our model in words, an undertaking that enabled us to observe our mutual disagreements and understandings of our model and work accordingly.

Co-writing was a journey in which we rediscovered the milestones we passed through in the years, and the picture of our journey suddenly became clearer and at the same time more complex. We had to re-ask ourselves the question of whether the groups we established contributed to effectively counseling cross-cultural groups and also address the inherent conflict they were created to bridge, i.e., the Palestinian-Israeli conflict, or whether they just intensify it. We realized that although we have assumed particular stations during our journey, each participant also interacted amongst both of our unique styles during the different phases of the counseling process. During the writing of this chapter, we re-lived the difficulties of establishing and guiding such a complex group. The process enabled us to refine very special and endearing moments, and revisit interesting people that touched us in a special way during our journey.

At first we were enthusiastic about the inter-personal interactions and its unlimited potential, which gave birth to a unique creation, along with the ability to achieve a mutual goal, i.e., bridging our two seemingly separate worlds. We revealed to each other some of the most intimate parts of our being, without knowing where this writing process would lead us to, and we also questioned whether we should focus on ourselves or on the group. Eventually we were both hurt and overwhelmed by intimidating feelings, resulting from an overpowering love-hate relationship, attraction and outright repulsion. This level of exposure and intimacy led each of us to close down before the other.

From that point, the focus of the subject matter shifted from us to the group, and we seldom sat down to write together. Thus, we felt protected from the process of writing and the feelings evoked in each of us as well as between us.

At the end of this co-writing process, we felt the beginning of a sobering maturation, alongside the naivety we shared at the start of writing this essay. Today we face the challenge of continuation. Where do we continue from here? Will our working relationship endure and improve? How can we evolve together from this seemingly interpersonal stalemate? Despite our growing and sobering up of our phenomenological fields coupled with the narrowing of the passion in our souls, we both feel very connected to this "baby" and will continue to cultivate this project, even though our external environment surrounding both of us is so frustrating.

Sa'ed Tali, Lod, Israel
Oshrat Mizrahi Shapira, Ra'anana, Israel

References

Allport G. W. (1954). *The Nature of Prejudice*. Reading, MA: Addison-Wesley.

Back, K.W. (1972). *Beyond Words*, Baltimore: Penguin Books.

Benne, K.D., Bradford, L.D., Gibb, J.R, and Lippitt R.O. (Eds.) (1975). *The Laboratory Method of Changing and Learning*, Palo Alto: Science and Behavior Books.

Boal, Augusto (1981). *Poeticas of the Oppressed, Theater of the Oppressed*, Theater Communications Group. New York, 1985.

Buber, M., (1981) *Besod Sia'ch Jerusalem*: Mossad Bialik.

Burton, J.W. (1969). *Conflict and Communication: The Use of Controlled Communication in International Relations*, London: MacMillan.

Cahanov, Maya and Katz, Israel (1980). A Survey of Dilemmas in Guidance of Dialog Groups Between Jews and Arabs in Israel, *Megamot*, 29-47.

Kecman, J.E. (1979). An international approach to conflict resolution and its application to Israeli-Palestinian relations, *International Interactions*, Vol. 6, No. 2, 99-122.

Kelman, H. C. (1979). An interactional approach to conflict resolution and its application to Israeli-Palestinian relations. *International Interactions, 6 (2), 99-122.*

Lev-Algem, Shulamit and First, Anat (2000). The circle of fringe: from community theater to mass communications, *Kesher*, 28, 82-94.

Pettigrew, T. F. (1998). Intergroup contact theory. *Annual Review of Psychology*, 49, 65-85. New Haven, Conn: Yale University Press.

Steinberg, S. (2002). *Typology for Discourse Classification in Conflict Groups, in Group Dynamics in a Multi-Cultural Society*. Lea Cassan, Rachel Bar-*Ziv eds., Cherikover, Tel-Aviv, 65-74.*

Triandis, H.C. (1983). *Essentials of Studying Cultures, Handbook of Inter-Cultural Training*, D. Landis and R. Brislin (Eds.), New York: Elmsford.

Section Three

bridging the interpersonal

X. THE GIFT

By Mark McConville, Ph.D.

Introduction

Several years ago, I sent a gift to a new friend. We had met at a Gestalt writers' conference, and she had been very supportive and generous with her feedback. I wanted to say thank you, and hit upon the perfect way to do so. We shared, it turned out, an affection for baseball, and I could think of no more perfect gift than a baseball cap representing my home town team, the Cleveland Indians. It's a terrific looking hat, I thought to myself, with the smiling red face of Chief Wahoo, the team's mascot and logo, looking out from above the brim. I bought the hat and sent it on its way, and then enjoyed that feeling of inner warmth that comes when you have found the perfect gift, and given it straight from the heart. I was pleased with myself.

Weeks passed, and then several months, and I heard nothing back from my friend, which perplexed me. When you give a gift from the heart, you like to know how it is received. And then finally, after three months, came her note. Thoughtfully written, carefully, even affectionately worded, it concluded "and so, even though I know you sent this gift with the best intentions, I cannot bring myself to accept an article whose logo is so offensive and demeaning to so many Native American Indians. I hope you can understand."

Understand? UNDERSTAND? Hell no, I don't understand. I sent you a gift, a thank-you, not a political treatise. Whatever Chief Wahoo symbolizes to you, to us Clevelanders he's a symbol of civic pride, a baseball team and a community that has come back from the ashes. I resent being re-cast from a caring friend to an insensitive bigot. I'm angry, and hurt, and No, I don't understand.

More than anything, I was bewildered. Yes, bewildered. That's exactly the right word, especially because as my initial reaction began to fade, I became aware of a nagging, uncomfortable itch on the underside of my awareness. I recalled seeing the American Indian protesters outside the stadium during the Baseball World Series, with their placards reading "We're a People, Not a Mascot." And I remember my discomfort then, knowing in my heart they were right.

WIW Bewilderment

In the politico-socio-racial subset to which I have assigned myself, Well-Intending-Whites (WIWs), this experience of bewilderment is not entirely uncommon. I have had the experience before, and have heard it described by other WIWs. In its typical form, it goes something like this: Some sort of social situation is unfolding: a conversation, perhaps a group session, a faculty meeting, a parent conference. People are interacting with one another, and the interaction seems to be going along fine. People are making sense, perceptions are being expressed, ideas articulated, differences are being aired. And then someone, inevitably a Person of Color, brings up race as an issue, a current issue, present in the room as we speak. "You wouldn't be saying/doing that if I were White..." the person might be saying. Racism is here, I'm being told. But I am bewildered, because I don't see it.

This experience of bewilderment, I believe, admits of two components. The first is some degree of defensiveness, often fueled by anger or hurt at the implication of bigotry. It may be openly expressed, or may be silently harbored. It can take various forms, but usually includes a perception of the offended other as overly sensitive, and therefore as responsible for being offended.

Why are they making such a big deal over a logo, when the real issues -- jobs, education, political representation -- would be more legitimate targets of their energy. For heaven's sake, I don't get bent out of shape over that insulting Notre Dame University logo that depicts us Irish as angry, brawling midgets. I could get upset every time someone alludes to us Irish as rigid, or combative, or alcoholic, but I choose not to. Why do they choose instead to be offended?

This defensiveness is often supported and bolstered by some sort of comparison, inevitably unfavorable, to one's own reference group. And it is here, it seems to me, in this space of bewildered defensiveness, that White experience often closes down. This is the familiar stopping place, where subjectively at least, people are inclined to throw their hands in the air, shake their heads, and walk away. It is essential, I think, that we recognize this, and that we become more public about our struggles to push through the stuckness to a fuller awareness of what happens at the racial boundary. And at least one way to do this, as a White, is to stay more fully with the experience of bewilderment, to hold it open to the scrutiny of examination.

For bewilderment contains a second component hidden within its folds, a component less clear and more deeply embedded in the ground of the experience. It is a vague disquiet, a confusion. It is a sense of something in my ground, just beyond the borders of my awareness, something I may be missing. It is a dawning sense of my own ignorance, and with that, a realization that I am not as innocent as my good intentions claim. Beyond my intentions, there is an impact of my behavior on others, and an uncomfortable realization that I'm not owning enough responsibility for that impact, and worse yet, that I am not owning up to my responsibility for this ignorance.

These half formed awarenesses are fueled by my knowledge that bigotry indeed exists, that it is all around us, that it permeates the air we breathe. It is, in other words, the simultaneous prehension of my innocence and my guilt, my non-racist intentionality and my immersion, and participation, in an atmosphere saturated with inequity and bias. This is bewilderment.

Figure-Bound Experience

Confusion has always been a most powerful motivation for me, and I have been wrestling with the confusion of this, and similar, experiences, for years now. As a Gestalt therapist, my response to confusion lies with phenomenology, the careful description and explication of experience. Understanding the organization of an experience has always held the power to release me from its grip. It therefore, feels natural to turn to the tools of Gestalt therapy's phenomenological method in order to make sense of this bewilderment. In particular, as pointed out by Barbara Thomas (1997), the Gestalt notion of figure and ground is especially helpful in understanding the nature and power of "ism" experience.

In the earliest research and theory of Gestalt psychology, ground was shown to exert powerful, silent contextualizing forces on aware, figural perception. This principle has been demonstrated experimentally at every level of experience, from the simplest forms of visual ground to the most complex phenomena of cultural and historical context. In every case, ground serves to shape figural perception, and to do so in a manner that co-constitutes the apparent properties of the figure itself.

In a laboratory situation, when an upright focal object is placed within a tilted framework, it will eventually appear mis-oriented itself, relative to the orientation of the context. The more the framework itself is out of awareness, that is, the more it becomes an invisible organizing aspect of ground, the more dramatic the figure's mis-orientation becomes.

The effects of ground, in other words, are intensified as they recede qua ground and are collapsed onto figure. Another way to say this is that when ground is silent, invisible, figure ends up bearing the weight of ground, in so far as a perceiver attributes to figure the forces emanating from context. When a painting in a gallery is given just the right frame, and the lighting and location are perfect, it is the painting itself that gets the credit, while these contextual influences remain hidden from the untrained eye.

Blaming the Victim

The effects of this simple principle in everyday perception are everywhere, and nowhere more dramatic than where matters of culture and race are concerned. One example that comes to mind is the death of Edmund Perry in 1985. Perry, an eighteen-year old African American youth, grew up on the mean streets of Harlem; but in spite of this, he had attended, on scholarship, the nation's most prestigious prep school, Phillips Exeter. In the summer of 1985, about a month after graduating with honors from Phillips Exeter, with the world at his feet and full scholarship offers from Yale, Berkeley, and Stanford in hand, Edmund Perry was shot and killed while robbing a New York City undercover police officer.

I remember the reactions of several of my White friends at the time: This kid had everything, opportunities the rest of us only dream of. How could he make such a stupid decision. What was he thinking?

There is a tendency for Whites, taking for granted our ground conditions of empowerment and support, to focus exclusively on the figural phenomena of choice, personal decision-making, and individual opportunity. Like the subjects in the tilted framework experiments who lose awareness of context, we tend unconsciously to collapse ground onto figure. In other words, when evaluating the likes of Edmund Perry, we are inclined to psychologize the sociological ground, to interpret its organizing influences as emanating solely from the individual person. We remain simultaneously ignorant of the powerful influence of his ground in shaping his options and possibilities, and ignorant of the disorienting effects of our own ground in shaping our perception and evaluation of him.

To evaluate Edmund Perry out of context, as if his fateful, mis-guided choice that day were nothing more than a matter of individual choice and decision making, is to heap upon the figure, in this case, a young man who may as well have journeyed from his home in Harlem to the Moon, the extraordinarily complex and convoluted weight of ground. And ground, in this case, included the invisible effects on this young man of becoming an outsider simultaneously in an alien, racially hierarchical culture, and on the streets of his own neighborhood. When we miss the ground from which such decisions arise -- and let's face it, as Whites, we miss it all the time -- we are prone to amplify the role of figure in organizing the field, and this creates a skew in our thinking and perception.

Horatio Alger

I'm proud of my success. I had to overcome a lot to get where I am today. I saw the opportunity, and I made the most of it. My parents were both second generation Irish Catholics whose ancestors arrived in this country in flight from the Great Famine and Anglo-Protestant oppression. My ancestors were virtually penniless when they arrived, and had made a life for themselves by dint of hard work and perseverance. I remember my father telling me that any man (sic) could make his way in life if only he took responsibility for himself, took hold of his bootstraps and pulled himself up. This is what he had done, and it was what he expected me to do.

Accordingly, when I look at my personal history, at my educational, occupational, and economic accomplishments, I am inclined to see them as psychological, rather than as sociological or historical phenomena. My accomplishments seem to me the consequences of personal choice and hard work, matters of figure in other words, not ground. The problem with this line of thinking is not that it is false (because it is not simply false), but precisely that it is figure-bound, which is to say, blind to the silent contextual factors which either support or impede achievement.

Harlon Dalton (1995) has spoken of this type of thinking as exemplifying the myth of Horatio Alger, the author whose stories celebrated the rags to riches opportunities of American life. The myth, Dalton points out, conveys three basic messages: first, that we are all judged on the basis of merit. Second, that everyone has an equal opportunity to succeed. And third, that life is ultimately fair, if only one is willing to work at it. It is not difficult to see why this myth appeals to those of us in this culture who operate from a ground of support and empowerment. Like plants whose roots soak up the nutrients of their surroundings, we blossom and fulfill our potential. To the extent that we have done so, and being blind to the influences of ground, we tend to exaggerate our personal responsibility for our development.

Both of these situations, that is, blaming the victim, and buying into the Horatio Alger myth of success, share the same perceptual distortion of collapsing (thereby denying) the effects of ground into figure, and holding figure responsible for factors which far exceed its intrinsic being and behavior.

Figure Bearing the Weight of Ground

Recently, I attended a diversity workshop where a fellow student, a white woman, inadvertently confused the names of two African American women also participating in the workshop. The White woman was sharply rebuked by the woman whose name she misspoke, who pointed out that she had spent a lifetime of invisibility in a culture where Whites often do not see Blacks in their individuality. The White woman hung her head in shame, and slowly dissolved into tears.

Was she guilty of failing to see the other women in the full dignity of their individual identities, of reducing them, in racist fashion, to perceptual categories? This was the spontaneous interpretation of her behavior acknowledged by many people in the room. But was this interpretation an accurate assessment of her individual personhood? I think not. Her participation up to and following that moment was exemplary for Whites wishing to do the work of diversity, a model of open-mindedness and authenticity. And in her wider life (I happen to know this woman fairly well), she doggedly lives out her commitment to these principles.

So how are we to understand this momentary transaction, this "blooper," (as the leaders of the workshop labeled it)? Certainly this white woman did not deserve rebuke. Does this mean that the African American woman was over-reacting, making something out of nothing? Some people might be inclined to say so. But if we write off the offended woman's challenge as an over-reaction, are we guilty of minimizing and rationalizing the cultural sediment of racism? Some people might be inclined to say so. How are we to escape this conundrum of interpretation?

It seems to me that when Whites and People of Color come together to do this work, to interact and learn in contexts of openness and vulnerability -- then moments such as this are inevitable. And in these moments, it is figure which does, and indeed must, bear the weight of ground. It is the momentary interaction, innocent by itself, which picks up the embedded forces of ground, invisible in their own right, gathering and reflecting them as a lens gathers and focuses diffuse ambient light. We could argue the correct interpretation of the White woman's behavior, but that would be to miss the point.

The point is that we Americans live in a culture and in a history where our ground is shot through with the sediment of racism. And as Ralph Ellison (1994) showed so brilliantly, this ground has conspired to deprive African Americans of their visibility, to reduce them to a nameless, faceless They. And however innocent a figural behavior, it is always from this ground that its full meaning emerges. Our bloopers are not so much to be defended and rationalized as they are to be accepted as opportunities to make ground visible.

What To Do?

As a white person, I have struggled to identify in concrete terms what I need to do to dis-embed myself from the ground into which I was born. And my objectives in doing so are more than a little self-serving, for I am convinced that any system of privilege not only oppresses the disenfranchised, but poisons the spirit and diminishes the humanity of those who are advantaged.

Like many people, I keep a personal journal. Over the years, I have written to myself on this subject of race and racism, attempting to define the concrete nature of my personal work to be done in this area. Though I am naturally reluctant to share thinking that reveals my ignorance, my occasional bewilderment, and, indeed, my ground of privilege, it seems worth the risk. But in advance I feel compelled to admit that I am more than a little embarrassed at my own naiveté, and know full well that many readers are miles ahead of my personal learning curve. Following are some of my notes to myself, culled from my journal, and edited slightly for the present context.

Learn to See the Invisible

As a White man, many of the problems of empowerment have been solved, both by me at the level of figural existence, but more importantly, for me by the ground-tradition into which I was born. Power achieved, at least for the well-intending, is power forgotten, power which has receded to ground, power which has become invisible as an organizing context of perception. This is true in any interpersonal field. If you want to know where the power is, or, more importantly, where it isn't, don't ask those who have it. Ask those who don't. Children, for example, often have a much more accurate perception of where the power exists and how it is used in a family system than do their parents. They know what they can and what they can't get away with, far more accurately than do the adults in the system.

The same thing obtains in larger levels of system; in our culture and society at large, for example, where race is concerned. The eventual product of this sort of figure-bound enculturation is that, whatever its intentionality, it spawns for the empowered an ignorance of racism as a structure of ground. And in so far as I permit myself to remain confluent with my ignorance, as long as I fail to push myself to see the ground structures of my and others' experience, I am part of the problem.

Explore the Historical Ground

An educated reader, I am embarrassed to admit, for all of the reading I do, that I have read relatively little history concerning the development and perpetuation of racism in America. My historical knowledge has been about on par with the average ninth grader. I knew the American Civil War ended over a hundred years ago when the Northern states (the Good Guys) freed the slaves (the Unfortunate Victims) from the Southern states (the Bad Guys). I was relieved to be part of the good guy camp (I recall my parents speaking proudly of our hometown, the Lake Ontario port of Rochester, New York, as an integral part of the Underground Railroad that sent escaped slaves to Canada).

What I didn't know, or perhaps had forgotten, was the extent to which White America systematically conspired to keep free Blacks "in their place" during the years both preceding and following the Civil War. When a Black artisan class of skilled workers emerged in the mid 1800's, in the time when American labor was beginning to organize itself, systematic (and successful) efforts were made to deprive them of the opportunity to practice their trades (Ignatiev, 1995). This is just one small example, but what shocks me the most is the extent of my own complacent ignorance of historical ground, in light of the fact that it is precisely this sort of ignorance that fuels the blaming the victim mentality of so many White Americans.

Learn the Meaning of Being White

As a White man living in a White culture, the meaning of my race has been largely invisible to me. The feminist historian, Peggy McIntosh, has challenged this colorblind myopia successfully with her description of white privilege (McIntosh, 1989). McIntosh writes, reflecting an experience that is common among WIWs, that she had become accustomed to seeing the various ways that People of Color are dis-advantaged in this culture. But then it occurred to her to reverse the figure-ground organization of her experience: "As a white person, I realized I had been taught about racism as something that puts others at a disadvantage, but had not been taught to see one of its corollary aspects, white privilege, which puts me at an advantage," she writes.

I recently had a simple experience that highlighted for me the blindness of Whites to White privilege. Together with an African-American colleague, I was facilitating a diversity roundtable discussion with the faculty of a school where I consult. The participants included fifteen teachers, fourteen of whom were White, one of whom was African-American. In the course of the discussion, one participant raised the following provocative, hypothetical question: If each person had to choose between changing their gender or their race, which would you change? The participants wrestled uncomfortably with the dilemma, agreeing that this was a most provocative and difficult question. Except for the African American woman, who stated flatly "For me, that's an easy question. I'd choose to be White." An embarrassed silence fell over the group. "But why?" asked one of the White participants finally, adding, "You seem so proud, so confident, as a Black woman." "It has nothing to do with pride," she answered. "Why would anyone choose to stay perpetually in the one-down position?" (Of course, the same statement could be made across the gender boundary, but this apparently was not the point she wished to make.)

In the silent moment that followed, the obvious was revealed to me. As well-intending Whites, we were thinking, "You [singular] are as good as we." As a minority, she was saying, "You [plural] have advantages we don't have." Specifically, as well-intending Whites, we miss the forest of racial inequity for the trees of our individual good intentions. In the card game of life (if I may permit myself such an analogy), I have no difficulty making a space at the table for a Person of Color, and for regarding that person with the respect and honor he or she deserves. I am likewise comfortable enough speaking up and challenging other Whites at the table who would seek to bar that individual from the game, or conspire to deal them fewer cards than the rest of us. But I am pained and ashamed to admit that despite my good intentions, the deck itself is stacked in my favor. But this is undeniably the case, and it is time for me to say so.

This realization comes painfully to me, particularly in light of my own cultural and racial heritage. My people were Ulster Catholics, and before they fled the Irish famine of the mid 1800s, had lived under as harsh an economic and civil enslavement as the Western world has ever known. According to Ignatiev (1995), "Eighteenth-century Ireland presents a classic case of racial oppression. Catholics there were known as native Irish, Celts, or Gaels (as well as 'Papists' and other equally derogatory names), and were regarded, and frequently spoke of themselves, as a 'race,' rather than a nation."

Indeed, the historian W.E.H. Lecky had noted that "the most worthless Protestant, if he had nothing else to boast of, at least found it pleasing to think that he was a member of the dominant race" (Ignatiev, 1995). And as a race, Irish Catholics were systematically deprived of every human right imaginable by their Anglo-Protestant oppressors, eventually surrendering a million of their numbers to genocidal starvation in 1846-50.

When they arrived in this country, my ancestors were by no means "White," because in that era White privilege was extended only to those of Anglo-Saxon, Protestant heritage. Irish Catholics, particularly the desperately poor immigrants of the famine years, were reviled and excluded from the body politic. Together with free Blacks, they occupied the bottom rung of the socio-economic ladder. (One common racial slur of the era was to call Blacks "smoked Irish" and black-faced minstrel shows sometimes denigrated African Americans as "no better than common Irishmen.")

The immigrant famine Irish, having themselves been the victims of relentless and cruel racial oppression, should have been natural allies of America's oppressed free Blacks and slaves. Indeed, the great Irish leader Daniel O'Connell orchestrated a potent appeal to all Irish Americans to join forces with Black Americans on behalf of their freedom and dignity. Treat them, he wrote "as your equals, as brethren. By your memories of Ireland, continue to love liberty, hate slavery.... and in America you will do honor to the name of Ireland" (Ignatiev, 1995: 10).

But it wasn't to be. The Irish turned their backs, and, even worse, their boot heels on America's Blacks, climbing over them as they clawed their way up the racial ladder. In the end, the Irish became White, and in so doing, re-located the color boundary to roughly its present day position. As a race, my people were given an opportunity to change the face of America for centuries to come. And we blew it. This is not the sort of history I enjoy reading. It is not what I want to teach my children and grand children. But read it and teach it I must.

Don't Overestimate the Importance of Good Intentions

In those situations where I have witnessed a Person of Color become offended by well-intended White behavior, my first impulse has always been to focus on the innocence of the intentions. In the case of Chief Wahoo, the Cleveland baseball logo, I detect no intention to malign or demean. Its meaning, for those of us who count ourselves among Cleveland's baseball fans, has more to do with civic pride, with our city's recent history as the butt of national jokes, now rebutted as our team, like the city itself, fights back and establishes itself among the winners.

But good intentions, I am quickly learning, are not enough. And in so far as they blind me to the impact of my behavior on the other, good intentions are indeed part of the problem. Every behavior is defined by its intentionality and its impact, and the impact of my behavior on the other is every bit as real as the intentionality with which it is launched. Whenever I find myself bewildered by someone's response to an action of mine, it is because I am blind to the ground of their experience. My advice to myself here is simple: get interested in the impact, particularly when it surprises me.

Don't Underestimate the Importance of Good Intentions

The other side of this coin is that if I am going to wade into the sensitized field of diversity, of gender and race and sexual orientation, and particularly as a white male, my good intentions are the only thing I can count on, the only thing that dis-embeds me from the racist, sexist, heterosexist ground into which I was born. I have met too many entitled, empowered Whites without good intentions to believe for one minute that good intentions don't count for something. My advice to myself: hold on to my good intentions for dear life. There will be moments when they are all I will have to keep me from drowning.

Talk to Other Whites

I have discovered in myself the curious tendency to turn to People of Color for support in my own work around the diversity issue. It usually takes the form of a silent request for acknowledgement and confirmation that I am on the right track. And from time to time, I have encountered a response, usually politely offered, which says in essence, "This is your work; you figure it out." It has dawned on me recently that Whites don't talk enough with other Whites about these issues, that we become cognizant of diversity concerns only when there is a Person of Color somewhere in the field. But this isn't right, clearly, if we are truly committed to the work. My advice to myself: promote White on White dialog about racism and diversity issues. We must do our part of the Work, and this includes offering and giving support for this business of making ground visible.

Remember the Wisdom of Gestalt

I have wasted a lot of my own energy trying to "do it right" when interacting at the color boundary. I've labored under the illusion that if I try hard enough, if I am attentive enough, I can avoid the sins of our racist society. I am beginning to see that this is nonsense, and it is nonsense because it flies in the face of Gestalt wisdom. Gestalt therapy tells us that the road to change is through heightened awareness of what we already are. I have found myself, like so many of my therapy clients, trying to make myself into something better than what I am before cultivating a rich awareness of what I am to start with. My advice to myself: the work is not, paradoxically, to make myself a paragon of racial blindness; the work is to discover how I participate, and how I have participated, in the racist culture that blinds me.

The Gift

So I am now ready to complete the circle. So long ago it seems that I sent that hat, and received that note, and found myself bewildered, hurt and angry by my friend's rejection of my gift. I would rather brush aside the incident, to leave it buried in my journal, than to reveal this whole business of discovering my participation in the racist structures of our common ground. But staying with experience, sifting it and making it public, has always proven itself the most powerful tool for growth. For isn't this what Gestalt Therapy, with its paradoxical theory of change, teaches us?

And bewilderment? Bewilderment, it seems to me, contains in miniature the very essence of this phenomenon -- WIW racism -- the blindness to the structures of ground, but also the seeds of curiosity that can lead us to uncover these same structures. Of course, this all seems obvious to me as I write this, and, as I said before, I am more than a little embarrassed by the labor required to see it. But so be it. This was my friend's gift to me, and for this I remain in her debt.

Personal Account

Writing this piece, *The Gift*, was wildly different from any other writing experience I have ever had. First of all, it is more a story than a piece of professional writing, and it is a very personal story at that. It began in the mid 90s, and emerged most directly from my experience at the Gestalt Institute of Cleveland, where I am a member of the faculty. At that time, we were, as an organization, beginning to deal head-on with tensions rippling throughout our community related to race relations. From time to time, students of color would speak about their experiences of racism and racial insensitivity within the training programs. I recall two recurrent themes in my own experience at the time. The first was that whenever I witnessed or was involved in one of these incidents, I couldn't see any racism at all. I privately felt, in most instances, that the students involved were deflecting away from their own growing edge issues by framing the interactions as racist. Crying "racism" seemed to me like playing a trump card that interrupted the process of examining ongoing contact process.

The second recurrent theme, and the one that most intrigued me was that I found myself completely unable to voice my experience openly. I was mute. Paralyzed. Why, I wondered? I began to explore my lack of voice in a series of conversations with Diane Nichols, an African American woman who was in my psychology practice at the time. Those conversations proved to be transforming for me, and led to the writing project that became The Gift. What

I came to realize was that I was locked in my individual, egoistic perspective, failing to grasp the wider context and the experiential point of view of the "Other." This failing, I soon realized, is the essential structure of racism. And I myself, I realized with a dawning sense of sickness and shame, participate in racism in spite of my intentions and beliefs to the contrary. This writing project was my therapy. It took me months to complete, and documents my journey from shame and defensiveness to ownership and openness. And with this shift, of course, I found my voice. I am honored to have this piece included in the present volume.

Post script: my writing was triggered by a very specific incident – a reply from a colleague informing me that in good conscience she could not accept a gift I had sent her, on account of it's racially offensive nature to American Indians. I have long admired this women for many reasons, but none more than her courage in making this reply. She is Lynne Jacobs.

Mark McConville, Cleveland, OH, USA

References

Dalton, Harlan (1995). *Racial Healing*. Doubleday, New York.

Ellison, Ralph (1994). *Invisible Man*. Random House, New York.

Ignatiev, Noel (1995). *How the Irish Became White*. Routledge, New York.

McIntosh, Peggy (1989). White Privilege: Unpacking the Invisible Knapsack, *Peace and Freedom*, July/August .

Thomas, Barbara (1997). *Integrating Multicultural Perspectives in Gestalt Therapy, Theory and Practice*. The Gestalt Institute of Cleveland Voice.

XI. "It's Greek to me!"

*By Edna Manielevitch,M.Sc. and
Talia Levine Bar-Yoseph, M.A.*

Introduction

"Its Greek to me!" is a common phrase describing a total lack of understanding of another's words, expressions, or explanations. This phrase became alive, actual, and literal for both of us when we were invited (on two different occasions) to train others in Greece.

How on earth can we train Greek-speaking people while speaking English, we wondered, however well spoken as a second language English as a medium would be? Training in Greece highlighted our awareness of the issue of cultural differences and of cultural gaps further than many other cross-cultural encounters we had ever experienced. Hence, this essay attempts to look at the special contribution Gestalt theory and practice possess when the trainer(s) and the trainees come together as a mixed cultural group.

What a context: Talia, on one occasion, Edna on another, in both cases the situation entailed an Israeli trainer whose mother tongue is Hebrew, training in English a group of Greeks who speak no English. Of course, there would be a translator who would translate everything both ways. But exactly how comforting would that be? How would we know that the translations would be exactly or in close proximity to what we would be relating?

We were already accustomed to a diversity of languages in our professional lives. English, Slovak, Czech, German -- all languages Talia had faced as a trainer, and Edna as a trainee -- are not all dead languages and have many sister languages in Europe. Israel, after all, is a country composed of numerous cultures; hence, an immigrant's land. So the Israeli ear is used to a Babel of sounds. Greek was this very ancient language. It was for us one of a kind and resembled no other language we knew. Ninety-nine percent of it was utterly foreign to us. We therefore had no linguistic familiarity to hook on to.

Working in such a context, where one of us had been the trainer from a different culture was for Edna the seminar in Greece; and for Talia, training seminars in Germany, and in Austria, and in the Slovak and the Czech Republics. We both, furthermore, have had experience working with Israeli Arabs; however, not as trainers. At this time, in this essay, we propose to look at the benefits as well as the loss in this kind of training.

Regarding the training taking place in Greece, the variables we had before us were:

- A foreign trainer (we were each there for a similar event at different times)
- An Israeli trainer teaching in English via translation
- A foreigner to the Greek culture and to all participants
- Little cultural support
- No ground to rest on
- An interested group of human beings, all there by choice, aware well in advance that the trainers were foreigners

As Israel and Greece are geographically close, the Mediterranean culture could be assumed to be familiar. This in itself could be fine support somewhat, or a possible pitfall, if we were to presume familiarity. The infrastructure that we hoped to build on included some cultural familiarity, on top of a fundamental choiceful interest, and a will to enter a relationship. We were excited about having certain basic questions answered – namely: how all of the variables were going to work in a place where there was no common linguistic culture, where we lacked the most basic tool of communication: namely, language; or how we might succeed in expressing our subjective experience where the common ground was so linguistically scarce.

However, we had another asset -- a sound theory to rely on, Gestalt theory, which supported this meeting in the field of not knowing.

Learning to Trust

This visit to Greece became a fantastic opportunity to fully experience the value and power of the intent for a dialogic relationship. How by itself might it hold the infrastructure for a relationship, we wondered? We were to discover, however, that the interest and the intent held the meeting together when there was no common language other than the will to meet. We had no doubt that there was a will to meet; or perhaps more than a will - a genuine interest, wish, desire, and effort.

In the actual training in Greece itself, highlighted for us, among other things, was the major role of familiarity itself as an essential ingredient for maintaining self-support and for sustaining support from the instructional/learning environment when we tried to communicate with others from a different linguistic culture. I, Talia, had a blissful moment when I heard the name Achilles pronounced exactly as it is pronounced in Hebrew. It was a poignant moment of realization of how essential familiarity was for me; so much so that I stopped teaching and shared my experience with the group. I, Edna, heard a word that sounded like "paradigma" only to find out to my dismay that, unlike the Hebrew or the English meaning, it meant "for example" – something very different from the meaning of the word familiar to me.

This brief experience highlights for us the danger aspect in presuming a familiarity of any kind or degree. Such an experience served as a much-needed lesson in humility, and supports a much-needed, however tedious, discipline of checking one's understanding.

Edna's experience evoked in me, Talia, a recollection about a time I had lectured on phenomenology in the Slovak Republic. I led an ongoing training tailor-made for a group of Czech and Slovak professionals, yet another challenge in the bridging of the divide by language. The training occurred three to four times a year for eight years; two trainers traveled with me each time. The trainers were mostly the same people, even though at times others contributed a trip or two. Amongst us were two English, one Irish, one South African, and an Israeli.

The challenges lay between us the trainers on the cultural front as well as between the trainees and us. At least we, the trainers, could communicate in English, even though it was not my mother tongue. I am saddened thinking about all those trainees I, to this day, never had an unmediated conversation with. There were people who invited me to touch their soul, to meet them in various ways, who experienced me at my best and indeed my worst, yet never ever could we meet speaking the same language.

Yes, we met in different ways; still, one essential way was missing. Furthermore, even with those who comprehended English on varying levels, most times conversations bumped along on significant efforts, or on a careful use of words here and there, and very close attention even: in short, with quite a lot of discourse-enhancing interruptions, with our experiencing fully the essence of interruptions in contact.

So as I was lecturing on phenomenology -- there was a number of times I used the phrase subjective experience. I always had a strong, continuous concern about how the translator might be handling my terminology. I could never, until they took the Gestalt exam years later, fully know what they had understood and what they had reconfigured in their own mind.

As I was listening to the translation, waiting for my turn to continue, I heard the word "obyectiva," which apparently is the Slovak word for "objective." In Hebrew, the word is "obyectivi." My ears perked up. I stopped the translator, telling him I thought he was wrong. Faced with my sudden chutzpa, the room grew silent. Between the three languages -- Slovak, Hebrew, and English -- and relying on my years of hearing a mixture of foreign languages, I could pick up a fundamental mistake. Subjective experience was being erroneously translated as objective experience.

It was a tough moment. I was the guest, the foreigner, even though the teacher. I explicitly doubted the accuracy of the translation in a language I knew not. My support for this action was my rich background in listening to a mixture of languages, my trust that the dialogic stance to a relationship would help me sail through and my integrity in actually being unequivocally certain that what I was teaching was Gestalt and that I intended to be understood.

Translators

In the absence of a common language, the role of a translator becomes essential. In general, translators at times are neutral; at other times, they can be hostile or competitive, and often totally unfamiliar to specific scientific nuances in terminology. In the specific incident of Talia's described here, the translator was a member of the training group, a lovely man who meant well. He might have felt embarrassed, which was tough both on him and on Talia. She had to protect the teaching and the feelings of the translator and the group, as well as hide a small sense of satisfaction at picking up the fundamental mistake.

In one particular experience of Edna's, there was a lovely Greek lady who was assigned to be the translator. She was not a member of the group itself. How was she to be treated, as a translator per se, or as a participant as well was an all-important question? The choice to have her participate seemed to be the right one; however, it presented a complex situation, as most of the time she was wearing the translator's hat, a role that was making her seem to be a "representative" of the trainer (the true source of professional training in the room). On the other hand, part of the time, she was regarded as a member, experiencing and sharing her experience like all the other participants. Hence, I, Edna, experienced firsthand a mixture of gratitude and frustration.

In both cases, that of Talia and Edna, a part of the energy in the field was taken by the need to distinguish between the different roles and the fluctuations between them. However, over time, Edna and Talia both have come to the same realization that there may very well be little support for us when working with a translator in a different culture from ours. There is often no ground on which to rest in such cases. We have had to learn to trust before we had a relationship. Unlike the familiar therapeutic/training context where trust is gradually built up and upon as the therapy/training situation evolves, here we had to trust even before we knew who the group and the translator would be.

Realizing that, trust became the support we needed, we have learned to let a stranger initially handle our professional integrity while walking into the darkness of linguistic understanding of what we were about to say to a group in a new room. In translation/lecture situations, we, of course, could not follow the translator or the trainees.

In a way, the seminar room under such circumstances will feel as if it had an invisible wall/boundary between the trainees and us. Unlike the usual experience of Gestalt training where the unmediated relationship is a basic feature of the learning, under these new circumstances, there was always a mediator to the relationship and to the content the trainees received.

However, as essential and necessary as it was, trust alone could not suffice.

Questions as Phenomena

In Greece, The Slovak Republic, and elsewhere, as we have noticed in our practice, our own similar histories of growing up in an immigrant country, and our shared or individual intention toward focused listening (rather than switching off) when we do not understand the trainees' language, all help the matter along a great deal. This meant for us trainers having to be even more aware of what was going on without the support of comfortably knowing that our instruction and their comprehension were being fully mediated by linguistic cues.

Gestalt is about dialogue, about making dialogic contact, and about being oneself at the boundary. From a phenomenological perspective, it's a small miracle whenever any two individuals actually meet and maintain high quality contact where each has his/her subjective experience, even when both share the same cultural background. It becomes harder when we are from different cultures. It becomes even harder when we throw in a third person: the translator. The contact is mediated through the translator. What happens to the process, what happens to the quality of the contact? What happens to the trainer at every single moment?   And what happens to the participant's process?

The figure encompasses what the participants are saying in the moment; however, to understand what a particular participant is saying, and to comprehend how it is that this person may be participating, all verbal communication is mediated by another. The trainer has to listen to what images, meanings, and discourse strategies the translator is delivering, conveying, and relating. Attention is split between the participants speaking through the translator -- to the way he/she is in this moment -- and the voice of the translator relating the content of what the participant is expressing. All the variables are constantly present: eye contact, paralanguage (intonation, pitch, stress), facial modes of expression, and body tonus -- all of which may not match our own habituated manners.

Is the translator a part of the ground only? This is a question one might answer positively. However, we found the answer to be rather more complicated in the mediated training process. When we speak, we make eye contact -- or not, depending on our own cultural norms -- with the person we are talking to. With whom do we make eye contact in a psychotherapeutic training context? It is natural for the trainer to maintain eye contact with the participants, but how is it to be effectuated under these circumstances, where translation intervenes, mediates? How is it for the participants? The much-needed verbal translation becomes a buffer between the trainer and the trainees. Under these circumstances, there could always be the danger of the mediating intervention turning into an interruption.

Can the foreign trainer maintain contact with the participants when his or her attention is divided among so many variables? What happens to a participant's process while the trainer is listening to the translator? Does the participant ever feel in contact or perhaps lost, as the trainer's attention seems to fluctuate between him and the translator? In this field, is communication being mediated or unmediated? Is it being cued correctly or miscued?

In the need to understand the answers to all of these questions – which is another way of saying, to understand what is going on in the moment -- the trainer might focus on what the translator is saying and break eye contact with the participant. This is a rather natural behavior, but it takes significant effort to control. How is it for the participant? How does the translator feel, especially if he is also a participant trainee? Is the translator just a part of the ground? Though translating is his job, isn't he sometimes inclined to throw in some of his own ideas? The field is composed of a swirl of questions.

The Phenomenological Perspective

This long list of complex questions and thoughts – which we actually address here outside of addressing the training itself – suggests a situation in which after every segment of speech a pause for translation ensues, and where there is the ultimate lesson in retroflection for all of us, including all we wanted and did not want to know and experience about retroflection.

In retrospect, being in this situation is paved with human beings holding their breath and this is a sure recipe for fatigue and bodily distress. Again we found out that the way we are at the boundary is what counts the most. To our great satisfaction, we learned in both our respective experiences that the genuine will to be in contact helps overcome the barrier; and, in fact, in those moments of having to listen to something one did not understand, we are so immersed in the wish to stay in contact that it became almost tangible. It was apparent that both trainer and trainee were present for one another.

Nonetheless, for both of us as trainers, these experiences have been rewarding, for we have been able to find out that the dialogic stance (Hycner & Jacobs, 1995), when both parties are present and willing to acknowledge and include one another, proves to be a very effective tool in overcoming what may initially seem to be so insurmountable. The co-created field is characterized by the genuine wish to make and maintain contact of all the parties who partake in the situation: trainer, translator, and the group members.

The field, like always, becomes the common ground, and the field has its own intricate ways of making figures surface and recede. The growing awareness of that turned out to be another source of support, initially for the trainers, and gradually more so for the trainees.

Phenomenology, another pillar of Gestalt, turned out to be a powerful ally, both in highlighting differences as well as in bridging them. Both of us found out that the lack of a common language made us more sensitive to the need to understand the way the participants were configuring the field. This common Gestalt practice became more crucial under the circumstances. Interestingly enough, it was easier for us as trainers to practice humility, as we did not have a common language to serve as a common ground.

Hence, we could not rely on our ability to understand the spoken words. Making contact was happening in many ways: eye contact, gestures, body tonus and expressions, physical proximity, and tone of speech; but all these had to be supported by making meaning. So, although the simultaneous translation slowed the process down, it was essential for checking once and again whether both participants and trainers were able to see each others configuration of the field.

Every thought took practically twice the time to be expressed once in each language. Every question went through two mouths and the emotional experience was thereby both experienced and mediated. Hence, under the circumstances, the field, constantly in flux, becomes unfamiliar and more complicated. However, focusing on the here and now, on what was actually happening in the field, was something we could all witness and share. Sticking to descriptions of what was going on, without assuming to have prematurely understood and taking the time to explore the meaning was more easily invited as we were stripped of the linguistic common ground. The application of the phenomenological method, were much needed tools that proved very beneficial in the multi-cultural context (Spinelli, 1989).

Conclusion

A meeting of a multicultural group constitutes a field filled with introjections and projections. Each culture contains and maintains introjects that have been accumulated and integrated into it throughout the centuries of its existence. It is very easy to make the other cultural group a subject of projections of what one believes his culture is not. Disentangling what was an individual configuration from what was collective or cultural was one of the figural issues in these seminars, making the contact alive and vibrant, allowing all of us to explore what was happening to us at the contact boundary. This, too, provided a lesson in humility. In the wish to meet, we had to assume a non-assuming position, not taking anything for granted.

All the above turned out to be a unique experience for all who shared it. The seminars ended in both cases in a euphoric feeling of actually having experienced an "I – Thou" contact. Edna recalls one of the participants saying: "It feels as if we all know English." The quality of the contact made the issue of the language recede into the ground, becoming almost marginal. At the end of the eight years of training in the Czech and Slovak Republics, Talia was told she used to relate to comments before the translation was completed and at times before it started. And believe me, I, Talia, really absolutely do not speak the language. This feedback caught me by a total surprise. I have not noticed this phenomenal resonance before.

We hope that our case-brief exploration of how Gestalt theory's emphasis on the dialogic stance, phenomenological work, and on the experiencing and sharing of experiences, can help bridge cross-cultural gaps more, thereby enabling human beings to meet more fully and comprehensively in places of very little common ground, in order to establish mutual common ground.

Personal Account

Writing about our experiences in cross-cultural encounters presented both of us with an opportunity of writing together.

For me it proved to be the final stepping stone from being Talia's trainee to entering a collegial relationship – moving from a 'trainee's' to a 'trainer's' culture. Being able to look at similar experiences from a trainer's point of view turned out to be both novel and enriching experience. Struggling with the need to write, sharing sensations feelings and observations, arguing a bit, discussing the similarities and the differences bore fruit, however short.

Edna Manielevitch, Jerusalem, Israel

References

Hycner, R. & Jacobs, L. (1995). *The Healing Relationship in Gestalt*, The Gestalt Journal Press, Inc.

Spinelli, E. (1989). *The Interpreted World*, Sage Publications, London, Newbury Park, New Delhi.

XII. Uncovering Unity in Diversity

By Holly Timberlake, Ph.D.

I came from a middle-class, upwardly mobile family who had moved, when I was four years old into a newly developing suburb of a medium-sized Midwestern United States city. We were Protestants, though religion, as it turns out, was never really important to either of my parents.

Our town was highly heterogeneous. There were the Italian Americans (who all went to the Catholic school until 9th grade) and, by the time I was in high school, three African American families (who just happened to live in three prominent upper middle class homes in a row), and all the rest of us. My father's attitudes were racist, and as I grew up they became decidedly and more blatantly so, while my mother would never have admitted being racist, one of her favorites of my college boyfriends was Chinese from Hong Kong, but to even talk of dating someone who was Black brought fear and panic—worry about what her friends would think. Oddly, out of this pot, grew my two siblings and I, all of whom have grown up to actively work for the elimination of prejudice, especially my brother, who among other intercultural involvements, has been a member of the Urban League in Detroit, and has, with his own money, renovated buildings in inner-city Detroit to create space for the support, development, and showing of inner-city and African American art, and myself.

My first memory of cognitive dissonance created by racial prejudice occurred when I was nine years old. My mother had just opened a private kindergarten when my sister was born. She needed someone to help care for my infant sister. Josephine had been a housekeeper at my grandparents for a number of years (my grandmother was a teacher and my grandfather, a manager of a drug store.) She began taking care of my sister. Josephine was Black. Oddly, I can remember her from my grandparents' place, but remember no interactions with her, no real being with her, no personal relationship, and no physical touch—no real contact at all. Why? Why would I not remember any contact with a woman who cared for my sister? It disturbs me to think that I was, at the time, that much in the sway of my parents' beliefs about the world. Yet I know I was.

One day, probably shortly after she began caring for my sister, I walked to the kitchen doorway and watched her giving my sister a bath in the sink. Did she know I was there? Probably. Did I say anything to her then? I doubt it. For I have always remembered feeling intensely confused and even scared, not understanding how my parents could trust this Black woman with their infant daughter. I have no specific memories now of what I'd heard from my parents about people of color, but I do know that it must have been blatantly racist for me to worry about my sister's safety and feel befuddled by my parents' decision. In fact, my father--more than 35 years later--had on more than one occasion, verbally threatened me with violent action to express his rage at the diversity work that I have done. As I sit here writing this down, I notice my chest tightening, my heart beating a bit faster, a light tingling in my chin, neck, and arms, tension spreading. Staying with my body, I can feel my stomach begin to churn. I feared my father, and also learned much from him about what and who I didn't want to be.

Yet now, as I write this, I experience a deep gratefulness for this incident and for Josephine. This dissonance, for which I can remember no resolution, became the ground of my active interest in the larger world and in diversity. I imagine Josephine having the presence and the heart to feel compassion for a young girl struggling to make sense of what has been called a schizophrenic split in this country's collective awareness, created by the presence of racism. Still, it bothers me.

In my early, pre-pubescent teens, prior to events and dynamics that contributed to an incremental loss of self-esteem so familiar to so many, many women, I'd begun to become disillusioned with my culture. Unsure now what brought this on; I perceived a lack of heroism and altruism. I saw people not standing up for what they believed in; they complained and did nothing. They mowed their grass, watched TV, went to parties, and weren't heroes and heroines. This bothered me then, now I know it says a lot more about me and what I value and am driven towards!

It was about this same time that I recall having what felt like an empathic experience of being Black and having people stare and look down on me, cross to the other side of the street to not pass by me, throw stones at me, or even kill me; all of this only because my skin was a different color. I was learning of the Civil Rights Movement from watching TV, since I wasn't learning about it in school or from my family or church. No one was taking responsibility for teaching children about such an important powerful moment in this country's life, unless one had the good fortune to have parents who cared and understood. Most Caucasian parents were still too somnambulant.

This momentary empathic resonance was a powerful moment to a 12 year old girl. This I tried to explain to my mother but received no emotional or empathic response from her. It seemed she didn't get it; I didn't understand then about dissociation and psychic numbing. My disgust at such discriminatory and oppressive behavior (though without that particular language) intensified my dissolution and my conviction to not emulate my elders in this.

Having had almost no opportunity for interaction with diverse others, I was enthusiastically looking forward to making friends with people of diverse backgrounds as a student at Kent State University. I was so surprised to discover that few, if any, of the African American students I met in my first months there had any interest in being friends with me. I felt rejected and retreated from attempting further contact for the next four years. I remember feeling angry at the rejection I experienced, taking it personally. Being shy, it was easy to retreat. I now know this to have been a common response then. While I've liked to think this rejection was not personally directed, it is also quite possible I acted in ways that belied my desire for connection. It is likely my own actions contributed to the rejection, or perceived rejection I experienced.

I had the odd fortune of living in the next town over from Kent State University where 13 students were shot during political protesting of the Vietnam War in May of 1970. That fall, my first quarter of college, I was graced with an English professor whose goal was to have us get in touch with our deeper, inner selves through writing. When she read of how disillusioned I was with my culture, she helped me to see that there were heroes and exemplary individuals within the White culture; something in me healed a little at this. The next semester, in the spring of 1971, I took her multicultural literature course. The writings of George Jackson (1970), Franz Fanon (1965), and Vine Deloria (1996) left indelible marks on my psyche and spirit. For me, it was a way of opening myself up to the wisdom of different perspectives--of gathering information about the wider world of humanity and doing a bit more to replace the prejudice lingering in my being. I thrilled at the introduction to people who fought for what they believed in. I found heroes to emulate from a distance.

Shortly after I graduated with a degree in Philosophy, I was introduced to and became a Baha'i, drawn to belief in the oneness of humanity. For the first time in my life, I began to connect with people from multiple ethnocultural backgrounds where we all believed in eliminating all prejudice from our hearts, to create communities based on love, justice, and equality. I began to see celebration of this diversity as essential to the evolution of humanity, and to see it as a core focus of my spiritual development.

As an adult, I came to more fully recognize the unearned privilege conferred on me by my Whiteness (which I had first glimpsed when 11 or so). I continued to expand my knowledge of and my friendships with people of color, as the director and program facilitator for a community group created to increase interracial unity and reduce racism in my town, I held monthly "Eliminating Racism" gatherings at the university and in my home, taught a course in diversity issues relevant to counselors, was a consultant in cultural diversity, and wrote my dissertation on the need to remove racism (as well as sexism and materialism) from our theories of supposedly healthy development. And, I'm sure, made many mistakes and missteps along the way.

Literature on group identity development often says that we must explore the roots of our own cultural heritages, our history, to know who we are. But as aware as I have been of these issues for as long as I have been aware of them, I have never felt the need to do this. What I do feel is the need to understand the history of women's oppression and to heal myself from wounds hundreds of years, even thousands of years, old. These roots I have definitely sought out for years.

Still I have thought much about this supposed need and as a result have come to the conclusion that I am a "cultural creative," one who, for a myriad of reasons, is more drawn to developing a world-centric orientation, rather than a culturally embedded one. I have realized that culture has little or nothing to do with the questions of who I feel closer to, or resonate with, of who shares my most sacred and valued beliefs about life and humanity. As an adult, I attribute much of my learning and growth to those like myself, to people who carry within them an expansive perspective about the world, who thirst for the rich garden of diversity. My connections with them have increased and deepened my awareness of myself and of life's possibilities and assisted me in becoming a much better human being.

With an eye toward contributing to the development of a global theory of human development, I have contemplated the effects of both prejudice and myopia or ethnocentrism on the human experience and on human development. What follows are my thoughts arising out of this consideration.

One of the underlying beliefs forming the foundation of this effort is the belief that humanity is again at a transformative time of great significance. We are for the first time in recorded history in the midst of globalizing our involvements, our politics, our finances, our decision-making, our languages, and life. Everywhere, life is being altered by increasing diversity, from the socio-political structures that characterize public life, to our own personal experiences of others and ourselves. All the world stands on the brink of evolutionary and transformational changes necessary to avert crises of global and far-reaching consequences.

Having observed on-going de-contextualization and re-contextualization or self-organizing of the sort suggested here, we are beginning to alter, expand, and transform our understandings of what it means to be human. For example, people whose values had more often been placed on intellectualizing are beginning to recognize the information that is lost, the experience that is lessened by not attending to our feeling states, while those who have perhaps focused on the spiritual aspects of life are coming to see benefits in incorporating a more material orientation to life. The tendency to exalt oneself, to wall oneself off from others, to make condemning judgments against those considered different, is rampant throughout the world. The more prejudice and superiority a group accepts about itself, the less it will be able to recognize the value in the perception, and the orientation, of the other.

Humanity is like a human body; the body is humanity and each cell different, unique, and important, and necessary part of the whole, not really self-sufficient, or whole without the other cells.

It is astonishing how little attention has been paid to the very real effects of institutionalized oppression (classism, racism, sexism, etc.) especially from the oppressor side. The pervasiveness of this omission of oppression in the literature supports McIntosh's suggestion (1989) that there is a taboo operating in the mind set of the Western dominant culture, such that we are trained not to see the reality of oppression and injustice (McIntosh, 1989). The definition of the concept of taboo includes these connotations, "a ban or inhibition attached to something by social custom or emotional aversion . . . a proscription devised and observed by any group for its own protection" (American Heritage Dictionary, 1969: 1308). A taboo against seeing certain aspects of reality is a human phenomenon and is, theoretically, to be found in all cultures. Certainly, the subjugation of women is a fairly universal prejudice and oppressive dynamic; prejudice based on skin tone is also one that is fairly widespread, ablism is another, as is classism.

Recognizing these distortions within the Western, mechanistic worldview, I suggest that the taboo phenomenon is a universal one as is the worldview that one's own culture is superior; however, when we expose this phenomenon through mutual conversations about it, we become subtly or acutely transformed as our dialogues head us into a new more expanded paradigm of human life and development; and as we transform, so we transform our cultures.

Experiences of oppression are institutionalized deeply and philosophically in the formation of language, the construction of both thought and the experience of reality, and therefore in what are considered of value. This oppression or narrowness based on the exclusion and rejection of the other is detrimental, even at a philosophic level, to all humanity – whether in our roles as oppressor or oppressed. Citron (1969), in summing up the effects of racism on White children, argues cogently that prejudice significantly restricts individuals' ability to perceive the truth of things. He explains that when the illusion that the prejudice represents reality is believed, "It is impossible . . . to deal accurately or adequately with the universe of human and social relationships [and ideas]. . . . [The child] also learns salience, that is, what portions of his environment [or experience] are important to him, and to which he must react" (Citron, 1969: 13-14).

Perceiving only a portion of one's own experience, the rest is discarded, denied, and disowned as "not-self." One thus learns not to trust one's own perceptions, one's own logic and intuition; one learns not to see what one sees, and must rely blindly on tradition or authority for one's understanding of reality, hardly knowing and often denying that this is so.

Citron (1969) further points out that this creates a "dependence on a psychological and moral crutch which inhibits and deforms the growth of a healthy and responsible personality. . . . [They] are robbed of opportunities for emotional and intellectual growth, stunted in basic development of the self so that they cannot experience or accept humanity" (Citron, 1969: 15-16). This socialization pattern robs us of our ability to be fully present in the moment, requiring we reclaim the absent parts of ourselves to achieve full contact. These dynamics are at work not just in prejudicial thinking, but also in cultural trances, and in low self-esteem, and distorted perception of self and other.

In a similar vein, Kremer (1996) emphasizes the importance of recovering the indigenous minds of us all. He shared an old Nordic tradition that "The movement into the future is possible only if we remember the past" (Kremer, 1996: 28). His discussion of the importance of cultural or racial remembering parallels the process of personal healing from emotional trauma, in which it is necessary to remember the past so as to be whole, and to recover parts of the self that were locked away by the experience of trauma and loss. I believe this is why knowing the history of women is more important to me than of my various European heritages, for it is as a woman that I have been most affected by oppression. I have been wounded by the injustices experienced by women everywhere. If we need to recover what has been stolen or wounded as cultural groups to feel whole, it is what has been stolen from me as a woman that I need to reclaim.

Culturally, these logical and mythic dimensional differences are reflected in some of the following distinctions identified as axiological values: Eastern traditions generally emphasize internal, or contemplative validation, polarities which inherently contain their opposites, and collectivism, the Afrocentric worldview is characterized by emphasis on spiritual essence and oneness of being, and interdependence, and the Western on individualism and dualistic or dichotomous thought.

Take, for example, epistemology, as exemplified by the variations on the nature of science and knowing. Western science has been epitomized by the "scientific method" in which a very precise series of steps is required to determine the probability that something might be true. The scientific method requires that all extraneous information be eliminated from considerations, so that only the most powerful explanations for an hypothesis remain. This reductionistic thinking, in which the probable influence for a certain hypothesis is separated from everything else, is the outcome. And this has come to characterize much of Western thought.

Given that older cultures (for example, Native American, African, Chinese) have logics and epistemologies that are constructed of more inclusive and expansive processes than the reductionistic dualism of Western thought, Myers (1988) has suggested that perhaps dualism, as the fruit of reductionism, is itself a distortion of a more expansive epistemological system (Myers, 1988). Pre-Socratic thought was far more unitive. The activity of description and categorization for the purpose of control and prediction was given great impetus through Aristotle's philosophy. Western thought traveled a road towards reductionism by emphasizing only one side of the polarity of separation and connection. The Western worldview became dominated by external and scientific validation, separation and autonomy, independence and objectification, and the manipulation and acquisition of things/objects.

Yet the pendulum of Western reductionism has begun swinging back towards the center. Indeed, in the movement away from reductionism multiple influences have been introduced that have been bringing more wholeness into our knowing, communicating, experiencing, and researching again. In some cases, the influence is from the reclaiming of ancient wholeness, in some, opening to perspectives that have maintained more epistemological wholeness; and from the combining of the indigenous and ancient with the new co-creative perspectives. All these energies and more are now contributing to a shedding of ways of knowing that are now too divisive and limiting to contribute to the well being of the whole.

Native Americans, "Look at life….and come to….knowledge" totally differently from Western methods (Colorado, 1996: 6). In my words she argues that an aspect of the colonialization in other parts of the world in concert with a superioristic attitude, only the West could have science. The rest of the world's cultures also have unique philosophies, but it wasn't considered that anyone else could have science" (Colorado, 1996: 6). It's important to add that while she states that other countries could have philosophy, Deloria's (1996) comment below suggests a lack of, at the very least, respect about Native American philosophy. Further, there was no acknowledgement that there could be other logics, such as the di-unital logic of African thought.

Colorado describes indigenous science as a "way of bringing people to a higher knowledge . . . . [N]ative scientists, through their rituals and songs, are working all the time with energies -- the energies of the earth -- in a way that is just as precise as the way Western scientists work (Colorado, 1996: 6). Deloria (1996) points out that tribal people are just as systematic and philosophical as Western scientists in their efforts to understand the world around them, caring about finding the "proper moral and ethical road upon which [to] . . . walk. Observing the environment, and from ceremonies, dreams, and visions (so both individually and communally) interpreting messages received by spirits is the source of knowledge (Deloria, 1996: 38).

Taoist thought symbolizes polarity as inherently composed of its opposite. The yin-yang symbol depicts the knowing that each pole contains within itself the opposite of the other. It "is the interlocking, melting together of the flow of movement within a circle. The similar -- and at the same time, obviously contrasting -- energies are moving together . . . . The whole idea of a circle divided in this way is to show that within unity there is a duality and polarity and contrast" (Huang, 1973: 12).

Afrocentric logic is di-unital, reflecting the union of opposites (Myers, 1988). This union is described as spirit manifesting, life as, at once spirit and matter, a consubstantiative perspective of the whole being in each of its parts— or holigraphic, as we have come to understand. It follows that self-knowing is the epistemic base, and knowing comes through as imagery and rhythm.

Women have begun identifying ways of thinking and of communicating that integrate body awareness and intuition with externally learned knowledge which resonates for them and holds up to rational evaluation, reclaiming their authentic and unique voices (Belenky, et. al., 1986), and their self-esteem, from the oppressive trances of speaking the "cover story."

Jergen Kremer (1996) has pioneered a way of communicating he refers to as "participatory concourse," that is applied to qualitative research (Kremer, 1996). He explains that by allowing ourselves the freedom of concourse based on conscious participation in the phenomena and the possibility of metaphoric knowing" (Kremer, 1996: 35), we are capable of recovering embodied knowing, a more full awareness and experience of ourselves and life, and dialoguing in a way that "allows us to appreciate scientific achievements without denying the body, the heart, sexuality, gender differences, and the divine (Kremer, 1996: 35)."

So some of us in the West are beginning to open to life and ways of knowing that reincorporate our bodies, feelings, intuitive connections to wisdom in the universe, ones that are inherently unitive and connected, that move, and flow and have rhythm and harmony. All of these elements, taken together, might well be essential aspects of removing the veils that distort perception, thought, and feeling, so necessary for developing a unity-in-diversity perspective. In other words, we are beginning to heal from the negative effects of the inherent splitting associated with dualism that has cut us to our quicks. And in doing so, with the help of the elders and our brothers and sisters from around the world, are reclaiming and developing essential communication tools upon which transformation into a global and more just world will derive.

Furthermore, to attempt to see a phenomenon in its wholeness, relationally speaking, requires us to open to multiple perspectives and to experience the contact boundary as a prism, rich and full and deep of meaning and possibility. The perspective that we can not know or see all there is to know, see, and experience; because the whole hasn't completely revealed itself, or will reveal itself differently as the prism shifts, and that there is always more beyond our conceptual grasp, is one that helps us to become more open. The degree to which we are able to do so is limited by the remnants of our cultural trance, by our lack of knowledge and awareness, and by our psychological mind set, attitudes, and our belief structures. This is to say that what we have not healed affects the very patterns of our thoughts and our ability to perceive a more expanded figure, from a more expanded ground.

We are now more aware that the survival of the whole depends on the abilities of parts to stretch themselves at the contact boundary to expand their experience and perspectives to include, recognize, and at some level, accept other angles of diverse cultural experiences of reality, including interweaving of psyche and spirit, spirit and matter, and felt bodily experience, etc.

Further, expansion of our understanding at these levels is enriching and growthful. This brings together the two foci of this chapter: the threads of healing from and eliminating prejudice and the importance of developing a more expanded, global grounding in the world, or worldcentric perspective. To create the most enriching and growthful intercultural contact, each of us needs to commit to twin intrapsychic missions. The first is to create or encourage an internal environment in which signs of prejudice more easily rise to figure where they can be healed. Secondly, it is necessary to understand that our assumptions about how the world works or should work are, too often for the world's good now, culturally bound, distorted and superioristic. Understanding both these motivates us to transform the ground of our awareness and comprehend the worlds of possible constructions of reality. Not only does this prepare our ground for deep and meaningful intercultural contact, but we also begin to be able to envision a world based on justice and love. With these twin movements of healing and growth, we begin to be the change we want to see; we become powerful, transformative change agents in the world.

Wolff (2004) articulates qualities and levels of deep dialogue better reflect on the dynamics of people coming together to share meaningful dialogue. He posits five stages or descriptive places in the process of coming to share deeply in groups. The first he calls "positioning" or getting to know one another by the use of "I" statements that introduce one to others, a process of "serial monologues," that emphasize personal history. The second stage is "initial connectedness," in which we become aware of who the others are in the group. Threads connecting comments begin to be made. "I" statements are focused more on awareness of what others have shared (Wolff, 2004).

In the third stage of "emergence," moments of silence are noticed as reflection on what is being shared increased, the quality and the energy present deepens as meaning is made from the threads that have developed. "Co-emergence," the fourth level is where new levels of meaning are generated and thoughts and feelings shared add to the meaning being created. The consciousness of the group moves in response to emerging themes. Deeper trust is evidenced through new insights, more silence so that interplay develops between the two. The final level of deepest dialogue is "dynamic silence," in which there is no ownership of what is said. Voice emerges from group consciousness, and a sense of a larger presence is often felt. New meanings of the whole emerge. As resonance increases, silence deepens, a kinesthetic experience of the whole is felt, and a synchronistic element is perceived to what emerges. New meaning unfolds from the willingness of each to suspend belief and judgment and let their beings interact with new information and perspectives. A sense of excitement is felt as each one experiences the living interconnected flow of thought and feeling (Wolff, 2004).

This articulation of the depth of dialogue combined with the Gestalt cycle of experience creates a spiral that is, because of the ebb and flow of conversation, a kind of stylized graphic depiction through which to view what happened in the group.

How then might all of this come together? I want to discuss this using as illustrative, observations from a group of people who gathered to interlogue with myself and Anita Jackson, Ph.D., who co-facilitated the groups, about questions of human development dynamics from diverse perspectives. This was part of an early effort to contribute to creating a theory of human development that was not ethnocentric, not carrying elements of dominance-based thought and ideology, one that might focus on universal elements of psychosocial development. Such a theory, it is maintained can only be unfolded through the voices of many representing the world of humanity, not just from one person trying to create a universal theory for all. The group consisted of academicians, therapists, and cultural diversity trainers from diverse backgrounds.

It was a wonderful group of people who freely came for no other reason than to share with and listen to each other about our thoughts and feelings on healthy human development from the vantage of our own perspectives. There were no credits or benefits offered other than the opportunity to engage in such sharing. Therefore, they were all intrinsically motivated to do this. The six of us were of African, Hispanic, African American, and European American descent and culture. Three of us were from this country (USA) and three from elsewhere (Peru, East Africa, and Ghana). There were two men and four women.

We had much in common: education (all were Ph.D's, doctoral or master's level students in Counseling and Human Development), so we all valued education and helping and teaching others. Four of us were from families who were monied and/or had strong social standings in our communities. Those of us who did not, came from families where education and the professions were highly valued (both European and African American women). Obviously, we all had or found the means to attend college. We all value and promote cultural diversity in various ways. Some of us had come to this country and experienced the challenges and growth of learning to live in the ethnocentric American culture where, depending on the color of your skin and your gender, you are more or less likely to experience discrimination. Additionally, we all knew one another through various academic and professional activities.

The group gathered together for the purpose of discussing healthy psychosocial and spiritual development. We consulted on questions of the nature of healthy development and the relationship between healthy adults and the psychological health of their upbringings. We discussed the varied ways that our childhood experiences seemed related to our choices as adults. We looked at our experiences of feeling connected to and different from our families. We observed that oftentimes the path to "healthy development" passes through unhealthy territory. What occurred with these groups was a powerful flow of thought and feeling in which all the elements of the contact cycle were enthusiastically enjoyed, with a growing depth of feeling.

We opened by posing the following question: what was your own gendered and cultured experience, not what you were told it was or should have been, but what did you experience? Rather than comments couched in "my culture," members talked about their personal experiences in ways that included cultural differences as part of the description of a fuller experience. A white male from the Plains in the United States spoke of the powerful and loving presence of women in his life as a child, especially his sisters. A woman from Peru talked of the linearity of her upbringing, and the lack of flexibility in expectations.

Almost immediately, a member threads the two comments together, adding to both, and interweaving her own statements about her upbringing. From this moment on, in the interlogue there is an interweaving of the larger of meaning of what is being discussed in almost every comment. Everyone talks about their own families and how experiences, whether positive or negative have powerfully contributed to choices and values now, but little is actually said about cultural differences. What happens is much richer, in a way. We share the inside of our lives, thereby gazing into the richness of the variety of cultural experience.

From a prominent family in rural America, where the daughters get the education, because the men will do the physical work to and the one son sees himself more aligned with the sentiments of his sisters than his father; to a wealthy and powerful, yet highly respected family in East Africa, in which a daughter exalts in giving money to the workers and helping those who have less; to the extended family experience in Northern Ohio in which the children spent childhoods full of adventure and creativity, feeling at home and secure throughout the neighborhood filled with various family members; the high expectations, that left no room for divergence in a wealthier family from Peru; or in the emptiness of a middle class Caucasian family in Northern Ohio, caught up in being upwardly mobile, caught in appearances what they received from them, we were all witness to a world wider than we knew. No one had to stretch to wrap their minds around the differences presented by the others.

Described through the personal, lived lens that interwove cultural elements in the narrative, we could all see the differences, and yet could understand them much more as human experiences. To my absolute delight, the sharings so supported my belief that each culture can learn from every other culture, and that we all need to learn from each other to grow and develop at this critical juncture in human history. I felt so enriched by what I learned about human life around the globe. There was something in the personal sharing of a lived life with its details, with all the colors and emotions connected to the person's memory that gave breath to their descriptions. It was as if, in the sharing, I received the energy of what each person was sharing, in that moment, living in the beauty of their experience.

Early on in the dialoguing, a concept that one would bring up would be used by another to further reflect on deeper elements of their childhoods. For example, a comment of the distancing that came from a materialistic, urban life, sparked thoughts about attachment and what attachments may not be so healthy, so that attachment, itself, was seen to need contextualization. Attachment was one of the first themes that ran through our discussion of our childhoods. We talked of attachment to the land, to animals, to others in our families, to a way of life, to expectations. This in turn led to thoughts and feelings of not being accepted, of not feeling that one belonged. For some the greatest experience of this was within family, for some it was in school, and for some it was the experience of discrimination based on race and gender, whether it was the experience of being an African foreigner and woman or of being an African American woman in higher education.

The theme that emerged at the end of the first group was that we all experience some fragmentation from wounds throughout our lives, but that if we have a viable enough field, a background of support that sustains us, we can create ourselves in healthy ways. We can create wholeness out of the disassociative split of modern life, of life as a disenfranchised person or member of a disenfranchised group, as long as we have the ground, some stability underneath the dysfunction.

Experiences were heard and reflected upon without any outward signs of anyone being challenged by the worldviews of any other. Of course, there may have been some discomfort experienced that wasn't voiced, but if so, it was minimal. So minimal that during second gathering, the need that emerged and was the main focal point of the conversation, was about our need to challenge ourselves further to find areas of discomfort, to find our limitations, or the places where we began to share and recognize our own cultural embeddedness and ethnocentrism. We talked of inviting a Ku Klux Klan member, of talking about homosexuality, or religion, of something that would perhaps touch some raw places inside, some places in need of healing, some way to grow together through our differences.

Even in the short span of two gatherings, changes in perspectives were heard. One member originally framed the distortions about which we were talking as those of the Western worldview which has been imposed on all people worldwide, to seeing that "every world view is distorted to some extent and that every person upholds some distortions to some extent. I probably always knew that but never really brought it out as clearly in my thinking." She went on to say she saw how all cultures have negative and positive traits and issues with superiority and inferiority, and that there is an importance and power in being able to expand oneself to incorporate all the multiple perspectives we encounter.

The awareness that emerged in the group was that there is greater inner peace that comes from not feeling that we have to defend who we are because of fear and use power over others. The more we expand ourselves and discard unhealthy limitations and distortions of perspective, the more balance we create, the more love and peace that enters our hearts and our lives, and the more we are able to resist the impetuous scramble towards fear-based politics and religion, thereby decreasing the violence perpetrated in this world from institutionalized levels.

Perhaps we were all a bit surprised at the easy flow between us all. We began to desire to challenge ourselves, to push the boundaries, to find out where they were, what it would be like to experience them, how we would move through them to a resolution of contact on the other side, and how all this would deepen our connections to one another. We made suggestions of how we could dig into the dark underbellies of our own limitations, believing somehow that this was necessary in a multicultural context to grow.

This was to be the next step in our explorations, but sadly, it never happened. I have wondered since if this was so, because despite our desire to push the boundaries, there may also have been some fear. Just enough, perhaps, that we didn't make the extra effort to find a way to continue when it became more difficult, when there were finals, and then finals were over and people's schedules weren't compatible over the summer. And the energy faded.

I debated on whether or not to let the reader know of this ending. I would like to "end" the experience on a positive note and ignore any disheartening end to what had begun as a highly energized and enthused opportunity. The last group meeting took place at the end of a spring semester. Two of the participants had been graduate students, two were professors emeriti, and two of us had completed our Ph.D.s. One went home to Ghana for the summer, one, who lived two hours away, was not teaching over the summer, so wouldn't be available, and one was getting ready to move to another city and university for her Ph.D. work. These life trajectories, on the surface, contributed to the dissolving of the group.

So perhaps life just intervened in ways that over complicated this effort in lives already too hectic and full. Since challenge is often our best motivator for change, such movement would, no doubt, bring much change and growth. But I think I learned this. With a foundation of openness and acceptance in an atmosphere of choice, there is such beauty possible in the coming together of people from around the world. It is an act, sometimes heroic, that generates so much hope for the future, so much belief in the goodness of the world of humanity that we should avail ourselves of it as often as we can. I am delighted and a bit astonished at how deeply we were able to communicate about our lived experiences. I believe we all walked away richer and wiser both of ourselves and of others. I believe we would all do it again; we just didn't, yet.

Personal Account

The opportunity to co-write a chapter in this book with a colleague who was someone who lived for me in that expanse somewhere between friend and acquaintance was one that I looked forward to with delight. I had known that she had done some similar writing with women of color and I was anticipating the intimacy and the process of delving into unexplored depths of knowing and experiencing. I believed that the request for dialogic or co-written text was one that would provide more of the exhilaration of human exploration that, like many of us writing in this book, I cannot get enough of! And I eagerly jumped on board!

This is how this experience began, but our lives began to diverge. We lived in different cities, many miles apart, and both our careers were turning into some new pathways that resulted in us not being able to hold the center of our projects connected with and written about in this chapter. I ended up writing the chapter alone.

I never would have noticed to such a degree the isolation of writing alone, had not the project began as a joint effort. There is such power in the sharing of hearts and minds, in the fleshing out of the nuances of difference and agreement. There is so much more knowing that becomes available when we bring all of who we are to the table. And while we can still do this writing alone, the human interaction, the energetic dynamic that is created when two or more come together is not touched or plumbed.

It was then, a gift, both in the presence and the absence of a writing partner and it affected both my experiences of figure and ground throughout the writing process and even now as I pen this bit of introspection. I can see what was, what might have been and what is popping into the screen of my mind like different angles of a prism—all illuminating the same configuration in many of its potential array, thereby revealing itself as a very full activated, yet still full of potential, experience. I have grown from it, grateful for her presence and accepting of her absence.

And wondering, if the truth be known, if losing her as a writing partner didn't have to do with some insensitivity not recognized on my part that she chose not to address. I do not have the answer to this. Then I wonder if my saying it diminishes in the reader's mind the validity of what I write. Yet, to write with integrity, I feel I must end by opening this door that cannot be closed in this particular instance. I write this to honor the challenge and the hope of coming together across barriers that can make intercultural connecting a sometimes precarious pursuit. I write this in the hope that we all continue to acknowledge and bring down the barriers to full contact in our own behavior, when we discover them, taking responsibility for our insensitivity, lack of thoughtfulness and compassion, our territoriality, and our fears—all those dynamics that are truly at the ground of our disconnections with one another.

Holly Timberlake, Stow, OH, USA

References

Belenky, M. F., Clinchy, B. M., Goldberger, N. R., and Tarule, J. M., (1986). *Women's Ways of Knowing: The Development of Self, Voice, and Mind.* N.Y.: Basic Books, Inc.

Citron, A. (1969). The rightness of whiteness: World of the white child in a segregated society (pamphlet). Detroit: Ohio Regional Educational Lab.

Colorado, P. (1996). Indigenous Science: Dr. Pamela Colorado talks to Jane Carroll. ReVision: *A Journal of Consciousness and Transformation*, 18(3), 6-10.

Deloria, V. (1996). If you think about it, you will see that it is true. ReVision: *A Journal of Consciousness and Transformation*, 18(3), 37-44.

Fanon, F. (1965). *The Wretched of the Earth*. London: Macgibbon & Kee. Huang, C. A. (1988). *Embrace Tiger Return to Mountain: The Essence of Tai Ji*. Berkeley, CA: Celestial Arts.

Jackson, G. (1975). *Soledad Brother*. Chicago, IL: Laurence Hill Brooks.

Kremer, J. W. (1996). Evolving into what, and for whose purposes? ReVision: *A Journal of Consciousness and Transformation*, 18(3), 27-36.

McIntosh, P. (1989). White privilege: Unpacking the invisible knapsack. *Peace and Freedom*. July/August.

Morris, William, (Ed.), (1969). *American Heritage Dictionary*, Boston, MA: Houghton Mifflin Company, 1308.

Myers, L. J. (1988). *Understanding an Afrocentric World View: Introduction to an Optimal Psychology*. Dubuque, IA: Kendall/Hunt Publishing Company.

Toms, M. (1991). *At the Leading Edge: New Visions of Science, Spirituality, and Society*. Burdett, N.Y.: Larsen Publications.

Wolff, R. A., (2004). Developing Deep Dialogue: Can the assessment of dialogue contribute to its effectiveness? in ReVision: *A Journal of Consciousness and Transformation*, 26(3), 23–27.

XIII. Culture and Body

By Michael Craig Clemmens, Ph.D.
and Arye Bursztyn, M.F.A.

Intentions

Our intention is to examine field as co-created through bodily experience. A field body perspective identifies the physical co-constitution of relationship, systems, and culture. This allows us as therapists and our clients to explore the greater context of our mutual experience. The figures that emerge for our client can become fuller for both them and us when experienced in a cultural context. This approach is not one of forcing a cultural lens upon what emerges for clients. Rather, we are acknowledging that the fact of field sui generis may be culturally and bodily embedded, shading more light on the experience of our clients and ourselves.

The body emphasis of Reichian therapy and early Gestalt therapy were responses to the over-inhibited repressed white professional culture (Reich, 1945; 1972). Although this emphasis may not fit other cultures, it was a response to the cultural bodily conditions of Western culture. Attending to body as part of the relational field is to be culturally sensitive. Secondly, cross-cultural contact in therapy can be enlightened by attending to differing embodiments and different interactive processes among members of a culture.

Our essay is the result of our shared experiences. As body-oriented Gestalt therapists working in different cultures, we have worked together in multicultural training programs and workshops. In our individual practices we have worked with individuals, couples, and groups from different and mixed cultures. From these experiences we have developed some curiosity and awareness of the relationship between culture and body. The need for analytical and methodological culture and body research seems obvious, and yet a review of body therapies will show that the literature, though significant, is not abundant (Frank, 2001; Kepner, 1993).

We have two intentions in sharing our research experiences at this time. First, we want to heighten practitioners' interest in the relationship between body and culture. Our perspective is that of a unitary field (Parlett, 2000). We believe that each person in his/her body exists amidst a field of other relationships, and in a field of history and social structures, all of which co-constitute or influence bodily phenomena. It is not enough to understand individuals only in the context of their own character/personality (Johnston, 1994), their family of origin or of their own body structure (Lowen 1967, 1971; Keleman, 1985).

Widening our lens to include the relationship between culture and body can lead us to more complex figures and the differences that may emerge that are more than individual but also field. As part of a field perspective, the individual is not a dualistic "mind" or "body" but a unity. When people know, they know through their visual, auditory, and kinesthetic senses (Markova, 1996). Throughout this research, we will be attempting to hold in value all three modes of sensing. The biggest challenge for us, and perhaps the reader, is to transcend our Western bias of auditory/verbal and visual realities and to describe the kinesthetic aspect of culture.

Secondly, we want to offer some skills and guidelines in attending to the cultural aspects of bodily experience. We have spent much of our professional life attending to embodiment. Embodiment refers to the physical (space) and to the immediate (time) of self in relation to the other. Embodiment is always present centered, occurring in the here and now. It is the turn of my head as I listen to you or the heaviness in your chest as you remember your mother. In cultural embodiment, there are also numerous examples. It is the way we sit in rows or stand in circles for a wedding service or funeral. It is the way that Navajos crouch and sit alongside the road as they talk to each other.

Throughout the process of this discussion, we observe how aware we have been and must be of the challenge of putting somatic experience into verbal form. Our goal in dialoging and sharing some case examples is to make this work more flesh and blood for the reader. Therapy, including Gestalt therapy, has strong, enormous verbal/cognitive biases, orienting us to value or describe what can be processed and expressed in language. The images and sensations we offer are clearly a gestalt of embodied culture as we see it. From this bodily field perspective, culture is our bodies moving in relation to each other in a developed pattern.

This pattern is ground for those of that culture. Within each existing pattern (culture), possibilities of movement and structure are enhanced and are more likely while others are not enhanced and are less likely. What feels familiar and normal in one culture may seem foreign in another. An excellent example of this is the dominant American value of looking square in the eye when talking to another, which over time has morphed into good eye contact -- a standard bias of most American counseling and training programs, and a value of a particular culture (White) and perhaps not of others, such as Native Americans or of African Americans (Sue & Sue, 1990).

Practitioners frequently give lip service to attending to body experience, often moving quickly to body experience as symbolic or metaphorical. The emphasis on body as metaphor is an artifact of our analytic archaeology (Kepner, 2001). Our interest, as Gestalt therapists should also be on the phenomenology of body and culture, the lived experience. The worst disservice we could do is to arrive at cultural categories, having reduced individuals and groups to a priori assumptions. With pre-determined cultural categories, we can easily fall into stereotyped, discriminatory pits. We would rather look at the experience of difference, the inner images and feelings attached to the bodily experience within a culture.

Our experience is that the skill required to attending to body and culture is to transcend viewing the individual in isolation by seeing him/her physically in relation to others. We can do this not from a set of body culture categories but in dialogue, remaining phenomenologically curious about our client's experience. Our challenge is to remain aware that our perspective, our feeling, and our own bodies, are always influenced by our own embodied culture. Every meeting we have with another is influenced and shaped by our mutually embodied cultures.

This particular experience is of the field incarnate, the lived embodied field. Previous knowledge about someone's body and culture are best removed to the back burner and should not be our leading focus. Part of this challenge is to develop and maintain our own body awareness as part of a culture: how we carry our history/culture in our movements, gestures, orientation of our eyes, tone of voice, use of touch, and proximity with others.

Culture
Culture is the creative adjustment of a group of people over generations-it is implicit and in ground.   --- Leila Guitterez

Culture and body have been viewed mostly from the perspective of touch and physical contact (Montagu, 1978) and physical space or proximity (Hall, 1966). Fisher (1973) points out the relationships between boundary phenomena and cultural body practices; for example, Americans spending so much time in cars as external boundaries to compensate for our weak personal physical boundaries. Berman (1989) describes the physical disconnection in Western culture resulting in a "basic fault" reflected in our treatment of animals, our architecture, our need to reconnect with our physical and primitive self. The latter can be seen in the rising interest in solutions to such contexts, such as shamanism and ecstatic movements.

A Gestalt approach to culture allows for the unification of what is split or unacknowledged by traditional therapies, such as, body, spirit, and culture. In order to unify what has been split, we as practitioners must immerse ourselves in the field incarnate and let go of our theories about self, body, and culture. We must immerse ourselves in the field of cultural embodiment by feeling our sensations and remaining curious about the other's sensations. Both "body" and "culture" are well structured and are normally (Dare we say abnormally?) co-constructed in a way that they would go unnoticed, cunningly hidden in the background.

Our being in our own bodies and noticing the implicit, which is that, which is part of the ground, infinitely aid re-experience or first-time experiences. The field as we constitute it in the moment can include all of the elements of body and culture. We would be more conscious of this phenomenon were we to but look and not take for granted cultural/bodily biases, such as, notions of "good contact" or functioning. Awareness will lead to making creative adjustments. We understand creative adjustment to be emerging within the context of the field in which it exists: the cultural contexts where the field differs among many peoples. And, of course, we see many people in our offices, at our workshops, and in consultative settings.

Culture is a larger level of system beyond the self, the dyad, and the family. It is shaped by all of these levels of human interactions and shapes them as well. The following section elaborates the development of Gestalt and body as we move beyond the individual to the field in which he/she is embedded.

Gestalt and the Body
Gestalt therapy has always valued physical experience as an important aspect of the individual's mode for creating contact (Perls, Hefferline & Goodman, 1951). The degree to which body is emphasized varies among Gestalt practitioners and has evolved over time. The following outline identifies salient Gestalt approaches developed over time. Gestalt awareness of the body entails intervening with individuals (primarily) through the awareness of physical experiences.

The range of Gestalt approaches in working with bodily experience seems to follow the lines of psychotherapy from a more neo-analytic approach (influenced by Wilhelm Reich) as developed by Frederick Perls (1969) to a more relational field perspective. This early approach involved undoing retroflections (muscular inhibitions) analogous to Reich's character armor.

This early research has led us to view body structure as a retroflected core. Body structure refers to the inherent muscle, skeleton, and fascia patterns enervated by the self in relation to others. Structure is not a fluctuating process as such but is rather a frozen or fossilized process. What begins as a creative adjustment to field conditions of threat, lack of nurturance, and so on, develops into a pattern that limits and determines possible future movements or reactions of the body. The emphasis in such cases is primarily on the individual and his/her inhibited self. The interventions include expressive movements, such as pounding or yelling, screaming, or repeating particular movements. The intention of these experiments is on discharge and releasing holding patterns (Kepner, 1993).

Body as Metaphor

Fritz Perls also emphasized and developed a generation of Gestalt therapists who worked with Body as metaphor in which individuals would play their disowned body parts. These approaches (Smith, 1985) acknowledge the interpersonal elements related to the individual's expression (or more accurately non-expression), and are primarily individually focused. This view is one of impasse; that the individual was out of touch with his/her core self which if not interrupted would be expressed. The answer is to "undo" the retroflections and bring the individual more "in touch" to directly experience the inhibited feelings, thereby restoring full functioning. This approach continues to be the emphasis of deep tissue and expressive work. Typically, the role of the group is of support or as audience rather than to be interactive. The cultural bias of this early approach lies in the emphasis on body as inhibited and bound up. This is more typical of Western Europeans and North Americans than of persons of other cultures.

Body as Support for Contact

Laura Perls (1992) in her writing and teaching emphasized what she called "supports for contact." By supports for contact, she meant those aspects of the individual's physical organization that enhanced or delimited his/her quality of interaction with self and others. Body for Laura Perls was a support that enhanced the self to experience the environment and make "contact." Her background in dance and movement underscored the physical aspects of experience. The emphasis in this work is less of the cathartic contact or discharge and more of those aspects of body that support interaction and functioning (Perls, 1992). The work of Frank (2001) is an example of the continuation of this approach. It is implicitly and explicitly interpersonal since the development of the capacities for interaction are learned and developed in relation to the other. Interventions include emphasis on breathing, postural support, and restoration or development of subtle self supporting movements (Perls, 1992).

Body as Self/Ownership

Kepner (1993) framed the body in terms of a process, emphasizing the degree of experienced ownership or body as self. In Healing Tasks (1995), he further clarifies the field conditions that support a lack of ownership and desensitization -- namely, the experience of environmental trauma. His emphasis on the other is primarily in terms of the creative adjustments individuals make to survive. This enormous contribution is relational, contextualizing the person's bodily process as interpersonal. Interventions and experiments emphasized at this level include sensation development to support ownership, undoing fixed patterns and developing physical patterns to support choice.

Body As Relational Field

In the last few years there has been a re-emphasis in Gestalt therapy on field theory (Wheeler, 1991, Parlett, 2000). Field theory as discussed here includes the whole of experience but has not emphasized field as a physical phenomenon. Recently, Guitterez (1998) has expounded on Wheeler's structures of ground outlining what she calls GS levels (level of the ground structures that include culture and bodily experience).

Embodied Culture

In Israel, we know so well to be sensitive to cultural differences. Even dogs learn to discriminate between different people according to their ethnic origin. A dog in an Arabic village would recognize a Jewish man as a target for barking and vice versa. A dog in a Jewish village would bark at an Arab passer-by. Dogs, like people are well equipped to detect cultural differences that are expressed through nuances of body structuring, smell, and so on.

Embodied Culture - The Field Incarnate

Culture is embodied. Rather than conceptual, embodied culture is lived in the flesh, moment-to-moment, filled with memories, expressions, movements, sweat, sinew, viscera, and breathing. This is the physical living of culture. There is no culture without embodiment. We learn, teach, and maintain our culture through our physical experiences of touching, being held, speaking, and interacting in groups (Montagu, 1978; Guitterez, 1998). It is a shared field (Parlett, 2000) literally handed down from generation to generation. This is our home culture, the matrix of body movements and sensations that we feel as a connective web, the field incarnate.

Is it not radical to consider that not only do we in our solitary Western view manipulate the environment (Perls, Hefferline and Goodman, 1951) but our self as environment also? Our embodied culture calls to us, influences our bodily patterns, and shapes us in ways that we are often not aware of happening. This notion of body is then closer to the shamanic and ecstatic. We can try to transcend our culture but only with awareness. We are embedded in a field that can only change with our need for and willingness to create awareness of how we might be different.

The Field, as referred to in Gestalt theory, is a conceptual framework that includes our body-experience. It may include our physiology on the inside, our contact with gravity on the vertical axis, and the intricate ways, on the horizontal axis, in which we "do" ourselves in relation to our communities and "are being done" by them.

Our experience in exploring body and culture is that field is physically co-constituted and maintained. Feel yourself in your home town, village, or neighborhood. You attend church, temple, or a sporting event. As you enter the situation, you organize your body in relation to how others do; you know a priori how to be with others. The circle around you is an organism, breathing, chanting, or cheering.

This is different from the individual's awareful movement and gestures. The embodied culture is an interaction of unaware movements that are typical or embedded in the common field.

Dialogue: Two Examples of Embodied Culture

Michael: I have recently spent time with my son and his friends who skate and use skateboards. What strikes me when I am around them is that this is a culture. Their culture has its own language, clothing, manners, gestures, and movements. The culture has its elders and icons (for example, the American Tony Hawk). Through mostly nonverbal interaction, the elders pass on the language, skills, and embodiment to the younger and newer members. As I move into the skating building with them, I am aware of how differently I move than they do. Clearly, I am a visitor. The new culture is more than a generational experience; it is an embodied field co-created out of shared purposes. The purposes seem to define themselves in contrast or opposition to the dominant culture (differentiate) and band with similarly oriented people (confluence). It is similar to the experience of gangs with a "we" on the inside of the circle dressed differently and a "they" on the outside.

I bought a pair of sneakers designed for skateboarding for my purpose of supporting my arthritic feet. One of the skaters commented on these shoes but my need was different. I did not move or shuffle the way they do. The field was not organized for me, even with the same shoes. My purpose was different; my culture was different. I was a visitor not even trying to fit in.

It is a culture of moving across the field. Like Wheeler's (1991) reference to Lewin's example of the field which changes depending on the conditions of either a lover's picnic or war. In these large empty rooms with ramps, the skaters move in a particular shuffle and leap in the air, complimenting or commiserating with each other with in-group cultural terms like "soul grind" or "Oley!" In my body I am aware that I don't move this way.

Arye: As a choreographer/dancer, I was interested in identifying this "gestalt" even before I was aware of gestalt terminology. It was most natural to begin pursuing this interest when I left Israel twice. My first opportunity occurred when I studied dance in the United States of America, and secondly, during my stay in Japan. On the background of the foreign culture, I could see better where I stood. The work resulted in a full evening solo performance called "A Tin Soldier on the Sea-Shore of Jerusalem." Performed nationwide (and also in the States) it was followed by meetings with the audiences. It became clear how powerful, how evocative and how problematic it is to bring up issues of culture that are embodied, that reside within the soft tissues of our physical being.

The dance consisted of four parts: First, the childish, "young" image of Israeli identity, with an intense, acrobatic movement language derived from my children's free dancing: running, spinning, rolling upside down. Second, there was the lyrical, spiritual, feminine inner-figure, gently flowing, undulating upwards. Third, I presented the tormented image of an old man, unbearably slow, with a body that is a minefield, exploding at every step. The fourth and final part reveals the soldier, with an arrogant, sarcastic, over-masculine movement-language, and a parody of the Macho image.

These were the four inner-figures, four qualities of my identity as an Israeli man, and each one of these images has its own embodiment and its own movement-language and all were "different" as experienced by myself and by the audience. Those figures were a phenomenological portrait of my embodied culture, and recognized as such by other members of the same culture.

As a therapist, I wish to consciously discern elements of the embodied culture in my client's body-process, bring them to my awareness and to his, and even creatively and expressively with the possible movement-language or dance that may come up.

Body, Culture, and Gender

Michael: As I hear your description of these young men, I wonder about body, culture, and gender. Another entire issue is the way culture trains us in our bodies, and here dance (and sports) plays a major role. I am thinking of the hordes of young obedient girls dressing up in tights, placing their left hand on the bar at the Ballet studio, ready for their *"plies"* in front of the mirror and the dominant presence of the authoritative ballet teacher. They are molded, deconstructed, and reconstructed en masse towards their gender roles, cherishing the ballerina image. Same with us guys, with our leather jackets, with our shoulders squared and raised, with our swaying and bending of elbows, obediently (and eagerly) marching to our ball games and ultimately and tragically to the military service, where ownership of body (and life) is transferred to "king and country."

Visiting Culture and Home Culture

The examples above from our lives illustrate the experience of difference when visiting a different culture. Embodied Culture is unaware, a part of experience that is so assimilated that it is now ground rather than figure. These physical movements and patterns are part of our culture, a given. Because we live, move, and act in patterns constantly, embodied culture is usually out of our awareness. We don't notice how we move, hold ourselves, and use our voices when we are among those who do so similarly. It is only when field conditions are ripe that our embodied culture of origin is in our awareness.

Arye: Walking down an alley in Tokyo together with my dance-company colleagues, somebody comments about me walking like a "bully," ready to strike back. I am made aware of my constant alertness. Did I bring it with me from home in Israel? Are we really so self-guarded here?

A famous Japanese choreographer brought our particular dance company from "the West" for a particular production. I was a bit embarrassed at that time to hear that we, the foreign dancers, had body types that were different from Japanese dancers. We were told that local dancers have physical proportions less beautiful than our own. I wondered about this self-perception and didn't quite understand it, as I did not see any outstanding difference. Was it an objective difference that I was unable to see? Was it a cultural prejudice? One way or another, on a cultural level we may have very specific experiences of ourselves in relation/comparison to others.

As a dancer I was also made very aware of my culturally–based limitations. I participated in a Butoh dance production in Japan. Butoh is a form of avant-garde Japanese dance, based on traditional Japanese culture in a very undermining, rebellious way. Was it really possible for me to embody this dance form? On the surface, maybe; but deep down inside, obviously not.

Could a non-Israeli dancer convey the same information as I did in my dance? I would think probably not. Even classical ballet, the great equalizer of human bodies, looks so different with dancers from different cultures.

Visiting Cultures

So there are differences when the same physical process is embodied in different cultures. But I wonder about the experience of sameness/difference and what stands out for us. The image that occurs to me in this process is like fruit ripening, when the less obvious fruit becomes vivid and there for the picking. Ripening happens when we look at ourselves, feel what we are doing in concert with others, usually at a ritual or event. At a funeral, we are sometimes so heightened in our awareness that we become aware of how we move in relation to others in our clan. This is familiar to us within our family, this culture. We know how to move, where to sit. We know what fits in this situation with little cognitive processing. As we meet the mourners, we drop our heads and speak softly (in some cultures) or wail and move about (in others). But we know: it is in our tissue. The ripening or heightened awareness reinforces the sense of the culture joined together.

But when we make contact with another culture, our awareness ripens to the contrast. A boundary becomes clear as our awareness of the differences heightens. The differences in embodiment are felt. For example, if I arrive at the New York airport and then fly to St. Thomas in the Virgin Islands, I notice people move more slowly in the latter. Their voices share a melodic quality and they tend to stand up straighter (their spines are consistently more elongated). The tourists leaving to return to NYC seem to be moving a little slower than they were back in that city before. Why? What I believe is that this group of people has shared a field of embodiment. It is not that an individual or a group decides to move a certain way. Rather, it is the repetition of unconsciously moving confluently together and sharing certain contextual cues that evoke and maintain the "Big Dance."

The brain always recognizes the set-up or staging, on cue. This experience gets encoded out of our awareness. But as visitors or strangers to certain new rituals, we can become aware of new patterns and consequently feel what we are doing. But eventually, like the tourists, the new-shared embodiment also becomes background until arriving back home. This is the process of awareness of differences.

Another possibility is to not notice or be aware of the boundary, by desensitization, thereby decreasing sensate awareness. A third possibility is to experience the boundary of embodied differences and then attribute negative qualities to the other. An example of this is the tourist who mimics the way people from different embodied cultures talk and walk. Or the therapist who responds to the more apparently subdued client of another culture as depressed and moves to "help them undo their retroflections." This is the stance of fixing the other's embodiment based on a cultural bias. It is also an organization of the field as correct and incorrect in functioning. All embodied cultures are biased, in the sense of selecting and encouraging some physical aspects and not others.

When we are not aware of our own embodiment and its cultural rootedness, we are more likely to act out of our biases and proceed without awareness. So bridging between embodied cultures is based upon awareness and enough sensation to know the differences accompanied by curiosity to explore them.

Depending upon field conditions, differences might become figural or not. Arriving in Chile, Arizona, I am immediately aware of how much physically bigger, noisier, and verbal I am than the Navajo customers at the Laundromat we are all using. In this situation, I want to blend in by lowering my voice. I can feel myself slump in the chair making myself smaller. In a few days this way of organizing myself becomes a pattern and less in my awareness. This is another aspect of the phenomena of visiting a place; the initial heightened sensation is gradually replaced by the new embodiment of this culture.

Of course, I do not have the history and other aspects of this culture; my experience is not as rich. I am only visiting. But I am doing more than taking pictures; I am becoming part of the picture. To continue with the visual metaphor, it is as if my visit into another culture is an overlay of one photo over another. I cannot fully leave my embodied culture yet I can begin to move with the background of my home culture and the foreground of the new visited culture. Simply, I will never be a smaller Navajo but I become less noisy, less verbal and more attentive to non-verbal facial cues that are of that culture. My accommodation to smallness is created in other ways.

Another response accommodation to a visited environment is to become constantly aware of my own familiar embodiment. This process is one of holding on to my own known embodiment. Newly immigrated people often hold onto this process, usually in groups. Again, it is not usually a wakeful decision, but rather a connection with being the way I am. Power and dominance of privileged majorities (White Americans) is an important field condition of this visiting. It may be what keeps the experience of visiting lasting for generations. The inflexibility of the dominant group occurs in not merging or assimilating any of the embodied culture of the visiting group. In terms of the most extreme of polarizations, I am reminded of a phrase I heard from a Midwestern American minister whose comment about a reggae concert was that "we don't move that way."

Body and the Gender Culture

There are many cultural differences between genders (Tannen, 1994; Kraus & Ullman, 1998). Physical embodiment is only one lens. When working at a gender boundary, I encounter the dilemma that mirrors back to me more than just my cognitive understanding of these differences. I/we have biases through which we perceive physical differences in between and within genders. Since my childhood, I have been encouraged to stand tall, throw my chest out, to literally take up as much space with my body as I can. This is an entirely different experience of embodiment that women are socially acculturated to experience. The potential differences are myriad and yet offer potential for either a very powerful awareness or ignorance.

Awareness of how we as men and women organize our bodies can be studied but that is only a brush stroke: an abstraction disconnected from the immediate field. The real work is to be fully attentive in the moment for differences and for how we feel moving in the world that way. How is the world experienced differently if I organize my body in this different way? Can I even use my body this way? What are the implications of power, flexibility, and receptivity? Such are the dilemmas of cultures embodied around gender. This particular kind of embodiment can become so much a part of our immediate experience, and so very much of a co-constituting of the field that we can only be curious, attentive, and notice our own embodied bias shaping itself.

A good example of this is Lowen's concept of the bioenergetic valuing of the "phallic character" as being the goal or ideal for human development (Lowen, 1967; 1971). This is clearly a traditional male value where discharge, independence, and competency are the highest valued aspects of development over relatedness, reflectiveness, and collaboration. A parallel bias that is often rooted in the culture of gender is the emphasis-value of affective expression. Some female (and male) therapists consider a session successful when the client cries. While the expression of emotion can be a powerful cathartic release and movement through painful experiences, such an expression can also become polarized. Other aspects of bodily experience, such as physical groundedness or expressive anger, can be devalued or seen as mere male rigidity.

Arye: A good example of the embodied difference of culture and dominance comes to my awareness when walking back home from work during a dark evening hour. I am suddenly filled with an acute feeling of gratitude for not being a woman. I can imagine how fearful I may have been if I was a woman walking downs this dark path.

Michael: I feel this kind of experience often when talking with female clients who have been abused or physically assaulted. Their culture is physically different. They organize the field and their body differently from how I do; and for them different situations have more threatening meanings and consequently engender different bodily reactions. My male gaze suggests to me that it is a physically different world for them. Often my work in therapy is to do the very thing you mention, imagine and physically attune to what that experience must be like.

Embodied Culture and Clinical Implications

From this discussion some elements of Gestalt therapy seem essential when working with embodied culture. The differences and similarities of the therapist and client can be understood through the lens of a phenomenological and dialogic approach to these differences. It is useful for us as clinicians to understand the characteristics of different embodied cultures. McGoldrick, Giordano, and Pearce (1996) describe ethnic differences and characteristics and their relationship to clinical practice. This profound contribution provides invaluable background to understanding what is ethnically typical in therapy. Similar works describe differences in whites and people of color, that is, differences related to power, privilege, and attitudes towards change (Plummer, 1997; Thomas, 1997).

Arye: Another example is a Contact-Improvisation dance class for women that a friend of mine teaches in an Israeli prison. Among other things, she has remarked on several occasions to me on the great difficulty these women have in changing levels of position, i.e., moving between standing, sitting, and lying down. These movements necessitate some flexibility in quickly releasing and folding joints. What may be the relevance of this seeming inflexibility to being a prisoner? Whatever the answer may be, any attempt to work with these women would take into account their physical organization embedded in the cultural field.

"To influence someone in any serious way, it seems to me, is to have an impact upon that person somatically."   --Morris Berman (1989)

Skills for Attending to Embodied Culture

This discussion so far has been about the notion of embodied culture. What is significant is how our experiences of embodied culture(s) shape our clinical practice. The first stage of this process is sensitization to the client's embodiment. The second stage involves choosing whether or not we attend to this, or whether it is a significant aspect of the field. But the capacity to even have this choice is based on the therapist's attention to bodily/cultural organization, both of his/her own, and the client's. The actions I take when I am with someone who embodies a different culture is based on the field conditions of the relationship, my own capacity to work in this way, and the client's interest in this as a part of the figure and process at any given moment. The following are skills for attending to embodied culture.

Being An Awarefully Embodied Therapist

In order to attend to my client's (and our own) embodiment, I need to be sensitized, not just perceptive (seeing, hearing, and sensing) but also fully present (Perls, Hefferline & Goodman, 1951), that is, feeling myself in the moment. I need to be aware of how I move, sit, breathe, gesture. When I am embodied, I am attending to my own physical experience in the moment. I sense myself in relation to others and how I organize myself/ourselves. Without this awareness, the notion of embodied culture is a notion. The downside of this a priori knowledge can be that we make assumptions about someone's culture based on what we have read or experienced. We can also be unaware of our reactions, movements, and assumptions about the impact. This can create a fuzzy and assumptive field where we intellectualize rather than attend to our experience.

Sensation and Awareness

There is a significant difference between sensation and awareness. Sensations are the raw substances out of which awareness emerges and are later mitigated by language. We can describe our sensations by staying with a particular tactile experience of, say, tightness or tingling or numbness before we move to what such a sensation reminds us of. One way to attend to our clients' sensations is to pay close attention to sensation language; this is especially useful when working with clients of different cultures. Furthermore, our attention supports the development of sensation in them and the development of their awareness of having meaning-driven sensations, even when they don't give voice to the sensation.

On the other hand, if I choose to disclose my own physical experience, I can offer a crisp sense of myself in the room. The third advantage of using sensation language has to do with attunement. I often find myself sitting like my client, "trying on" their gesture, experimenting from where in my body my voice has to come to sound like them. In order to support this kind of elasticity, I need to be aware of my habitual body patterns (body structure). This allows me to better attune to the client's patterns and remain aware of my own, shuttling back and forth. This is all-important at the individual and dyadic level.

When there are cultural differences, my attention to my own physical process can support staying aware and curious about my client's cultural embodiment. I become more potentially attuned to my client's physical experience by being in touch with my own. This is in contrast to the practice of either bracketing off my own sensations or of joining with the client without any obvious measure of self-awareness. The more I myself, however, am aware of my own physical process, the more I co-constitute a field where my client does the same.

An attuned awareness, of course, means that I am using myself like a tuning fork or a Tibetan bowl, where the vibration resonates inside of me. The bowl or fork is always still within me, forged in my culture. But the more sensitized I am, the greater the opportunity for feeling new or different vibrations, feeling the contrast or similarity. This approach can also seem odd to people from cultures (Western European) where boundary or attunement are experienced verbally. Conversely, some cultures may not even use language to communicate the most heartfelt experiences. Remaining attuned to these differences in field conditions is the ongoing skill of the therapist, a discovery rather than a pre-knowing.

Case Example

Michael: I·met Rolfe in a training group in Scandinavia. He is Swedish and carries his body fluidly with a cool expression on his face. As he spoke about himself, I was struck with how unanimated he sounded, how flat and monotonic his voice remained while discussing his father's suicide. I could feel my own throat tightening and my pulse quickening. My eyes felt heavy and thick, almost on the verge of tears. As I looked around the training group (all Scandinavians), I was also stuck how calm everyone looked.

At this point, I became aware of having a number of choices with the differences between how I felt and how he looked/sounded. I could share with Rolfe what I was experiencing while he spoke. The other choice that I took, however, was to become curious about how he used his voice and breath. I began to breathe like him and noticed the entire room also began breathing in a slow but deep rhythm. I did this for a few minutes. When I spoke to him my voice had the same tone as his. I found that I could say anything and yet my tears subsided. I did share this with Rolfe and the group.

We developed an experiment of attending to our breathing in this manner. What emerged out of this process was a theme of keeping hushed voices at a funeral or during painful times in the Scandinavian culture. What also became clear was that a number of the group members had suicides in their family experience. I embodied with Rolfe and the group by noticing my breathing, my throat and chest, as we dialogued. As I looked around the room, I drew everyone's attention to the embodied field we were creating in the moment.

Attention to the Embodied Field

As discussed earlier, individual bodily experience is culturally embedded. To fully appreciate and work with an individual's moment-to-moment experience, it is important to recognize aspects of an individual's field that may be connected to culture. The field transcends the individual and the individual's milieu" (Parlett, 2000). The field suggests which cultural body elements shaped and shape the individual's anatomy.

Knowledge of the role of field in body-oriented work includes the role/relationship of the client and therapist, the differing gender and power influences, and the immediate and long-term forces that led to the consultation. Such knowledge encourages us further, namely, to be attentive and attuned to the embodied cultures of all people in the room.

The process of attending to culture/body as part of the field is one of questioning and directing awareness. If the field is the ground in the moment (Wheeler, 1991), then attention to the field enlarges the ground out of which awareness and meaning emerge. The two skills I need the most in order to attend to the concept of body/culture at play are 1) the skill of noticing my assumptions about physical movement, expression, and structure; 2) the skill of attending to how the client's bodily experience may be embedded in a larger cultural pattern different from my own.

Case Example

Angela is a new client referred to me for body work. She is a muscular woman with a thick chest and back. Her hair is cut very short and she wears athletic clothing (sweat suit and workout shoes). She tells me that she is 'of course, a lesbian' and that she was referred by her partner (a therapist) who felt she should see a man, someone like me.

I was aware of how many stories I could generate from what she already said and from her sheer physical presence in the room. Ironically, we were dressed similarly and had almost the same body shape. The assumptions I had about her body shape were based on how I got that way - playing sports and weightlifting. This was my most immediate assumption, which I kept reminding myself to not believe too strongly. What also stood out for me was that Angela was focused on my being a male in some way.

I decided to ask her to say more about how my maleness was significant to her and also to pay attention to her physical experience as she spoke. She immediately asked me if I was going to do the same. This sounded like a good path since we could both take more responsibility for the contact. She shifted in her seat to face me, tightened her hands into fists, and held her breath. "You first!"

As I told Angela about how I experienced myself as a male in relation to her, she listened intently. When I shared my experience of feeling tense in my head, she laughed. Without any question from me, she said: "So are we going to butt heads?" I did not have this image but encouraged her to pay attention to her head. She thought for a while. For Angela, the entire situation, being sent here, the way I looked to her (like a big block), and my gender felt to her like a "head butting situation."

This was entirely different from my early image that we were similar; she now anticipated us as butting heads. We later experimented with embodying both butting heads and some opposites, such as relaxing our necks and heads and then attending to the difference in our individual and collaborative experiences. What strikes me about this encounter is that Angela's embodied culture, which included considerable conflict with "butt head" men, including my appearance and my psycho-physical responsibility to "keep my head," co-created a specific field that we were now both experiencing and experimenting with. My assumptions about how she developed her body type were wrong. She grew up in an environment where she had to brace herself repeatedly to absorb both physical and verbal blows from her father.

This process of attending to the embodied field in the moment led to our clarifying the different engendered meanings that Angela and I carried. She was later able to explore the potential of softening and expressing more emotion in relation to me and to others. This new skill developed over time because we mutually paid attention to what her physical organization supported her to manage. Secondly, by attending to my assumptions about her body structure (which were embedded in my own male sports culture), I was able to hear and see her in the contexts (field conditions) out of which she developed.

Dialogic Process

I am interested in dialoging with my client about their experience. My intention is to offer them the ways I experience them as physical and to encourage them to dialogue with me about what I observe in their physical patterns. By offering my own sensations, I am acknowledging both of our experiences as forming the field itself.

Case Example

Rose is from Argentina. She often looks far away as if she is sleeping. As I catch her eyes when I am dealing with others in the training group, she appears to be aware of the process. Her physical process is paradoxical in that she seems to be out of contact and yet deeply attuned at the same time. One of the group members once asked her about what she was doing. There are many times when initially this conversation has a hostile and accusatory tone with statements like "Are you part of the group or not?" I asked both Rose and the other woman, Eleanor, to talk about what they are experiencing and doing in their bodies. As Eleanor talked, Rose's eyes rolled back in her head and she smiled.

This act of course, brings on another level of accusation. So I then asked Rose what she was doing with her eyes. I told her I was very curious about this motion. She said, "I am seeing pictures of scenes as she talks. I am visioning her words." We continued to dialogue, drawing Eleanor into the process. Rose rolled her head and fluttered her eyes even more. Now Eleanor wanted to know what Rose saw when she talked, and "How does she do that!" This led to a dialogue between the two of them about Rose's culture of shamanism that she was raised in as a child. I responded to Rose by telling her I could feel her eyes on me during the group. This, in turn, led the group to a deeper discussion of all the physical and non-verbal ways that we were affecting each other. This moment framed a significant connection and widened the group's field. Without our willingness to dialogue about our physical experiences, the group's process may have remained at the traditional serve and volley verbal interaction. Rose might have been marginalized based on the group's body assumptions.

Phenomenological Stance

Michael: Some of the criticism of Gestalt therapy has been based on our tendency to be White European, Judeo Christian in our approach (Plummer, 1997; Thomas, 1977). At times we may overemphasize certain body movements or gestures out of this culture/body bias. A common example of this is the value frequently put on clients facing and looking directly at us. When working with a Japanese or African American client who is not looking directly in our eyes, I want to avoid assumptions about this behavior; rather than assume this is a deflection or avoidance of "good contact."

The dilemma is that I am part of the field. I cannot stand outside of my perceptions as if they are objective (Sapriel, 1998). But a phenomenological stance in attending to body is to attempt to be aware of my assumptions (both cognitive and physical) and to offer behaviorally descriptive observations. For example, I describe the muscles in my client's face, his/her eyebrows, rather than to talk about his/her affect or feelings. Part of the phenomenological stance is what I am seeing and hearing that leads to the conclusion of grief or terror.

Perception is not only culturally biased, but also personally biased and based upon some data that we usually synthesize into a conclusion. For example, if I see someone's eyes narrow as they look at me, I can quickly synthesize this into a conclusion that they are angry, holding back tears, suffering from an allergic reaction. All or none of these may be true. My point is that while we attend carefully to language, frequently therapists comment on body language (a conclusion) or affect (a softer, more gentle conclusion). But verbal language is often the figure or summation experienced based in a background of physical movement and expressions.

A classic mis-attunement in Gestalt therapy may be based on assumptions of a different embodied culture where privacy and physical space are managed by averting eyes, or where looking directly into eyes is experienced as a challenge. A contrast to this is the amount of physical space taken up by an American from the West. In that culture where there is enormous physical space available, the freedom to move around and "looking square in the eyes" is both common and a value of an honest person.

The biggest challenge is to not make quick meanings out of body movements, gestures, and patterns of group physical interactions. I am interested in exploring the client's experience and in describing the client's body process while remaining open to correction /clarification. This requires staying longer at the level of sensation, attending to movement, gesture, breathing, and speech descriptively. That is, I should not jump to the thematic level so rapidly but rather spend time and awareness in sensing. In order to do this, I must be sensitized, paying attention to my own embodiment. I must know how to see and to describe the physical behavior of individuals, pairs, and groups.

Case Example

Raj and I sit across from each other in my office. He is a first generation Indian and I am a fourth generation white man of Irish/Dutch/German origin. He has come to therapy complaining of headaches. His headaches have been determined to be psychosomatic, as he explained to me. He started the session by telling me the names of all the physicians who had determined this diagnosis. He then looked at me and smiled, his face uplifted with open eyes and a slightly open mouth.

I was aware of both smiling back at Raj and resisting this at the same time. My mouth seemed to lift upward each time he smiled; yet I didn't feel either pleased or happy. This happened about five times until I began to notice tightness in my forehead. As I felt my own headache emerging, I became curious about what he/we were doing. There was something about my desire/refusal to lift my facial muscles into a smile. I was also aware of his repeated smiling at me. What was it about this situation that we were co-creating that supported his uplifted beaming face? This process took about five minutes as he talked about his headaches.

I decided to talk to Raj about what I noticed in him and in my own physical experience. After I did so, he rubbed his head and asked: "You think smiling gives me a headache?" I replied that I was not sure about him but this was what was happening for me. We devised an experiment where we tried to smile and pay attention to our heads. Soon Raj became aware that the more he smiled the greater tension he felt in the place of his frequent headaches. This led to our discussion of him smiling with me. Raj talked about respecting me as the doctor, the professional. This was for him, an Indian man, an important role. As he said this, he smiled and then nodded his head: "This is what one does with a professional person in India." So, I observed, Raj becomes aware that he has been in situations where he has been meeting many American professionals, first in job interviews and then for medical consultations. He looks at me again and says: "A lot of smiling!"

The field Raj and I co-created involved us playing out the roles of the smiling Indian man and the professional white American expert. By noticing what I was drawn into, Raj and I were able to identify our cultural and cross-cultural embodiments. The phenomenological stance here did not involve bracketing-off in a pure sense; instead, it was about noticing how I was perceiving and physically behaving. Ironically, Raj's headaches decreased through his awareness of how he used his face to manage contact, a behavior that he identified as part of his embodied culture. From a traditional Gestalt perspective, Raj's behavior could be seen as an attempt at confluence. My interventions with Raj emerged from attending to my experience being with him. He and I behaved and organized our bodies in relation to each other. This became the figure of the session. By remaining aware of how I was co-regulating the field (person of power; to smile or not to smile), we expanded his bodily awareness of adjustment beyond the individual and interpersonal level to include embodiment of culture.

Concluding Thoughts

Arye: Body-focused Gestalt allows me to approach differences with phenomenological tools, casting away stereotypes, codified body language and prejudices. I do my best to be very aware of my own ground, my own bias, and the eyeglasses through which I perceive others. Only then, hopefully, will I be able to work with clients through their introjects, patterns of confluence, or culturally trained retroflections. In this respect my dance of bringing to awareness some inner cultural figures is still ongoing.

The relationship between body and culture is inextricable. Each culture has its own rituals, movements and patterns. These patterns both develop and maintain the culture. Assumptions based in our own culture can lead us to differing and sometimes mis-attuned choices in therapy. The myth of the objective observer is only half the dilemma. There is also a myth of the objective feelings, that all bodies are the same. Different cultures develop differences in bodies, cultural field-conditions, affect rituals, patterns of movement, values, and judgments about bodily experience and development.

We live in a world where cultures both overlap and at times seem hardened into ethnic silos. Increasing numbers of people travel between cultures and reside in different cultures. The speed of travel, global business, and electronic media bring movements, its body styles, habits, customs, and us into contact with different cultures. The inherent White European assumptions of Gestalt therapy (a culture itself) are assumptions embodied often out of awareness. The corresponding dilemma is the Western tendency to idealize other cultures (particularly people of color) as being ultimately more spiritual, more embodied and more contactful. This lens also may obscure our awareness of the cultural body relationship; it is our cultural postcard, a snapshot rather than an immersion in the embodied field of that culture.

We have intended this study to offer some possibilities regarding attending to the relationship of Body and Culture. We do not suggest this is the only bodily figure to be worked with cross-culturally nor that culture need always be figural. But the presence of body and culture is always part of the field. It is only through attention to field conditions that include our own bodies as co-organizers of the field with our patients that biased assumptions can be suspended on both sides. Awareful suspension (rather than denial of assumptions) is the path to a phenomenological stance and a dialogic process that makes contact possible across and within embodied cultures. Perhaps what we create in intercultural, inter-embodied therapy are new cultures, temporary field conditions that allow us to attend and be curious on the sensate level. Perhaps the therapist, at best, helps co-create not only a shared language, and shared ideas, but also a new embodiment out of which awareness and change can emerge.

Personal Account

Michael: As I remember our process of writing this Chapter, I am struck how the influences of culture managed our work. The two of us sat at computers sending across cyberspace ideas, feelings and experiences that we lived separately and collaboratively. We were both moving in our bodies dancing across the keys and listening to the sounds and movements around us in our two different worlds. You in Tel Aviv and me here in Pittsburgh, Pa. I look out the window and see six inches of snow and red brick houses. People walk by, trudging along against the cold . I remember Tel Aviv and imagine an entirely different view out your window. But at the same time, during this writing process we were connected by our curiosity of these embodied differences. We had to get back to our bodily experience sometimes to connect, to describe through our own movement, sinew and breath what we meant and were trying to communicate. It was not enough that we had shared history before, each time we had to reconnect across our cultures. Many times we would ask each other what do you mean by that word? Can you translate please? Our struggle to do this mirrors the challenge of working across cultures and the wisdom that our bodies provide as the embodiment of connection and difference.

Michael C. Clemmens, Pittsburg, PA, USA

Arye: As I respond to your writing, Michael. I can imagine your presence, the way you wrinkle your forehead, the shine of your eyes, the dimensions of your body, your smile when my comment strikes home. Would I be able to write similarly· if it was in my language, Hebrew? Probably not. "Strike home" would make no sense, and maybe the intimacy of the physical description might feel awkward. Somehow, "talking" to you across the e-mail takes me, in my imagination and feeling, to Pittsburgh, or to "Gestalt land" with its particular ethos and sensibilities. I find myself softer, less guarded, and more open. It is as if talking "about" culture and body with you takes me somewhat out of my "cultural body," and into a more personal relationship with you. This reminds me of how fluid is this field of "Body" we talk about. How we constantly keep changing and re-structuring ourselves in the process of relating, even when it is a trans-Atlantic relation like ours.

Arye Bursztyn, Tel Aviv, Israel

References

Berman, M. (1989). *Coming To Our Senses: body and spirit in the hidden history of the west*. Seattle, Wa: Seattle Writer's Guild.

Clemmens, M. C. & Bursztyn, A. (2003) <u>Culture and Body-A Phenomenological and Dialogic Inquiry.</u> *British Gestalt Journal*, Volume 12 No. 1.

Fisher, S. (1973). *Body Conciousness*. Englewood cliffs, N.J.: Prentice Hall.

Frank, R. (2001). Reaching and being reached. *Gestalt Review* (4) 4 301-308.

Frank, R. (2001). *Body of Awarenes*. Cambridge, MA: Gestalt Press.

Guiterrez, L. (1998). *Ground Sequence Model*. Unpublished paper, Gestalt Institute of Cleveland.

Hall, E. T. (1966). *The Hidden Dimension*. NY: Anchor Books.

Johnston, S. (1994). *Character Styles*. New York: Norton.

Keleman, S. (1985). *Emotional Anatomy*. Berkeley, Ca: Center Press.

Kepner, J. (1993). *Body Process: working with the body in psychotherapy*. San Francisco: Jossey–Bass.

Kepner, J. (1995). *Healing Tasks: psychotherapy with adult survivors of childhood trauma*. San Francisco: Jossey-Bass.

Kepner, J. (2001). Gestalt approaches to body oriented therapy. *Gestalt Review* (4) 4, 262-266.

Kraus, M.A. & Ullman, D. (1998). Feminist relational theories & Gestalt therapy: a lively dialogue. In *The Gendered Field*, GIC Press Monograph series. Ullman, D.D. & Wheeler (Eds). Cambridge, Ma: GIC Press.

Lowen, A. (1967). *The Betrayal of the Body*. N.Y.: Collier.

Lowen, A. (1971). *The Language of the Body*. N.Y.: Collier.

Markova,D. (1996). *Open mind: exploring the 6 patterns of natural intelligence*. Berkeley, Ca: Conari Press.

Montagu, A. (1978). *Touching: the human significance of the skin*. N.Y.: Harper.

McGoldrick, M., Giordano, & Pearce, J. K. (1996). *Ethnicity in Family Therapy*. Second Edition. New York, London: The Guilford

Press.

Parlett, M. (1997). The Unified Field in Practice. *British Gestalt Journal*, 1, 16-33.

Parlett, M. (2000). Creative adjustment in the global field. *British Gestalt Journal*, (9) 1, 13-2.

Perls, F. S. (1947; 1969). *Ego, Hunger and Aggression*. New York: Vintage Books.

Perls, F., Hefferline, R. & Goodman, P. (1951). *Gestalt Therapy: Excitement and growth in the human personality*. New York: Julian Press.

Perls, F. S. (1969). *Gestalt Therapy Verbatim*. New York: Vintage Books.

Perls, L. (1992). *Living at the Boundary*. Highland, N.Y.: The Gestalt Journal Press.

Plummer, D. (1997). A Gestalt approach to culturally responsive mental health treatment, *Gestalt Review*, (1) 3, 190-204.

Reich, W. (1945; 1972). *Character Analysis*. New York: Simon & Schuster.

Sapriel, L. (1998). Intersubjectivity, Self-psychology and Gestalt. *British Gestalt Journal*, 7, (1), 33-44.

Smith, E. (1985). *The Body in Psychotherapy*. Jefferson, N.C.: McFarland.

Sue, D. & Sue, D. (1990). *Counseling the Culturally Different: theory and practice*. New York: John Wiley and Sons.

Tannen, D. (1994). *Gender Discourse*. New York: Oxford Press.

Thomas, B.Y. (1977). Integrating Multicultural Perspectives in Gestalt Theory and Practice. *The Gestalt Voice* (6)2, 1-9.

Wheeler, G. (1991). *Gestalt Reconsidered*. New York: Gardner Press.

Section Four

bridging in therapy

XIV. FOR WHITES ONLY

By Lynne Jacobs, Ph.D., Psy.D.

I was startled when I first greeted my new patient. She was a tall (5'11") African American. I collected myself as quickly as possible, hoping not to insult her with my initial shock.

On the phone, I'd had no inkling that she might be black. In fact, I had expected to meet a young, possibly quite shallow white woman. My reasons were that her voice had sounded young and thin, much like the infamous "valley girl" popularized in the '80s (the "valley girl" was a comic icon of U.S. culture, caricaturing shallow, vapid, materialistic, self-absorbed culture of some white, suburban middle-class families).

As Joyce began to tell me the story of her decision to seek psychotherapy for herself, I chided myself for my assumption that I would be meeting a white woman at my waiting room door: Joyce had not "sounded" black. I was also amused and only a little chagrined as I saw myself continuing to encounter my disparaging stereotype of how shallow Joyce must be if she speaks with a "valley girl" lilt.

Joyce was seeking therapy because she was unable to overcome serious depression and waves of anxiety that had beset her for about 14 months, ever since a male lover had broken up with her in a hurtful and inglorious manner.

I was still trying to make sense of our beginnings. Joyce was obviously intelligent and psychologically astute, although more perceptive about others than about herself. As she settled in, her voice even deepened and became more resonant, much to my relief. But I found myself wondering why she had chosen to see me, a white therapist, rather than one of the many black therapists who practice in the Los Angeles area. I wondered if she knew of the availability of African American therapists, if she purposely chose a white therapist, or if the fact of our race difference was unimportant to her. That last thought embarrassed me, confronting me with the reality of how her race WAS important to me, and I felt vaguely guilty, as though I ought not to be having any awkwardness or discomfort, or to be thinking of her as, among other things, a "black" woman. I was being bitten by a common bug in our culturally diverse and racially divided country, and it is an element of the subjectivity of most white therapists. I call it white anxiety. I shall discuss it further at a later point.

This is almost a stream-of-consciousness article. I have used the writing here as a chance to reflect and to learn. I can only hope it is not as difficult to read as it was to write. The reader is warned that the article does not flow smoothly from one idea to the next. It jumps and twists in a reflection of the jumps and twists and side-trails my heart and mind took in the process of writing, which became an encounter with my "whiteness." It jumps from one scene to another, from attempts at reason, to emotional memories, to passionately held beliefs and aims.

I am reminded of June Jordan's 1981 reference to an interview with Toni Morrison about her book, *Beloved* (2004). Morrison spoke of pulling readers out of their familiar world, wrenching them into a strange and terrifying world, much as had happened to the Africans who became slaves. Whenever I try to walk through the minefield of explorations in race relations, I have the experience she describes. Familiar moorings and sensibilities are wrenched away. I have entered a strange, shadowy landscape that at once pulls me in and repels me. I am afraid; I am fascinated; I am impelled by my wish to contribute to the healing of the racial divide, and to heal myself.

The next thing I must warn you, the reader, is that every time I have sat down to write this piece, the reasoned passages that I have mentally crafted disappear, to be replaced by passionate polemic at the keyboard. I am uncomfortable writing this essay, I am anxious, I feel exposed, I dread being judged. And yet I want to contribute, in some small way, to healing the wounds of racism. I am writing a plea for my fellow white therapists to be cognizant of the effect of our dominant status on how we think, act and feel in everyday life, and in the consulting room.

The title of this paper is rich with multiple meanings, just as is any examination of, or dialogue about, race -- certainly in American culture. One meaning of the title is to serve as a reminder to me of who my audience is, to whom I wish to speak.

I am a White clinician writing to other white clinicians -- most especially White American clinicians -- about the phenomenology of whiteness for American Whites, and its various implications for our work as therapists. The title, "For Whites Only," is also a bitter reminder of how charged race matters are, how exclusionary white thought tends to be, largely unbeknownst to whites. "Whites only" was once a cruel segregationist clarion call, raining daily degradation down on Black Americans. Unfortunately, there are still deeply embedded "whites only" constructs of thought and ideology that permeate our culture, largely outside of ordinary everyday awareness. These embedded mores affect our daily conduct and the conduct of our therapy, both with whites and people of color. Americans practice in a cultural field shaped by history and current practices which once existed "for whites only ".

I feel almost embarrassed by the depth of my passion against racism and prejudice in American culture, most especially about subtle, often unrecognized forms of white racism and racial insensitivity. It puts me in a curious position: Throughout my life, I have been asked to account for why I am so impassioned. And I certainly can think of influences in my life that might at least partially account for it, such as the fact that I was raised in an area of the U.S. that had a marked "color line." In fact, my parents belonged to a small advocacy group that fought to remove impediments to housing integration in our town on the outskirts of Washington, D. C.

There are also more uniquely personal, as opposed to sociological, threads of my life history that incline me to feel a close identification with disenfranchised people. And yet, being asked to explore where my interest comes from seems to me to be a way of participating in the very racial insensitivity I am attempting to overcome. For the question supposes that I am a bit unusual, and should account for my difference (How often I have heard African Americans complain of having to "explain" their "difference" to well-intentioned but ignorant Whites!). The more intriguing question for me is why so few Whites are even aware of, and distressed by, the extremity of the racial divide in the U.S.. How is it that an interest in one of the most cancerous problems of American culture is viewed as unusual and in need of explanation when a white person expresses interest, and yet it is viewed as self-evident -- if a bit overwrought, from the perspective of many Whites -- when expressed by a person of color? The fact that the question hovers in the air at all is, I believe, one of the manifestations of how isolated Whites are from a problem in which they are dominant participants.

As an example of the problem of lack of awareness among Whites, I had a conversation recently with two white colleagues; one had been raised in east Texas -- part of the American south -- and the other had been raised in Los Angeles, California. Both had attended "all-white" public schools. The southerner said that the shadow of knowing that he and the entire white community were doing something morally egregious hung over all, even the segregationists.

The Angeleno had given no thought at all to her all-white schooling. Unlike the situation in Texas, the segregation in Los Angeles was not accomplished through the use of visible and tensely enforced laws, but rather through the more hidden processes of real estate brokers, mortgage lenders, and various other social and political practices that allowed the segregation to be seen as "accidental" rather than designed.

For the southerner, our racial history is a major part of his sense of identity as an American, whereas for the Angeleno, it is a minor theme. I contend, however, that the racial divide in America has shaped what becomes (or does not become) figural in her sense of herself and others as thoroughly as it has the white southerner, or any black American, but the shaping factors remain lodged in the background, an ignored dimension of her field; whereas for the white southerner, the "racialization" of his consciousness can more readily become figural.

Whiteness

I have identified myself as a white person, and an American, two signifiers that are often treated as if they are interchangeable -- at least by White Americans. Authors generally do not use the signifier of "White," or "Caucasian," unless, as I am doing now, the author needs to establish whiteness in relation to non-whiteness. In most other instances, there is an assumption, at least among Whites, of whiteness unless stated otherwise. The assumption of whiteness is not ordinarily figural. It is simply one of the many background assumptions that, without awareness, shape the world-view of most White Americans.

If you are a white reader, imagine yourself with a patient. You most probably thought of a white patient (certainly the overwhelming majority of my current and former patients are white). But the fact of their whiteness was probably meaningless to you. In all likelihood, the meanings to each of you of working together as a white dyad have rarely become figural. I can think of only a few white patients in my current practice who give any thought to the fact that we are a white therapist-patient dyad.

"The most striking characteristic of whites' consciousness of whiteness is that most of the time we don't have any. I call this the transparency phenomenon: the tendency of whites not to think about whiteness, or about norms, behaviors, experiences, or perspectives that are white specific" (Gotanda, 1997: 72-3).

Examine this quote from Jane Flax (1990), below. She is writing about the lack of consciousness among males of the context of "maleness." I shall amend her paragraph by substituting racial terms in brackets next to her gender terms.

"Rarely have male [white] scholars self-consciously studied the "psychology of men [whiteness]" or "men's" history [history of whiteness] or considered the possibility that how men [whites] feel about women [people of color] and their own gender [white] identities may affect every aspect of their thinking about and acting in the world. This denial of men's [whites'] own location in and determination by gender [race] systems has practical consequences as well. Male [white] scholars tend not to read feminist [antiracist] theories or to think about possible implications for their own work. Women [people of color] are left with the responsibility for thinking about gender [race], but because we do it, such work is devalued or segregated from the "mainstream" of intellectual life" (Flax, 1990: 24).

I could just as easily have substituted "heterosexual" for male, and the paragraph would still have much evocative power and heuristic value. Males, whites, straights, all occupy positions of unmarked, dominant status in our culture, and studying any one of those perspectives would be illuminating. In fact, Barbara Thomas, who has developed a curriculum which integrates gestalt theory and multicultural perspectives, makes a good case for how the exploration of any multicultural theme is likely to increase our skills as a therapist for any patient, because learning about other cultures enriches our ground. It expands the range of themes that might emerge into figural awareness as we listen closely to all of our patients. She writes:

"Phenomena such as the invisibility of culture and privilege, the operation of the "absent standard" and the heightened visibility of tokens provide excellent examples for teaching the concept of figure/ground.... Development of theme is an important component of Gestalt Therapy process. Within this context, knowledge of other cultures, sub-cultures, ethnic and social groups can be conceptualized as material which increases our sensitivity to themes which may arise in our work with clients. By enlarging our ground we gain access to possible themes which otherwise would not become figural for the therapist who does not share the cultural background of the client" (Thomas, B., 1997: 6-7).

Having witnessed the phenomenon with some of my colleagues (and having participated in it myself), I concur with her warning that there is a danger of applying one's cultural knowledge so rigidly or enthusiastically that the uniqueness of the patient is annihilated. I am sure we have all had the experience of talking with someone who "knows" us because they claim to be familiar with our culture. The "knowing" stops at the level of cultural generalization. I have certainly had that experience in conversations about my female gender. Somehow, general statements about the cultural norms of a different group sound most offensive to me when they are spoken with conspiratorial delight with, or pride about, one's knowledge of the "other"; and especially when the speaker is a member of the dominant culture. It is ironic -- because although certainly some knowledge is better than none -- that the uniqueness of individuals is still ignored, and a major complaint among African-Americans, for instance, is that they are invisible.

I would expand Thomas' thesis a step further. Gestalt field theory posits that reality is ambiguous, open to multiple interpretations, and is perspectival. Therefore, learning something about other cultures and sub-cultures also helps therapists to contextualize, and therefore become more aware of, and relativize, our own cultural norms. This seems to be an especially important heuristic tool for American White therapists, because we are less likely to have encounters in our daily lives that open the doors to such awareness.

As I noted above, for various personal and political reasons, racial inequality burns my heart. Moreover, insensitive and ignorant use of power makes me irate when I am not demoralized by it. These passions show in my choices as a therapist: I gravitate towards theories that call upon therapists to be continuously self-reflective as to their impact on their patients (in gestalt therapy, this shows in our commitment to the necessary awareness of our impact that a dialogic relationship embodies). Self-reflectiveness and openness to correction by the patient are the best safeguards against ignorant abuse of our power as therapists.

So while I think it behooves White therapists to be open to learning from and about our patients from other cultures in order to work more sensitively with them, I also value such study and engagement for their value in helping white therapists deconstruct our own "whiteness," and in so doing help us to recognize the white norms and advantages we tend to accept as universal givens. Such deconstruction, or contextualization, is part of the process of equalizing power between races, one encounter at a time. Although I feel awkward and anxious in this process, as I said earlier, I also feel inspired by it. I agree with McConville's (1997) assertion that "any system of privilege not only oppresses the disenfranchised, but poisons the spirit and diminishes the humanity of those who are advantaged" (McConville, 1997: 13).

White Privilege

"White skin privilege" is a term that came into popular usage in the liberal days of the Sixties and Seventies. It was a way of connoting the cultural and social advantages of whiteness in American culture. One of the white skin privileges exercised by most of us who can lay claim to it is a total lack of consciousness of our whiteness, as described above, and therefore of the privilege that comes with it.

To become aware of our privilege as a reflection of our whiteness immediately contextualizes something that for most whites is experienced as a universal, not perspectival truth. Contextualizing our privilege immediately makes our empowerment something which is fluid, and may shift and change, rather than something that is eternal and immutable. When such notions are raised in gatherings of whites, one can often detect an uncomfortable shifting of chairs in the room.

Peggy McIntosh (1995) believes that whites are taught not to recognize white privilege. She writes that white privilege is "an invisible package of unearned assets that I can count on cashing in each day, but about which I was "meant" to remain oblivious. White privilege is like an invisible weightless knapsack of special provisions, assurances, tools, maps, guides, codebooks, passports, visas, clothes, compass, emergency gear, and blank checks" (McIntosh, 1995: 77).

The signifier of whiteness and white skin privilege is the white, Anglo-Saxon Protestant (WASP). I have the look and carriage of a WASP, and am treated accordingly. Actually, I am not a typical WASP, but was raised very much as if I am, which is again a white skin privilege. I am the grandchild of immigrants. My maternal grandfather was born in England, and was WASP. But my other grandfather was a Jew from Poland. My two grandmothers were both Irish Catholics; one arrived in the U.S. at age 17, and kept her brogue until her death. As McConville (1997) has pointed out, in the ever-shifting boundaries by which whiteness is defined, Irish Americans were initially considered non-white.

So, technically, I am not a WASP, but I most certainly am white, and I look like a WASP (blonde hair, light complexion, light eyes); and in one of the conceits afforded to Whites in this country, I was raised as if I came from no culture in particular, but was simply "American." It was as if my family had sprung up suddenly on American shores through the process of spontaneous generation. I never had a sense that we came from somewhere else first.

Of course, WASPs do have a specific culture, and "whiteness" is a historically situated, sociopolitical designation (Hale, 1998). WASP cultural norms include a valorization of individualism, stoicism, and conquering or rising above obstacles (as opposed to "adaptive fatalism") (McGoldrick, Pearce, and Giordano, 1982). There is a strong emphasis on the nuclear family, and on "correctness," on having the family and its individual members successfully achieve whatever values are held in esteem at the time (McGoldrick, et al., 1982). These values have come to be fused into what Margaret Mead called an "American culture." They constitute an invisible standard by which others are measured, and the measuring happens without our awareness because Whites do not recognize the standards as cultural norms. Rather they are assumed to be universals of healthy or correct living (Thomas, 1997).

The invisible standard wields an enormous power at all levels of culture and government, in large part because it operates as a silent, unacknowledged background; so the various mores that comprise the standard are taken as objective givens rather than as perspectival. I shall explore this further in a later section on Social Darwinism.

Racial Consciousness

I was intrigued by a reference Thomas (1997) made to a statement by Carter (1995), pointing out that all people go through a developmental process in the formation of a racial identity, and that their developmental stage may be more crucial than their color when it comes to cross-race conversation. In writing this article, I have had many associations to my own history, and most of my associations have been about my whiteness as a racial phenomenon rather than my WASPness as a cultural phenomenon. I certainly have a sense, heightened in the process of revising this article, that the development of my racial identity is a developmental process, activated even as I write.

I find myself wondering again how much to tell of the details of the development of my racial consciousness. The details seem mundane in the telling, although they are emotionally powerful to me. Probably more important than any particular story, however, is that my mother and her family were always racially conscious. My grandmother was an Irish Catholic, my grandfather an English Baptist. They had witnessed and had been hurt by religious intolerance often enough that it was a small step for them to develop antipathy for intolerance and discrimination of all kinds.

My grandmother and my mother and father all were active, to varying degrees, with groups that sought to equalize justice and opportunity between Blacks and Whites. It was not uncommon in my house to view our life stories through a racial lens. I can cull out two major trends in the development of my racial consciousness. The first is that, unlike McIntosh (1995), I was aware very early in my life of my white privilege in conjunction with my awareness of black disenfranchisement. The second is that I have a lot of what I call racial self-consciousness.

Of the first trend, learning about racism has always had a two-fold focus of attention for me: "what it means to be black in America" and "what it means to be white in America." They go hand in hand for me, having grown up in a town where the differences between white and black were quite visible. As I described earlier, I was raised in an area of the U.S. that had a prominent, albeit de facto, "color line." Whites lived in the suburbs surrounding a city largely populated by African Americans. This was the metropolitan Washington, D.C. area. The area was also a focal point for the legislative thrust of the civil rights movement. The inequities of life along the color line are seared into my racial and social consciousness.

The second theme I can cull out is one of racial self-consciousness. My interest in race matters makes me acutely aware of racial differences. I tend to be very interested in talking with others, white and black, about racial issues and experience. I have a sense that this is a "stage" along the way in the further development of my racial consciousness and sensitivity. What I imagine is that if I had the chance to engage in race-based dialogues to my heart's content, I would no longer seek that kind of conversation at every opportunity. The problem for me now is that, when my conversational partners are African Americans, I run the risk of rendering them invisible again if at that moment they are in a more color-blind mind-set. I do not move easily from racial consciousness to color-blindness, and both mindsets are necessary for intimate contacting between blacks and whites. This has implications for therapy, which I will address at a later point.

At any rate back, to my story. You can see from what I have written that I made the usual white background assumption that unless I picked up evidence to the contrary, the woman I was to meet would be white. Joyce is a sociologist with a particular interest in racial consciousness, and racial experiences in LA. When I did ask her, in our second meeting, if she had given any thought to finding an African American therapist, she said that she had gotten my name from a colleague she trusted (a white sociologist whom I had seen for therapy a few years earlier), and the referral was more important to her than color. My question also seemed to raise her level of defensiveness slightly, and I knew that she was already quite embarrassed that she was seeking therapy in the first place, so I did not inquire further.

Several weeks passed and the therapy lurched along with few references to her race, and none to mine. She would occasionally mention a difficult interaction or situation, and in the process of exploration I sometimes asked her for the race of the person with whom she was struggling. She would appear relieved and identify the person as white. At that point we would explore the possibility that the difficulties arose in part as a result of the racial prejudices or ignorance of the other person. But I always had to initiate the race-based discussions.

I continued to be uneasy that we had not overtly acknowledged our racial difference. I could not see that she was uneasy, but I was. I became tangled in doubts of almost obsessive proportion. The doubts took my thoughts in various directions. I was reluctant to impose a figure into her process of talking about her own interests if that figure was an enactment of my anxiety. I wondered if perhaps I wanted to offer an African American therapist so that she would leave and relieve me of my anxiety. Or, I wondered, perhaps I wanted the overt acknowledgment of our racial differences so that I could establish myself as different from "those other" whites. Then again, I wondered if perhaps I needed the acknowledgement of our racial difference because I was not as developed, in terms of my racial consciousness, as I thought I should be. On the other hand, I hoped that maybe, just maybe, such an acknowledgement might be helpful to Joyce, who might need me to take the initiative.

One of the striking "symptoms" of my anxious self-doubt is the harsh tone of self-doubt and self-criticism in them. This is a not uncommon experience for other whites who are racially sensitive. This may be a manifestation of white guilt, something else I will also address at a later point in the paper.

White Anxiety

I am anxious when I meet a new patient who is from a cultural, ethnic or racial group different from my own. I am also anxious when I begin to work with someone from a markedly more elevated social class than mine. Some of my anxiety is a simple fear of strangeness or newness. That anxiety is quickly overcome by establishing contact and getting to know the patient a little better. Then anxiety turns to interest. Some of the anxiety is a heightened concern about whether I will be competent with this new patient. This concern, common at the start of any new therapy, is heightened by my worries that I am a "multicultural illiterate." Finally, there is a darker anxiety that nibbles around the edges of my awareness, lingering for some time, specific to working with African American patients. I think it has to do with a vague feeling of threat to my sense of innocence or goodness. I anticipate that our work together will throw me into an encounter with my complicity with white privilege, and also that our relationship will have an edginess based on the patient's silent accusations of me for enjoying white privilege, and of my racial guilt and shame.

One day Joyce started talking about the details of a study she was conducting. She mentioned that she always had to allow twice as long for interviews with white people than with other interviewees. She said it took the white interviewees an extra hour or so to become comfortable enough with her to speak freely and openly. They had to overcome their anxiety over whether they would make a racial faux pas, and their worry of being harshly criticized by my patient. She said that the whites in her study lacked a vocabulary for addressing multicultural themes, whereas the other participants were highly articulate.

I was reminded, as she spoke, of my first few awkward sessions with her: my anxiety, confusion, twinge of self-conscious shame; not knowing how to acknowledge our racial difference, not knowing how much it "ought" to matter. I decided to tell her what I was thinking. I described the tangle of doubt and confusion I experienced in not knowing whether I was being more racist by mentioning race, or by not mentioning race. We both had a good laugh, and the atmosphere between us underwent a palpable change for the better. I believe that this was a signal to her that we could talk about the effects of racism on her life, but also, and perhaps more importantly for the development of our relationship, that we could also talk about my "whiteness," and my racial consciousness, and about how both of these factors influenced our work together. We have both been looser, freer, with each other since then.

Often, my biggest problem during the course of treatment with Joyce was that I believed I must resist my temptation to engage in talk about race matters. She has people with whom she engages freely in such conversations, but I don't. I am hungry for the chance, and she is astute and articulate about racial themes. I remember a visit I made to the Gestalt Institute of Cleveland, and how nourished I felt by frequent conversations about race matters. Their integration of multicultural consciousness with gestalt theory and training looks seamless to me from the outside. I especially relished conversations among Whites about race matters. I found several other Whites who were passionately interested in deconstructing whiteness and in attempting to cross the racial divide, and even one white man who had read many of the same books by African American writers that I had read. I was in "race matters" heaven.

Once, shortly after my visit to Cleveland, Joyce and I were exploring her distaste for public speaking. We began to look in greater detail at different public speaking experiences she has had. Joyce is a perfectionist and loathes showing her vulnerability or awkwardness to all but her dearest friends. She feels threatened with exposure when she speaks in public. We had explored the familial roots of her perfectionism and to some extent the race-based roots as well. I suggested we explore more closely whether there were any differences in her experience based on subtle differences in her speaking contexts. It turns out that one particular speaking engagement had been easy, even relaxed for her. The difference was that her audience had been primarily black, not a common occurrence for her. This experience allowed us to examine more closely an internal critic she had, who turns out to be white. She has begun to wonder if her strongest sense of shame is in relation to this white critic.

Although this was a surprising and freeing discovery, it has also been enormously painful for two reasons. The first is that she feels diminished by her vulnerability to "white" judgment. Her mother crusaded very hard to inoculate her against the stings of encounters with white prejudice. Second, she feels mournful and almost overwhelmed by the realization that no matter what she does, she cannot escape prejudice, racism, and the wounding that come from breathing the air, all of which makes her invisible as a person. West (1994) refers to this as the "white normative gaze," and asserts that Blacks must be able to gain some distance from this gaze in order to know themselves deeply.

The dilemma of invisibility is quite figural for her now. Joyce is considering branching out from her institution, where she feels strangled, into doing independent consulting. She has been puzzled by her inability to write a proposal for funding. We have come to understand her inhibition as related to a fear of being totally invisible as she reaches into the white world for recognition. Her sense of herself as invisible is not a new awareness. But she is surprised and chagrined to see just how much the effects of racism continue to impinge on her. I remember in one poignant session we saw how much of her life was dedicated to proving herself to Whites. With sadness and bitter resignation, we mourned together that she would never be able to prove herself, once and for all, to the White World.

White Guilt

After Joyce left therapy with me, I thought of some of my White patients, and the struggles they face when they stand on the verge of personal and professional risk of the kind Joyce faces. For most, some sense of personal efficacy can carry them across the threshold. Joyce knows that all of her efficacy may not mean anything; so she is robbed of a sense of personal agency at a time when she needs it most. It was a moment of stark awareness of how different two lives may be based only upon a difference in color. I was reminded of a passage written by white author Willie Morris, in his autobiographical book, *North Towards Home* (1967). Morris was born and raised in Yazoo, Mississippi. In his autobiography, he reports on a letter he received from an African American man who had read an essay Morris had written about pleasant memories of his childhood in Yazoo. The letter writer asserted that he, too, had been raised in Yazoo, and that "Your Yazoo is not mine."

Trustworthy colleagues, to whom I am grateful, criticized my first draft of this paper, because they found in it an agenda to win the understanding and approval of my Black colleagues, and by doing so, to expiate my guilt. Interestingly, in attempting to explore the phenomenology of being white in racially charged America, I had neglected to explore a very common phenomenon known as "white guilt" but I had brought it to life in action in the construction of my paper. I felt chagrined, embarrassed, and guiltier still, as I did not want to "use" anyone, particularly my African American colleagues in that way. This time I shall not omit a discussion of white guilt

I am particularly interested in how White Americans, such as Morris, come to terms with their complicity in something larger than themselves that oppresses others but not them. How do they reconcile their simultaneous responsibility and their good will? I wonder where we might derive a sense of goodness and dignity when we live a life shadowed by racism and white privilege. I also remember reading The Autobiography of Malcolm X. I had finished reading it about a month before Martin Luther King was assassinated. I was a senior in high school, and I realized, to my horror, that my suburban school education was a lie. We were being fed a highly sanitized, white-dominated vision of American life and politics.

My interest in reconciling the shadows and light of guilt and innocence reflects not only my racial sensitivities, but also my family history. My personal history and my racial/social history at times converge in shaping my consciousness and politics. In my family, there was also a "sanitized" version of who we were as a family, and it differed greatly from my direct experience of serious, messy family disturbance. And much like Blacks at the time, I could not find a voice for, or others who could listen to, my perspective and my pain. Within my family I came to feel ashamed, guilty, dirty, and plagued by doubts about my personal goodness and dignity. So the parallel currents of racial sensitivity and personal history drive my question about complicity, responsibility, and goodwill that Morris addresses.

Probably better known to most of us than our race-based anxieties is our race-based guilt. Many of us feel guilty about the history of slavery and inequality that is so inherently contradictory to our democratic aspirations. The ugly and self-defeating combination of anxiety, guilt, shame, and ignorance makes it all but impossible for even the most minor of cross-race interactions to proceed with the natural grace that is common in White-White interactions. That is partly why this paper, as I write, is so graceless. I am strongly aware that a graceful paper would be a lie of sorts, a sanitized and careful tiptoe through a highly charged, incredibly complex and tangled emotional landscape. My guilt is part of what fuels my passion to try to set things right.

Social Darwinism, Belonging, and Superiority

Certainly one of my most guilt-provoking reactions when faced with the realization of my privileged status and freedom is my smug sense of "belonging." My heart may be big enough to want all of us to belong, but there seems to be another current of thought and feeling that captures me, the one where I feel vaguely superior by virtue of the fact that I "belong." At such a moment I am confronted with one of the unshakeable consequences of having come to maturity in such an individualistic, competitive, and racialized culture: for me to be "inside," someone else must be "outside." Another remnant of my acculturation into the strong individualistic ethic of WASP American culture shows in my private thought that if any particular patient is so alienated, so much "outside," perhaps his or her outsider status is somehow deserved.

This phenomenon of blaming the victim emerged from the "Social Darwinism" of the late 1800s and remains present as a background influence today. Social Darwinism combined the individualistic values of Protestantism with capitalism and Darwinian evolutionary theory to create a social/scientific theory that held that those who succeeded in the new industrial culture of the U.S. were those who worked hard and had the proper genetic endowments (survival of the fittest), and those who were impoverished deserved their poverty by virtue of their personal weaknesses and deficits. It is a profoundly racist theory, whose currency in the U.S. was born of the anxiety and defensiveness of white property and factory owners at a time when immigrants and newly freed slaves were flocking to work for them, but threatening their secure sense of place and of ownership of the resources and the culture of America.

It is only a small step to go from the notion of personal failings to the notion of defects and weaknesses of a racial or cultural group. Thus, the dispossession and disadvantages of African Americans in the U.S. have been attributed to personal defects of character and ability of the African race rather than to racism in American culture. Even such seemingly benign assessment instruments as the intelligence test began in the racist crucible of efforts to prove the inferiority of African Americans by measuring skull sizes. It is extremely difficult to convey the strength and embeddedness of Social Darwinian thought. It is an aspect of our cultural, social, historical field, shaping quietly and pervasively our figure-formation process.

One small example that might be useful is the example of psychological studies done in the 1970s on a phenomenon called "field dependence/independence." The gist of these studies was various experiments designed to test to what degree research subjects' perceptions were influenced by field conditions. The prevailing wisdom of the day was that relative field independence was a sign of mental health, whereas field dependence was a sign of weakness. Until well into the 1980s, there was no critical appraisal of the individualistic ethos that permeated the conclusions drawn from the research findings. Current criticism argues that an already shaped and presumed sense of individualism privileges field independence in one's research at the expense of observations regarding interconnection. Ironically, the research findings were organized according to the researcher's "field dependent" embeddedness in their very own WASP and Social Darwinist perspectives, which would prize individualism; latent, prevalent field conditions remained in their background, never to be brought into the foreground for examination!

I remember going "on strike" in 1961. I was 11, President Kennedy had been inaugurated, Martin Luther King was one of my heroes, and I thought now was a time to take a stand. So I wrote a letter to the President asserting that I would no longer recite the daily Pledge of Allegiance to the flag of the United States. Schoolchildren throughout the country recited this daily pledge as a morning ritual to begin the school day. But the last line read, "with liberty and justice for all." Where was the justice for so many African Americans who were still prevented from voting in the American South? So I announced to the President that I would not recite the pledge until Blacks could vote.

My point in telling this amusing and fondly remembered tale of my childhood is that I have not been ignorant of the racial politics and inequality in this country, and yet, despite the racial sensitivities I have worked conscientiously to develop, I am engaged in a never-ending battle to deconstruct and dis-embed myself from the remnants of WASP, Social Darwinist acculturation. I frequently encounter moments of what McConville (1997), in describing cross-race conversations, describes as "bewilderment."

"It is a dawning sense of my own ignorance, and with that, a realization that I am not as innocent as my good intentions claim. Beyond my intentions, there is an impact of my behavior on others, and an uncomfortable realization that I'm not owning enough responsibility for that impact, and worse yet, that I'm not owning up to my responsibility for this ignorance" (McConville, 1997: 3).

"These half formed awarenesses are fueled by my knowledge that bigotry indeed exists, that it is all around us, that it permeates the air we breathe, even this air, right here, present in this room, as we speak. It is, in other words, the simultaneous prehension of my innocence and my guilt, my non-racist intentionality and my immersion, in an atmosphere saturated with inequity and bias. This is bewilderment" (McConville, 1997: 3).

"Whenever I find myself bewildered by someone's response to an action of mine, it is because I am blind to the ground of their experience. My advice to myself here is simple: get interested in the impact, particularly when it surprises me" (McConville, 1997: 14).

To McConville's (1997) painful and inspiring description, I would add that the bewilderment is also a sign that we are also ignorant of an important dimension of our own ground. Which brings me back to Social Darwinism and to my own bewilderment. I remember my bewilderment upon first reading a seminal book on institutional racism by William Ryan called *Blaming the Victim*. One form of institutional racism he deconstructed was the notion that the reason African Americans as a group were unable to attain economic equality, even after legal equality had been advanced greatly and educational opportunities were supposedly more plentiful, was that the impact of generations of racism and slavery had yielded a culturally deprived Black community.

I regret to say, but must, for the sake of my argument, that his reasoning created a moment of bewilderment for me. I had been thinking that the notion of "cultural deprivation" was a more compassionate understanding of the struggles of poor urban African Americans than the ideology I had heard spouted that they were simply lazy and eager to take advantage of the welfare system. But Ryan pointed out how the notion of cultural deprivation allowed governments to focus the problem within the victim instead of within the field. An example he used was that of schools. I present a lengthy quote below to provide an example of his deconstructive thrust that was so enlightening to me (emphasis my own):

"[The researchers] found that lower class children, particularly lower class minority children, have had less exposure than middle class children to certain kinds of experiences that are helpful in the school situation.... Middle class kids are better able to distinguish between words that sound alike, are better able to perceive colors and shapes, and, in imitating their parents' speech, have learned to talk in a style similar to that of most teachers. Thus, the middle class child is somewhat better prepared for the school experience than is the lower class child. But it would not be unreasonable to present this proposition in its reversed form: The school is better prepared for the middle class child than for the lower class child. Indeed, we could be tempted to state further that the school experience is tailored for, and stacked in favor of, the middle class child (Ryan, 1971: 35)

While many white Americans may not have heard of the concept of Social Darwinism, it is so closely linked with WASP values, and with science, that we were all raised in its thrall, regardless of our racial or ethnic past. Tracing Social Darwinism as a historically situated political device has helped me contextualize some of my own norms as they have come into my awareness.

Although my intention here is to make various meanings of "whiteness" more figural, in order to illustrate more fully the impact of the Social Darwinist ambience on my own forming figures, I turn to another relationship in which I have superior social standing compared to Susan, a white lesbian patient. She was repeatedly sexually abused in childhood. Our therapeutic relationship has been emotionally intense and quite stormy at times, knotted with distrust, testing, mutual defensiveness, and yet deeply honest. She yearns for an intimacy with me that feels safe, not threatening. She reported a dream to me: "We are at a party, but not standing near to each other. You are carefree, and happily eating a delicious filet mignon steak. I am in a shadowy corner, relegated by my health problems to eating vegetables. I resent your greater freedom to taste rich foods."

Susan's dream brought home to both of us the painful mix of feelings that were evoked after sessions in which she had felt particularly close to me. She bemoaned the resentment and envy she experienced when she felt at once close to me and yet alienated because of my "heterosexual privilege." At one point she spoke bitterly of how if each of us met our respective lovers outside after the session had ended, I would be able to walk off hand-in-hand with my male lover, while she and her female lover would have to walk with a discreet distance between them or risk ostracism or worse.

My own reaction to this dream was a complicated one. I was mournful, sobered by the reality of her disdained minority status. At the same time, I felt a sense of patronizing smugness at the sureness of my sense of belonging and safety relative to the wider culture. I then felt ashamed of myself, and guilty to be reveling in my status as cultural insider. I also felt proud of myself for being able to help unearth and face squarely the painful gap between us that existed in that moment of realization. I imagined myself in her shoes, and began to burn with humiliation and anger. All of these reactions tumbled pell-mell throughout my body.

In this moment it was crucially important to Susan that I reach across the space between us with heartfelt understanding of how different we were, and how unfair it was that, through no doing of her own, she was an outsider, and I was an insider. It was equally important that my efforts to feel my way into her bitter outrage and sense of victimization not be motivated by my wish to "close the gap" between us; to attempt to erase, if only in the moment, the bitter truth of our different standings in the culture.

Whether working with gay and lesbian patients or with people of color, I find I must resist the temptation to be self-effacing. I am tempted to do or say something that brings me into closer alignment with the patient's sense of being disenfranchised. I think I am trying to avoid my guilty feelings of smug belonging, and also to reduce the strength of the patient's envy. I have found that it is better for our work if I can simply "take the heat" while knowing full well that the patient's envy and my guilt are consequences of my privilege.

Another patient, Carla, a terribly isolated young black woman with daunting fears and inhibitions, was struggling to establish a foothold in her profession. She never mentioned our race difference, and was uncomfortable on the rare occasions when I made my whiteness more figural. I finally asked her why that area of discussion was so off-limits. She said with some trepidation that she was afraid that our connection would break entirely if we talked about our racial differences because there were dimensions of her life that I could never fully understand. She thought that she was damned either way. If I could not understand her deeply, she would be lost and alone once again in a painfully familiar psychological landscape. Yet if I endeavored to understand her -- as if I thought I actually could grasp in all its depth what it means to be black in this culture -- she would then lose all faith in my self-awareness, and my racial awareness. Carla was hopelessly despondent at the end of the session.

It happened that our local paper that week posted an editorial about the racial divide, and about how Blacks and Whites could begin to meet each other without rendering Blacks invisible if Whites acknowledged the unbridgeable gap of understanding that exists between a life lived with privilege and one lived under the constant shadow of racism. I brought the editorial with me to our next session. To my surprise and delight, Carla had read the same editorial and was quite receptive to placing our relationship in the context of "meeting-by-seeing-where-we-cannot-meet." She was relieved and heartened also that I had not been insulted, and had not wanted to give up, even when she felt hopeless. Over the course of our work together, she gained enough confidence and trust in me to tell me some excruciatingly painful and shameful stories of her childhood, something she had thought she would never be able to do.

White Shame

A moment like the one between Carla and me is pregnant with the awful possibility of shame for the patient; shame over expression of hurt and bitterness, shame over caring about being an outsider, shame over being exposed as an outsider at a moment of vulnerability in the presence of an insider. Des Kennedy (1998) said that shame is represented by the statement "You are without meaning as a person in my world" (Des Kennedy, 1998: 94), a sentence that would resonate powerfully with my patient Joyce as well as with Carla and Susan. Of course, the moment is also pregnant with possibilities for healing, because there is a good chance that the patient will be exposing herself to another --the therapist -- who cares and can stay in contact, and by being there and being affected, the patient may have the experience of actually having meaning to another.

The moment is also ripe for guilt, shame, and defensiveness for the white insider therapist. I certainly feel guilt over the privileges I have, heightened at moments when someone I care about who is an outsider is acutely aware of my privilege and his or her disenfranchisement. When that someone is African American, I sometimes burn with a sense of shame, not just about present injustice, but about history as well.

In the case of Susan, I was singed with a complex sense of shame and guilt. I felt some shame over a moment of pleasure I had had with her recently. She had affectionately referred to my style of attire as "dyke chic." I had been flattered by my temporary admission into being an insider in her outsiders club. Now I felt ashamed of my selfish experience of flattery. I felt guilty that I could move so easily from inside the straight world to inside the lesbian world and back to the straight world again; whereas she could not. Her "straight life" left her with a secret life. I felt ashamed of availing myself of the pleasure, from the safety of my dominant-culture status.

At various times, Susan and I speak freely of the complicated interplay of our gay and straight lives. But at this time, I said nothing of my own self-absorbed doubting. I simply felt her outrage and hurt along with her, and the shadows of humiliation that hovered in the air. And I felt my own outrage and heartache along with all else that I described above.

Shifting Relational configurations

The twists and turns in my relationship with an African American patient, Louise, have been instructive for me about the shifting figure and ground of our racial differences and of my whiteness. I will never forget how she first introduced herself to me. She had seen me give a lecture on shame at a local clinic. She said she knew she needed to look at shame in her life; after all, she was "black, lesbian, and a woman: a three-time loser." She said this with amusement, and a glint of defiance in her eyes, but her sense of shame was also palpable.

Over the course of our work, she asserted that her lesbian identity was more of a home to her than her black identity. She said Blacks were intensely homophobic. Our relationship, as it progressed, was generally comfortable, graced with humor, exploration, and also laced with occasional fits of exasperation on both our parts. In the early days, Louise seemed quite closed, mistrustful, and provocative. I was dogged in my pursuit of the "Louise-behind-the-armor" (her description), alternatingly gentle and sassy with her, and occasionally defensive when I felt hurtfully dismissed by her. We could talk about all of this openly, freely, and with vigor.

We have come to feel quite close, intimate, and trusting of each other over the years, and what is intriguing, is how little we talk about our racial differences. We do sometimes talk of what "blackness" is to her, and what my "whiteness" means to her, but more often she seems to engage with me in a way that renders our race difference irrelevant. In these periods, our differences of race and sexual orientation are in the background, not because they have been suppressed, but because we are, for the moment, busy with another way of relating. I cannot describe well what the other way is, except to say that we sometimes end those sessions with a feeling of having emerged from an altered state, maybe a state where perhaps our intimacy had transcended usual parameters by which we define ourselves.

I have brought the wisdom gained from Louise into other cross-race or cross-orientation therapy relationships. I am more keenly sensitive to the times when my patients want a chance to just talk as if we can know each other very well, way under the skin where those categorical differences do not live.

The therapeutic atmosphere is a play-space, where only the limits of our creativity affect the permutations of the therapeutic relationship. I have many identities with any given patient, and they with me. Relational configurations shift with the shifting figure/ground of contacting and of awareness.

In the shifting figure/ground of contacting, various self-states, or organizations of self-experience, are activated. Each of these self-states is also a self-with-other state. I think that when a therapeutic process is going along well, there is an easy suspension of the givenness of one's identity, and patient and therapist readily engage in various constructed relationships. For instance, there may be times when a male therapist is a mother to a patient's hungry-baby self.

When I work across racial lines, the givens include my white self and the patient's black self. These givens tend to be experienced as givens, the same way gender is experienced as a given, because they are treated as immutable facts in subtle and gross ways, in the preponderance of our everyday lives.

Of course, the meanings of this givenness are constructed, and the therapeutic process involves continual co-construction and deconstruction of various meanings, including the meanings revolving around racial identity. Some of this constructing and deconstructing process occurs when patient and therapist find different self-organizations being activated by each other. For instance, at times when Susan speaks with some embarrassment about her sex life with her lover, she is strongly aware that I am straight, whereas at that moment, I am usually not very much centered in my straight sexuality. Rather, I have entered her sexual/relationship world, and the category of gayness or straightness (hers or mine) has faded to the background.

At times when Joyce is speaking of her encounters with white racism, she looks up with a sudden shocking remembrance that I am white; whereas I may have been unaware for the moment that she was talking with white-me. Her look of shock and fear alerts me to be cognizant, once again, of my whiteness as a powerful part of her visual field as well as of her emotional field. Sometimes with Louise I am aware that I am a white person listening to a black person, while what is figural for her is that she is lesbian, speaking with a straight person. Any one of these moments where we are mismatched has the possibility of opening up a chance for therapist or patient or both to dis-embed themselves from a culturally constructed self. However, they are each also moments in which my misattunement may be hurtful to the patient.

These shifting relational configurations are important to me as a reminder that there may be long stretches of time where my African American patients and I are working on issues that are experienced, for now, as deeply personal and "color-blind." At such times, it is important for me to de-center from my own racial self-consciousness. And yet, I think it is also important for me to keep in mind the different worlds we enter when the session ends.

Final Thoughts

Given the impossibly complex dynamics of power that run throughout the ground of any black-white interactions, I sometimes feel pessimistic about whether it is really possible for White therapists and African American patients to establish a safe enough climate for deep, transformative therapeutic work. The very structure of therapy replicates the power structure that has disenfranchised them. We meet at a place of my choosing, and the times and fees are more for my convenience than for theirs. The power imbalance lives in the room. And while it may be merely a personal issue for a white person, the racialized grounds we bring to the meeting make it more than that when the patient is not white.

But my work with Carla leads me to think that the one thing that may be affirming for a patient in this situation is the very fact that the intimate contact of therapy changes both participants. When a white therapist, representative of dominance, power and privilege, is willing to be changed by close engagement; the power balance shifts for both of them. I doubt that African Americans often have the chance to have a white person listen closely to African Americans recounting the experiences of their lives. When so many of their experiences are implicit criticisms of the therapist's cultural status, generally African Americans are only heard by insisting on being heard. In the consulting room, the atmosphere can be one where their experiences and perceptions are welcomed, not just tolerated. Could this possibly be a healing dimension in a cross-racial dyad? I feel presumptuous in even suggesting it, but I think it might be so.

The process of writing and re-writing this paper has raised for me more questions than it has answered. After my first draft, I wondered whether I ought to *not* accept African Americans as patients. I looked back upon the work I have described above, and I wondered if I have been too race-based in my orientation to the African American patients, or in a way the opposite, not sensitive enough about the impact of my whiteness on them. I felt in need of instruction, but probably more important, in need of consciousness-raising discussions about whiteness. I am also acutely aware of how much I value and enjoy working across racial lines. I learn so much, but I wonder whether I get more than I give vis-à-vis my African American patients.

By the time I did some more soul-searching and reading and conversing in response to the criticisms of the first daft, I had a sense my own racial consciousness had shifted and developed. For one thing, my ease with the fact of my whiteness, and its concomitant privilege, has increased. Although I strongly disagree with Carter (1995) who asserts that the most developed of racial consciousness would include the experience of pride in my whiteness. I think "white pride" is a problem, especially since "whiteness" is an arbitrary and political, rather than racial, category anyway! Ethnic pride makes more sense to me. I can take pride in various ethnic influences on my development and on the development of the broader culture, but the assertion of a "white" identity, I am convinced, now more than ever, is a major stumbling block to racial harmony.

For another thing, my ease around people of color has grown enormously. I do not find myself worrying about intruding; I do not feel shy about engaging in race-based, as well as other, conversations. I no longer see such an "other" when I look at someone who is African American. This is hard to explain, because I do not mean to say that we are alike, another person and myself. And yet, now I have done more of my intellectual and emotional homework so that there is increasing overlap in the grounds, or fields, which shape our consciousness.

An interesting question in my mind is, what about white therapist-patient dyads? So often the question is raised, ought an African American work with an African American therapist? Ought a lesbian work with a lesbian therapist? The push in that direction has to do with a search for the best conditions for the enhancement of an affirmative identity. But when I think about Whites, I wonder if we would not be better served by working with someone who is not from our culture. Because of our very dominance, the cultural themes that may be shaping our problems, even how we frame what our problems are, are in the background. The same is likely true for our therapists, and hence we may not be able to raise the questions that may be most helpful for us to explore!

I also wonder if I should notice whether a white patient never notices his or her whiteness. I have found that I feel free to contextualize comments in terms of gender, or to WASP culture. But rarely do I contextualize patients' themes in terms of whiteness. Helping a patient to understand how WASP values have shaped his or her phenomenology is not the same as helping a patient to understand how racial thinking has shaped his or her phenomenology. Racial thinking is rarely figural when I am working with a white patient.

Finally, in a surprising irony, as I have explored my relationship to my whiteness, and traced some of the sources of my interest in black-white relations, I find myself interested, as never before, in working with people from diverse backgrounds. Despite my doubts, pessimism, and worry, I wish to be able to work competently with African Americans. Also, in the process of wending my way through contextualizing my whiteness, my interest in culture has expanded, and I feel some excitement at the possibility of working with people of other cultures and ethnicities. This is a confirmation, once again, of the paradoxical theory of change. By staying with my experience as it evolved, twisted, turned, by not throwing anything anyway, I end up changed, and to my delight, more open to, and inclusive of, otherness.

Personal Account

One of the most interesting and perplexing aspects of writing this article is the tension that developed between my aims and the aims of the editor and originators of the book project itself. It seemed only right that a book exploring bridging the divides between differing cultures of all kinds, would utilize co-authorship format. Such a format could bring together people from differing cultures, and the ensuing conversation would be part of the texture of the book, the ground from which the particular articles would emerge.

I preferred to write my article alone, and efforts to persuade me to find a co-author were to no avail, even though I knew this placed a burden on the editor, disrupting the structure and aesthetics of the book project. Generally, I prefer writing on my own, as writing solo is certainly more efficient than co-writing. But there is more to my decision than this stylistic preference.

I **had** to write my own story. When I was asked to join the book project, I declined at first, claiming (truthfully) my cross-cultural illiteracy. But I changed my mind the next day, realizing this project afforded me an opportunity to have a reckoning with my own "race-consciousness development." I had been so moved when I had read earlier drafts of Mark McConville's personal odyssey through his own consciousness-raising process, I became eager to use writing to continue my own explorations.

I am also, quite possibly, enacting the very thing I describe in my article as the WASP cultural norms. There is an emphasis on individual achievement, not collective achievement. And the sense of place, or belonging, that allowed me to insist on doing it my way.

The explorations were much harder emotionally than I had anticipated, as I have pointed to in my article. And although I had a vague sense that my first draft had a subtle agenda to win approval and recognition from my African American colleagues, I was not able to make that agenda figural without the help of some insightful editorial questions from Tali, and some thoughtful and kind conversations with some colleagues.

So ultimately, although I am very gratified to have had the opportunity to write this article on my own terms, the article became different, vastly improved, "cleaner" and more useful for my development by the dialogues into which my first draft drew me. I am not surprised by this; I have tremendous faith in dialogue. I am, however, deeply grateful for the honesty and insights of my colleagues and of Tali, the editor.

Lynne Jacobs, Los Angeles, CA, USA

References

Carter, R. T. (1995). *Race and Racial Identity in Psychotherapy*. New York: John Wiley & Sons.

Flax, J. (1990). *Thinking Fragments: Psychoanalysis, Feminism, and Postmodernism in the Contemporary West.* Berkeley: University of California Press.

Gotanda, N. (1997) "Tales of Two Judges," in Lubiano, W. (Ed), *The House That Race Built.* NY: Vintage Books, Random House, 66-86.

Hale, G.E. (1998). *Making Whiteness: The Culture of Segregation in the South, 1890-1940.* NY: Pantheon.

Jacobs, L. (2000). For Whites Only. *British Gestalt Journal*, v.9 #1, pp. 3-14.

Jordan, J. (1981). *Civil Wars.* NY: Touchstone.

Kennedy, D. (1998). Gestalt: A Point of Departure for a Personal Spirituality, *The British Gestalt Journal*, Gestalt Publishing, LTD, London, v.7, n.2, 9: 88-98.

McConville, M. (1997). The Gift. in McConville, M (Ed.) *The GIC Voice*, Cleveland.

McGoldrick, M., Pearce, J., and Giordano, J. (1982). *Ethnicity & Family Therapy.* NY: Guilford.

McIntosh, P. (1995) "White Privilege and Male Privilege: A Personal Account of Coming to See Correspondences Through Work in Women's Studies." In Anderson, M., and Collins, P., (Ed.'s) *Race, Class, and Gender.* NY: Wadsworth Publishing.

Morris, W. (1967) *North Towards Home.* NY: Dell Publishing.

Morrison, T. (2004). *Beloved.* NY: Random House, Inc.

Ryan, W. (1981) *Blaming The Victim.* NY: Vintage Books.

Thomas, B. (1997). Integrating Multicultural Perspectives in Gestalt Theory and Practice. In McConville, M (Ed.) Cleveland: *The GIC Voice.*

West, C. (1994). *Race Matters.* NY: Vintage Books.

X, Malcolm, Haley, A., Davis, O. (Afterword). (1975). *The Autobiography of Malcolm X.* NY: Random House, Inc.

XV. THE UNIVERSAL LANGUAGE

By Anne Teachworth, CGC, CPC, DAPA
and Lenny Ravich, M.A., CGC

Background on the Co-Authors' Culture by Anne
Of all the workshops I have ever presented outside of the United States, the lifestyle of the Hebrew people in the Orthodox religious community in Jerusalem remains, without a doubt, the most dramatically different culture shock I've ever experienced. It is this experience in Israel in the late Eighties that I chose to write about for a book on bridging the cultural gap because the learnings I brought back with me from my Israel trip are still the most important I have ever had as a therapist. Indeed, it is still amazing to me seventeen years later that the Gestalt approach could facilitate for me such profound contact with a people who lived in a culture so different from my own.

As an American gal born in the Deep South and living in the midst of the historic French Quarter of New Orleans, my background was quite different from the Israeli people. But, unfamiliar as their culture was, I was already somewhat familiar with the idea of religious strife. Born to a Jesuit-trained Pope-abiding Catholic father and a Sunday School-teaching hymn-singing Protestant mother, I had been uniquely primed on a daily basis in childhood to relate to the conflict in the Holy Land, first-hand. There had been many times when I felt as if I was growing up in the midst of a Holy War myself.

My co-author, Lenny, is himself a living bridge across American and Israeli cultures. A former Connecticut Yankee who has lived in Israel for over thirty-five years, Lenny is in a perfect position to share with you his experience of my workshops there, plus give some inside information on the population and customs of the Jewish participants. Born an American Jew, he came to Israel in his thirties, married a Sephardic Jew, and raised his family there.

Well-familiar with the Hebrew religious customs in Israel, he can explain to our readers many of the cultural situations I couldn't understand at the time. He has been in the Israeli Army and knows the drill, the risks and the rewards. In addition, he attended all seven of my workshops in Israel, and as a therapist himself, had already worked with some of the Hebrew-speaking participants before they came to my Gestalt workshops there.

Lenny's Note to the Reader
The idea to invite Anne to Israel came after I had studied with her in 1986 on a visit to see my sister in New Orleans. I was so impressed with her Gestalt Institute there that upon my return to Israel, Susie Lanir, my co-therapist, and I decided to model a Gestalt Institute in Haifa after Anne's. We knew we needed some Gestalt training to do that so we began by asking Anne to come teach us in Israel. It was a Jewish idea….we could stay home and learn, save on travel costs and make some money, too. To quote an Arab-based proverb, "If Mohammad wouldn't come to the mountain, we would get the mountain to come to Mohammad."

Background by Anne
Indeed, getting me to go to Israel truly was like moving a mountain. It

is important for the reader to understand that prior to receiving this invitation to teach in Israel I had never even been to Europe before, much less the troubled Middle East. Although I was ready to go to the Holy Land for openers, my family and friends weren't at all happy about it and did their best to talk me out of it. All we knew in the US about Israel then was it was a dangerous place to be, so dangerous that none of my six sons wanted me to accept the invitation and, in fact, not one of the three teenage ones would agree to drive me to the airport.

Each of them excused himself by saying that if anything happened to me in Israel he did not want to be known in the family as *The Brother Who Had Helped Mom Fly Off To Her Death.* Finally, the oldest one relented and drove me on the condition that I never tell any of his brothers, if, in fact, I ever returned to tell anyone. So I boarded the plane with that ominous warning lingering right under the little bit of courage I had mustered about going off alone to a faraway land long known for its Holy Wars.

As I said before, as a child, I had indeed gotten more inside information about religious differences than I wanted to know, particularly about the Catholics and Protestants. As a wiggly little girl, bored with sitting still and quiet like the grownups at a Latin Mass, I had always begged to go to my mother's Protestant church for her Sunday School class. But my Catholic father had lovingly explained to me that it would be a mortal sin.

"What, Daddy, is a mortal sin?" I had innocently asked. "It means something that you go to hell for doing," my peaceful loving father had answered solemnly. Even at six years of age, I had a hard time believing God would send a little girl to hell for wanting to go to her own mother's Sunday School classes. My father said he didn't like believing that God would do that to me either, but he couldn't take the chance. So I wasn't allowed inside her church. Thus, began my love of forbidden fruit, especially forbidden religions.

My mother thought the Catholic Church oppressive, controlling, and hostile to her Protestant religion, and verbally regretted the paper she had signed years before agreeing to turn over the raising of her future children to my Catholic father in order to marry him. Now resenting that she had forfeited the rights to her maternal territory without much of a fight, my mother was catching up quick with her own private little protest every Sunday. But protest as we may, neither one of us could disobey my father in any matter. She never did, nor did I… at least not until after he died, that is.

My parents' warring religions, however different, were similar to each others' in a couple of important ways. Both were Christian faiths who believed in Jesus and in both the Old and New Testaments of the Bible. But their religions were different in that my Catholic father prayed to the Blessed Virgin Mary, while my Protestant mother didn't ever pray to Jesus' mother at all for reasons I couldn't understand as a child.

Nevertheless, as an adult preparing to lead a workshop in Israel not only for non-Catholic, but non-Christian people, I knew I was way outside of my father's introjected permission range and way into the "forbidden." Jews, like Catholics, didn't have Sunday School; they didn't even go to church on Sunday! Their holy day was Saturday.

Other than that, I knew little of the differences between the Christian and Jewish religious practices. I did know that Jews didn't honor Jesus as the expected Messiah; nor did they honor His Mother Mary in any special way. I was curious to find out more about who these people were. And to make it even more confusing, I had read that Christians, Jews, and Muslims all honored Abraham, historically the father of all three religions. Muslims differed from Christians though on which one of Abraham's sons was his rightful heir.

Judaism and Christianity both traced their lineage to Abraham back through his second-born son, Isaac, by his wife, Sarah, while the Islamic Muslims laid claim to this patriarch through Ishmael, Abraham's first born-son by Sarah's Egyptian handmaiden, Hagar.

Lenny's Comments

In a historical sense, both the Jewish and Christian religions were originally Semitic, whether they liked it or not, since Abraham came from the city of Ur, in the land we refer to today as Iraq. There were other religious facts Anne was to learn over the course of her time in Israel. Jews not only didn't believe in Jesus as the Messiah or in the New Testament of the Christian Bible as Catholics and Protestants did, but only in what Christians referred to as the Old Testament. To Jews, there is nothing at all "Old" about the Old Testament, or Old Covenant, which is called the Tanakh, or Bible. The first five books of the Hebrew Bible constituted the Torah (or Revealed Teaching), and are the holiest books of Jewish scripture.

The Muslims' holy book is the Quran. The Muslim Quran coincidentally narrates the Annunciation of Jesus' birth to Mary by the angel Gabriel in ways very similar to the Christian and Hebrew Old Testament Gospel narratives; however, the Quran, unlike the Hebrew religion, does depict Jesus as a messiah figure. But trying to explain the different meaning of 'messiah' as held by Muslims in the short time Anne would be in the Middle East would surely be confusing to her. It was confusing to a lot of us who lived here in Israel.

Strangely enough, the Muslims' great prophet, Muhammad, had accepted that Jesus was a prophet, but had not accepted Jesus' divinity as Christians did. Muhammad also recognized the Jewish Torah, even though neither the Jews nor the Christians had reciprocated by recognizing Muhammad as a true prophet.

Anne's First Journey To Israel

Because my first workshop was scheduled in Haifa the last weekend in December, I left New Orleans on the evening of Jesus' birthday, Christmas Day, 1987. Flying an American airline with a change of planes in Brussels, I was due to arrive at the Tel Aviv airport on Dec. 26th after fourteen hours airborne.

On the flight from New York with me were several Israeli residents, most noticeably, six Jewish men dressed in black suits and top hats, with long braids hanging down on each side of their face. I had first noticed their group standing apart from everyone else in the airport and praying intently as we waited to board. They were the "ultra-religious," another passenger told me, who usually flew El Al, the Israeli airline, mostly for the tight security always in place there. I had to wonder if the 'men in black,' as I called them, would find it necessary to pray as hard as these men were if they had been boarding an El Al flight instead. I swallowed my concern in one big lump and started my own Hail Marys, thankful that these guys were also doing their own religion's part to keep my first overseas flight in the air.

Flying trans-Atlantic is much like going to camp or attending an intensive weekend workshop retreat. Within a few hours of takeoff, most of the passengers had started talking to the people sitting next to them. Close quarters produced a quick situational intimacy among us.

By the time we arrived, we had eaten a few meals together, slept together, and shared our histories, in particular, the main purpose of each one's trip to Israel. Several aboard were Christian tourists who, unlike me, were with a tour guide. But like me, most had never been to Israel and didn't know what to expect when they got there. However, our education would begin before we arrived in Israel.

In Brussels, on the stopover, I quickly learned the meaning of the word 'kosher' when the 'men in black' on board wouldn't let the plane take off until their special kosher meals had arrived from the airline caterer. "Kosher?" I asked, and a Hebrew passenger explained, the term meant food prepared according to Jewish law and pre-approved by the Rebbe.

"Rebbe?" Rebbe, he said, meant Rabbi: the holy man in charge who tells religious Jews what they can do and what they can't do. Somewhat like the Pope who was the Catholic representative of God, I reasoned, still in the habit of comparing everything to my own culture.

Lenny's Insider Information

Just to note, whenever Orthodox Jews write the word "God," for theological reasons, they spell it "G-d." When Anne uses the word, we will leave it as "God," but when she quotes an Orthodox Jewish client using the word, we use the Jewishly correct way: "G-d."

Another thing, the ultra-religious 'men in black' as Anne calls them are really called Haredim (meaning something like 'Those who tremble in awe before "G-d"). They study the Torah; the collected First Five Books of Moses of the Tanakh, in a place of study and prayer called a Yeshiva and eventually might become scholars and rabbis, or "rebbes" themselves.

The Haredim are supported by the Israeli government and are exempted from military service in the Israeli Army, which is often a point of resentment with both Israeli men and women, since compulsory service is required of every Israeli citizen from 18 to 55 years old.

That very year Anne came to teach here, I myself had already spent my compulsory one month a year reserve duty in the Israeli Army. My two sons were both full-time soldiers. My young daughter would also be required to serve her required two years once she reached 18 years of age.

Anne in Bethlehem

One of my main reasons for wanting to go to Israel came up in idle passenger conversation early in the flight. The 'little Catholic girl' in me had always wanted to see where Jesus was born. The Christian tourists on board were going to Israel for the same reason, but were already scheduled to go to Bethlehem the following week with their pre-arranged tour group. Lucky for me, my seat mates, a Hebrew university professor and his wife, both born in Israel and living in Bethlehem, offered to take me to the Church of the Nativity upon our landing in Tel Aviv. I gladly accepted.

What I found as we drove into Bethlehem hardly matched my childhood expectations of Jesus' birthplace. I was not at all prepared for the multicultural extremes I experienced as we approached the Church of the Nativity. Bright multi-colored Christmas lights were strung everywhere. Several Arab protesters wearing traditional red and white checkered headscarves were all around us shouting protests and waving their arms in the air.

In obvious contrast, several Catholic nuns and priests waited silently in their traditional black religious garb, some with rosaries in their hands. It was a strange mixture of American and Middle Eastern cultures. Souvenir carts offered both Christmas and Islamic items to the tourists, but no Jewish souvenirs. There were no 'men in black' there, either.

TV newsmen were everywhere filming everyone and everything. Israeli soldiers with loaded M-16 rifles stood somber guard a short distance from the church. Others manned security checkpoints from behind barbed wire. An alarming sight! My Jewish friends, not the least bit interested in Jesus, all too used to the soldiers and rather bored with the protesters, too, sat down to wait while I took my place in line to enter the Church of the Nativity with the other Christian tourists.

I hadn't heard there was any out of the ordinary uprisings in Bethlehem when I made my plans to come. Just the 'normal' trouble in the Gaza Strip, far away from where I would be, I had mused. For a few minutes, I worried that my sons had indeed been all too right about the danger. Fear began to drown out my sense of adventure. In whispered tones, I stepped back out of line to ask my Israeli friends what the problem was. The man's answer was an insight into protesters that I have never forgotten to this day.

"There is no uprising now," Shlomo said to me. "These protesters are regulars who show up in Bethlehem every year around Christmas time because they know there will be news cameras here from all over the world. Protesters and terrorists *both*," he emphasized, "like to go where they know they will get international TV coverage." I never forgot that Israeli man's casual insight into the Arab-Jewish conflict or my experience of it first-hand.

There in Bethlehem, for the first time in my life, I went through the electronic scanning devices that are now commonplace in all airports. Three security checkpoints had been set up for Christian tourists who wanted to get inside the Church of the Nativity. At each one, a fully armed Israeli soldier searched my purse and snapped my camera once or twice checking to make sure it was not a bomb. Much too close for comfort, I flinched each time someone ahead of me in line handed their camera over for inspection. Surprisingly, my video camera was allowed in unchecked, maybe because it was already on, maybe because so many TV news cameras were already rolling that mine just fit right in.

The Church of the Nativity sits on top of the cave where Jesus was born. Crowded in closely together, about two dozen nuns, priests, tourists and I cautiously descended approximately eight roughly hewn steps into a small grotto-like area under the church floor. No one had asked me for a Press Pass yet, and still amazed that my lone video camera had gotten this far, I proceeded to film the very spot where Jesus had lain in His manger almost two thousand years ago. My spirit jumped for joy that I had been brave enough to make this journey by myself and fulfill my childhood wish to come to the Nativity site. This side visit to Bethlehem was already well worth the risk, even now as I reconsider the trip these many years later, especially since I have the video film to go with the pilgrimage stories I tell my grandchildren.

Anne's Arrival in Haifa

Staying with Susie Lanir and her family in Haifa was a cross-cultural experience in itself. Originally from New York, Susie had come to Israel after college and married an Israeli-born university professor whose German Jewish mother had survived the concentration camp. Together with their son and daughter, Susie and Yoram lived in a lovely nine-room, two-story villa in an upscale neighborhood called Carmel on the edge of a hill directly across from a rather shabby-looking Arab community.

The fragrance of the flowers in Susie's lovely garden behind her house was in sharp contrast to the fact that her front yard contained a small bomb shelter stocked with gas masks for the entire family. "Any for guests," I asked?

"Not to worry," Susie had answered when I arrived in Carmel the night before the workshop. "There is no trouble now. No missiles have landed here since the Six Day War. Besides, the sirens will blow very loudly if we need to go into the shelter. You'll hear them, for sure," she comforted me.

I tried to relax. The friendly atmosphere in Susie's home helped. Lenny came over. We laughed and joked over dinner. I fell in love with Falafel - fried chick pea patties on pita bread with humous and pickled veggies - the Middle Eastern version of a hot dog with chili, pickles and onions on a bun.

My bedroom window overlooked the beautiful Mediterranean Sea and I awoke the next morning to the familiar sight of a clear blue sky, much like looking out my bedroom window in New Orleans. Outside I could hear children playing. I lay in bed and smiled, noticing that Jewish children's laughter sounded the same as American children's. Even though I couldn't understand a word of what they were saying, their joy was unmistakably the same. Dogs barked the same, too, as they played alongside the children. Mothers' fussing tones sounded the same, too.

I began my day by walking through Susie's garden again. The weather was much like being home. I smiled, realizing I had come round the world horizontally on the 30th parallel. The olive trees were a different shape and of a much smaller size than the stately moss-covered New Orleans oaks I was used to. But my favorite flower, the red geranium, was the same and abundantly in bloom in Israel. For a moment, I was back on my own balcony in the French Quarter appreciating my own flowering pots.

From the mosque on the neighboring hill floated the unfamiliar solemn sounds of devoted Muslims as they began their day by calling one another to witness before Allah. The melodic haunting cries reminded me somewhat of the Georgian chant I had grown to love in the Catholic Church. I stared across the hill surprised that an Arab community lived so very close to Susie's house in Haifa. They would have been neighbors in every sense of the word except for the small valley and the huge religious gaps that separated them. I tried to imitate their sing-song prayers.

On the plane I had heard about a Wailing Wall in Jerusalem but was told this was definitely not it. That would come in a later visit to Jerusalem. The prayerful chanting stopped as suddenly as it had started just as we were getting in the car to go to the workshop.

Later, as we drove directly under that Arab side of the hill across from Susie's house, Lenny punned that "This was where Israelis often go to get stoned." But I knew he wasn't referring to marijuana. Cautiously, I kept my eyes glued to the top of the ridge, expecting to spot rock-throwing Arabs, but none threatened the roadway this morning. Or dared to.

Anne's Comments on Being in Israel

In late 1987, when I arrived in Israel for the first time, the Gaza Strip along the border to Egypt was rapidly becoming the scene of major conflict. Palestinian Arabs were resisting the steady flow of Jewish settlers who were moving into Gaza to stake a claim to what they also considered 'their own' historical homeland, politically referred to as the Occupied Territories. The Palestinians also viewed Gaza as 'their' land. As more and more fenced Hebrew-speaking towns sprang up there, sporadic conflicts erupted. Israeli soldiers were sent in to protect the Jewish settlers from what they called, 'Palestinian insurgency.' It was an area of daily conflict no one knew how to resolve.

All this background is to set the scene, inform the reader, and reiterate that what I knew mostly through newspaper and TV before I came to Israel had little comparison to the actual experience, valuable lessons, and insights that I gained by actually being there. Here's the story of that learning.

Lenny's Account of the Workshop in Haifa

We held Anne's first workshop in Haifa on a Saturday and a Sunday at the Rothenberg House on Mount Carmel. We simply titled it a "Gestalt Workshop." More than fifty non-Orthodox participants pre-registered. Anne had requested we ask them to bring a photo of themselves as a child. The workshop was intense from the minute Anne entered the room. She formed a circle right away and walked around inside it, making eye contact with each participant, reaching out her hand to everyone there and repeating each one's name until she got it right.

"Shalom," she said nodding both at each person and their photo, making a point of getting each participant and their little Inner Child welcomed into this workshop. Then she put all the people into two circles one inside the other and had the people in the inner circle tell the people in the outer circle what they had most wanted to hear from their own parents. Then those in the outer circle did the same.

The first individual work was with a middle-aged woman who had always kept her hands and fingers well-covered with an oversized sweater. Anne tenderly exposed her hands and fingers by gently rolling up her sleeves. Tears rolled down the woman's cheeks as she made contact with Anne and with her own vulnerability. Another piece of Gestalt work involved a dream where Anne had several members of the group represent and role-play the different parts of the dreamer's fantasy, reliving it once as the woman had dreamed it and then role-playing it once as she wished the dream had ended. Magically, even the most reluctant people in the room, the ones who had come only to observe, were getting actively involved.

Anne's Account of the Workshop in Haifa

Before I entered the workshop room that first morning, I remember thinking that perhaps I had been over-ambitious coming here. Even though Susie, Lenny and I had joked and talked in English in the car, the morning drive here had reawakened my fear. Perhaps the Israeli people, the language barrier, the political diversity, and the conflicted environment of this strange land could be such unknowns for me that I might not be able to make true contact with the group. I did not want to only teach them theory or do a demonstration of Gestalt Therapy. I wondered if any of my learnings from my first Gestalt teachers, Mary Ann Merksamer and Leland Johnson, both Americans, would work under these very different conditions. My training with Laura Perls, surely would help though. She was Jewish and not American-born. As German Jews,

Laura's mother and sister had died in the concentration camps.

Fifty people were in the workshop room when I walked in. I didn't know any of them and most of them didn't know each other, so what I had learned in Gestalt training years ago about the inclusion stage of group process was going to be very useful. I decided to begin the workshop by having all fifty participants stand in two concentric circles facing each other.

I walked around to each person, introduced myself, took several willing hands in mine and looked each person in the eye as they said their name directly to me. The Hebrew names were so unfamiliar to me. I could not even begin to pronounce most of the guttural sounds. Simply nodding, I repeated each one's name back to them until my pronunciation got close enough that the person finally nodded in recognition.

Whenever a participant said nothing back to me, I remained quiet while we either looked at each other directly or away and back. Gradually, the tension melted. The room consisted of fifty strangers when I first walked in, but this basic Gestalt contact-withdrawal exercise had connected me to them and them to each other even before I'd finished going around the circles. We had become one group in spirit. Though different languages still separated me from them, a similar purpose and energy had joined us. The different religions would not be a problem after all. My Protestant mother would have loved these Jewish people. I could feel her presence here with me smiling over my shoulder.

I was, however, definitely unprepared for the experience of having an Israeli student I had never met standing alongside me translating every word I said into a language I didn't understand. But I knew I had to get used to it. Already I had noticed how quickly the participants who had spoken English to me at first had quickly regressed to using their native Hebrew tongue when expressing their deeper feelings. However, I began to notice that their tone, rhythm, and volume still sounded much the same as it would have been in English. Although the words were unfamiliar, their emotional delivery was very familiar. "Process, not content," Laura whispered inside my head.

I particularly remember how an exchange with one of the participants in the opening round later evoked a powerful piece of delayed grief work. A well-tanned muscular young woman in her late thirties, quite pretty and speaking perfect English, had described herself as a Zionist when I first made contact with her. Now, staring at the floor, she hesitated several minutes before raising her head to look me in the eye. She began to sob when I asked her to tell me her name again.

"My name is Yaffa," she tearfully told me. "When you first looked me in the eye, I felt sad for my father who has just died. I am the daughter of a Holocaust survivor who would never look me in the eye like you did. All my life, my father said he couldn't let me see the pain he carried in his soul, but I've always longed to know who he was. He never talked about Auschwitz but I knew from my mother that his parents and brothers had been taken there along with him and were never seen again. I loved my father so much but he died without ever letting me know what had happened to him there. He said he wanted to protect me from the unspoken horror he had been through. And now he is dead, and I can never get the close contact I always hoped for with him." As I listened to Yaffa, I remembered my own closeness with my deceased father and tried to imagine what her father's deflection had been like for her. I couldn't. My father would have been sad not to be close to his daughter.

I asked Yaffa to remember her father as he was a year before he died and she described how each time she looked at him, he would lower his head or look away. Then I suggested she put her father in the empty chair and ask him to look at her, telling him that she needed to see him looking at her once before he died. "Abba," ("Father") she pleaded beginning to use her native Hebrew language as she spoke to him in the empty chair. And so the standard Gestalt chair work began, but it quickly became significant when I asked her to sit in the empty chair and become her father.

Cautiously moving over to his chair and looking down at the floor, Yaffa began to role-play the spirit of her deceased father reluctantly complying with his daughter's wish for contact. As his eyes came up to look at hers in the empty chair, it was as if a demon had jumped out from inside her/him. I flinched as I saw the intensity of 'his' pain exploding out from her eyes. Most of the other participants jumped back in horror as she screamed out the imploded agony her father had kept hidden inside himself all those years. With it, exploding from his daughter's mouth came the repressed `survivor' shame that he had tried to hide from her. In the here and now of that room, we as a group went back with him to that concentration camp as he confessed his agony at being helpless to save his family who had disappeared one by one into the gas chambers.

As we listened to Yaffa crying, moaning, and sobbing, I realized that her father's unresolved feelings over his family's deaths, and his unexpressed anger at his own powerlessness to stop it from happening had been silently introjected into Yaffa's unconscious mind. Her father's deflected grief over his childhood family had prevented him from having any emotional closeness with the daughter he loved. She, in turn, had 'inherited' his process of deflection. It was the beginning of my awareness of how often secret emotional traumas and behavioral patterns of dealing (or not dealing) with intense feelings are passed down from one generation to another non-verbally.

Yaffa (whose name I later found out meant 'pretty woman' in Hebrew) told me later that all her life she had been afraid of this quiet beloved man but had never before known why. Now, she finally understood the introjected reason. Like him, she had never been able to feel close to anyone she loved, either. Now in retrospect, she began again speaking to me in English. "Love hurts, is what my father always told me. You know, it's strange. I have been a dedicated Zionist all my life and always committed to never leaving Israel. But the truth is, before I did this work to release his agony from inside me, I was actually afraid to leave Israel. I did not think I could feel safe anywhere else in the world. Actually, I didn't ever feel safe in Israel, either. Now I would like to visit abroad. I feel unafraid for the first time in my life."

I couldn't help but contrast Yaffa's statement about losing her father's introjected fear of ever leaving Israel with losing my and my sons' fear of having me come to Israel in the first place. And with that contrast, came the sudden realization that I no longer felt afraid to be in Israel. It had been a sacred moment to meet both her father in her and my father in me. I felt incredibly welcome as part of this group and surprisingly safe in this troubled land. Our cultural differences had been bridged through the depth of this intense personal meeting with the four of us.

My fear was being replaced with a strong sense of purpose. In order to stay centered and protect my Inner Child from all the Holocaust memories I would hear at the workshop, I began to meditate alone in the garden at each break to center myself in the now. As a child, I had watched RKO Pathe News films in the movie theatres that showed American GIs liberating emaciated Jewish survivors from the concentration camps at the end of WWII. Here in this workshop were some of these very same survivors and their grown children. I didn't know it then, but the Jews in therapy in Israel at this time were among the very first to break the silence of shame and tell the world of their trauma in the ghetto and the camps. I felt honored to be here with these heroic people as they finally released their long-hidden feelings from that horror.

I remember next the Israeli captain who said he needed to cry over the killings he had seen and done in war. He spoke of how hardened he had become. However, he suspected that holding in years of accumulated sadness was the cause of his severe headaches. Try as he may to release the fountain of tears he knew was inside, he couldn't get over his own learned resistance. To him, crying was weak.

Susie had told me stoic reactions were coping skills that were taught in military training. In addition, she had said, working with a female therapist would represent a serious gender issue for most Israeli men who were not used to taking a woman's direction. Nevertheless, here he was asking me if I could 'make him cry.' It was a retroflection worth undoing.

I had him begin by remembering the last person he had seen crying, and, of course, it was a female, his mother. I instructed him to put his mother in the empty chair, and to watch her cry as he was leaving for his last tour of duty. Next, I had him sit in her chair and be his mother, showing us her facial behaviors, biting his lip, sniffling, swallowing, and imitating the sounds of her crying, pretending to wipe her tears from his face, and making his chin quiver as hers had. Then I had him return to his chair, mimicking her and saying, "I'm crying about...I don't want to cry about..." over and over again.

Within minutes, and much to his surprise, his own sobbing began. Like a kid with a new toy, he'd cry, feel the wet tears on his face, and all of a sudden, stop crying, laugh for joy, and then go back to crying some more. During the rest of the workshop, whenever anyone else cried, he would smile and let more tears come to his eyes as he joined them.

Lenny Describes Anne's Second Visit To Israel

One thing is necessary to understand about our Gestalt Institute's success in Israel. Religious Jews believe that the harder a thing is to achieve, the more quality it possesses in the end. Students who were living in the Gaza Strip on the western side of Israel had found it excruciatingly difficult getting to Haifa in the northern part of Israel for workshop training. Often it took these students at least three hours driving to reach us.

With their wives, several of whom were pregnant, they usually made the trip to Haifa through hostile Occupied Territories crowded into two bulletproof cars with their M-16s within close reach. The travel conditions were often made more difficult by having to dodge the rocks and Molotov Cocktails being thrown at them by Palestinians who lived along the way. However, it was somewhat of a holy journey for them to get to us during the week to study in Haifa, but the fact that it was difficult for them to accomplish only added to their Jewish dedication to do it.

On Anne's second visit to Israel, a young religious man from the Occupied Territories by the name of Mordechai organized a workshop with her with the Orthodox Jewish community. Even though he was an ardent student of Gestalt who had been studying with us in Haifa, Mordechai had been unable to attend Anne's first or second workshop there because it had been scheduled on a Saturday and Sunday, instead of the middle of the week training we usually did. Strict observance of the Sabbath began at sundown on Friday for all religious Jews and continued until sundown on Saturday. So Mordechai had arranged for Anne to do a Sunday and Monday workshop in a private home in West Jerusalem, which is the Jewish sector of the city.

So telling our students in the Orthodox religious community that my Gestalt teacher was doing a workshop there on a Sunday and Monday was not difficult to sell to them, just difficult to sell to their Rabbi since Anne is a Catholic and a woman. It must be taken into consideration that those in the religious communities who wanted to attend Anne's Jerusalem workshop had to have the prior agreement of their Rabbi in Jerusalem. Getting his approval was a feat of magic since it is well known that, in the past, this Rabbi had only approved workshops by Jewish teachers and therapists who were males. But it happened, nevertheless.

Mordechai, who had organized this Jerusalem workshop and who would also serve as Anne's translator, brought with him his wife Dina, the only daughter of the patriarch Ya ' akov. They were both Lenny and Susie's Gestalt students. But the thirty-five or so participants there were mostly Orthodox religious women who lived in West Jerusalem. Several others had come with Mordechai from the Occupied Territories in the Gaza Strip at his urging. It was their first workshop, too.

Unlike Anne's Haifa workshop, there was almost no opening inclusion process here with this group in Jerusalem. Nor was it necessary anyhow. The Orthodox communities already knew each other well. And there would definitely be no hand-holding permitted here. An Orthodox religious person is not allowed to touch a person of the opposite sex unless married to them. Anyhow, these participants already had their own community established and it was obvious to me they just wanted their time with "my Gestalt teacher" who, they were sure, could give them wise answers to their dilemmas, much like their Rebbe did.

Anne Describes Her Second Visit to Israel

The following year, two two-day workshops were scheduled for me on my return visit to Israel - a second one in Haifa for the non-religious Gestalt students and a new one with the Orthodox religious community in Jerusalem. For this new group in Jerusalem, I had been instructed to dress according to the Orthodox women's dress code: high-neck, long-sleeved blouses and long skirts with stockings. The Orthodox women also had to cover their heads with a scarf or hat, but I was exempted from this part of the rule.

The Holy City was on a hill and as we drove up the winding road to Jerusalem, I noticed the many burned-out wrecks of Israeli Army bullet-proof cars and trucks alongside the road. I was told that these war wreckages had been left there in respect for those who had given their life to defend Israel and were now proudly displayed for all to see.

"Reminders of the Independence War in 1948," Susie had told me, "Lest we forget." But forgetting inside Israel would be difficult. Moving slowly along ahead of us was a convoy of Army equipment and soldiers. This time, a cannon sitting on a flatbed truck in front of us harmlessly aimed its nozzle into our windshield as we drove into the Holy City.

Somehow it all seemed familiar now. The people of Israel were living on a giant Army base ablaze with flowers. It was quite a polarity. As we drove along, I thought again about the many religious differences between the Christians, Jews, and Muslims in Israel.

Amidst the many polarities, I found yet another striking similarity, namely, that Jerusalem was a Holy City to all three religions and that the Jews and Muslims had fought over the city many times in the past. I learned from my friends that at the beginning of the 19th century, under European influence, the Old City had evolved into four sectors referred to as 'quarters.'

The Jerusalem of today was sharply divided into four dramatically different cultures, architectures, and lifestyles, like a pie cut into four equal wedges. There was a rooftop in the exact center of the Holy City where a tour guide regularly took tourists to show us the four distinctly different quarters -- Christian (Catholics and Protestants); Jewish; Muslim; and Armenian (Catholic) --which could be clearly viewed from an overhead vantage point.

However, most of the Catholic and Protestant Christian holy places in Jerusalem, the guide had wryly noted, including Jesus' crucifixion site, were actually in the Muslim quarter of East Jerusalem. The one exception was Jesus' birthplace, which, of course, was miles away in Bethlehem. For the first time, I realized Bethlehem, a Christian holy site, was now under Muslim control, not Christian or Jewish. That was rather disconcerting news to me.

Anne's Workshop in Jerusalem

The workshop for this Orthodox community was held at a private home in Jerusalem. Some of the homes in this Jewish quarter of Jerusalem were much newer than others, but all looked similar since they were entirely monochromatic. I learned that, for centuries, it had been required that houses there could only be built with the light tan-colored stone from the area, called Jerusalem stone.

I entered the workshop location through a wooden gate into another lovely garden filled with red geraniums like those at Susie's and on my own balcony in New Orleans. Somehow, even though Israel was thought of as a desert, flowers grew profusely there. I was told the soil was magic and that was why the tourists were always trying to sneak some of it out of the country with them when they left, even though that was against government regulations. Most Israelis believed the earth and water to be holy. I was beginning to understand why just looking at their gardens. The blooms were larger than I had ever seen and the colors more vibrant. It was its own Findhorn garden.

Inside the simple stucco house, eighteen unknown people were already sitting in a circle on the floor cross-legged in the well-known Gestalt group style waiting to begin. Silently, they greeted me with shy smiles and respectful nods. I wondered what they had been told about me and what their expectations were of "Lenny's teacher," a female Gestalt workshop leader from America. Most of the women there, I had been told, had never been to a workshop before, and very few of the religious men from this Orthodox Jerusalem community had ever attended weekday Gestalt classes in Haifa.

The organizer, Mordechai, who was to be my translator, was a redheaded, freckled-faced young man in his mid-thirties who lived in the Occupied Territories with his wife Dina and six children which he didn't look old enough to have. Mordechai had a decided peaceful look to him that concealed his reputation for throwing Molotov cocktails out the window of his bullet-proof

Mercedes, by which he kept Arabs from approaching his car on his drive back and forth to Jerusalem. Nevertheless, later on that morning, when friendly Mordechai invited me to come visit his home after the workshop, I immediately declined. The initial fear was back and was most definitely my 'mother' this time.

Lenny's Comments

The participants, half of whom were not from Jerusalem, were recruited by Mordechai, and had driven in from the settlement towns in Yehuda and Shomron in the Occupied Territories. They were among the hundred twenty thousand Jews living in the midst of more than two million Palestinians in the West Bank. I did not know if I could sensibly explain to anyone the political tensions that existed in Israel. Often volatile, the conflict erupted regularly into bombings, street fights and warfare. We who lived here had gotten used to it but the more I tried to describe it, the more outrageous it seemed and the more Anne got nervous about being here. So I stopped. She needed to work.

Anne Speaks of the Jerusalem Participants

Because this was a workshop for Orthodox Jews, I had expected that the 'men in black' would be present, but these religious men were dressed more like the hippies I knew in America with their drawstring pants and loose fitting gauze shirts. Each man wore the mandatory religious skullcap on his head. I called it a "yamaka" (yarmulke) but was told those caps were called that only outside Israel. The 'kippah' as it was called inside Israel, was the name in Hebrew. Either way, they looked like the schoolgirl beanies I'd worn back in the days when it was mandatory for a female to have her head covered inside church. Several of the Orthodox women here not only covered their heads with a scarf tied behind their ears, but also wore a wig under it. I knew it couldn't have anything to do with vanity because it certainly was not attractive. But the women did not seem to be interested in that at all. I wondered if they were purposely trying to make themselves unattractive to men. *Why?*

I was informed that a religious man here could not touch any woman other than his wife, and that this rule also applied to my translator, Mordechai, who was not even allowed to shake hands with me when we met. Initially, my impression of these Orthodox religious people was similar to having walked backward 1500 years in time. Their lifestyle was so dramatically different from mine in Metropolitan New Orleans.

Did they know I was Catholic? But it was too late to ask Lenny and Susie for more particulars. Neither of them knew most of these new Orthodox religious people either. "Ok," I told myself remembering Mary Ann Merksamer's teachings. "Deal with what is, instead of what isn't," she would say. What choice did I have but to do that? The work would begin without my ever having a chance to ask the participants what their expectations were of being here with me. I was deep in an unknown culture and didn't know what to expect of them either. Unlike the Haifa workshop before this one, most of these people already knew each other well. But I hadn't gotten to meet any of the participants individually before we started and definitely could not do my usual hand-holding opening circles here. As I wondered how to make contact, to my surprise, I was told the group was ready to get to work and had already decided who would be first. So I would have to cross that bridge when I came to it, if I could ever find it. "Stay centered," Laura Perls would have said and

"Breathe."

The pre-chosen volunteer was a heavy-set, wide-eyed sweet-faced young woman about thirty years old named Bathsheba, who looked to me like she was still reeling backwards from shock. Bathsheba trembled as she began to tell me about her trauma. As per the Rabbi's instructions, Bathsheba had been made to carry her unborn child dead within her for two months before giving birth to the stillborn baby girl. I shuddered with her as she described the ordeal and tried to process my own identification with her at the same time.

A mixture of relief followed by guilt flooded my mind. I had given birth to six live babies myself and, unlike her, had stopped before my luck ran out. I had had no miscarriages, no traumas and no girl babies. Only sons. I remembered that Bathsheba from the Old Testament had given birth to a stillborn male infant as punishment from God for her relationship with King David. But this rather docile Bathsheba didn't seem to have disobeyed God, or had she? Was there something I didn't know about her history? Indeed, there was plenty I didn't know about her religion.

Lenny's Commentary on Bathsheba's Work

The name Bathsheba means "seven years old" in Hebrew. Coincidentally, this dead infant was to be her seventh child. According to Jewish tradition, an embryo has no identity until it is born, and so the dead baby girl was considered to be a "nefel" (an aborted one). Because of Hebrew law, a baby born dead could not to be buried alone in her own grave. So the Rabbi had instructed that Bathsheba's baby be buried with a recently deceased woman, a stranger whose name had to remain completely unknown to Bathsheba, and it was also required that the whereabouts of this woman's grave be kept secret from her, too.

After years living in Israel, I had grown used to the Rabbi's control over his people's lives but I knew it was completely foreign to Anne. Even Anne's Catholic Pope had no such power over his people.

Anne's Account of Bathsheba's Work

As Bathsheba told me her story, her trembling increased. According to the five stages of grief that I had learned from Elizabeth Kubler-Ross, Bathsheba was clearly still in shock, the first stage. I wondered how much grief work if any she had done to release this traumatic experience and doubted if she had ever gotten to or through anger, the second stage. I asked Bathsheba to lie down on a mat next to the wall instead of sitting up, mostly to give her body the needed support for the intense emotional release that was imminent.

On second thought, I realized that moving the mat to the center of the floor might have provided better positioning for me in the group as I worked with her. Had I chosen to sit behind Bathsheba instead of in front of her, I could have seen the other participants, too. But by the time I realized my logistic error, Bathsheba was already shaking so hard, I could not move either her or me around. So I began the work with my back to a circle of people I didn't know.

From the first moment as Bathsheba began telling me how much she wanted to die, I felt afraid. Not of her feelings, but of my dilemma. At that moment, I instinctively knew she was either holding in her anger at God for her baby's death or at the Rabbi for having her carry a dead infant to term. I had no idea why the Rabbi would insist on this and assumed it must be religious law. I wasn't going to question her about it at this point. The issue was her feelings about the baby's death, not my curiosity about the Rabbi's instructions.

More importantly, how on earth was I going to deal with her introjected barrier against releasing that rage to either God or the Rabbi here in this Orthodox group? Or was it my own introjected barrier? Frantic, I began to stall to give my therapist-self time to think how to work with her diplomatically.

"Are you angry at your doctor?" I asked first. Mordechai translated, but Bathsheba's head shook "No" clearly enough for anyone to read without his help. It occurred to me to avoid the anger issue altogether and save my own position and reputation. It would definitely be a smarter choice to avoid having her express the verbal content of her rage here. Would it be ethical for me to ask this client not to talk, just let out the sound of her feelings instead? That was a redundant question now. Bathsheba was already wailing at the top of her voice.

"Are you angry at yourself?" I asked. Mordechai translated as Bathsheba screamed out another "No." I could just have her exaggerate her shaking, but her shaking was now at maximum intensity. "Are you angry at your husband?" I asked next, stalling my way along. Mordechai looked at me helplessly without bothering to translate as she screamed out another "No."

What to do? I was running out of time. Who to ask? The therapist in me needed answers I could not get from me or her or him. I quickly glanced sideways over at Lenny and Susie, wishing I could take a time out and confer with them as Bathsheba thrashed about on the mat. Was it permissible in her religion for this woman to be angry at God? I had no idea. Fear grabbed hold of me. How could I help her release the rage that she was repressing without putting me in jeopardy with the Rabbi?

Laura would say "Use your own background," but my American Catholic background would not work here. I needed some common ground. Biblical Bathsheba wouldn't do. This Bathsheba here hadn't broken any of God's laws. She had followed the Rabbi's rules and her child had died anyhow. It did seem unfair. I would have been angry if it had happened to my baby, I projected.

With my back to the crowd, I began to pray. Would I get thrown out if I even suggested to Bathsheba that she might be angry at God for her infant's death? I had no problem being angry at God myself. In fact, at that very moment, I was so furious at Him I couldn't even pray in the respectful Catholic girl style I had learned in school.

"I can't believe you did this to me, God," I silently told Him off. "This is not fair. You bring me all the way here to Israel to work with Your Chosen People and then you start me off with this impossible situation. Now You better come up with an idea of what to do to get me out of this mess You put us both in." Still fussing at God in my head, I looked at the still trembling Bathsheba and silently added, "And make it quick!"

I sat quiet for a moment, concentrating on keeping my own breathing steady and deep. I needed all the self-support I could muster. Bathsheba stared at me, frightened by the emotional intensity she was feeling and desperately hoping I could come up with a miracle to make the uncontrollable shaking stop. Where were my trainers when I needed them? A Mary Ann thought stayed with me: "Be your breath, in and out."

Leland Johnson had always focused on the breath, too, and talked about 'the existential alone point.' "What do you do when you don't know what to do?" he had quizzed me over and over. "One day you will find out. Well, you breathe, and you stay centered," he would guide. "Just breathe and wait." And so I breathed and waited. And waited, and breathed. And then, believe it or not - and I could hardly believe it - Amen! Inspiration came in the form of an idea to tell an Old Testament story that I most certainly knew a Jewish crowd could relate to. I thanked God for both His helping hand and His innate cleverness.

I began by reminding Bathsheba about the time God had asked Abraham to sacrifice his son. "I'm sure Abraham didn't want to do that," I told her, "and, you know, it's possible that Abraham might even have been angry at God for wanting him to do that," I suggested cautiously. "And when Abraham raised his hand with the knife in it, maybe he was raising his fist at God, too. Maybe he told God he was angry at Him, even though he intended to follow God's will anyhow. Maybe you might tell God the truth, too, if you are..." But before I could finish the sentence with "...angry at God," Bathsheba had already exploded with such intensity that her body physically lifted off the mat. For minutes on end, she beat the mat, shook her fists in the air, and screamed what even to my un-Hebrewed ear, could only be fury at her G-d.

When her anger finally calmed down to simple sobbing, she began rocking the baby/pillow I handed her. As I joined her in saying goodbye to the infant, I heard rustling sounds coming from the participants in back of me. What would the outcome of eliciting this woman's rage at G-d be for me? At best, I might be escorted out of the workshop or at worst, escorted out of the country. But now my joy for Bathsheba and not my fear for me was filling my heart. Here in front of me sat a calm Bathsheba, smiling through her tears, and reaching out to me. We hugged and I tried to prepare myself to face the awful music that might be waiting for me in the group.

Only a few of the participants in the group were dry-eyed as I turned around. Three of the women were quietly sobbing, still being comforted by the woman next to them. The rest of the participants were smiling at me. Several of the women went over to hug Bathsheba and most surprisingly, as Mordechai told me, five of them said they, too, wanted to work on their anger at God. By the end of the day, His heavenly ears must have surely been burning!

On the way out the door, I asked Mordechai what the Rabbi would do when he heard about this anger work. He laughed. "What do you mean – 'when'? He already knows. The Rebbe knows everything his people do. Several of us told him at the lunch break." Amazed that the Rabbi had allowed me to continue, I asked Mordechai what his response had been. "The Rebbe said he liked what you are doing. He said to tell you that he was glad you were helping his people tell G-d the truth about how they feel about Him.

The Rebbe said that whenever people tell G-d the truth, they get closer to G-d, so to thank you." Those words are forever etched in my mind. Through Mordechai, that Rebbe gave me a new understanding of the Jewish religion that was surprisingly similar to the confessional where we Catholics went to tell God the truth. Indeed, the Rebbe had shared his personal feelings about my work. Instead of just giving Mordechai a simple approval for me to continue, he had reached out to make true contact with me, and by crossing that bridge, he had gotten our very different religions much closer to each other. I liked him even though I never would meet him.

Lenny's Comments on Bathsheba's Work

When Anne asked Bathsheba if she could get angry and shout at G-d, there was a hushed silence in the room. As Bathsheba began to rage against her Maker, Susie and I sat by completely shocked. It was an accomplishment that I have never witnessed or ever attempted previously in working with this religious community. Obviously, we Jewish therapists had never dared contradict the Rabbi's instructions to a client in any way. Anne's introjects might have stopped her from being angry at her own Catholic father's rule, or the Pope's, but it hadn't stopped her from challenging the Rebbe's. Expressing her anger at having to follow his religious rule was however the missing piece before Bathsheba could let go of her dead baby. Maybe it was the missing piece for Anne, too.

Susie and I watched stunned as Anne then gave the woman permission to re-enact her pregnancy and dialogue with the dying fetus, telling her baby girl how much she loved her and had wanted her to live. Finally, when Anne suggested she say "Goodbye" to her stillborn baby, Bathsheba began to cry softly and naturally, rocking the imaginary infant in her arms. I watched as she softly lay the dead baby/pillow down on the mat, patting it as you would if putting an infant to sleep.

After Anne's workshop, Dina, Mordechai, and Bathsheba enrolled as students at our institute in Haifa. Bathsheba continued to study with us for eight years and eventually became a trainer for two years before she started her own Gestalt and Psychodrama groups. She is quite successful today as a Gestalt group facilitator in Jerusalem. She had her tenth child a year ago.

Bathsheba came back for a refresher course in Tel Aviv last year and I presented her with an inscribed copy of Anne's book, _Why We Pick The Mates We Do_ (1997), a gift Anne had asked me to bring to Bathsheba for her counseling practice even though Anne knew it very likely that the Rebbe had 'picked' Bathsheba's mate, and most definitely had to approve every female's choice of a husband. Fifteen years later, while preparing to write this chapter with Anne, I telephoned Bathsheba to ask her for memories of her Gestalt work with Anne.

"I was in a state of shock after having lost my child that previous year. I lived in a split," she said in the telephone interview with me. "Part of me was alive and part of me was dead. I felt I didn't belong anywhere, that I was not truly alive anymore. I had been ready to commit suicide before I came to that workshop. It was my last hope. I was in despair but Gestalt saved my life. After this experience of fury against G-d and having the opportunity of speaking to my unborn child, I got up from the floor as if magic had occurred. I felt integrated. I had completed my unfinished grief business and was alive again."

Mordechai's wife, Dina, waited until the end of the second day to work with Anne. She told us that her father had murdered her mother in front of her and her six young siblings. Because he was sentenced to prison, the young children were orphaned. Dina and Mordechai, just newly married, had 'adopted' all of them. Dina's quandary now was her father's insistence that she bring the children to visit him in prison, which Dina said she couldn't do, even though the Ten Commandments clearly state: "Honor your mother and father." Her work concerned her wrath at her father and the conflict concerning the Rabbi's instructions.

Anne's Account of the Second Day

A slender woman in her early thirties, her dark hair covered with a scarf tied behind her ears, Dina told me she had waited until the last hour to speak out because she had to work up the courage. "But after watching you work with the other people for two days," she said, "I am convinced you can tell me the right thing to do."

Now all experienced therapists know how to deal with a client's projections and why to not buy into them. My Gestalt teachers had taught me to give questions back to a client, but never answers. "Thinking you know what is right for a client is surely an ego issue for the therapist to deal with," Leland Johnson had insisted. "Answers are just your projections onto the client." So I knew I wasn't going to tell Dina what to do, even if I thought I had the solution she was hoped for. But not knowing the problem, I asked her what it was. Then I knew for sure I didn't have an answer for her, or even a good question.

Dina's problem was that her father wanted her to visit him in prison with his other children and the Rabbi said, "Go." She wasn't sure whether her murdered mother would want her to do that. And besides, Dina couldn't forgive her father. And her religion wouldn't allow her to disobey him or the Rabbi.

I remembered that feeling from my own childhood. Dina was sure I could tell her the right thing to do. I knew I couldn't. All I could do therapist-to-client was help Dina release her conflicted feelings. Would that be enough for her? Dina looked at me expectantly as I debated with myself regarding what my own 'right thing' to do was, not hers.

"Well?" she said, confident in her projection of a grand solution coming from me, "What should I do?" she asked me as I was asking myself the same question. The truth still was I didn't know. Maybe I was overwhelmed. I'd worked four full days in a row. Maybe I should have taken a break today in the afternoon instead of working straight through. That's what Laura Perls would have done.

I lovingly remembered how Laura had taught me to pace myself in workshops to avoid getting overtired like I was now. "Stop and rest," she had said. "Take a break." Too late for that now! "Anything you use comes from you as an individual therapist," Laura was talking to me in my head again. "Be yourself and speak your own truth" is what she had meant.

I remained quiet for another moment and then simply told Dina the truth that was foreground for me at that moment, not therapist-to-client, but person-to-person. My own truth. "I don't know," I said. She stared at me in disbelief. "What do you mean, 'You don't know?' I've watched you know what to do with every other person in this workshop and you dare say 'I don't know' to me?"

Certain now of my honest response to her, I repeated it. "Dina, the truth is I wouldn't know the right thing for me to do if my father had killed my mother. I wouldn't know what to do either." She turned away in anger and disbelief and stomped out of the room. I watched her go without saying another word. Inside me, Laura, Mary Ann and Leland were all OK with what I had done. So was I.

Lenny's Account of the Second Day

The last piece of work in the religious community that day involved Dina's sister who had a dream of a monstrous fish chasing her. This woman was also the daughter of a man who had killed her mother because 'God had told him to do it.' Dina's sister was petrified even telling Anne the dream, and shocked at the thought of accepting herself as powerful when Anne suggested she role-play the fish. She shyly refused the suggestion, since owning her own power is forbidden to married women in this religious community.

Only men, according to Hebrew teachings, are allowed to be dominant and powerful. Of course, Anne didn't know that when she suggested it to her anymore than Anne knew that none of Bathsheba's prior therapists had ever dared to facilitate anyone's anger at G-d.

Anne accepted the woman's religious introject easily, and simply asked the young woman to shiver out the fear she was feeling in her body about having been asked to be the fish, and she did as Anne asked. The young woman was then able to describe the fish to us but not role-play it. It was, however, a way for Dina's sister to safely begin discovering her feelings without crossing the boundary of her religious and cultural introjects about women. The shivering was a unique way to non-verbally relieve the pressure of the fear she'd been retroflecting since the dream.

Anne Describes Her Third Visit to Israel

In 1989, after my third annual workshop in Haifa, I traveled once again to the Holy City, to do a second 'weekday' workshop in the West Jerusalem sector for this same Orthodox religious community. As before, the workshop was scheduled on a Sunday and Monday since religious Jews could not attend on the Sabbath.

Feeling fully welcome and safe, I was returning to see friends now. Going in with the full approval of the Chief Rebbe under my belt this time, I eagerly entered the gate into the same flower-laden garden I had remembered so well from the previous year. Only this time, several of the women were gathered outside the house to greet me. As I approached, the giggling crowd stepped away to reveal a smiling Bathsheba holding a newborn infant in her arms. When I came nearer, she held the infant out to me.

In Hebrew, translated by one of the women, Bathsheba said, "My new baby girl is one month old. I named her 'Shavuoth,' which in Hebrew means 'Feast of the Harvest.' The work you did with me last year saved my life. I never even thought I could be angry at G-d. It was too scary. But that's exactly what was wrong with me. Surprisingly enough, G-d didn't seem to mind. See - He even gave me another baby girl." Her face was beaming as she looked at her infant. It was a beautiful sight. I walked into the house carrying Bathsheba's eighth child. As I entered the workshop room, Mordechai rushed over to me, calling out loudly in English for Dina, his wife. "Come over here and give Anne a hug from me so you can give me her hug back."

Instantly, I recalled the rules about married men not touching any other woman except their wife. But it was Dina touching me that I was thinking about. Would she listen to her husband and come over and hug me after the last workshop when she had been so angry with me? Walking up slowly, Dina hugged me without a word and then promptly transferred the hug to her husband, now standing next to both of us with a big grin on his face. Turning to me, she said, "You know, I was so angry at you after the last workshop when you didn't know the answer to my problem. At first, I was angry that you had helped everyone else solve their problems, but not me.

For all these years since my father murdered my mother, I have been feeling so stupid for not knowing what to do. Must I obey the Rabbi and go see my Father or should I be loyal to my mother, disobey the Rabbi and not visit my Father? It was driving me crazy. "One morning a few weeks after the workshop, I suddenly realized I wasn't as troubled anymore about whether or not I should forgive my father and go visit him. I wasn't feeling so stupid about not knowing what to do anymore either. I had been so angry at you. You see, I thought you really did know and just wouldn't tell me. I had never believed you really didn't know. I thought you were so smart that you would surely have the answer.

"And one day, I realized you really didn't know. I had been so angry at myself for not knowing what the right thing to do all this time was. I had always thought I was so smart, too, but I had been feeling so stupid. So when I forgave you for not knowing, I could forgive myself, too. No one would know what was the right thing to do, would they? No matter how smart they are.

"So that very day I decided to just do what the Rabbi had told me was the right thing and I went to visit my father. After all, the Rabbi is supposed to be the smartest person around here. I still haven't forgiven my father though and I am at peace about that. You know, I don't think I could've forgiven myself for being stupid unless you were willing to be stupid, too." And with that, Dina gave me a big hug. I thought of my own mother who had always said, "The Lord works in mysterious ways." All over the planet, too, Momma.

The rest of the group gathered around me in a circle. This time, we said our hellos to each other and exchanged catch-up news before the workshop began. I touched the hands of all the women before we began. Later that day in the workshop, I was in such synch with the group's energy, I no longer had to wait for Mordechai's translations. I don't know exactly how it happened but while working with Avi, one of the men, I actually forgot that I couldn't understand Avi's language. Mordechai said I was replying as if I knew what Avi had just said in Hebrew.

Bewildered, Mordechai even asked me if I had learned Hebrew over the last year and I told him "No," but somehow I didn't need his translations anymore. I had reached the point of simply paying attention mainly to Avi's body and his breathing, not listening to his words but instead to the sound of his voice. At that moment in Israel, for the first time, I realized what it was like to be in spiritual contact with a client's humanness and his spirit both. I could feel it in my heart and it wasn't confluence. I had crossed the bridge that separated 'us' by language and religion. My father in me had crossed over, too.

Years ago in Gestalt training, my dear teacher and close friend, Mary Ann, did an amazing piece of work with a French participant without benefit of a translator and no one in the workshop ever realized Mary Ann didn't know French. Mary Ann had told me that would happen to me one day if I would take my attention from the client's words and instead focus on the client's body, feelings, breathing, voice tonality, volume and rhythm. "Follow the process, not the content."

It is in that essential way that people the world over are alike," she said. "Regardless of how unfamiliar their language, religion, and customs may be - feelings sound the same the world over." Emotions in the Israeli people were indeed the same ones I had experienced in all my years of working with American clients. There were no new feelings being invented in this country, and I have not found any new ones in other countries since. We are all using the same ones. I had to come to the other side of the world to understand what Mary Ann had said about the universal language of humanness.

"*We are all one energy field.*" Let's call it LOVE.

Lenny's Summation

The reaction to Anne's visit and her therapeutic work earned her more invitations to the Holy Land. On her next trip, she did a workshop for therapists in Jerusalem that was sponsored by Burt Meltzer, a psychologist friend of mine, and then another for him in the south of Israel on a 'moshav,' which was the farming community where he lived. In addition, Anne did her regular yearly Gestalt workshop in Haifa for us and another one for the religious community in Jerusalem.

Of course, Susie and I grew light years as a result of Anne's visits with us. So did our workshop participants and our Gestalt Institute in Haifa. My thoughts now seem to merge on the belief that Anne exuded some sort of trust in her contact, and people went from cure to cure because of their faith in her. It was like watching participants stand in a bread line, each awaiting his or her turn. All of the work was deep, and a respected hush came over the room whenever Anne spoke…maybe it was her Southern drawl that hypnotized them. Anyhow, the Israeli participants all listened with very high positive regard, waiting for the wisdom that they knew was sure to come, and most often did.

I remember the profound work that was accomplished and the incredible closeness that was established among everyone present at Anne's workshop especially considering the major cultural and religious differences she started with. The deep personal contact we felt still lives inside all of us who were there and we still remember those times together with much love.

Anne's Summation of Her Experiences in Israel

What I discovered as a Gestalt therapist working in that troubled land has stayed with me since and remains so dominant in my consciousness to this day as one of the most profound learnings of my life. I am now certain that whatever vast differences exist among people in other cultures, regardless of how many unknowns stand between us, true contact will indeed occur if we can only meet the universal humanness in one another face to face, spirit to spirit. No matter how different the cultural beliefs, lifestyles, religions or languages may be, human emotions are the same everywhere, and recognition of our mutual emotional similarities is at the heart of true contact for people who have been locked into conflicts the world over or at home.

And somehow in spirit on one of my trips to Israel, my parents had quietly reconciled their Holy Wars. I can now imagine being a child sitting alongside them at church as they enjoy the love they always felt for each other. Whose church really doesn't matter. The love does.

The dead are invisible. They are not absent.
- St. Augustine

With Dedication and Appreciation

To my parents who are no longer separated by religion:
Edward Peter Schekeler, who died July 30, 1961, in New Orleans
Eunice Kellogg Schekeler, who died May 25, 1983, in New Orleans

And to my Gestalt teachers who are also still alive inside me:
Laura Posner Perls, who died July 13, 1990, in Germany,
Mary Ann Merksamer, who died November 8, 2003, in California
Leland Johnson, who died November 10, 2003, in Germany

Personal Account

Traveling backward in time has its own pitfalls....some of the memories that were foreground for me had been enhanced by having already told the story several times over to my students here in New Orleans. Some of the memories that were foreground for Lenny had escaped me altogether; however, reading his account brought back the experience in a flash.

Co-writing with a friend on the other side of the world presented its own challenges. I had hoped to create our chapter in the style of Barry Stevens and Carl Rogers' book *Person To Person*, where each chapter is an alternating dialogue in response to the other's previous one. But that did not happen.

Once I started to write, as always, I became immersed in the experience, wrote fast and plenty, forging ahead of the memory check-ins with Lenny. He was fine with my prolific sentences and let me take the lead in the writing, liking better his position of commentator and collaborator rather than co-author. Several times we remembered not just different things, but things differently.

When we first began exchanging memories, I couldn't tell you if the woman I worked with in the opening round had her arms covered and I rolled up her sleeves, or if she had her sleeves rolled up and I rolled them down. But amazingly enough, as Lenny and I continued to share our accounts, I began remembering the contact I had with the participants, and like a video playing in my head, the pictures, sounds and settings came back full color, full feeling.

And so it was with this chapter as it emerged....we began to realize that Lenny was remembering from the outside observer position and I from inside the experience working with the person. And in that way, we put it all back together. Tears came to my eyes often as I relived a lot of those moments.

Once again, as I wrote, I was rejoicing at the opportunity I'd had to fulfill my childhood dream and journey to Israel. Once again, I was revisiting the bonds I had formed with the people there. I would like to thank my teachers for the gifts they gave me that helped that happen and for these precious Gestalt memories.

Anne Teachworth, New Orleans, La., USA

References

Augustine of Hippo. (400/1993). *Confession: Books 1-xiii*. Translated by F. J. Sheed et al. Indianapolis, IN: Hackett Pub Co.

Kubler-Ross, Elizabeth, (1999). (Reprint Edition) *On Death and Dying*, NY: Scribner.

Perls, Laura, (1977). *Interview with Laura Perls*, Conducted by Edward Rosenfeld, May 1977, NY: The Gestalt Journal Press.

Teachworth, Anne, (1997). *Why We Pick The Mates We Do*, Metairie/New Orleans: Gestalt Institute Press.

XVI. PSYCHE AND CULTURE

By Lolita Sapriel, MSW and Dennis Palumbo, M.A, MFT

"Each culture...is a repository of some good thought about the universe; we are valuable to each other for that."   --- Barry Lopez, *Arctic Dreams*

Introduction
        We are all products of our culture, and as psychotherapists, we need to be aware of our cultural biases, and of the personal/social context that inevitably affects the way we organize meaning for ourselves and our clients. In this essay, we regard both Gestalt therapy and intersubjectivity theory (a relational, context-based psychoanalytic theory) as being ideally suited for cross-cultural application. Both approaches reject the notion of only "one truth," both are contextual and field-theory based, and both respect the phenomenology of subjective experience. In addition, we posit not only that each individual is part of a social culture that must be understood and appreciated, but that, analogously, each individual can be viewed as a unique *culture*.   Hence, a therapist's assumptions that individuals from the same culture automatically share a personal similarity and shared symbolic meanings might obscure his/her appreciation and investigation of individual differences in the patient's personal universe.
        We therefore posit that meaning is always context-dependent. The more dissimilar a patient's experience or culture is from the therapist's, the more difficult it becomes to differentiate behaviors and attitudes emerging from the patient's immersion in his/her original culture.   Such moments reflect instances of individual psychological difficulties, thereby differentiating difficulties arising out of attempts to adjust to a new culture. In this same way, we have observed of ourselves that our cultural backgrounds influenced specific patterns of family interaction, and marked certain self-states as preferable.
        Factors such as these contribute to the "fixed gestalten" or "organizing principles" of each therapist. Stolorow's (1998) term "organizing principle" is defined as "fixed and invariant recurring patterns of experience arising out of one's earliest repeated interactions in one's intersubjective relational field...precisely, the term refers to the invariant, thematic patterning of experience (structure), rather than patterns of experience (content). These patterns are often unconscious or out of awareness, while nevertheless shaping our view of reality (Sapriel, 1998: 37).
        Two clinical vignettes will demonstrate how both the therapist's self-organization and the patient's organizing principles co-create meaning within the therapeutic dyad.
        But first, one brief note about us: we represent two very different cultural backgrounds: one, a woman, is a Sephardic Jew from Egypt, with an amalgam of both Jewish and Middle Eastern cultural influences; and the other, a man, is of Italian American origin. We will address the "intersubjective" process arising from the collaboration of two such culturally different authors writing together.   In our co-authorship, we have to address male/female cultural socialization as well as East/West cultural differences, amongst others.

We have also noticed that our working together emphasizes one overarching fact -- namely: whether as individuals, or as persons from diverse cultures, it is not uncommon for the strivings of individuals for self-definition and self-expression to give rise to the fear that expressions of difference may jeopardize connection and relatedness. In other words: How can my "I" include "you" without either of us surrendering our uniqueness, and express instead the moment-to-moment dance that constitutes relatedness?

Culture and Psychotherapy

As psychotherapists, we occupy a position of authority and influence with the clients who come to us in need. Often, in our professional training, therapeutic theories or developmental models are presented as if they describe universal givens, and the ethnic or cultural biases underlying these theories are rarely addressed. For example, it is axiomatic that Western culture favors individuation, separateness, verbal skills, and goal directed behavior. These have also, coincidentally, been identified in the West as masculine goals. In contrast, many Asian or Arab cultures prize communitarian goals, connectedness, relatedness, and non-verbal attunement; often identified by the West as feminine qualities. First, we must understand and be aware of these cultural presuppositions, while sidestepping the pitfalls of stereotyping. Then we must work to accept and acknowledge the difference so as to engage in a dialogue that does not require obliteration of those differences.

A partial list from M. McGoldrick, *et al.* (1996: 12) offers an almost humorous example of such well-known biases, the "sound bytes" of cultural stereotypes: The English worry about dependency and emotionality; the Italians about family loyalty; the Chinese about harmony; the Jews about their children not being successful; the Arabs about their daughter's virginity, and so forth.

As psychotherapists, whatever our theoretical orientation, we are constantly and inevitably organizing meaning and seeing patterns in accordance with our own personal/cultural history. We are products of our own upbringing and the culture from which we come. We are products of our professional theoretical orientations. These various cultures inform our ideas and our habits of how to respond to our clients. What we observe clinically is inevitably influenced by our theoretical and cultural and personal psychological lenses. These ingrained views of our world and of how we make meaning are referred to by Stolorow as "organizing principles".

We have chosen to work from both a Gestalt therapy and an intersubjectivity theory model (one humanistic, the other a relational psychoanalytic theory) because we see them as consistent with a multi-cultural view. Both theories hold that human development is contextually based; that is the meaning of behaviors or attitudes arises in part from our personal/social context, rather than from a universal given.

For example, Mahler's (2000) developmental theory of positing separation and individuation as the healthy maturational goal is now understood to be culturally based (Mahler et al, 2000). This bias becomes apparent when working with many Asian-American clients in the U.S., who must come to terms with the conflict between a culture of individuation and that of one valuing greater interdependence; where "even older Asians tend to live with their parents and carry out parental wishes, and expect their children to do the same" (Yi, 1998: 309).

The tendency to pathologize such behaviors as indications of emotional enmeshment is increased, using Mahler's developmental scheme, since it does not acknowledge an origin of acculturation. The therapist must understand the context of the client and the preferred values of the culture of origin. In another example, an Indian mother in treatment in the United States reported that she could not say no to her child. Viewed from within a Western perspective, this could easily be understood as pathological boundary disturbance, a confluent state. However, within the Indian culture, mothers apparently don't habitually say no to their children; they find ways to distract them instead (Roland, 1999).

Increasingly, the United States is becoming a multicultural environment, and the salad bowl rather than the melting pot is the newer model, wherein each ethnic group seeks to retain its individual flavor. Therefore, it behooves us as therapists to increase our understanding of the cultural differences that can affect developmental and relational patterns.

In an interesting analog to the dialogic construct in both Gestalt therapy and relational psychoanalytic work, Grudin (1996) suggests that "cultural diversity at its best is a dialogue of cultures in which interaction with the exotic or 'other' instills compassion, sophistication, a sense of alternatives and intellectual curiosity" (Grudin, 1996: 138) This stance reinforces the notion that the intersection of the subjective world-views of disparate cultures has the same potential for growth and mutual understanding as does the therapeutic dyad created by the subjective views of patient and therapist. This definition is remarkably compatible with Levine Bar-Yoseph's statement that "Gestalt offers a field perspective that allows/enhances difference and believes that a dialogue is possible only where there is a difference" (Levine Bar-Yoseph, 2005: 6). However, as Grudin (1996) warns, we must also guard against certain presuppositions regarding a patient's cultural heritage, such as stereotypical ethnicity," which encourages us to diminish 'ethnic' people in two ways: we may underestimate the extent of their individuality and we may assess an ethnic characteristic as a limitation without appreciating its role as a cultural strength" (Grudin, 1996: 138).

We include these considerations in our attempt to weave an understanding of our own cultural heritage with that of our patients, and, with it, an appreciation of the larger field created by our authorial dyad. Just as our perceptions emerge from the amalgam of cultural and interpersonal influences in which we were formed, so too are the therapeutic theories to which we hold allegiance equally congenial to us as a result of these formative factors -- regardless of our insistence that, upon sober reflection, we find their intellectual soundness obvious. We intend to show how our individual cultural background affects our co-authorship. We also intend to demonstrate, via the clinical vignette, how as therapists we use our awareness of our cultural/psychological organizing principles as a bridge to understanding the world of a client with different cultural and psychological world views.

In this regard, we are greatly indebted to the classic work by Atwood and Stolorow, *Faces in a Cloud* (1994), wherein they first promulgated the notion that psychoanalytic theories are products of the subjective perspectives of their developers. They used psychobiographical analyses of Freud, Jung, Reich, and Rank to illustrate how these individuals' primary relationship patterns later found concretized expression in their theories. Atwood and Stolorow say: "It is our contention that the subjective world of the theorist is inevitably translated into his metapsychological conceptions and hypotheses regarding human nature...[and that] rather than being results of impartial reflection upon empirical facts accessible to everyone, they are bound up with the theorist's personal   reality..." (Stolorow & Atwood 1994; 5). We would assert an additional proposition: that every theoretician is also embedded in a specific cultural context which finds its way into his/her theories.

Thinking contextually requires us to articulate and question the personal assumptions underlying our theories, and to be aware of the inevitable cultural biases inherent in our choice of theory. It is crucial both to maintain a stance of respect for individual differences and to understand specific cultural differences.

Differentiating so-called "normal" development in one culture from individual psychopathology is made more complex when early relational patterns may be so different from the prevailing Western/European norm. The intersubjective field is much more complicated when taking into account multi-cultural factors. The more remote a culture is from our own, the more difficult it becomes to make such differential diagnoses. Our focus becomes one of assuming less and inquiring more. Even if a client "explains" their context to us, we still can never "inhabit" the phenomenological experience of their context, and so the contextual flavor of an action or thought is more difficult to assess.

Historical Antecedents

We draw on several historical antecedents for thinking contextually. Field theory and dynamic systems theory are helpful paradigms in this endeavor, both emphasizing interconnectedness and the mutuality of influence; the notion that any movement, anywhere, changes the meaning of the whole. Our thinking is also informed by the hermeneutic tradition, a philosophical stance which, according to Gadamer (Orange, 1997) means that we only "understand from within the context and perspective of tradition...and that 'there is no understanding in isolation'" (Orange, 1997: 72). Gadamer asserts that our subjective "prejudices" are inevitable and must be tested in dialogue (Sapriel, 1998: 43). From the humanistic-existential tradition, we draw from Husserl's phenomenology and its respect for subjective experience, although we eschew the Husserlian notion of "bracketing" as inconsistent with Field theory (Sapriel, 1998: 11-12). What we mean in this regard is that bracketing refers to the attempt to observe behavior with presuppositionless eyes. In a field theory view of reality, that is an impossible feat, as no observation can be arrived at outside the field.

We also draw on Gestalt psychology with its emphasis on figure/ground. From the psychoanalytic tradition, we draw on a more recent relational construct: Stolorow, *et al* intersubjectivity theory, which "...addresses primarily the larger relational field....[and] offers a 'lens' through which to illuminate the personal subjective world of an individual in the context of a specific relationship with a specific other" (Sapriel, 1998: 2). In this context, we see Gestalt therapy and intersubjectivity theory as complementary, since both reject the notion of the existence of "one true reality." They are both process theories, contextual and field-theory based. Both focus on the phenomenology of subjective experience and are therefore both eminently suitable for cross-cultural application. Schein's (1985) definition of culture as a term "reserved for the deeper levels of basic assumptions and beliefs that are shared by members of an organization that operate unconsciously and that define in a basic 'taken-for-granted-fashion' an organization's view of itself and its environment" (Schein, 1985: 6-7).

Schein (1985) highlights the group quality of this experience, with its shared history and shared boundary (Schein, 1985). This definition is not confined to organizations, and extends to social groupings of all sorts. Using this definition as an analogy, we can see how any individual within an organization or social cultural context can be seen to hold a unique set of organizing principles, beliefs, and world view. We posit that each individual belongs not only to a cultural context of shared meanings which must be understood and respected, but that each of us could also be viewed as a distinct and idiosyncratic culture of one. This perspective prods us to question our assumptions of like-mindedness based on external cultural similarities, so as not to obscure the appreciation and investigation of subjective differences in the meanings of each individual's inner universe.

This issue is commonly seen in discussions, for example, where members of the gay or lesbian community wonder whether they can best be understood only by a gay or lesbian therapist. Or similarly, African Americans might wonder if they cannot be understood by a white member of the dominant culture. Carried to an extreme, can only a female therapist understand a woman; or a male therapist a man? This is one way to illustrate what we mean to highlight; that each of us is individual and unique in our inner worlds, as well as in the structure of our brains! So we must not assume similarities of experience just because of external similarities. Price Cobbs, M.D. and his co-author, William Grier (1968), in *Black Rage*, emphasize this point when they state that even when both therapist and client are African American, no assumption of similarity of experience or personal meaning should be taken for granted.

Stolorow (1997) points to Mikhail Bakhtin (1981), whose theory of dialogic contextualism also articulates this very same principle: "The words most associated with his work...are dialogue and heteroglossia. By the latter he seems to have meant the multiplicity of potential meanings in any utterance -- that each word and expression belongs to the particular language of a particular speaker in a particular dialogic context -- there are no 'neutral' words and forms" (Stolorow, 1997: 73; f. Bakhtin, 1981: 293). Furthermore: "Each word tastes of the...contexts in which it has lived its socially-charged life; all words and forms are populated by intentions. Contextual overtones are inevitable in the word" (Ibid: 73). None of us, though we may come from the same culture, uses even the same word in the same way. Whether verbal or non-verbal, meanings are layered, contextually determined, and imbued with affective and idiosyncratic shadings. Even gestures apply in this context: "nonverbal communication is often culturally or racially bound; signals take on different meanings among different cultures or races" (Moore, 1986: 149).

We two therapists -- one male, one female, both from vastly different cultures, but both belonging to families that were part of the immigrant experience to America -- examine our own personal and cultural organizing principles, in order to illuminate the interface between our subjective world views and the subjective worlds of our respective patients. We believe that the way we have come to understand our personal perspective inevitably influences the clinical interaction in our dyad. We further believe that a dialogic process is one in which meaning is co-constructed by both participants. In that spirit, any case presentation would be unfair and incomplete without also including an exploration of the therapist's (not just the patient's) subjectivity.

A caveat: while both therapist and patient contribute to the emergence of meaning in the therapeutic relationship, the therapist remains the therapist, using his/her clinical expertise to bring previously unilluminated dynamics into awareness. However, when presenting a clinical example from an intersubjective, contextual vantage point, the therapist's organizing principles need to be articulated, along with the patient's. This dual articulation is not to be confused with a therapist's self-disclosure. Though "each is a full participant and contributor to the process that emerges...[and]although the analysis is always for the patient, the emotional history and psychological organization of patient and analyst are equally important to the understanding of the clinical exchange" (Atwood *et al,* 1997: 9). We also concur with Aron (1996) that the equal importance of both does not in any way remove the fundamental asymmetry of the therapeutic relationship.

That said, this paper will also include biographical information from each of the two therapists, as well as each of the patients. For the sake of clarity, each author chose to focus on only one core "organizing principle" arising out of each author's cultural background, as well as out of each author's personal psychological history, to illustrate the co-construction of the dialogic dance. It is understood that many other organizing principles are always in operation, but will not be the focus of this paper.

Lolita Sapriel's History

I was raised bilingual in French and Arabic in Egypt until, at the age of seven, we arrived in the United States, where I began to learn English. Writing on the role of bilingualism and biculturalism as a crucial component of development, Perez-Foster (1996) suggests that "we possess dual templates through which we shape and organize our world...two different symbolic worlds that must coexist, cooperate, and probably compete to ultimately form the illusion of a harmonized bilingual self" (Perez-Foster, 1996: 101). Language is not only the carrier of cultural values, but also of the felt sense of self in a particular culture. Hence, certain of my developmental memories are accessible affectively only in the language in which I first experienced and conceptualized them. For us to be multilingual is also to be multicultural, and to be therefore aware early on of the relativity of personal meanings.

My family was part of the Sephardic Jewish community that emigrated from Spain in the 15th century and settled in the Middle East. In Egypt, the British and the French embodied the dominant cultures, and families of European origin sent their children to non-Arab schools. Since my family was steeped in the French educational system, I attended a Catholic convent school. Although, paradoxically, we were part of a Jewish minority living among the Arab majority, my family identified with the French colonial culture. I grew up thinking I was French.

Not surprisingly, integrating ourselves as an immigrant family in the United States was fraught with ambivalence. My parents came from one culture and we, their children, were straddling two. Contrary to many other ethnic groups (and unlike Dennis Palumbo's experience in his Italian American family), my family did not view assimilation into the dominant Anglo culture as desirable. They made every attempt to retain our culture of origin, sending us to French schools on Saturday and providing yearly trips to France. However, we were never actually French; so it seemed that the Jewish aspects of our culture were less valued. Furthermore, our Sephardic Jewish roots were entirely different from the Ashkenazi Jews who predominate in the U.S. We spoke Ladino (Turkish and Spanish), not Yiddish. We ate dates and rice at Passover (not apples and gefilte fish), and in general embodied a Middle Eastern and Mediterranean cultural identity, and not an Eastern European one.

The idealization of all things French included the adoption of a Cartesian attitude in which all intellectual pursuits were valued: "I think, therefore I am" was our childhood motto. Logical and rational thought prevailed, with a concomitant devaluing of emotional and affective experiences. Simultaneously, all positive affective memories were wedded to my parents' childhood in Egypt, which was pictured as a wonderful, mysterious, vanished time in history. Arab food, music, language, and Egypt itself were evoked on a daily basis, with feelings of regret and nostalgia. The affective heart of our family was Arabic, the intellectual and cognitive center of our family was French. Once in the United States, my schooling, including all graduate level professional studies, was in English.

The gradual integration of these multiple self-states happened slowly over a lifetime, like the gathering together of multiple strands of colored threads, later to be woven into a multi-colored tapestry. A trip back to Egypt as an adult in my 30s (for the first time since my departure at the age of 7) unleashed a flood of emotional memories, and brought closure to a felt experience of a life-long split.

As an adult professional teaching psychoanalytic and Gestalt theory in French in Quebec, I integrated the language of my childhood with the formalized learning of my second country. However, my decision to become a psychotherapist evoked fear and puzzlement in my family. They had no idea what that profession entailed, and it appeared singularly lacking in the all-important security that my family required.

This multicultural background made for some interesting and mutually exclusive patterns of relating that, as later organizing principles, formed the core of my self experiences. My family's dynamics combined Jewish, Arab, and European influences, all forming an uneasy alliance within me.

The authors of *Ethnicity & Family Therapy* describe Arab family patterns, wherein "men are given duties...toward wives and children, wives are given instructions as to how to treat their husbands, and children are advised to honor their mothers....[and all]are expected to view the good of the family above the fulfillment of individual wishes" (McGoldrick *et al,* 1996: 338). The father's authority must be respected absolutely, and neither the wife nor the children are encouraged to explore ideas or share in the decision-making. "Arab children...are not encouraged... to be individualistic and separate from their parents" (McGoldrick et al, 1996: 338).

Of Jews, they observe: "Jews historically have perceived themselves...as part of a cultural-ethnic-national body. Their fundamental membership was bestowed by birth rather than by belief or practice" (McGoldrick et al, 1996: 611). The minority of Jews in America are of Sephardic roots; the majority are from Eastern Europe. However, regardless of the cultural background, in Jewish families, parents continue to expect "geographical as well as emotional closeness from their children," even after marriage (McGoldrick *et al*, 1996: 613-14). Family connectedness is a powerful value. A typical parental response to a child's divorce can be "How can you do this to me?" (McGoldrick *et al*, 1996: 616). Education and professional achievement are central values. Verbal skills are highly valued, and children are encouraged to voice their opinions. Mothers exercise authority at home.

However, there are still remnants in Jewish thought (particularly in Eastern Europe) that see women as subordinate, and men give "thanks to God that thou has not made me a woman." (McGoldrick *et al*, 1996; 621). "In the traditional Jewish nuclear family, the mother is considered the nurturer of the entire family, including the father. She continually outdoes herself in caring for others, foregoing satisfaction of her personal needs...no sacrifice is too great, ...her implicit mission is to work primarily for the development of others" (McGoldrick *et al*, 1996: 625).

In my family, my father held absolute authority over his spouse and children. The Arab, not Jewish attitude towards the woman prevailed. Jewish valuing of education was juxtaposed with the Arab prohibition against independent behavior. Guilt or shame was the price exacted for questioning paternal authority. Both the Jewish and the Arab traditions conceptualized attempts at differentiation as disloyalty, disobedience, or selfishness. And both cultures saw the woman's role as a pervasively self-sacrificing one.

Conflicts between the patriarchal, old-world authority, as opposed to the more egalitarian model in the U.S., were inevitable, particularly regarding notions of freedom, autonomy, and the right to self-definition (now also extended to girls!).

My personal experience in Gestalt therapy highlighted the difference between the cultural "fixed gestalten" of my culture of origin, and those of the therapists who were embedded in the dominant Western culture. In its own historical reaction to the overly-intellectualized Freudian psychoanalytic tradition, Gestalt therapy in the 1970s valued feelings over thought, thus providing support for the validation of personal experience and affects, and a counterbalance to the overvaluing of intellectual processes in my family.

Gestalt therapy awakened and strengthened my awareness of autonomous strivings, while simultaneously underlining the nature of my dilemma. However, even in the therapeutic setting, the strongly held societal and therapeutic values of autonomy, individuation, and separateness at times intensified my sense of shame. Signs of interdependence tended to be framed as "field-dependency," while difficulties with autonomy were often viewed as pathological "confluence." Under the heading of "self-support," individuation and autonomy were clearly viewed as maturational goals. Sensitivities to the other's state of mind, which often resulted in difficulties setting boundaries, were viewed as symptoms of individual pathology (that is, projections, introjects, and so forth), rather than as understandable and valid context-dependent behavior.

These ethnocentric and subjective biases in Fritz Perls' explanation of Gestalt theory were never explored, and the theory was applied without regard to differing cultural norms. Unfortunately, field theory was an aspect of Gestalt therapy that received less attention at that time, and an "isolated mind" view prevailed over the more contemporary, contextually-based "intersubjective" view. Moreover, the lack of a coherent developmental theory also left unexplored early child-caregiver patterns of communication and their legacy, not only in the patient, but also in the here-and-now therapist/client relationship. Only recently have the field theory aspects of Gestalt theory earned a greater emphasis, such that Gestalt therapy is now better-suited to understanding the individual in the field, to viewing behaviors as emerging from a context, and to addressing the individual's ability to creatively adjust to that context. This perspective was heightened for me when later therapeutic encounters from a Self-psychology and intersubjective approach articulated more clearly the notion that "selflessness," in my particular family, represented a legitimate expression of hundreds of years of certain cultural values -- notably, wishes for relatedness and connectedness. Understanding why I had encountered such difficulties in attempting to shift these "fixed gestalten" greatly helped me to decrease shame. It then became possible to shift from an experience of automatically and reflexively feeling compelled to maintain an attitude of utter selflessness (so as not to jeopardize needed ties to the "other"), to one with an enhanced capacity to choose when and how to organize decisions around my own priorities. The element of choice, which had been absent, was now possible.

Cultural implications are inevitable. Had my family remained in Egypt, it is possible that my mother's intelligence, wit, and sophistication, allied with her subservient position, would have marked her as an exemplary wife. I would have been raised with fewer internal conflicts, and with the experience of looking up to a mother who fulfilled her role so well. Once in the U.S., however, seeing her daughters achieve an autonomy she never could, heightened my mother's pain, as an awareness of her own longings, and the impossibility of overcoming the legacy of her upbringing, surfaced. And it was, sadly, more difficult for her daughters to admire her position.

Dennis Palumbo's History

My childhood was markedly different from Lolita's; not only in ethnicity and environmental influences, but in how it was explicated by my caregivers. As a third-generation Italian American growing up in the Eisenhower 50s, the expected and continually reinforced notion was that one's identity was American. The Italian cultural influences were threaded in a more clandestine way throughout an extended family which (unlike Lolita's) prized assimilation and acceptance by the dominant culture as perhaps the greatest achievement, and the primary sign of success as an individual.

From an early age, I was encouraged to view academic (and therefore financial and professional) success as my prime responsibility, and the best way to bring honor to my family. Both parents had been raised in the Depression, and promulgated the values of hard work, consistency, and initiative. However, though my father owned and managed a popular neighborhood grocery store, I had been made aware since school age that a blue-collar job was not to be considered. My options, spelled out quite explicitly, were doctor, lawyer, engineer, or -- the acceptable fall-back position in any Italian-Catholic family: priest.

It is crucial to remember that my family was third-generation Italian. According to the authors of *Ethnicity and Family Therapy*, first and second-generation Italians traditionally looked askance at higher education and a professional life as potentially divisive to family cohesion (McGorlick et al, 1996: 343). The prevalent wish by Italian parents was that their (male) children go into the family business, usually blue-collar, and one unlikely to necessitate leaving the tight emotional and geographical confines of the neighborhood. My father, for example, was expected to take over one of the family's five grocery stores when he returned from duty in World War II, regardless of any personal ambitions he might have -- which he dutifully did.

For my family, as for many other third-generation Italians, this all changed with the educational and technological fervor of a burgeoning post-war America. Values shifted from the more insular, constricted ideal of the "immigrant" experience, to those wherein "rising in life," educating oneself, and achieving social assimilation predominated. The more explicitly Italian aspect of experience was now situated almost totally in the domestic realm: unquestioned belief in the idea of family as the foundation of life; a subtle distrust of non-Italians; disdain for any non-Italian foods;   strict   adherence to rituals such as Sunday family dinners, weekly visits to grandparents, attendance at Mass, and First Communion; and rigid gender roles in matters of work, child-care, and respective family responsibilities. My father worked at his job (which was rarely discussed with his wife) and paid the bills. My mother raised the children, ran the house, and negotiated social obligations.

This cross-hatching of Italian Mediterranean influences and what one might call the stereotypically "American" or dominant-culture virtues of higher education, assimilation, and professional success, contributed to an interesting amalgam of organizing principles. A vivid example: as a small boy, I was once romping playfully with a group of Italian bricklayers who were building a stone wall in front of my house, when my grandmother (the family matriarch) pulled me away from the dirt-and-sweat-covered laborers, whispering urgently in my ear, "See why you must get all A's in school? So you don't end up like them." The fact that I was enjoying being with the workmen was either ignored or unnoticed. Then, in the kitchen not five minutes later, when I asked for a peanut butter and jelly sandwich, I was teased for "eating like a medigan (American)," instead of requesting some more appropriate Italian lunchmeats and cheeses. A double-edged message, familiar to many who've descended from immigrants, was conveyed: be who you are and yet strive to transcend it.

For purposes of our discussion here, the non-culture-specific aspects of the child-caregiver patterns of communication, and their resultant meanings for both authors, will not be explored. We understand that such delineations between specific, interpersonal experiences of the child and his caregivers, as opposed to what might be termed the sociological/cultural/ethnic contributions to that same system, are impossible to sort out. For example, was the pervasive exposure to my grandmother's narcissism, as opposed to her Italian heritage, more formative for me? Similarly, it is not easy to differentiate whether Lolita's legacy from her father was due to the particularity of his character traits, or that of his Arab patriarchal views. Nevertheless, we are concerned here with the cultural matrix out of which certain beliefs were formed, and their effect on the therapeutic dyad, and so such artificial distinctions seem necessary.

This dual desire by many Italian Americans for both ethnic solidarity and dominant-culture acceptance has risen recently to expression in pop media. A specific, striking example is from the film *The Godfather (1971)*, in which Don Corleone, having made his family's fortunes from illegitimate activities, dreams of a legitimate high-level professional life for his college-bound son Michael. "I never wanted this for you," the aging Don tells his son. "For you I wanted Senator Corleone, Governor Corleone" (Puzo, 1971). We hesitated to use this example for fear of reinforcing a personally offensive and patently untrue stereotype about Italians and organized crime. However, the film's resonance with audiences of all ethnic backgrounds speaks to the power of its depiction of the immigrant American's yearning for, and the price exacted by, success and class acceptance.

Throughout my college years and thereafter, my professional ambitions moved along in accordance with the requirement to achieve. Then, in my mid-30s, while in personal psychotherapy (and training) in Gestalt, I expressed powerful yearnings for the trainer to admire my progress, both personally and professionally, and experienced shame at both the yearning itself and its disclosure. Later, therapeutic experiences from an intersubjective perspective highlighted the context-dependent nature of the emergence of such yearnings. In other words, these old longings to be admired and attuned to were inextricably related to the particular situation co-created by this particular therapist and myself, and the ways in which our communication mirrored my early childhood experiences, including the cultural matrix of which they were a part. Further work entailed the struggle to delineate between two often-intertwining poles: my appropriate longings for positive mirroring, for both my feelings and my creative expansiveness, versus a lifelong requirement to "perform" at a high level of competence to maintain crucial emotional ties.

Adding paradox (or is it irony?) to the mix, I thought -- with the typical grandiosity of the young -- that I had rejected the familial demand for professional success by leaving engineering school to become a writer, and ultimately a psychotherapist. Both career choices caused great consternation in my family, the former involving financial risk, the latter being simply unfathomable. However, and to a large extent outside my conscious awareness, my requirement to succeed at a high level in both professions was proof of the on-going grip of the ingrained familial imperative. This organizing principle was successfully hidden from me by my outward repudiation of what I recognized as culturally-imposed values and expectations. Thus, in my work with patients struggling with issues of career success and personal authenticity, I had thought myself freed of these underlying dynamics (and their meanings), and therefore in no danger of what relational theorists term a "conjunction" with such patients. (A conjunction arises when the therapist's and client's obvious "similarities" appear to eliminate the need for further inquiry into the precise meaning of the client's subjective experience). As my clinical vignette will show, however, I was premature in my belief that I had transcended this cultural/familial organizing principle regarding achievement.

Case Presentations

We both found it useful to articulate how each of our own individual personal/social/cultural backgrounds contributed to the elaboration of specific "fixed gestalten," or "organizing principles." We used our self-awareness of our cultural organizing principles as a bridge to understanding the world view of the client in his/her culture. We chose to focus on only one pervasive thematic organizing principle, and chronicle its appearance in our therapeutic work with our clients. We also demonstrate how the client's cultural background impacts his/her organization of meaning and the intersection between our two world views. Sometimes cultural issues are explicit foreground between therapist and patient, and sometimes they remain background.

Lolita Sapriel's Organizing Principle

The experience of self and other, specifically the requirement for selflessness, grew out of my cultural and familial roots. As a woman, the spoken and unspoken requirement was to anticipate the emotional needs of others and immediately (reflexively) provide for their well-being. Their needs invariably outweighed my own, to the extent that access to my needs was problematic. Attempts to differentiate and act from my own perspective were labeled selfish, and when they evoked my father's hurt disappointment and my mother's unspoken sadness and depression, for me, inevitably, guilt was the result.

These pervasive, non-verbal signals reinforced my sense that no personal goals could come before the emotional needs of others in relationships. Causing any pain, distress, or disappointment to the "other" left me feeling vulnerable to experiencing myself as "bad" and "unloving." My dilemma, familiar to many, was to learn how to make room for another person in a relationship without losing myself through accommodation; or, conversely, defend against that accommodation by maintaining rigid, isolating boundaries. It is an understanding of how this cultural and psychological organizing principle of selflessness emerges to co-create meaning in the therapeutic dyad that will be addressed.

Lolita Sapriel's Clinical Vignette

Carol is a professional woman in her 40s, highly intelligent and articulate when not constricted by shame or fear. She was referred to me because of her long-standing depression after several prior therapies. Inquiry into her cultural background revealed that she came from a white, conservative evangelical Christian family, and that she was raised in a typical American city, in a middle-class neighborhood. Religious teachings held central place for her and further reinforced her family values. Self-control in all its forms was highly valued in her family. She described this control as being on many levels. There was emotional control ("Good Christians don't feel angry or depressed."); perception control ("I wasn't supposed to see or hear things."); mind/thought control ("Think only on that which is pure, good, honest, holy, and so on"); and behavior control ("I was GOOD!"). Carol told me that one of her favorite childhood acronyms was "JOY: Jesus first, Others second, Yourself last!"

She described her mother as selfless, but depressed and burdened; her father as a successful professional who never talked about his or others' feelings. She cannot recall any early memories of being held or rocked or touched, except if she were ill. Early childhood needs and feelings were shamed, verbally or non-verbally, rather than attended to. It seemed that any feeling states other than cheerful ones were there only to be judged as "good" or "bad" in God's eyes, never to be understood or valued in their own right.

This attitude was further complicated by the fact that she was a particularly sensitive child, responding intensely to light, noise, and other stimulation. Out of this interactive matrix, she was left with the sense that her sensitivities were shameful defects, not assets to be proud of. Within the fundamentalist Christian culture, anger is not a valid emotion, as it contradicts the edict to be grateful and cheerful. Her primary survival strategy in this atmosphere was to become utterly self-sufficient, selfless, and numb/restrained in all her feelings. Within her devout, evangelical Christian culture, these aspirations to selflessness were viewed as desirable.

For many years, the cost to her of this state of mind was that she existed out of awareness. The shift from her family to a Theological Seminary came as a sort of culture shock to her, as for the first time she was exposed to differing, though still Christian, ideas. The further step of seeking therapy was another, more radical, journey, since apparently entering psychotherapy is viewed as tantamount to leaving the Christian culture.

Her prior therapy treatments were experienced by her as traumatizing, for various reasons. Her first therapist, who had been loving and nurturing, holding out the promise of hope in a human relationship, died suddenly after only nine months of treatment. In addition to her understandable grief and disappointment, the death of this therapist confirmed her worst fears: that her needs were indeed so burdensome to others that she "destroyed" all her relationships. Two other therapies also ended prematurely, and badly.

For a variety of complex reasons, the combination of her pervasive sense of hopelessness and despair, along with expressions of frustration or disappointment, contributed to prolonged, seemingly irreversible negative therapeutic impasses. Complex intersubjective interactions no doubt contributed to this state. Whether the fit was bad, or whether the therapists involved did not adequately handle their own defensiveness, or whether adherence to certain theoretical cultural points of view led to these impasses -- are all difficult to assess and are beyond the scope of this paper.

Suffice it to say that Carol was told she "was never satisfied" and that "nothing that was done for her was ever enough." These verbal responses, coupled with her therapist's irritation, dovetailed seamlessly with her own deeply ingrained organizing principle -- namely, that her feelings, needs, and her very being, were unwanted, unlovable, and dangerous to relationships that mattered to her. Carol herself believed that her holding differing views or experiences of the therapist than the therapist held of himself/herself further contributed to the difficulty. She was referred to me several months after the failure of her third attempt at therapy. Understandably, she was both desperate to find "a good fit" and terrified of a repeat performance. The first ten months of treatment were marked by hopelessness and despair, and the fear that I would not be capable of understanding or tolerating her. She wrote in her journal at home after each session and gave me the entries to read, always afraid that if I read them I would feel over-extended, and, inevitably, would come to feel burdened and resentful.

There were many instances of trial and error on my part as I attempted to understand her experience with me. For example, my periods of silence (which to me felt comforting, attentive, and quietly supportive) we came to understand were experienced by her as proof of my coldness, disinterest, or even distaste. (Neither of her parents shared their inner states, nor inquired with interest into her own.) We came to understand also how this evoked terror of her father's "silent disapproval and coldness."

Her pervasive conservative Christian belief system, coupled with her parents' unique personalities and relational patterns (a combination of the mother's depression and her father's narcissism), led to the deeply ingrained organizing principles that she is dangerous to everyone and that her needs "kill" relationships.

Carol is thus deeply ashamed of any need, feeling, or goal of her own, and numbs herself, while staying selflessly attuned to the needs of others. She must accommodate to, and be grateful for, whatever is given. To want something other than what is initiated by the other is to be ungrateful, selfish or thoughtless. Her muteness and paralysis during my periods of silence came to be understood by us as a product of this belief, since she organized my silence as unwillingness to know her. Through dialogue and empathic inquiry on my part, the two of us participated in co-creating a unique and inextricably intertwined system. She revealed with some humiliation that she needed my affect attunement (mirroring of her emotional states) to help with her self-regulation. After talking to me, even for a few minutes, she would feel calmer and less disorganized. Yet her conviction that her needs could only be experienced by me as an unwelcome intrusion motivated her to strive to eliminate them, even from herself. Her dilemma was agonizing. The oscillation between her longings for closeness and attachment to me, and her terror of being re-traumatized, informed all her experience. Loss was inevitable, hope too terrifying.

It seems reasonable to suppose that both of us being women might have made it easier for me to understand her experience of selflessness, even though our family dynamics were very different. Women in many cultures are socialized to be the caregivers and emotional caretakers of relationships. In our early sessions, I had asked her whether my being Jewish, and not Christian like her, presented her with a problem, since her upbringing was so specifically fundamentalist Christian. She denied any difficulty with that. She perhaps even experienced some relief, as she had been moving away from the rigid fundamentalist teachings for many years, trying to find her own voice. For her, being understood and feeling "connected" were far more important factors, although she did agree that she much preferred having a female therapist. She felt more hopeful that a woman might be more nurturing to the very young part of her. The difference in our religious upbringings continued to not be foreground between us.

The presence and articulation of boundaries is a complicated issue in any therapeutic relationship. In addition to the givens of fees and time constraints, there are the myriad relational co-created boundaries arising from the interactions within any specific dyad. As the therapist expresses his/her boundary, he/she also experiences an internal subjective meaning in the very act of setting such boundaries. The therapist needs to remain self-reflective of his/her subjective experience in relation to the client, and must also explore with the client the meaning any boundary may have for them (their phenomenology). Many things can happen when there is a consistent difference between the two subjective meanings each participant may give to the existence of a boundary.

When a patient consistently and intensely holds a view of the therapist that is quite different from the view the therapist has of herself/himself, the therapist's external boundaries may appear intact, but internally the therapist's sense of self may be compromised. A traumatized or abused client, for example, might experience a therapist's boundaries as cruel and the therapist as a perpetrator, while the therapist is experiencing herself/himself as kind and caring. To withstand being perceived so differently from one's own self-experience requires a strong and cohesive sense of self. A therapist who has not worked through specific early vulnerabilities and organizing principles, could over time, be triggered by a client who presents unworked-through early vulnerabilities of her/his own. If these differing and converging organizing principles from both participants are left unrecognized and out of awareness, they can never become a constructive part of the therapeutic dialogue, and, instead, will create an unbridgeable negative therapeutic impasse between the two participants. If these impasses are not successfully resolved, the therapist is unable to inquire empathically into the client's experience, because he/she is engaged in a defensive self-protective mode.

Carol believed that her two prior therapists had unknowingly over-extended themselves and, in her words, tried to give her what she needed, in the hope that this would help her deep depression. When their attempts did not give her what, in their estimation, she needed, and she remained upset with them or experienced continuing episodes of hopelessness, they reported that their experience of caring for her felt rejected. Again, for complex reasons not within the scope of this paper, premature termination was the result.

In order for me not to repeat these earlier therapeutic failures, I had to keep several thoughts in mind. The idea of differing but equally valid subjective realities had to remain foreground. I also had to remain aware of my authentic interpersonal boundaries with her, and not overstep them. My cultural and psychological organizing principle of selflessness was pervasively evoked and challenged. Several other cultural variables appeared to play a role as well. Her Christian religious upbringing, coupled with my Jewish/Arab upbringing, including our experiences as women, played a foreground role in our co-creation of meaning. My susceptibility to experiencing myself as uncaring, if I acted according to my priorities, when faced with her evident distress, might lead me to accommodate her, and then later harbor resentment, labeling her needs as too demanding. (This dynamic is not limited to the therapeutic relationship!)

Given my cultural background where female selflessness was elevated to sainthood status, any situation in which I made my needs a priority over hers (vacations, weekends, phone calls, and so forth) could evoke my dilemma. It became crucial to maintain an on-going stance of self-reflection. My sense of hopefulness lay in my desire to constantly understand her experience, rather than in a desire to fix, alter, or change her experience, (a tendency that might more accurately reflect a desire to decrease a painful self-state in me). Change does not occur by attempting to change the other's state of mind or belief, but by acceptance of what is.

Carol's responses to my limits are always mixed. She feels reassured and less lethal when I am not just selfless. To her, it must mean I'm able to take care of myself. Yet she also despairs, as it reactivates the dread that I will be so rigid that I will make no room for her and her needs. I call this the "there is room for only one person in this relationship" scenario. She has no blueprint for mutuality. She has told me many times that there was no negotiating or dialogue or protest possible in her family. She is also struggling with her internal cultural and religious requirement for selflessness and is therefore deeply ashamed whenever she needs me or brings herself to ask me for anything (such as to read her journal or a letter). If I appear tired in the session, she reflexively goes mute as she experiences herself as ashamed and bad for wanting anything from me at that moment. She is held prisoner by tight, invisible, and deeply ingrained religious and cultural webs.

Though my cultural background is very different, I can use my prior experience of cultural and gender-based reflexive selflessness to better understand hers. While hopefully no longer a prisoner of my own organizing principle, its echoes in my psyche allow me to attune to her painful dilemma: must she give up herself to have another; or give up the hope of another to keep herself? The field between us is constantly being re-configured in a dance of mutual regulation. My compassion for her distress must not lead me to overextend myself. On the other hand, adopting rigid rules of therapeutic behavior is not the answer either, as it would preclude my remaining open to her and the constantly re-configured field. Rather, my focus remains one of inquiring into and appreciating her experience.

I concur with Orange's 1997 statement that my stance be one of "continual self-reflection on the inevitable involvement of the analyst's own personal subjectivity....and [that] the stance of empathic-introspective inquiry...not seek to avert, minimize, or disavow the impact of the analyst's psychological organization on the patient's experience. Instead, it recognizes this impact as inherent to the profoundly intersubjective nature of the analytic dialogue and seeks consistently to *analyze* it" (Orange, 1997: 44).

Two examples illustrate this point. Early in our treatment, Carol expressed a fear that my drinking coffee during our early morning sessions meant that I could not be present for her. She "felt dropped" when my attention shifted. This was expressed with shame and terror that I would find her "too difficult" to be with. My powerful cultural dilemma was immediately evoked: whether to alleviate her evident distress by altering my behavior, or to maintain my habit and the comfort I derived from my first cup of coffee. It is important to note that she was not requiring I change my habits. What was being explored was an internal subjective state within both the therapist (my internal, culturally-based self-requirement to do everything possible to alleviate her distress) and the client (her subjective experience).

Since I was aware that I could not (without resentment) give up my coffee during our session, I needed to tolerate her distress non-defensively so that I could explore her longing to be close to me, to have my undivided attention. This required me to have within me an alternative organizing principle besides the one I grew up with; one that did not lead to my experiencing myself as bad or cruel if I put my needs over hers. Over the next few sessions, we explored the meaning of her subjective experience (without eliminating my phenomenology). We also explored her phenomenology, without eliminating my behavior.

After these sessions, Carol wrote in her journal: "I'm impressed that you don't seem to get upset when I feel bad..., even hopeless. I guess my hope is that you are one of these people who has (is it possible?) learned that feelings don't destroy or kill, they just exist to tell us more about ourselves.... [T]hey can even be welcomed by another person who doesn't share them (differences) (if that person cares about you at all)...." When I suggested that she "test the waters" by letting me know whenever she became aware of a difference with me, she responded with excitement and terror. She said, "Maybe this is something I can finally learn how to do: anger, conflicting needs, disagreement." We explored how, in her family, the eradication of personal differences had become the goal.

The second example had to do with her need for contact between our sessions (especially over my 3-day weekends). Without our felt connection, her ability to self-regulate disintegrated and she was less able to function, as all her psychic energy was funneled into self-regulation (eating, drinking, sleeping, calming herself, and so forth) Looking at this need contextually, we explored the various ways prior therapists had responded to her. One wouldn't work on weekends or make contact during long vacation breaks. (Carol felt starved in this relationship.)   Another exchanged messages with her every day and on weekends, and spoke with her for ten minutes every Sunday. This therapist later expressed resentment about "all I've given you." Her first therapist called her and spoke with her even when out of town on vacations, appearing genuinely willing and not burdened; unfortunately, this was the therapist who died suddenly.

Mindful of the necessity to be as authentic as possible with my boundaries, while still listening to her needs, we gradually, over a period of many months, co-constructed a rhythm of our own.   I acknowledged that having working phone sessions on the long weekend or on my vacations would not work for me. But I could see how my work schedule was not ideal for her needs. I was willing, therefore, to exchange messages with her. She could leave as many as she needed to, and I would respond at my convenience.   This evolved to usually once a day when we did not meet. On occasion, I called her directly and spoke with her. When this was done out of desire on my part, and not as a requirement of my being self-less, it presented no problem for me, and was helpful to her.

The multiple meanings given to our contact between sessions must also be understood and differentiated. There is a figure/ground relationship between two different functions that are being served, sometimes simultaneously, by my various responses to her.   One function of my responsiveness is a mirroring of her early emotional developmental needs and feelings; that is, early affect attunement. When our connection and bond were in place along this dimension, her ability to be calm and productive increased. The other aspect of my response is less obvious: namely, the meta-communication that if I were willing to leave messages for her (or touch her, or read her journals), it *must* mean that she was not repulsive or too dangerous.

Her fear/conviction that she was repulsive, or "too much," could be activated any time I called later than usual; or chose not to call on any particular day, or to remain silent during an emotional moment. This fear could not be addressed merely by my providing the desired response, since whenever I discontinued this, or failed to leave a message at a particular time of day, the conviction of her own inherent repulsiveness and dangerousness would resurface.

Stolorow (1997) describes the longing to be loved, held, and comforted as a natural developmental need; whereas the need to be constantly reassured that one is not inherently repulsive is an example of something gone awry. The figure/ground relationship between the two functions changes moment-to-moment, but both are always present. Together, we have come to understand her need to be included in my mind and heart as possibly an evocation of unmet childhood longings to be central in her busy, depleted, depressed, mother's thoughts. Winnicott (1989) refers to this as a longing to be the center of maternal preoccupation. Such an early child/caregiver configuration leads her to feel that she will inevitably exhaust my good will, or my physical and psychic resources, thereby proving her fear that she is deadly.

Conclusion

One final example: our work together had started at the time of my mother's death. Her own mother had died a few years before. Her much loved therapist had died the same month as my mother; several years prior.   So death entered our dialogue very early on. In one poignant session, in which we each, together, cried for our dead mothers, the unique and different meanings emerging from our cultural organizing principles were once again visible. Given my organizing principle, I became concerned that I had intruded on her session with my feelings (an example of my cultural assumption that empathy requires selflessness). My inquiry about this revealed that Carol had in fact felt reassured, comforted, and felt "met" by my willingness to show and share my inner experience. Simultaneously, her requirement of selflessness meant that she worried that the expression of her intense feelings would be experienced by me as coercing me into feeling something I didn't want to feel!

Summary

Our two organizing principles emerged again in the very process of talking together about my writing this vignette. In addition to meeting as two women from two vastly different social and religious backgrounds, we also represent the two different cultures of therapist and client. I worried that my writing needs would be intruding on her therapy. She seemed to respond enthusiastically, and participated fully in the process. However, further inquiry on my part revealed that my request had also re-activated a familiar organizing principle: once again, here she was having to put herself aside to take care of me and my needs. Both perspectives were true. The acknowledgement and appreciation of these differences was all that was required. No attempt was made to change or eradicate them.

Discussion of Case Vignette by Dennis Palumbo

Lolita has done a great job of delineating the ways in which a pervasive organizing principle, constellated around the idea of selflessness, was both interpersonally and culturally promulgated in therapist and patient, creating the potential for very different meanings to be assigned to a dyadic exchange. The therapist's silent attentiveness, which to her reflected an attempt to attune without judgment to Carol's affect states, was perceived (and organized) by the patient as a distancing, or lack of interest. Given the subject of this paper, what comes to mind for me is that Carol and Lolita, in this context, often co-created and lived within a subculture of selflessness. Each person's respective concept of selflessness – that is, its dimensions, origins, goals, and assumptions -- was different, a result of their differing families and cultural backgrounds. But the idea of selflessness, and its elevated status in each one's personal organization of experience, was a shared one. Thus, for both of them, negotiating meanings within this subculture of selflessness was particularly difficult.

The benefit of Lolita's own therapeutic work, especially involving the setting of appropriate boundaries, was evident in her ability to investigate the meaning of this boundary-setting for her patient. Here, I must confess, whether as a function of my being a male, or the elevated position my own intellectual and aesthetic pursuits had in my family, I would have been less inclined to explain or negotiate my boundary requirements. Since one of the ways my scholastic achievements were supported and encouraged in my family was for me to regularly go upstairs, shut the door on everything (and everybody) and study, I have a well-defined sense of my own requirements for personal space. Had I been a female in that same Italian family, regardless of aptitude or inclination, I doubt whether so much attention and appreciation would have been paid to my need for solitude.

One the other hand, and at the risk of a certain political incorrectness, what I imagine would be a difference in the way Lolita and I handle boundary-setting with a patient could merely be a "man/woman thing." Regardless of our two cultural backgrounds, and the particular dynamics in our families of origin, she and I live in a dominant culture wherein men are more often socialized to prioritize in favor of their goals, intentions, and immediate needs. For example, in the case of setting boundaries with the patient, a male therapist might find it less difficult to see his need for boundaries as an a priori given.

His clarity and lack of conflict around this area may derive from his reflected awareness of certain appropriate therapeutic goals of the treatment, or they may derive primarily from his being male; hence, his being accustomed to the idea that his goals and intentions are valid merely because they exist. Moreover, in such a scenario, a male therapist might find a female patient correspondingly less willing to confront him about perceived hurt or disappointment when faced with boundary requirements she finds distancing or abandoning.

From a relational perspective, an understanding of such issues is crucial if effective treatment across cultural divides is to occur. Regardless of the context, any two people in a relationship co-create a vehicle that illuminates, whether in or out of conscious awareness, concentric circles of meanings and assumptions.

These meanings themselves derive from the different origins in each one's personal and ethnic background. In other words, what we then observe are cultures within cultures, of shifting and reciprocal influence. As obvious as the sometimes unbridgeable chasm between male and female may be, also as subtle may be the differentiation between the ways one's concepts of selflessness informs one's affects, beliefs, and choices.

Any therapy starts a journey whose ultimate destination is not known. As previously noted, "Gadamer...states that 'the more genuine a conversation is, the less its conduct lies within the will of either partner.... [A] conversation has a spirit of its own.... [I]t allows something to emerge' "(Sapriel, 1998: 35).

This next vignette illustrates the direction of the therapeutic conversation that emerged when Dennis' central organizing principle was evoked with his patient's organizing principle. His dilemma was very different from Lolita's, however, centering more around a conjunction; an unspoken assumption of similarity between therapist and patient.

Dennis Palumbo's Organizing Principle

The predominant, often-articulated theme of my childhood was my parents' expectations of me in the world of achievement. Obvious dominant-culture markers were clearly defined and cherished: excellent school grades, with the resultant rewards and community appreciation; a high-level professional job, at which one rose to prominence; and a resultant social acceptance and assimilation. I recall that my mother often stated, though couching her words in humor that her goal for me was to be on the cover of *Time Magazine*. (Needless to say, I haven't made it yet.)

As I noted previously, however, my rebellious college years included the abandonment of engineering school and a fairly typical renunciation of my family's values, religion, and politics. (This was the 60s, after all.) As a professional writer, and then later a therapist, I've often continued to see myself as standing somewhat outside conventional thinking -- an iconoclast unfettered by the dictates of middle-class Italian aspirations toward social success and adulation.

Obviously, this somewhat grandiose self-ideal masked the depth and inextricable power of early childhood and cultural patterns of interaction that formed a potent organizing principle: namely, my requirement to succeed at a high level, regardless of what field of endeavor. This achievement was the necessary condition for me to feel worthwhile, cherished, and loveable. Therefore, even my rebellion (in career choice, politics, and values) had to be of a sufficiently well-thought-out nature, appropriately appreciated by peers, sufficiently enraging and inexplicable to family members. In short, I am my parents' son: I want my writing to be widely read; I want my work with patients to be successful, both for them and for me.

In the following vignette, we'll see how my struggle to keep this organizing principle in awareness contributed to a dilemma with a patient whose issues I somewhat grandly assumed I knew about all too well.

Dennis Palumbo's Clinical Vignette

Within minutes of my first session with Stan, a stocky man in his early 40s, he was telling me in great detail about his experiences growing up Jewish. Both his parents were professionals (physicians), as was his sister (an attorney), and he'd been aware since childhood that "great things were expected" of him. He'd been in therapy on and off for years, always with Jewish therapists, "who I knew would understand me," he explained. Since he knew I was Italian (he'd asked; I'd answered), I wondered aloud if he was worried that I wouldn't understand him. He laughed and said no, that we probably had the same kind of mothers: "Italian mothers are just Jewish mothers who can cook," he said.

Stan came into therapy complaining of depression and anxiety, the result, in his view, of painful career issues. He was divorced, struggling financially, and living in a small apartment that he described as "the stereotypical starving artist's garret." He was a published poet and novelist, but while his work had been well-received critically, he'd had little commercial success.

He claimed now to be uninterested in his writing, that it had all amounted to nothing. "I've wasted my life" was a common refrain in our early sessions together. "I used to think I was a failure because I'd tried to be a real artist, instead of some commercial hack," he explained. "But the truth is, I don't know if I'm really comfortable with the idea of success. Or at least, success as an artist. I should be doing something important in my life."

This theme of "doing something important" was woven throughout his conflicts around ambition and achievement. As a boy, growing up in a wealthy, socially-connected family, he'd been embarrassed by their money and big home. He was a self-described radical in college, marching against the Vietnam War and for civil rights. He thought then, and through his 20s, that a life "in the margins" of society, as an uncompromising artist, was the path of honor.

Naturally, he explained, this went against the wishes and hopes of his parents (particularly his dominating father), who'd envisioned a professional career for their son. From his mother, he received a shaming dual message regarding his feelings. He recalled in session the many times his mother, sensing his anguish over some scholastic or political issue, would urge him to share his concerns. Then, later on, seemingly burdened by his affective states, she'd protest, "Why did you have to unload on me?" "Maybe she was right," Stan said. "With me, nothing can ever be easy."

Later, his marriage to a woman who wanted a more stable life, including children, unraveled, largely because of his inability to resolve his central dilemma: career success versus artistic integrity. His wife saw his struggles in more mundane, though perhaps painfully astute terms: "You're addicted to struggle," she'd insisted.

Now, two months into the therapy, he felt frozen at a personal impasse: the conflict between deeply-rooted, familial (and, in his mind, specifically Jewish) requirements for high-level success, versus the pristine self-ideal of political/artistic integrity. The inability to integrate these two concepts leads often to self-loathing, which is itself expressed in almost grandiose terms: noble failure as a guiding image.

While our work together seemed at times unfocused or repetitive, our relationship was viewed by both of us as very congenial; we obviously liked each other, but more salient was a genuine intellectual/political/artistic kinship. We often discussed films, books, and the political scene with the relish of two academic colleagues of long acquaintance.

Moreover, I was aware (though did not disclose) that aspects of his narcissistic injury were due to elements in his childhood, particularly those revolving around parental expectations, that were similar to the ones I'd experienced. Finally, there was an explicit understanding between us that as a Jew and an Italian -- "verbal, passionate, neurotic smart-asses," in his words -- we were able to relate comfortably to each other. He trusted that I could empathize with his conflicts regarding financial success (dominant-culture acceptability) versus personal and artistic integrity. And I did: consciously and sincerely. And I stated this, repeatedly. He felt seen, understood, accepted.

In light of this seemingly perfect match, even to the extent of cultural similarities, I was puzzled at our lack of therapeutic progress. What I failed to see, in those early months of work, was the conjunction hidden in the intersubjective field created by our respective subjective worlds.

As someone who believed he'd transcended his family's requirements for acceptable success by choosing careers as first a writer and then a therapist, I felt I was uniquely qualified (both in terms of personal history and conscious intent) to stay with my patient's experience, to help him sort out what it was he really wanted to do, without having a stake in the outcome. But behind my liking of him, and our intellectual/artistic kinship, was this conjunction of which I was completely unaware: I, unconsciously motivated toward the familial imperatives tugging at him, wanted him to make something of himself; not in terms of obvious financial or professional success, of course. What our conjunction kept out of my awareness was my irritation and impatience with his dilemma of Success vs. Integrity. His inability to resolve it, and, more importantly, his continual expression of his self-loathing about it in terms of being a noble failure were unacceptable to me.

It was only a disclosure on my part one day, half a year into the therapy that the depth of this conjunction was revealed. He was complaining about the fact that an early novel was now officially out of print, and that all he had to show for it were glowing reviews in literary journals that nobody read. He hunkered down in his chair, sighed deeply, and said (once again) that he'd have to be satisfied with being "a noble failure." At that point, with some impatience, I disclosed that, based on how I was raised, noble success was the only acceptable stance. The problem was, I explained, that with the bar set so high, I often felt I fell far short. This intrigued him, and as we explored his reaction to what I said, Stan revealed his view of me as analogous to his disapproving father. "All this time, I always suspected you wanted to kick me in the ass." His yearning to be understood, and to keep receiving the balm of my empathy for his struggles (a provision on my part that masked the conjunction), kept him from ever verbalizing his belief that I was "secretly judging" him. He feared the price of such a "confession" to be the severing of the connection between us.

As we explored his fears about the loss of our emotional tie, Stan began also to make a connection between his mother's discomfort with his painful affect states and his own self-loathing about them. As a student, he was expected to excel, and, apparently, this excellence was to be achieved without struggle.

During one session, we actually formulated it as though it were a philosophical argument: Achievement should be attained without emotional struggle; such struggle is a sign of defect; marketplace success is the concrete symbol of achievement; therefore, struggle   hinders marketplace success. This simplistic formula Stan and I constructed as an intellectual project, demonstrated Stan's yearning to be seen, cherished, and actively enjoyed by others as the fully creative and emotionally vulnerable person that he is

These interactions were a revelation. We now understood how the similarities in our childhood experiences, embedded in a similar cultural matrix (his Jewish, mine third-generation Italian), disguised the requirement I felt to be seen as understanding, supportive, and non-demanding. This requirement was a function of a self-ideal that supported the belief that I had transcended familial values of success and attainment. For Stan, expressing his intuitive feeling that I secretly sided with the part of him that thought he should just "get over himself" (resolve his career conflict) would jeopardize our sense of connection.

Therapy moved forward from that point, with us now attempting to keep this conjunction in awareness. We can now even joke about my expectations of him and about how "us Mediterraneans" have to stick together in a "WASP world." Meanwhile, I struggle to contain my impulse to resolve his dilemma, and to keep in mind its origins in my organizing principles around achievement and around "reaching one's potential."

Discussion of Case Vignette by Lolita Sapriel

Dennis's vignette illustrates several critical points. He was able to track the course of the treatment, and identify the convergence of beliefs that gave rise to the impasse he describes. Initially, the apparent similarities of experience between him and his patient did validly increase his capacity for empathy with his patient's experience, and were the basis for an initial sense of bonding between them, as well as being a source of delight and comfort to both of them. However, as is true in any relationship, similarities can be highlighted in the initial stages of a relationship, while over time, the existence of inevitable differences must become the focus of inquiry. This is where an authentic dialogic process illuminated the existence of organizing principles in both therapist and client.

Very appropriately, Dennis inquired early on whether his being Italian, and not Jewish, presented an obstacle in the patient's mind, to his feeling understood. The patient wished to reassure him that Jews and Italians were very similar (the difference lay only in cooking expertise!). There might be an underlying assumption here that similarity is "better" than "difference." As therapists, we have all experienced how a therapy conducted along the lines of "having things in common" appears to run smoothly, until we come upon an unexpected and inexplicable impasse. I believe it was Dennis's courage in revealing his authentic reaction to his patient's noble suffering stance that began the process of awareness.

Dennis took the risk of voicing that he did indeed feel differently and this initiated a dialogue that then explored the conjunction between the two of them. The patient was afraid to reveal his fear that Dennis secretly thought of him as he thought of himself. He was apprehensive that, if articulated, that fear would lead to a loss of Dennis's empathy. Ironically, as long as the unconscious conjunction remained out of awareness, Dennis's impatience with his patient's dilemma could have been perceived as a withdrawal of that very empathy the patient was afraid of forfeiting. Once in awareness, however, Dennis was able to clearly articulate the underlying process; he accurately saw that although he had escaped the trap of siding with the content of his patient's dilemma, he had not escaped having a stake in the outcome of the dilemma itself: "Success vs. Integrity," as Dennis stated.

Had he been my patient, as a woman therapist I would not have had the same conjunction, as striving for one's ambitions and goals was not part of my cultural or gender-based organizing principles. I might have focused more on the dilemma around self-expression as it related to his mother; i.e., she would encourage him to express himself and then criticize him for burdening her. His working with a female therapist might have more quickly brought up those feelings towards me/mother. It seemed to have something to do with his dilemma around artistic integrity (self-expression) and around not feeling good enough.

Conclusion

Conjunctions can be much more difficult to identify because they engender a high degree of comfort and ease. Disjunctions, where the therapist and patient view meaning very differently from each other, are more visible, because they are often more painful. Additionally, it is important to underscore that in the therapeutic situation, therapist and client may be holding two very different organizing principles, without trying to eradicate such a difference, as if they are agreeing to disagree safely, without jeopardizing their relationship. Dennis remained open to exploring his own individual subjective experience, as well as his patient's. To do so required a degree of emotional honesty and integrity, since his self-awareness and subsequent self-disclosure flew in the face of his own self-ideal.

Overall Summary

In this essay, we have attempted to illuminate and explore two main points: first, that meaning is always context-dependent; and second, since psychotherapists are as much a product of their particular cultures as their patients, it is crucial that we be aware of our cultural biases, including but not limited to, those inherent in our therapeutic orientation. We have discussed the stereotypical assumptions embedded in various ethnic types, the ways in which cultural biases and specific familial dynamics can join in influencing the patient's organization of experience, and the always-present danger that the therapist's assumptions about the patient (either of perceived social/cultural similarity or dissimilarity) can obscure the appreciation and investigation of the patient's personal universe.

From a relational perspective, effective treatment in a cross-cultural context requires diligent, reflective awareness on the part of the therapist of the ways in which perceived similarities and differences can themselves be used as tools to make more explicable the patient's lived experience. Thus, hopefully, the therapeutic dyad, in all its shifting permutations and myriad array of meanings, can be a vehicle by which the patient comes to better understand, and ultimately embrace, the particular subjective world in which he or she lives.

Epilogue

Since one of the important points we are making has to do with the omnipresence of context and its importance, we deemed it appropriate to articulate the many layers of context suggested in this essay, and how they intersect with each other. In our experience of co-writing, we have a Jewish female born in Egypt, raised in a matrix of French and Arab cultures, who co-authors this paper with a white male, third-generation Italian American from Pittsburgh. The co-authors thus embody the cultures of man/woman, East/West, and Italian/Jewish. How did this mix of cultures affect the co-writing?

Our experience of shared authorship can be broken down along various lines. When the culture of gender is the focus, we came to understand how Lolita Sapriel's upbringing in a patriarchal and narcissistic power structure informed her concern about inviting Dennis Palumbo to join the writing team. She was excited by their common intellectual ground but experienced left-over echoes of her fear that as the male, he would want to be top dog, and overrule her thoughts and ideas. Like her father, hee might require her to subordinate herself to his ego. She was aware that this was a remnant of the attitude in her family of the devaluing of the feminine. Once she included Dennis in her process, she had to risk trusting that her ideas (and the words that conveyed them) would be respected. Once a dialogue between them was opened on this subject, Dennis was able to understand her concerns and to reassure her that he would not need to be dominant at her expense.

As for Dennis, the man/woman issue did not appear to be a charged one for him. As the person invited to join Lolita, he was pleased to be included and volunteered that he admired her intellect. This threw Lolita into some confusion as it challenged her organizing principle head-on that a man would demean her ideas! Dennis was more concerned with wanting to contribute appropriately without becoming unduly attached to his own words and ideas. His ego was more invested in his writing than in his gender. And, while he doesn't exactly relish being re-written (after years as a professional screenwriter), he wanted to mollify any lingering concerns about having to defer to him. (He thinks of himself as much too enlightened for that!).

In the editorial meeting between Lolita and Tali, it emerged that Lolita experienced her Jewishness only as a cultural context, not as a religious one; and equal, therefore to Dennis' Italian-American culture. Religious similarities or differences never entered into the dialogue. It was a non-issue. Interestingly enough, the Jewish/Italian cross-cultural context brought up only a positive charge. It is almost stereotypical that Jewish and Italian, as well as several other Mediterranean cultures, respond with a similar ethnic expressiveness. Our work process was smooth and flowing.

As Jews and Italians, we were both accustomed to a vivacious, lively mode of exchange; often interrupting each other, talking over each other, finishing each other's sentences. Ideas came in torrents, overlapping each other in stereotypically non-WASP fashion. Deborah Tannen (1990), a professor of linguistics at Georgetown University in Washington D.C., refers to this style as "cooperative overlapping," and describes it as typical of New York Jewish culture. Even our conversational pauses were the same (Frankly, they didn't exist!). This simultaneity of talk is experienced by likeminded people as warmth and rapport. In some other cultures, interrupting another person while they are talking is considered very rude.

Given one author with a very Mediterranean ethnic mode of expression, and one with a stereotypically Anglo Saxon or Nordic means of expression, we personally believe that such a cultural style difference might have automatically precluded joint authorship, or rendered it much less enjoyable, as long pauses to a Jewish or Italian may feel like lack of interest or rapport. The East/West differences were notable only in so far as they further bolstered the gender-appropriate behaviors for a woman raised in a patriarchal Eastern culture. However, as a boy raised in a strongly matriarchal family, Dennis grew up feeling a requirement to shine for both his mother and grandmother. As a result, he often found himself wanting to seem intellectually and rhetorically impressive to Lolita. Though able for the most part to keep this inclination in awareness, he could still feel its insistent tug at various times during the writing process.

In summary, once we had dialogued about our polarities in an honest, authentic manner and successfully addressed our cultural differences, we found that our cultural similarities became a great asset. Once trust along the man/woman cultural requirements was established through dialogue, the cultural matrix that was easy to bridge was the Egyptian/Jewish with the Italian/American. All in all, our shared experience was one of pleasure and trust in our co-authorship.

We stimulated each other to expand our views and an attitude of mutual respect prevailed at all times. The experience was very pleasurable and less lonely than either author writing alone. One other cultural context merits attention. Both authors were steeped in both Gestalt therapy and intersubjectivity theory. Hence, their professional cultures amalgamated a humanistic existential and a psychoanalytic relational position. These two therapeutic cultures differ in certain respects, and at times both authors experienced a dilemma.

From within the Gestalt culture, authenticity and appropriate self-disclosure are valued and not uncommon. From within the psychoanalytic tradition, therapist authenticity is less important, transference is the focus, and self-disclosure, while not prohibited, is less part of the culture. Attempts to straddle both led the writers to wonder whether they had deviated from the psychoanalytic culture by their level of personal self-disclosure; and had deviated from the Gestalt culture by their attention to transference and their use of psychoanalytic theory.

A final thought: in search of analogs to multiculturalism, we drew on a multi-disciplinary base for our quotes, mining research from philosophy, mediation, and cultural studies, as well as from humanistic and psychoanalytic studies. We found this inclusive approach not only intellectually exciting and expansive, but also a validation of the wisdom of drawing on a multitude of subjective and professional cultural views in the pursuit of full understanding.

Personal Account

During the years we worked together an Arab and a Jew, facilitating cross-cultural groups it was clear to us that we developed a specific model as we moved along. In coming to write the chapter we had to articulate our model in words, an undertaking that enabled us to observe our mutual disagreements and understandings of our model and work accordingly.

Co-writing was a journey in which we rediscovered the milestones we passed through in the years, and the picture of our journey suddenly became clearer and at the same time more complex. We had to re-ask ourselves the question of whether the groups we established contribute to handle and bridge the inherent conflict they were created to bridge – the Palestinian-Israeli conflict, or whether they just intensify it. We realized that although we have assumed particular stations during the journey, each participant wandered amongst them in different phases of the process. During the writing we re-lived the difficulties of establishing and guiding such a complex group. The process enabled us to refine very special and endearing moments, and revisit interesting people that touched us in a special way during the journey.

At first we were enthusiastic about the inter-personal interaction and its unlimited potential, which gave birth to a unique creation, and from the ability to achieve a mutual goal, bridging our two seemingly separate worlds. We reveled to each other some of the most intimate parts of our being, without knowing where this writing process will lead us to, and if we should focus on ourselves or on the group. Eventually we were both hurt and overwhelmed by intimidating feelings, resulting from an overpowering love-hate relationship, attraction and outright repulsion. This level of exposure and intimacy led each of us to close down before the other.

From that point on the focus of the subject matter shifted from us to the group, and we seldom sat down to write together. Thus we felt protected from what the process of writing evoked in each one of us and between us.

At the end of this process we feel the beginning of a sobering and maturing, alongside the naivety we shared at the start of the writing of this essay. Today we face the challenge of continuation. Where do we continue from here? Will our working relationship endure and improve? How can we evolve together from this seemingly interpersonal stalemate? Despite the growing in sobering up of our phenomenological fields and the narrowing of the passion in our souls we both feel very connected to this "baby" and will continue to cultivate this project even though the surrounding is so frustrating.

Lolita Sapriel, Santa Monica, CA, USA
Dennis Palumbo, Sherman Oaks, CA, USA

References

Aron, L. (1996). *A Meeting of Minds: Mutuality in Psychoanalysis*. Hillsdale, NJ: Analytic Press.

Atwood, G., and Stolorow, R. (Editor). (1994). *Faces in a Cloud*. Northvale, New Jersey, London : Jason Aronson Inc.

Bakhtin, M. (1981). *The Dialogic Imagination*. Austin: University of Texas Press.

Bar-Yoseph, T. L. (2005). (Ed). *The Bridge: Dialogues Across Cultures*. Metairie/New Orleans: Gestalt Insitute Press.

Cobbs, Price M. & Grier, Wm. H. (1968). *Black Rage*. NY: USA: Basic Books.

Grudin, R., (1997), *On Dialogue: An Essay on Free Thought*. Houghton-Mifflin Co.

Jacobs, L. (1995) Subject-Subject Relating: An Example of Optimal Responsiveness in Intersubjectivity Theory. (Presented at Self-psychology Conference, San Francisco, CA).

McGoldrick, M., Giordano, J., Pearce, J.K. (1996). *Ethnicity & Family Therapy*. Second Edition. New York, London: The Guilford Press.

Institute of Contemporary Psychoanalysis. (1999). Conference: *Multicultural Challenges to Psychoanalysis* Los Angeles.

Mahler, M. (1975). *The Psychological Birth of the Human Spirit*. In Mahler, S., Pine, F. & Bergman, A. (1975). NY: Basic.

Moore, C.W. (1986). *The Mediation Process: Practical Strategies for Resolving Conflict*. San Francisco: Jossey-Bass Publishers.

Orange, D.M., Atwood, G.E., Stolorow, R.D., (1997). *Working Intersubjectively Contextualism in Psychoanalytic Practice*. Hillsdale, N.J.: The Analytic Press.

Perez-Foster, R.M. (1996) The Bilingual Self: Duet in Two Voices. *Psychoanalytic Dialogues*, 6(1): 99-121.

Puzo, M., Coppola, F. F., (1971). The Godfather; screenplay after the novel by Mario Puzo; Paramount Pictures.

Roland, Alan. (1999) Verbal Communication. Conference: *Multicultural Challenges to Psychoanalysis*. Santa Monica, CA: January 23, 1999.

Sapriel, L. (1998) Can Gestalt Therapy, Self-Psychology & Intersubjectivity

Theory Be Integrated? *British Gestalt Journal,* Vol. 7, No.1. 33-44.

Sapriel, L. & Palumbo D. (2001). Psyche and Culture: an exercise in peer Supervision. *British Gestalt Journal.* Volume 10, No.2.

Schein, E. H. (1985). *Organizational Culture and Leadership.* San Fransico: Jossey-Boss.

Stolorow, R. (Ed), Atwood, G., Brandchoft, B. (1994). *The Intersubjective Perspective.* NJ: London: Northwale.

Tannen, D. (1990). *You Just Don't Understand: Women and Men in Conversation.* NY: William Morrow and Company, Inc.

Yi, Kris, Y. (1998). Transference and Race: An Intersubjective Conceptualization. *Psychoanalytic Psychology*, Vol. 15, No. 2.

Yi, Kris, Y. (1995). *Psychoanalytic Psychotherapy With Asian Clients: Transference & Therapeutic Considerations in Psychiatry.* Vol 32, Summer #2.

Winnicott, Donald W. (1989). *Playing and Reality.* London, New York: Routledge.

XVII. MIND THE GAP

By Talia Levine Bar-Yoseph, M.A. and Nahi Alon, M.A.

Part A: Talia

Delivering a lecture in Vienna in 1995 was one of the more difficult missions I had ever undertaken. I was invited to address a German-speaking Gestalt conference and presented a lecture titled, "Exploring a Meeting in the Middle Ground between Israeli Jews and Germans Fifty Years Later," without understanding a word of the German language. My attending a meeting between 'them' and 'me' (in English) marked an important change in myself and, though I did not know it at the time, it was destined to be an excellent beginning to a dialogue that I still carry on today.

There *they* were, attending of their own free choice, and as I stood in front of them of my own free choice as well, this meeting moved me well beyond measure, and I felt privileged to be there.

What started as another commitment to deliver yet another talk from a Gestalt perspective seeded in me involvement in the broader question of cultures divided by a common history. At the same time, I felt less and less capable of transferring my thoughts, research findings, and feelings to an expected professional lecture form. I had begun to feel a strong desire to shatter the usual forms – boundaries, really – of an academic delivery.

Writing became even more complex for me after the Israeli Prime Minister, Yitzhak Rabin, was assassinated on the November 4, 1995, the very month in which I had to lecture in Vienna. To make things worse on the personal level, a very close friend of mine committed suicide. The shocking phenomenon of one Jew killing another in the name of God and in opposition to peace took precedence over the intercultural issues I was getting involved with. Israeli internal affairs pushed aside any other figure/field/ground preoccupations abiding in me and soaked up a lot of my energy. Israel's internal affairs shifted me away from my intercultural interests, and I became someone different, internally.

However, even though I went to Vienna for the cross-cultural issue, I wanted to acknowledge the changing configuration of my phenomenological field. I appealed to my audience to allow a brief moment of tribute to the Prime Minister so recently assassinated and only then went on to speak of cultural differences between nations and between individuals. To begin with I assumed that a moment of silence would allow me to clear the ground for the appropriate figure. I then realized that an assassination of a Prime Minister struck a cord for people in the audience in a variety of ways. What seemed to be a personal need ended up being a powerful moment for many.

I asked them to shift their attention inwardly. *"Those of you who are willing,"* I suggested, *"please join me in an experiment."* A most suited idea in a Gestalt gathering as such. For a short while I guided them to pay attention to their inner-being in relation to the lecture title, their relationship to the subject matter and finally some sharing of the experience.

"Last May," I then moved on with my address, *"a close friend of mine jumped to her death from the 11th floor of a building, leaving behind two*

young daughters and a husband. For her, it was the only way out of feeling empty and redundant. Her mother, an Auschwitz survivor, committed suicide when my friend was ten years old. Dr. Orit Aviram, my research partner, suggested, 'You could start your lecture by telling your audience about yet another victim of the Holocaust.'"

"I cannot say for certain that my friend was a victim of the Second World War. However, could I say for certain that she was not? Is the answer important or is it yet another interruption to a relationship in the here and now? Or is it both important as well as an interruption to contact?"

"Growing up in Israel during the 1950s and 60s - I was exposed to the belief that it was always crucial to have the answer. Moreover, often the sense was that there was a high investment in the answer being positive, meaning she was a victim, almost regardless of the facts. The collective need, then, seemed to be, and still seems to be to this day, an investment in blaming, remembering and maintaining the victim position."

"A common survival mechanism consists of holding on to feelings as they were after the end of the Second World War. One of the ways to maintain history as "present" is to tighten the boundaries in order to not to allow fresh input. This choice of a way of being results in actively preventing contact. Many Israelis and Jews still refrain from using any German products, and would not travel to Germany. In fact, this is a common phenomenon amongst non-Jewish British people as well. A question to address is how is it that Germany holds the vast majority of the world's negative feelings, as if there were no others who shared the horror? This is a highly contaminated question, especially if presented in Austria."

I shared these thoughts publicly in Vienna and as quickly as I had stirred the pot, I was ready to leave it. However, that was impossible. One can't escape this topic, out of politeness or pain. So I continued relating to my Vienna audience what you continue to read here.

"There was not much of an option for a middle ground, either almost everything was associated with the experience of the Holocaust, or the survivor was simply to be left behind, and forgotten. As the latter scenario is unbearable and a middle ground did not exist, there was only one choice left - namely, to perceive events like my friend's suicide as living, or should I say "mortal," proof that the Jews continue to be victims of the Holocaust."

"The collective, therefore, can maintain the 'proof' that nothing has changed. The persecution, or the effects of it, are still happening. As long as there is a proof that the price is continuing to be paid, the ill feelings are justified and it is valid to hang on to them. This way of organizing the field strengthens the fixed Gestalt of holding on to the victim position. For people who went to hell and back, constructing the field in this way provides a constant reminder that they must stay on guard. Jews have experienced their world turning and twisting under the thumb of a monster one time too many. The risk of relaxing into believing that it won't happen again is great."

It is obvious that what I was saying was a) broadly generalized and b) my own personal way of understanding and constructing the field.

One of the strongest pulls in post-independence Israel in 1948 was the objective of the so-called "new Israelis" to move on and leave behind Eastern Europe in general and the pain of that time in particular. The "new Israelis" were composed of two main groups, each with a similar concern relating to the past. One group, attempted to configure the field of only recent Israeli history, a rather naive and grandiose objective. The other, comprised mostly of immigrants who assumed they could start afresh, attempted to cut themselves off from history on the surface, yet carried the memories of the Holocaust as a constructing experience which could not be erased.

Jointly, these groups presented a strong front. However, there were two clearly conflicting intrapsychic needs. One was to preserve the memory of the past. The other need was to create a free and safe country, detached from traditional roots, regardless of specific events like the war in Europe, or indeed the terror that immigrants from Arab countries had suffered. Israel possessed two polarities, two extremes, with little chance for dialogue.

I cannot possibly judge either of these two sides, their contradicting dreams and mismatched wishes. In any case, if I stay true to Gestalt philosophy, I cannot judge anybody's phenomenology - period. As a child, I was introjected with an overdose of both, and I creatively adjusted by closing off the horror that was too much for me. For a very long period, I held on to what by then had become a fixed Gestalt.

Theoretically speaking, I was a product of an educational system that in my case turned on its head. My overall feeling was that of "saturation": years of stories, horrific pictures from concentration camps, and awkward feelings about belonging to a well-rooted family in Israel (which meant I had no losses to report). All eventually took their toll upon me, one by one. My creative adjustment was to disconnect myself. The intensity, the anxiety and the need not to forget and let go brought about the opposite reaction from that which was desired by the educators: a fixed Gestalt that could potentially have been held forever.

Interestingly enough, the change in my position occurred at a specific time in 1993 as a result of what started as an innocent telephone call from Germany. Cornelia Muth had called to invite the head of the Gestalt Department at Metanoia London to contribute to a Gestalt gathering in Potsdam. The invitation came with no knowledge of my Israeli/Jewish origin.

I was surprised by the powerful reluctance that I felt and expressed it. For someone who perceived herself as not minding, I apparently minded strongly about going to Germany. I was confronted at once by how very partial I actually was. My acknowledgement of my feelings in conjunction with Cornelia Muth's persuasion led me to offer a workshop figuring around the exploration of the relationship between the Jewish/Israeli and German cultures in the here and now. A journey that started from the polarity of "Don't you ever forgive or forget" continued inward to the polarity of "Ignore it all, leave it behind" and settled in the middle ground of "Let us remember, yet meet one's self and one another as we are now."

At the present time, I wish to try to stay aware of my feelings and thoughts, while focusing on whatever emerges from a phenomenological stance. I wonder if I shall be able to hold on to my collective experience and find in myself a welcoming space for other collective and personal experiences. The basic question remains: Is there a way to maintain a relationship in the middle ground?

During my visit to Germany, I learned about a range of post-war feelings and reactions. All the people I met were seriously interested in a dialogue. They were open and willing to try to meet. Some of them, however, were rather pessimistic about the chances for a dialogue to develop. Outside the workshop, which held seventeen participants, I found the conference participants constantly making references to the war. I wondered whether it was evoked by my presence. The people I spoke to were surprised by my feedback, responding that this was how they had always been. Whether this was accurate or not, their phenomenology was of being "in it" a lot and of feeling shame, guilt, and self-criticism a lot of the time. We focused on exploring optional dialogue, at first in a nonverbal and then in a verbal way. We visited the fantasy world of the participants concerning Israeli beliefs. We then explored their fantasies about the Israelis' fantasies about the Germans. We attempted to create a bridge across the two cultures starting in a nonverbal dialogue.

A German history professor was rather skeptical when she told us about her life experience. She told us that some students actually used to leave the room when she lectured about the Third Reich. She started the workshop with two clay bridges pointing in opposite directions. The most she compromised was to have the two bridges pointing in the same direction. She would not put them together, as her friends requested, believing that it was impossible to put the Jews and Germans together.

Another university professor felt rather hopeless when he concentrated on the fantasies; he became hopeful when the idea emerged of using music as a bridge. My last example is a woman who thanked me for allowing her to feel able to breathe fully for the first time in over 40 years. She said: "In here," pointing to her stomach area, "is my history and I don't breathe here. In this workshop, I risked breathing in deeply.... I found out that I could breathe and stay alive." The power of this intimate statement left the room breathless.

Since all the participants were educators, they spoke about the different educational establishments in which they worked. The dominant feeling was one of guilt and of being blamed from within and/or from without. This feeling gave rise to similar polar reactions. Germans who suffered from their collective sense of shame and guilt hold on to these emotions, even though many of them were not even old enough in the 1930s and 40s to be involved. Many of them were not even born. Others were doing their best to push history aside, as if it did not exist. It seems reasonable in conjunction with the above, to look at a continuum where one polarity is the victim/blaming position, while the other is the guilt/shameful position.

As always, both polarities are in danger of being a fixed Gestalt. Each polarity is entangled in its own process, blocking away any information from the field that might confuse or rock its fixated configuration. By definition, each polarity is disconnected from the other. Hence, dialogue or meeting in the middle ground is out of the field of choice.

A lot of attention is paid nowadays to looking at the field. A number of prominent Gestalt thinkers have brought back the focus to Kurt Lewin`s field theory. Lewin (1989) identified that any place the field that is touched will affect the whole field, consequently changing it (Lewin, 1989). The affected field is different from the untouched field. Following this thinking, hence, any movement towards more contact between the polarities will affect the field.

In his book *Gestalt Reconsidered* (1991) Gordon Wheeler highlights the advantage of reaching beyond the figure and exploring the ground (Wheeler, 1991). In support of this comes Gestalt psychology, proving that a figure cannot stand on its own. A figure can form only against the ground it grows out of. In attempting to remove the ground, the figure itself becomes the ground, and a new, different figure now emerges. Hence, there is no possibility of sharpening a figure to dialogue with, unless it rests on the ground it has emerged from.

I returned from Germany determined to seek a way for a dialogue between polarities. Supported by the above perception and the fresh experience, my conviction grew in that it must be possible to bring along the whole experience and range of feelings, and have a dialogue. In fact, it's the only way to conduct a dialogic relationship. In whatever way, however small, one involves oneself in this vast issue, the field will be impacted.

The obvious happened. As I opened up to reconsider my relationship with the war, the Holocaust, and the people involved, I was flooded with emotion. I started to read, think, and allow the environment to impact me in a fresh way. Eventually, I ended up interested in three more defined figures:

1. Offering workshops focusing on dialogue between the divide, hence my participation in the Vienna conference and others.
2. Starting to co-create with Gordon Wheeler a book about cultural differences from a Gestalt perspective. (An idea which evolved to become this very book.)
3. Conducting phenomenological research (1995) with Orit Aviram comparing views of British and Israeli psychotherapists concerning their perception of Germany in the here and now.

Action soon followed:

The Vienna conference was devoted to an exploration of a dialogic relationship in the here and now. As I stressed earlier, my objective, fifty years after the war, was to explore a way to conduct a dialogue. In order to dialogue, one ought to explore and get acquainted with one's own phenomenology. At the same time, one needs to be open and interested in the phenomenology of the other partners in the dialogue. This intellectual book came into fruition—you are holding it in your hands. I soon realized that my preliminary step should be to learn more about subjective phenomenology of different peoples that were involved in the war. Hence, I conducted phenomenological research with Orit Aviram.

Forty Israeli professionals and forty British professionals were asked one open question: "What does Germany mean to you?" This way of posing the question invited spontaneous free associations, which resulted in immediate, unstructured rich and versatile reactions from the participants (Aviram & Bar-Yoseph Levine, 1995, unpublished). We have expected that:

1. The Israeli emotional response would be stronger than the British. This would then create:
   a. A polar attitude towards Germany.
   b. The use of more extreme definitions and terminology.
   c. The British response would be more moderate than the Israeli. This would then create:
   a. An attitude towards Germany as an equal country
   b. More moderate use of definitions and terminology.

2. Analyzing the data we learned that:
   The British related more to current politics: The Berlin Wall, The Reunification, and other perspectives and current issues of the European

community. Though they did relate to the Second World War, they mostly perceived the Germans as aggressive and a potential enemy. They remarked about the Germans` behavior as tourists and their eating and drinking habits, usually from a negative point of view. What was very clear was that the British looked the Germans in the eye, however negative or indifferent.

The Israelis, as expected, focused more on the Holocaust. On one hand, some emphasized that Germany was a negative and evil culture, and others expressed feelings of terror and dread. On the other hand, there was a very high regard and admiration of Germany as an origin of culture, music, and language. The Israelis held two polarities and from both they perceived the Germans as superior. The British held the middle ground, from which they perceived the Germans as equals.

The analysis of the many questionnaires, regardless of the participants' country of origin, revealed that the subjects expressed real anxiety concerning the repetition of the phenomenon, meaning violence originated in Germany.

I could not imagine a book about the bridging of difference without a chapter addressing some aspects of the Jewish-German relationship. Nahi Alon was my natural partner for writing. Nahi and I worked in a rather unusual way with Eva, a Holocaust survivor. We felt honored by her delight to write and being written about. Nahi and I perceived this piece of writing as a rich cross-cultural therapeutic journey.

Hence Nahi and I had made a choice to write about the therapy conducted by Nahi with a monk in a Tibetan monastery as a prelude to our work with a Holocaust survivor named Eva, whose story you will read about shortly in this essay. Therefore, the experience I have just shared with you while I was in Vienna describes the journey, which lead me and inspired me to create this book in general and of this essay in particular.

Nahi's ground contains Buddhist thought and hence we made a choice to write about the therapy conducted with the monk in the Tibetan monastery as a prelude to our work with Eva, so the reader would also meet Nahi's leading support and thinking in working with diversity.

Part B: Nahi & Talia

The fact that one person is capable of understanding another, in spite of vast differences of opinions, personalities, values, background, personal histories, and even different connotations of the same words, is by itself almost miraculous. This is all the more true when the interlocutors come from different cultures that may differ in the very basic notions about truths, right and wrong, social order, ethics, goals of life, change processes, and other human affairs. Different languages create further complications.

The single most important asset needed for interpersonal and cross-cultural dialogue is the readiness to acknowledge that the other person's view of the world, although different, is as valid as one's own. One obstacle to a cross-cultural dialogue is the human tendency to see one's subjective world-view as the 'objective' truth, as absolutely right, hence, to judge the other view as inferior to one's own, primitive, aberrant, disturbed, outright malicious, or simply as an incorrect opinion.

Another obstacle is the contrary tendency to look down at one's own culture as inferior or as lacking. Therapists may be as prone to demonization and idealizations as any other person. Pain, being a most private and idiosyncratic experience, is difficult to transmit even to very close people, let alone to total strangers. Moreover, understanding a particular, contextualized pain, its reasons and its cure, is culturally dependent to a large extent. For example, if a person being helped conceives of his situation as a punishment sent by God, while the helper sees it as the outcome of a parental neglect, the chances for a dialogue are minimal and for a joint venture they are meager at best.

Psychotherapy in a cross-cultural context therefore poses a major need on part of the therapist to respectfully learn the basics of the others' personal and cultural world, so as to create a common ground—without losing sight of one's own culture and therapeutic stance. The therapist has to pay special attention to what another culture has internalized as valid change process. For example, there is little value in using scientific or psychological reasoning in a culture that holds tenaciously to magical views. Therapy entails an ongoing two-way translation: the patient's private and cultural expressions of his/her experiences are translated into the therapist's inner language, and the therapist's responses are re-translated into the patient's language.

The less the patient is capable of freely moving between languages, the more the therapist is required to carry this burden and to 'speak the patient's language.' On the other hand, therapist and patient may share some basic assumptions and dispute others. In this case, when differences arise, these discrepancies may be beneficial. Whereas the common basis makes the patient feel understood and accepted, the difference of perspectives may create a sense of the opening up of new perspectives and options within the patient. Both experiences are essential to a new therapeutic narrative emerging (Omer and Alon, 1997).

Nahi: Many years ago I happened to stay in a Buddhist monastery in India for a period of study and meditation practice. A veteran monk of English origin approached me and said he had heard that I worked with hypnosis and thought I could help him with a rather focused problem. He described avoiding a particular meditation that was vital to his mental training and wished I could help him to resume the practice. I was not enthusiastic. I was to leave within a few days, and felt time was too short to engage in a therapeutic dialogue. Moreover, the cultural differences seemed insurmountable. He had long ago dissociated himself from his English-Christian culture and was versed in Buddhist life now, while I, a Jewish Israeli, had only a rudimentary knowledge of both his original and adopted cultures. I felt that he should ask his own Buddhist teachers for help. I shared my doubts with him, but he insisted and I decided to give it a try.

A few years previously he was to meditate on his past lives. Buddhists believe that world and mind have always existed, and therefore each being has had infinite kinds of reincarnations. Each of us has been at some point an arch-criminal, at others—a saint. Buddhist training of the mind requires elaborate meditation on past lives; he chose to meditate on a life in which he had committed the worst of crimes, a choice made on his own, as in the Buddhist practice there is no specification. (My therapeutic reasoning immediately wondered why this particular choice: Was this a negative self-image? A depressive tendency? Guilt?). He went into meditation (a hypnotic-like state) and experienced a horrifying vision. He saw a young man mistreating his parents. He got so scared with the thought that this image might represent a real scene from his past lives that he abandoned this type of meditation, never to try it again. (Was this a more general pattern of avoidance of emotionally-laden issues?)

I explained to him that in order to see what the difficulty was, we should go back to the original meditation (behaviorally speaking, I meant for him to re-expose himself to the frightening situation in a protected manner to overcome avoidance.) He accepted.

As soon as he tried for the first time, however, he burst into tears. He saw his deceased parents and was swept into a longing for them. Immediately, he got extremely furious at himself. "I go again into tears like a silly adolescent without any mental training, pitying myself, being overly attached, unable to control myself, trying to arouse sympathy like a baby!" This self-reproach could represent more general depressive thought patterns, such as all-or-nothing thinking, generalizations, title-giving, minimizing the positive, and exaggerating the negative, etc. (Burns, 1980). If this were the case, these thought patterns should be tackled before any specific content. I commented on the harshness of his self-attack. He retorted: "This is Buddhist mindfulness! One has to unflinchingly face one's limitations and analyze them so as to purify one's views! I may be a whining weakling, but at least I do not lack in self -honesty! You will realize that if you will keep on studying Buddhism."

I was facing a cross-cultural dilemma. What appeared to me in my own professional culture as a problematic and misery-producing tendency, appeared to him as the only spiritually correct attitude for a Buddhist to take. Was there a way to bridge these gaps and to find a view acceptable to both of us?

That night I thought of a way out of my dilemma. When he arrived the following morning, I met him with a written table, worded in Buddhist terms however, representing my own 'therapeutic' thought as well.

Self-cherishing	Negative-self-cherishing
One is perfect	One is nothing
One has only wonderful qualities	One has only lousy qualities
One is to satisfy all of one's desires	One is not to satisfy any desire
One should ignore all others	One should ignore oneself
One is more important than all others	One is less important than another

I informed him, "This table deals with Buddhist terms. I am not qualified to do that, but since you asked me, I allowed myself to form an opinion. The left column is about self-cherishing. I have learned this at your monastery, and I think it conforms to the Doctrine. Do you agree?" He did. Then I said: "The right column represents your approach towards yourself. It appears like mindfulness, but I am afraid it is no more than 'negative-self-cherishing' in disguise, a mirror-image which has the same basic faults."

He was extremely surprised and embarrassed, but unable to find flaws in my analysis. I continued, "There is another flaw in this attitude. I have learned in this monastery that developing compassion towards all sentient beings is a major goal in the training of the mind. Your attitude is definitely lacking in compassion towards at least one particular sentient being: You!"

Again, he was surprised. "This attitude is a source of suffering for you, and it is this attitude that prevents you from doing your practice, first by choosing the worst past life to meditate on, and than by not allowing yourself to be imperfect." He agreed. Then I persisted, "I think we can do some work together to overcome this obstacle in a way that will conform to the Dharma (the Buddhist doctrine). First, I'd like you to check with the Abbot (head monk) to see whether he approves of my understanding and work. We must be mindful that what I do will not run contrary to the Teachings."

He did consult the Abbot and showed him the table. He approved, and we started working. We met for eight hours in three days. As a veteran meditator, he was quite adept at self-training, introspection, and inquiry, a practice central to his adopted culture. I knew that once he got the idea, he could do a great deal of work on his own, much more so than my lesser-trained patients. And, in fact, in the following two days, he spent several hours meditating on these topics, gradually transforming his attitude into a more accepting and tolerant one. We together got to know his disturbing "inner critic," the harsh judgments it would pass on to him, its origin and the personal history that accounted for its tyranny.

In his language, our accomplishment meant "self-examination and purification." In my language, it was "changing negative self-statements," and in Talia's language, "enlarging the field of choice or reconfiguring of the field."

Only then, at the center of this achievement, were the monk and I able to deal with the specific 'stuck' meditation. I asked him to go again into a past lives meditation, but this time to be compassionate enough with himself to go to a most beneficial and happy past life. He gladly complied and experienced a most satisfying vision of having been a virtuous Abbot in ancient India.

In a different context, would I have agreed to help a person to improve on his or her past-life meditations? Would I have worded my ideas in a frame that is quite alien to me? Would I have asked to be approved by a religious leader? Would I have directly confronted or even opposed a patient's self-view? Probably not. I chose these ways because I thought that they were appropriate for the patient's particular culture and felt confident enough to enter this challenge. In fact, had I acted otherwise, the chances of missing the point would have increased.

Finding a conceptual framework that conformed simultaneously to our respective 'cultures' was a major step in working together. Utilizing the cultural elements of self-training and of philosophical inquiry conformed to the culture at hand and went along with the long tradition of the patient. My non-assuming attitude conformed to my status as a humble student of Buddhism. The Abbot's approval was vital to avoiding conflicting views or potentially dismissing my work as undeserving, and to gain synergy rather than conflict.

"Well," one may ask, "after all, this case is quite extraordinary. But how many times will I be called upon to treat a Buddhist monk in India struggling to deal better with his meditation? This is all totally different from my own everyday practice, in which I hardly experience cross-cultural dilemmas."

We believe that in today's world whatever might have been in the past, we felt that clear-cut boundaries between 'cultures' had been blurred, even though we are constantly faced with cross-cultural dilemmas in our everyday work. One could speak of "therapeutic cultures," of "cultures of countries-of-origin," and even of "personal cultures." Each of those "cultures" can arouse problems that have to be addressed. The case of Eva amalgamates a closer look at the aftermath of the Holocaust with an over-view of a multi-cultural therapeutic journey.

Eva

Eva, a Holocaust survivor, now in her 70s, came to Nahi for therapy many years ago, because she felt she could not cope well with life. Her life at the time was difficult and lonely, her past disastrous. It was not revealed until much later in therapy that Eva was only thirteen years old when she and her mother and brother were sent to Auschwitz soon after her father's death. Her mother and brother were sent to the gas chamber. She survived in the forced labor camps of Auschwitz, eventually, she was sent to the 'living-side' of the queue by Mengele the notorious Nazi doctor. After the war she, immigrated to Israel all on her own, and has lived ever since in great difficulty and pain. She had tremendous fears, her sleep was poor, she would often get depressed, and always felt like an abandoned orphan in spite of her successful work with children. Her relationships with men were complex and often ended in rejection. In spite of those difficulties, she has often maintained optimism, positive spirit, artistic sense and generosity.

Talia: Nahi worked with her for three years and then, because of his difficulties to pursue the therapeutic relationship as a sole therapist, Nahi invited me, Talia, to join as second therapist. We ran parallel therapies for three years. Nahi then left the relationship and I proceeded on my own with the client for another three years until a successful termination. In spite of considerable changes for the better, therapy did not alter Eva's self-perception as a chronically crippled survivor, who would need therapeutic crutches for life. "Hitler has lost the battle but won the war," she would say. "He left behind masses of profoundly crippled survivors whose mental wounds yielded damage for the mental health of generations to come." However, at the termination of therapy, she felt that not only could she deal better with life and with her past aided by the 'therapeutic crutches,' as she described Nahi and myself, but that sometimes she could manage with a good 'walking stick.'

Our narrative is not, and cannot be, coherent and smooth. One source of complexity is cross-cultural issues. First, Eva's Central European culture was different from our Israeli-born; second, her Holocaust past, not shared by her therapists, posed major therapeutic dilemmas and challenges; third, two different languages, sometimes incongruent, "therapeutic cultures" have evolved—Talia's and Nahi's, that differ, among other issues, on the question to what extent should the Holocaust be addressed.

We will present the two different therapies and try to see the cross-cultural issues involved.

Nahi: Eva asked for my help many years ago, when I was a relatively novice therapist. She had been dismissed from her job as the director of a children's crash clinic and, at the same time, she was asked to leave the room she rented in a family flat. Eva was devastated by the two dismissals: her work gave her a sense of purpose and meaning, and her lodging had given her a sense of family

I found that her grief for being expelled from paradise was inconsolable, and that any other view only evoked in her an acute sense of not being understood. I had to choose between dealing with the past and its impact on her present situation, or to deal with problem-solving. I opted for the latter. The problem was urgent, decisions had to be made, and there was no time for internal inquiry. Another reason for this line was her expectations that I would solve her problems for her.

In the past she had been receiving psychiatric treatment, and the psychiatrist, an elderly Holocaust survivor herself, related to her as an adopted child and would, in fact, do things for her a family member would do. After the psychiatrist died, Eva expected me to take over the same role, namely to speak to her landlord and take care of the problem. Her "therapeutic culture" collided with mine. Giving her practical advice rather than being her representative, was a reasonable solution for both of us in this 'cross-cultural' dilemma.

I suggested a line of action. She would tell the family she understood she had to evacuate her room (acceptance of the inevitable) but that she needed enough time to adjust to this difficult step. After all, their house was for her, a lonely orphan, a home, not just a lodging, and proper, necessary, steps toward separation had to be taken patiently (negotiating the details of how to deal with the inevitable.) This argument appealed to her, and she found that it was acceptable to the family also. They gave her six month's time, which enabled her to buy a small apartment and turn it into a cozy, hospitable home.

One of Eva's major difficulties was getting up in the mornings. "I don't think it's because we used to stand on parade at three in the morning, freezing with very little on," she would casually opine. She was completely oblivious to the possibility of a connection between her experience and her difficulties with 'the mornings' ever since. I chose again not to deal with the past, and also ignored the option of medication, because of the mistaken (and arrogant) assumption that hypnosis would be more appropriate. Once we started working as a team, Talia's different perception of psychiatric intervention enabled me to challenge my own. We had to bridge our difference in order to work well with Eva. When eventually she got medication the relief was immediate, and I had another lesson in modesty.

My feelings towards Eva were complex. A lot of the time I experienced compassion and appreciation, both with her current being and her tragic past. At other times, I experienced acute resentment at what I perceived as passive manipulative attempts to make me solve her life's difficulties for her. She was one of the loneliest people I have ever met and in conjunction with her previous experience with her psychiatrist, she turned into a needy clingy boundary-less client. Three years of dealing with her, left me exhausted and angry. I needed help that would share the burden, and at the same time would enable Eva to experiment with a different personal and therapeutic culture.

I asked Talia in. My thinking was that her being a woman from a different school of thought than me, as well as the fact that we worked together and were on very good terms would enrich Eva's therapy. I trusted that together we could better contain this complex therapeutic field. My suggestion was that Eva will continue to have two sessions a week, one with myself and the other with Talia. This was the best creative adjustment in order to not 'desert' Eva, yet survive working with her. Inviting a second therapist, enabled me to continue to be a good enough therapist to this woman who was almost destroyed by human cruelty and was so lonely with life.

Talia: Nahi approached me and suggested I "share" Eva's therapy with him. He presented his thoughts and concerns. It was clear we were embarking on a therapeutic adventure. However demanding and unconventional, it was deeply challenging and most needed for Eva (and Nahi). I was touched by Nahi's dedication, honesty, awareness and ability to ask for help. I accepted.

As a routine, Eva would meet each of us weekly. She loved it. She used to describe us as her separately living parents. She was delighted to have a separate relationship with each of us and cherished the three-way sessions we had periodically.

Eva sought my help with a wide variety of problems ranging from everyday trivial matters to the depth of existential questions. Eva wanted me to be her feminine mentor on the one polarity: to guide her through ways of using lipstick differently, to advise her where to shop for cloths, to answer questions like how to conduct a job interview, how to maintain relations with the few friends she had, could she go all the way to the other polarity, explore the past and incorporate it into the present, how to behave with new partners, and how to discern the processes that would prevent her from growing further. I found her need for 'trivial' advice contradicting to my, then, belief that only in-depth work matters. This was my growing edge challenged by Nahi's ability to see the essential contribution in the areas I belittled. Between Nahi and Eva I was tame. Interestingly enough, the questions of how to find new partners, Eva took to Nahi.

Nahi's emphasis on the present problems versus my emphasis on tackling the past was where the two different therapeutic cultures had clashed. We could reach a limited agreement, and what helped us cope with the culture gap was the respectful freedom we gave each other's ways of working, seeing the differences as assets and not obstacles. We were united in the wish to do our best for Eva. For me it was the least I could contribute to the world the way it was configured as a result of the Second World War.

Nahi: In retrospect, my decision to avoid the Holocaust background grew out of two sources: one was my conviction that whereas work with acute posttraumatic states should deal with the trauma, in working with chronic patients, the first priority was to stabilize everyday life, to strengthen self-support and leave the trauma for a later time. The other source was less conscious as I questioned the sense of: "Who am I to help with this unspeakable history? What do I have to offer? Can I do anything at all?" These were the questions that drove me away from facing such issues.

With Eva, I was at my best in dealing with urgencies that called for focus and dealing in the here-and-now. This by itself would be right had I not denied the importance of dealing with the past. Talia's approach overcame the denial and opened new avenues versus the ones I used. A more balanced attitude then evolved, which helped me to deal creatively in my own way with the past. There was one particular time Eva was mourning her situation as an orphan with no one to take care of her. "My father has died before I was even able to give him something in return for his giving", she moaned." I said, "Close your eyes, Eva, because I want to talk about fathers and giving." (The injuction to close her eyes was a frequent trigger for a hypnotic state.)

"Long before you were born, your mother told your father that she was pregnant. By the very fact of your having been conceived, they turned from being just a young couple into expecting parents. *And you did it without having to do anything.* Then you were born, and just by that he turned from a young man into a young father. And what a change*! And you made it without having to do anything, just by being there."* I continued to describe a young father's feelings as his small daughter grows. With these words I reviewed my own experience as a young father, not only her daughterhood. She knew my little daughter and liked her, and I sensed that Eva would experience my words on many levels. I   tried to guide her towards *feeling* her father as a living presence and not as a far-away memory.

Eva was deeply moved. She visualized vividly, and could identify with both little Eva and her young father, "You know, I feel now as if my father is guarding me from above, as if he is there right now. I know that from now on I will always feel he is guarding me."

And so it was, from then on, even on her worst days, Eva was able to hold on to the notion that her father was keeping an eye on her from heaven and that she was not an abandoned child anymore.

Talia: The Holocaust has been a heavily loaded issue in Israel for survivors and other citizens alike. The tendency of many survivors to keep silence was strengthened by profound ambivalence mixed with guilt among Israelis for 'not being there, for having it easy', Let alone the horror of actually learning the detail of what those people went through in Europe in those days. The sense of having no hope and not being heard coupled with the horror to listen and meet, lead to decades of a joint 'conspiracy' of silence, both in everyday life and in many therapies. Only decades after the Holocaust, was silence gradually lifting and a new and more accepting, respectful and compassionate perspective was emerging.

In psychotherapy this movement enabled therapists to be released from the guilty stance of "Who am I, non-victim?" to "Help the victims!" and to address Holocaust issues that beforehand had remained untouched. This broadening perspective, coupled with the lessons from the therapy experience with Eva, enabled me to realize for the first time that we all had been living in an "all-good/evil polarity" which prevented us from seeing the complexities of the situation, for example, the suffering experienced by many Germans and the suffering of millions of European citizens who also experienced the Second World War.

The   phenomenological   outlook   proved   to   be   invaluable   for transcending these polarities and for appreciating the validity of different points of view. My ability to open up to the complexity of the field was enabled by the work with Eva on a level of a rather "unaware fission." Years later in 1992, I was gently manipulated by a German colleague, Cornelia Muth, to conduct a workshop in Potsdam, a German city). The workshop addressed the probability of a relationship between the Israeli Jews and the Germans as human beings composed out of their entire phenomenological fields, this meaning a meeting allowing the past to be part of what is. From then on the fundamental importance of a cross-cultural dialogue, however painful, is strongly in my awareness.

It took Eva years to tell me in detail about her experiences in the concentration camp. Once she realized I was very interested, we could approach the matter openly. She, correctly, felt that talking about the camps was not invited by Nahi, hence, assumed the same about me. Nahi avoided dealing with the past and concentrated on improving Eva's present, justifying this choice by claiming that since Holocaust traumas could hardly be overcome, there was no point in dealing with them. I unwittingly introjected his approach, and at first, did not encourage Eva to talk about her traumatic experience. Luckily, the 'what is is' introject balanced out this stance.

In one session, Eva mentioned in passing an event from her time in the camps. She came to the session from her dentist and implied her teeth were in bad shape as a result of her being thrown repeatedly against the sharp edge of the pavement at the camp. The impact of her comment on me was shown on my face. Her sensitivity and need to explore that period in her life in conjunction with my authentic reaction broke the mold. Eva did choose to talk about her experiences and I was deeply interested. The 'rule' of not talking about the camps finally died a natural death.

The roles of "helper" and "helped" were not at all rigid between Eva and me. For example, she realized that as a young therapist I felt that discussing cosmetics with her was not 'therapeutic' enough. She consoled and encouraged me as 'the wise old woman' because cosmetics was one of her needs at that moment in time, and our relationship was a "mother-daughter-type", in spite of the age differences (I was twenty years her junior). The meaningful point for Eva was that I had grown up with a mother and was now a mother myself and thus could support her.

The ambivalence concerning the Holocaust in both survivors and therapists was exemplified in the way Eva looked at the notorious SS officer and physician, Dr. Mengele, the "Death Lord of Auschwitz " who would determine the new inmates' fate by pointing his finger either "to the right" which meat life or "to the left" which meant death.

Thirteen year old blue-eyed-long-blond-haired Eva arrived at the camp along with her mother and brother. It would be decades before Eva told anyone she was but a thirteen year old girl when she arrived at the camp. Mengele sent her mother and brother "to the left" which meant the gas chambers. However, something about Eva caught the attention of Mengele and he pulled her out of that queue and instead, sent her "to the right", which meant life. Not only did he assign her to a 'better' work camp, he continued to 'look after her' but, he did order 'medical experiments' on her body. Towards the end of the War, Germany retreated and healthy inmates in death camps outside of Germany were forced to march to Germany (i.e., the infamous "Death March"), but the weaker ones were exterminated.

By then Eva had significant problems with her feet. She could hardly stand, let alone walk. She was brought to the infirmary, probably as the first step toward the gas chamber. Again, Mengele was there. "It was inconceivable that he did not see I was useless" she said, "Yet, rather then sending me right away he pretended to be furious, in order to satisfy the Nazi camp commander, he slapped me fiercely, accused me of malingering and ordered me to return to the healthy ones. Thus he saved my life again!" Only God knows how Eva survived the March.

Another component in her positive regard for Mengele was the fact that like her father, he was a physician. Eva's father died when she was very young. She missed him and often felt she had repeatedly failed him. It was possible that in some strange way Mengele, through protecting her, got projected on to a lot more than he deserved.

Her attitude towards Mengele was very hard for me to stomach. From my cultural point of view, she was talking about a man who was personally responsible for the death of her mother, brother, and so many others. When I brought up the idea that she might harbor some resentment towards Mengele she rejected this notion vehemently. "He was an angel; he saved my life!" On the one hand, this was a creative adjustment made by Eva, that is, by finding a positive side to hell, she could survive better. On the other hand, this attitude demanded a lot of energy from Eva, and for Eva, it did appear to negate the world of horror Mengele was truly responsible for. In therapy Eva explored the process by which she developed this fixed, uncompromising position, and I explored my one-sided bias. This exploration bridged the "personal-cultural" barrier between us. I learned to accept the unacceptable – a positive side, for Eva, in that beast, Mengele. Eva learned that seeing more of the picture means more available energy, hence fuller life for her.

One day, Eva came to me looking stirred up and rather ashamed. She revealed her awful secret, she was hiding her real age all along. Eva had subtracted a few years from her age in order not to face the fact that she was an adolescent in response to all the difficulties that faced femininity and sexuality in the camps. She carefully chose to tell this life-long secret to a woman. Our joint experience was profoundly difficult and provided no less relief. Eva finally contained the shame she suffered as an adolescent. Opening up to the evil side of Mengele enabled her to address the feelings she had connected to her age while in the camps and I suspect this enabled her to develop a more satisfactory relationship with a man for the first time in her life, at over fifty years of age.

Nahi: A point of acute disagreement between Talia and myself arose when I decided to let Eva out of therapy. She was in conflict about two men she was meeting. One was a simple warm farmer, with little education and limited interests, who expressed openly and fully his willingness to be with her. The other was a well-educated lawyer who was by nature, complicated and very ambivalent towards Eva. He would often miss dates with her and then get angry at her frustration towards him. She was afraid to respond assertively, and would feel victimized and abused. Her other friend got the same treatment Eva received from the lawyer and Eva would complain about both of them in a repetitive, monotonous, whining tone of voice. As always, she would not consider taking any measures to change the situation, and would blame me for not understanding her plea. Maybe, she hinted, I should talk to the second, unreliable, suitor. I could meet him "by chance" and make him aware of both her merits and her needs. At some point I lost my patience and told her that enough was enough. I would continue treatment only if she stopped demanding action on my part, and either stopped complaining and accepted the situation as it was, or else take corrective action. I wasn't going to allow Eva to go on with her never-ending blaming paralysis. "Go home, contemplate the situation, make up your mind and make decisions. Call me only after you have a better way than the one you have been taking," I asserted.

She was shocked: "Are you throwing me out of therapy?"

"Yes, I am, indeed, until you adopt a more reasonable attitude."

An hour later a furious phone call came from Talia, who never shared my resentment towards and frustration with Eva. "Are you crazy? Rejecting Eva like that after all the work you have done to immunize her against rejection? You have retraumatized her by this forced separation." It was difficult for me to be in this conflict, but I remained undeterred. Eva should find a way to re-engage with me.

Three weeks later, Eva called. "You were right when you insisted on a revision. I hold no grudge. I have sent the lawyer to hell and announced to the farmer that we will attempt a better relationship. Will you accept me back in therapy?" "Of course," I said. Eva's old behavior never repeated itself again. It was Talia's turn to 'eat her hat'...

Years earlier, Eva was adopted by a well-known children's poetess, and they would hold reading-evenings together, and maintained a rather adult relationship. After her patron died, Eva's art stopped and her grief was debilitating. Years, and many therapy hours later, she resumed reading poetry on the memorial day of her deceased friend. This opened the door for a new career as an amateur artist. The "cross-therapeutic-cultural work" between Talia and myself reached the next level when Eva started to present poetry-reading performances which we both encouraged. Eva's art was a source of great satisfaction, however, it was also a great stressor because Eva was a perfectionist which she coupled with a merciless self-reproach that made her once again wish to quit her poetry-reading performances. We both supported her in her struggle to actively pursue her art, so Eva continued in spite of her acute fear. As a result of Eva's perseverance, she acquired a modest reputation in her community. Gradually she started to introduce poetry concerning the Holocaust into her events, until eventually Eva's poetry became the main topic

Talia: In her own way and by utilizing our interest and dedication in the most impressive fashion, and by encouraging us to accept her disability rather than assume she'd ever be free of a therapeutic support, Eva found more and more inner support. Eva moved away from her entrenched position of assuming she was chronically ill and would always need crutches to trusting that she can move away and return if and when she needed to. In other words, she gained flexibility, hence the choice to conduct a varied relationship with us. When Eva married a nice and generous widower, it was clear she widened her field of choice and finally applied her learning elsewhere. Therapy came to a natural halt. Her life was meaningful and satisfying at last. When I revisit that time in my professional life I feel deep gratitude to Eva and to Nahi for inviting me into their journey. I have learned through my experience that when the map and the territory don't match, the map is to be removed. Eva challenged any theory, right and wrong, any knowing and sense of arrogance I may have had, by her being. She taught me the depth of the word and this humbled me.

Nahi and I were invited by Eva and her first husband (now in her late fifties) to celebrate her life and the completion of her therapy during a dinner in the couple's home. Yet again, this dinner offered me another occasion to challenge the academic mold of what therapy is and adhere to my clinical instincts. A trait Nahi practiced naturally. We both dined together with the couple to commemorate the termination of Eva's therapy.

Nine years later we met again to discuss writing her story. She was delighted that we decided to write about her. "I decided to come out of the closet. People should know about the suffering and the pain of surviving" she exclaimed. She still held to her self-image as an invalid needing crutches for life. However by then, a meeting or two a year with Nahi were sufficient for Eva.

Nahi: Recently Eva asked me to resume therapy, this time "not for survival but for a better quality of life." The sense of urgency and of constant crises was no longer there for Eva. The therapy sessions went smoothly and were pleasant. Talia and I both agreed that Eva's old notion of the everlasting need for "mental crutches" was mistaken. Now Eva has grown legs of her own on which she can walk, not very elegantly perhaps, she still needs some support at times, but perhaps just a good walking-cane is now enough.

Talia: The process of writing paralleled the therapeutic process the three of us went through together as we each faced the same question. How can we collaborate to help Eva and remain who we are as human beings and professionals? At times we worked differently and separately only communicating and informing one another of what we were doing, at other times we collaborated closely to contain the field of pain and sorrow. Nahi and I explored our differences and made the best out of it. Nahi did wonders mindfully breaking the rules and solving problems. I followed in his footsteps as well and widened the work to explore Eva's traumatic experiences in the concentration camp and the impact it had on her thereafter. We can say that we made a good effort to stay as close to the boundary as possible, talking, meeting, arguing, disagreeing and at the same time respected one another throughout this process.

Finding a mutual language with Eva and the monk, and indeed amongst ourselves, demanded of all of us to meet at the contact boundary in full-awareness to the differences between us. Each of us, as therapists and the two clients brought strength into our interactions, which enabled the bridging of the gap between our different cultures. Nahi and the monk each stretched their perceptions to find a way to include the other into their visual world and this process helped the monk move forward. Nahi and I worked closely in order to help release Eva from the debilitating impact of the camps. This work introduced us to the edge of our capabilities. Only the dialogic relationship between the three of us could support us to end this journey on the right footing.

For me, Eva was the beginning of a one-way road towards addressing the bridging of differences and co-existences. For that I am in debt to her forever.

Personal Account

We were writing this essay for a very long while, agreeing and disagreeing both on current writing matters as well as revisiting historical issues from the therapy days with Eva. Part of our support system was years of working together in a multidimensional practice composed of therapists from a wide range of schools of thought. In adhering to the wish to write together we bridged yet again our differences through deep respect to one another.

What started as a work addressing cultural differences between therapeutic schools of thought, two therapists and a client, Israelis and Eastern European cultures, an Israeli and a Buddhist, also presented a male-female cultural gap. In fact I, Talia, found the latter to be the main obstacle to the completion of the writing. Nahi found my writing too emotional and I, his, too analytical. He ended up, cutting most of my more emotional and less focused contribution, as he saw it, at the same time welcomed 'Part A' of this essay which was written only by me, Talia.

To be fair it was upon my request from him to 'clean up the essay' that Nahi took this action (on Part B), during which he shortened a lot of his input as well.

An existential question presented itself to me. Can I live with the 'new' essay to which I now felt less connection? I realized we were facing the very question this book was born to address. How can one both remain true to oneself and co-exist with another who also has an internal 'truth' to adhere to. I decided to experiment with accepting Nahi's comfort zone as mine. In my (Nahi) view, Talia's ability to accept those latest changes symbolized the journey we took in order to complete this essay. I too faced the need to accept a piece of writing different to any writing I have completed before. I am moved by our ability to bridge our differences, yet again. Our infrastructure to this dialogue was paved with long-lasting love and mutual respect.

Talia Levine Bar-Yoseph, Jerusalem, Israel
Nahi Alon, Jaffa, Israel

References

Bar Yoseph Levine, T. and Alon, N. (1994). Petruska Clarkson & Michael Pokorny. (Ed). *The Handbook of Psychotherapy,* Routledge, London.

Burns, D. (1980). *Feeling Good: A New Mood Therapy,* William Morrow & Co. New York.

Dasburg, H. (1997). Verbal communication.

Lewin, K. (1989). *Resolving Social Conflicts,* Keter Publishing House Jerusalem Ltd. Jerusalem (Hebrew).

Omer, H. and Alon, N. (1997). *Constructing Therapeutic Narratives.* Jason Aronson, Northvale, New Jersey.

Wheeler, G. (1991). *Gestalt Reconsidered,* Gardner Books, Inc . New York, Sydney, London.

Epilogue

We've all come a long way, as readers, as authors, as culturally embedded beings, and as participant members of an emerging world culture, just in the course of this book's gestation, labor, and birthing. In the space of just a few years, we've seen fundamentalism and tribalism rise in nearly every culture of the world -- along with the birth of new hopes, new bridges, and ever-renewed courage by people all over that same troubled world, reaching out again and again to their fellow human beings, in spite of the difficulties, the heartbreaks, and the cost. Perhaps the world was ever thus -- with the forces of bridging and hope so nearly evenly balanced with the forces of separation and fear. The difference today is that these struggles are not local, but global; and the stakes are global as well.

Should we hope, or should we despair? Along the road to completion with this book, we've encountered that question again and again, both in the subject matter of these amazing essays and in their courage and spirit; and also in the actual process of working together to try to arrive together at this destination of a completed book. Together we have experienced deep recognitions and equally deep misunderstandings, including outpourings of compassion and support, along with deep hurts and the feeling of being unseen by a valued other. We have endured heartfelt satisfactions and hard frustrations and disappointments -- and that's all just between and among the authors and various editors of the book itself!

And we have survived.

If we've learned one thing together, it's the one fundamental lesson that, as Gestaltists, we knew already and should have remembered at every step: that felt experience trumps theory and good intentions every time! Translated into the particular situation of collaborating on the creation of a book together, we might express this lesson this way: talking about cultural differences and multicultural experiences is a kind of multicultural experience itself -- and will be subject to all the same challenges, stresses, hurts, disappointments, and moments of despair that characterize deep cultural differences wherever they are held and felt; including, most certainly, being subject as well to illumination, expansion, and the joy of being recognized by another being important to ourselves, utterly different from ourselves, and at the same time profoundly, passionately, like ourselves in the end.

Which is it: are we alike, or are we different? The answer is both, of course, but which is more basic, which one underlies and contextualizes the other -- our deep differences, at times seemingly so unbridgeable? Which one both underlies and grounds our ground of similarity of nature, the very earth that anchors a bridge at both ends, and joins it somewhere unseen, perhaps beneath a river or a gulf of contrast? It's fashionable these days, at least in the academy among non-sociologists and non-psychologists, to say that culture is all, is everything; that because there's no such thing as an unacculturated human being, there's therefore no such thing as humanity beneath, beyond, and within culture. Obviously, the fact that faithful authors and readers of this book have hung in this far together, and will steadfastly continue on to do the work we do, struggling to write works such as this one, across a vast apprehension of misunderstanding -- means that we respectfully disagree with these academics on this point.

If we focus through a broader lens for a moment – through that of the context of culture – we will come face to face with the odd fact that as humans, unlike practically any other kind of life in the world, we are a single interbreeding species, the cousin-descendants of perhaps as few as ten thousand individual members of a single tribe, survivors of an evolutionary bottleneck of only perhaps 3000 generations ago who then went on to populate the globe. What with the vanishingly brief timespan and the near-constant interbreeding since then, there hasn't been a moment for species divergence of any significance at all. We are all of us what we were a mere 100,000 years ago: meaning-making, storytelling, scenario-planning, imaginative apes, inspired with spirit and animated by the instincts of deep attachment, sociability, and collective recognition. Nor are these instincts wholly original to us: all of them are shared with our closest ape-cousins, and to varying degrees with all our more distant mammal kin.

What does that mean for us today? It means that a simple children's tale from the deserts of Asia can be lifted out and retold with the same enthralling effect to the children in a township in South Africa, or to an Inuit tribe in Canada. It means that the eyes of a parent may fill with unstoppable tears in Arizona or Argentina, from just seeing the pictures of a parent weeping uncontrollably over a lost child in Sri Lanka, Angola, or Iraq. It means that two lovers' eyes can meet on a lane in Brazil, thousands of miles from either of their homes, and they may defy everything -- family, religion, culture, law itself -- to cleave together as man and woman (or woman and woman, or man and man). All of this and more -- and yet we can't talk to each other? We're sorry -- we just don't buy it!

This is not to say it's a simple matter, talking to one another. Now, talking at each other -- that's easier. But how difficult can it really be to talk all the way across the countless ways each of us differs -- gender, color, caste, class, ethnicity, religion, sexual preference, etc. -- to the point of actually talking to each other, which means listening? Just looking around at any nation, any neighborhood, and any marriage is enough to give us a feel of the challenge.

That's the challenge that has been taken up so inspiringly and with such rich diversity in the pages of this book. What are the tools we bring to the task? Over and over in these essays we encounter the fundamental Gestalt tools we bring and draw on: the constructivist perspective itself, which explains that each of us co-makes a world, that each of these meaning-creations is valid, and that they must be understood internally first; the transformative power of dialogue; the brilliant Gestalt reminder of holism or metonymy, that the part doesn't just analogize the whole but is the whole itself and that we must therefore work it out right here and now, regardless of the fact that the whole will shift; the profound commonality of our shared grounding in embodiment, relational hunger, deep belonging, creativity, spiritual strivings; the tolerance of complexity, of ambiguity, and of the passionate messiness of life.

And beyond that, beyond the level of "tools" and "perspective": at its deepest heart, the Gestalt model is about hope -- that defining human hallmark of faith or creativity, which, after all, is the same thing, in the end. That a thing has never existed before doesn't mean it can't be fertilized, nurtured, and birthed into the world now. As humans, wherever we have known or imagined relationships based on profound identification with the whole, and profound commitment to the integrity and growth of each member part (in other words, a functioning human family), then to that extent at least we can imagine that same thing now, on a world level. And again, the world we can create together is limited only by the world we can imagine together.

May this book -- and even more, all the richly heartfelt work discussed in these pages -- be the shared contribution of all of us to this sacred task. As for the two of us, we began this project together, in a sense: one as a visionary, with a teaching and a dream; the other as nag and scold, pushing and prodding and criticizing (not always constructively) to stay with it and get it done. It is our rich privilege to end it together now -- and bring it to a new beginning, by putting it into your hands. If you take a single idea, a single criticism, a single moment of inspiration and heart for our common task from these essays -- then it is the world that reaps the fruits, and all its children.

We dedicate and rededicate these pages now to those children -- yours, each of ours, those of all the authors and editors and all the figures in these accounts, and then the millions upon millions across the world, who after all are all of our shared children also. May we and they have a better tomorrow.

Gordon Wheeler, Big Sur, CA, USA
Talia Levine Bar-Yoseph, Jerusalem, Israel

Publisher's Note

The concept of culture was first defined in 1871 by E. B. Taylor, yet, the term, culture, remains a word that has varied meanings (Taylor, 1924). In my work as the English editor on this anthology, I have crossed a bridge by engaging in a dialogue with Talia Bar-Yoseph, an Israeli, while well-anchored in my "Southern" American cultural values. My disadvantage: although I was well-schooled in my studies of the ancient Israelites, and very up on modern politics of the Middle East, I began my dialogue with Talia deficient in specific knowledge of Israel's modern cultural components.

As a result of this experience, I have concluded that culture is a communication which includes not only obvious verbal language, but also the language of behavior, how time is handled, attitudes toward work, play, and learning. Sometimes during my walk across the bridge to dialogue with Talia, I was acutely aware that both of us may not have correctly interpreted our communications. The bulk of the difficulties we shared in completing our work on The Bridge, in my mind, was directly linked to our native language orientations.

The greatest challenge with this manuscript involved looking at each author's chapter in terms of its overall proper English language structure while still allowing the heart of the author to resonate from the language of their native culture. This process included such rich and diverse cultures as Middle Eastern (i.e., both Israeli, Palestinian, & Egyptian), European (i.e., British, Austrian, Italian) and various sub-cultures representing the American authors (i.e., Hispanic, Russian, Westerners and Northerners, Southerners and Easterners – all of which possess unique cultural variances from the dominant American culture). None of their writings were independent of the author's culture, and as all the authors projected from their experiences, I too projected from my own cultural base as I traveled along their sentence structure(s).

In a world where communication is now instant from one continent to another as a result of Internet technology, most difficulties people have continued to experience are significantly tied to distortions in cultural meanings, and a failure to understand what each had wanted to communicate emotionally with words. In some sense, I suspect we are all not so far removed from the experiences described by the ancients in the biblical account of the Tower of Babel.

Language is culture, and *the* bridge we cross between cultures. And in a sacred sense, culture *is* who we are. Talia's anthology offers you an opportunity to share the cross-cultural contact the authors have made and surely will enrich your life in the future. Finishing this project has greatly enriched mine.

Deirdre Givens, New Orleans, La., USA

Reference

Taylor, E. B. (1924). *Primitive Culture*. 7th Edition. NY: Brentano.

Biographies

Nahi Alon, M.A. is a clinical psychologist and hypnotherapist who also studies and practices Tibetan Buddism and teaches Buddism psychology. Being a therapist in the Israel immigrant society with its various difficulties taught me to cope with traumatic realities, and to put much effort into trans-cultural work. I am also a glider pilot. Email contact: nahialon@012.net.il

Talia Levine Bar-Yoseph, M.A., former head of the Gestalt M.Sc. training, at Metanoia Institute, London, trains and supervises psychotherapists nationally and internationally. She is particularly interested in cross-cultural dialogue and has substantial experience as well in the treatment of Post Traumatic Stress Disorder. She has published numerous articles mainly in Gestalt journals. As Head of Choice Management Consultancy Ltd., she specializes in business consultancy, executive coaching, and team development, in Israel and Europe. Email Contact: t_choice@012.net.il

Mackie J.V. Blanton, M.S., Ph.D., is Co-Director of the Gestalt Institute of New Orleans where he is also the Chief Editor for the Gestalt Institute Press. He is an associate Professor of Linguistics at the University of New Orleans (UNO) for twenty-five years and a University Administrator of Diversity Education and Intercultural Administration for seventeen years. He is currently the Associate Dean of Student Affairs for Multicultural Affairs & Student Development. Over the years at UNO, Dr. Blanton's primary teaching, as well as his published research, has been in linguistics, *sacriture* (sacred discourse), and technical & scientific writing. Email contact: mblanton@uno.edu

Arye Bursztyn, M.F.A., is an Israeli dancer, choreographer and movement teacher and he is a Gestalt holistic therapist and group facilitator who has performed extensively since 1978 in Israel, Europe, USA and Japan. Arye studied far-eastern movement forms and martial-arts, energy-healing, body-work and group-facilitation and focused in recent years on Improvisational Performance, Contact-Improvisation and personal growth through Gestalt Body-Process. Email contact: aryeb@013.net.il

Michael Craig Clemmens Ph.D., is a Licensed Psychologist and trainer based in Pittsburgh, Pennsylvania. He is a professional staff member of the Gestalt Institute of Cleveland, and teaches Gestalt both nationally and internationally as well. He is the author of *Getting Beyond Sobriety*, published by Wiley Books, and has contributed articles to The British Gestalt Journal and The Gestalt Review. Email contact: MichGest@aol.com

Nigel Copsey, M.Sc is a Christian minister with a passion to integrate spirituality with mental health. He works with the community mental health services in inner London and for the Sainsbury Centre for Mental Health. He is also a humanistic psychotherapist. Email Contact: N.Copsey@btopenworld.com

Iris Fodor, Ph.D. is a professor in the Department of Applied Psychology at New York University, a Gestalt therapist and photographer. She is known for workshops and writings on women's issues and on integrating Gestalt and cognitive therapy. Her latest project is working with children and adolescents from different cultures using digital storytelling to create visual narratives. Email contact: ief1@nyu.edu

Deirdre Givens, M.S., MPS, CGC, Licensed Addiction Counselor, is the Director of the Addiction Training Program at the Gestalt Institute of New Orleans. Dee graduated from The Gestalt Institute of New Orleans in 1983, and then earned two masters degrees from Loyola University with honors. She serves as Chairperson of Education for the Louisiana State Association of Substance Abuse Counselors and Trainers and teaches Gestalt, Psychogenetic theory and Systems theory at the university level in addition to presenting her unique approach of assessing and treating co-morbid disorders such as trauma and addictions based upon Psychogenetic theory as a primary tool of assessment and treatment planning. Email Contact: DeeAmerican@aol.com

Lynne Jacobs, Ph.D., Psy.D., is co-founder of the Gestalt Therapy Institute of the Pacific. She is also a Training and Supervising Analyst at the Institute of Contemporary Psychoanalysis. She is particularly interested in relational processes in therapy, has authored numerous articles and co-authored with Rich Hycner, the article, The Healing Relationship in Gestalt Therapy: A Dialogic/Self Psychology Approach, published by The Gestalt Journal Press, New York. Lynne teaches and trains both nationally and internationally. Email contact: Lynnejacobs@mail.gestalttherapy.org

Vera Kishinevsky, Ph.D., was born in Russia in the former Soviet Union and immigrated to the United States with her family in 1978. She graduated from Odessa State University and, in 2001, received her Ph.D. from New York University. She works as a school psychologist and teaches graduate courses at Manhattan College in Riverdale, NY. Email contact: vera.kishinevsky@manhattan.edu

Anna Eva Kubesch, DSA, is a Social Worker, Gestalt therapist, Psychodramatist, and also does clinical supervision and coaching. Anna is a an independent Psychotherapist in private practice in Vienna (Austria). The main focus of her work include the following clinical areas: Fear and panic, depression, PTSD, and Second Generation (of the Shoa survivors). Anna has a special interest in Tango Argentino as "image of life." Email contact: Kubesch@psycho.at

Jim Kuykendall is a Gestalt Psychotherapist and Clinical Supervisor in Palliative Care. He has a private practice and teacher based in London, UK. Jim lectures internationally on therapy with young people and therapeutic approaches to bereavement. He has devoted 20 years of work to HIV and AIDS and bereavement counseling and has written extensively on this subject.

Philip Lichtenberg, Ph.D. is a Mary Hale Chase Professor Emeritus at Bryn Mawr College where he has taught for over thirty-five years. He is co-Director of The Gestalt Therapy Institute of Philadelphia and a member of the New York Institute for Gestalt Therapy. He has published six books and many articles. Email contact: plitchtenberg@erols.com

Edna Manielevitch, M.Sc., a psychotherapist, is in practice in Jerusalem, working with individuals, couples and groups. She studied Gestalt Psychotherapy in Metanoia Institute, London, and has a background in education and organizational counseling. She is a member of JGI - the Jerusalem Gestalt Institute. Email contact: ednam@bezeqint.net

Mark McConville, Ph.D., is a senior faculty member of the Gestalt Institute of Cleveland and a clinical psychologist in private practice. He is the author of *Adolescence: Psychotherapy and the Emergent Self,* and co-editor of *The Heart of Development: Gestalt Approaches to Working with Children, Adolescents and Their Worlds*, Vol. I & II.. He and his wife of 35 years are the parents of two grown children, and the grandparents of three wonderful boys. He lives in Shaker Heights, Ohio, USA.   Email Contact: markmcconiville@mindspring.com

Dennis Palumbo, M.A., M.F.T., is a psychotherapist in private practice in Sherman Oaks, California, specializing in creative issues, and mid-life and career transitions. He was formerly a screenwriter, most notably of the film "My Favorite Year", for which he was nominated for a Writers Guide of America Award for Best Screenplay. He has presented at workshops throughout the USA and Europe, and has a professional background in Gestalt therapy, group psychodrama, and intersubjectivity theory. His column, "The Writer's Life," appears monthly in Written By, the magazine of the Writer's Guild of America. His book, *Writing from the Inside Out: Transforming Your Psychological Blocks to Release the Writer Witting* (2000) and published by John Wiley and Sons, was based on "The Writer's Life" columns. Website: www.dennispalumbo.com

Lenny Ravich, M.A., C.G.C., is the Director of the Gestalt Institute of Tel Aviv and a graduate of the Gestalt Institute of New Orleans. Lenny is the author of *A Funny Thing Happened on the Way To Enlightenment*, published first in Hebrew in 2001 by Oranite Press, Israel and then in English in 2002 by the Gestalt Institute Press, New Orleans, Louisiana, USA. Lenny presents his "Laughter Is The Best Therapy" Workshops all over the world. His article on "Gestalt and Humor" is soon to be published in The Gestalt Review. Email contact: Lennyrav@zahav.net.il

Lolita Sapriel, L.C.S.W., is in private practice in Santa Monica, California. Formerly a trainer and past-president of the Gestalt Therapy Institute of Los Angeles, she currently teaches Gestalt theory and intersubjectivity theory to therapists in the US, the UK, and Canada. She is on the training faculty of Ryokan College and the adjunct faculty at Metanoia Institute in London. Her recent publication, "Can Gestalt Therapy, Self-Psychology & Intersubjectivity Theory Be Integrated?" appeared in the British Gestalt Journal. Email contact: lolism22@msn.com

Oshrat Mizrahi Shapira, M.A. earned her Masters in Theater from Tel-Aviv University and is a theater director and a group guide in the community. For the last eight years, she's been guiding dialogue groups. Oshrat is in charge of the community theater projects in the Hebrew University of Tel-Aviv and Haifa, where she also teaches community theater workshops. She has published various papers in the field of Community Theater. Email contact: oshratms@hotmail.co.il

Sa'ed Tali, M.A., is a facilitator who focuses on creating and developing dialogic contact among Israeli and Palestinian Muslims, Jews, and Christians through theatre theory and modeling. He is also a Senior Social Worker in the Israeli court of family issues, where he provides mediation and consultation services within the family.   Email Contact: saedT@molsa.gov.il

Anne Teachworth, C.G.C., C.P.C, D.A.P.A., is the founder and Director of the Gestalt Institute of New Orleans/New York and The Psychogenetic Institutes. Anne is the author of *Why We Pick The Mates We Do*, published in 1997 by the Gestalt Institute Press, New Orleans, Louisiana, USA. She has a chapter, "Three Couples Transformed" in A Living Legacy To Fritz And Laura Perls (1996) and a response in The Gestalt Journal to an article entitled "The Landmines of Marital Counseling" (4/2000). She has presented her Psychogenetic System of couples, parenting, and family counseling at workshops and conferences in the United States, Europe, Canada, and Mexico. Anne's radio show and monthly column "Ask Anne" provides psychoeducation to the general public interested in improving their relationships. Website: www.teachworth.com. Email Contact: Ateachw@aol.com

Holly Timberlake, Ph.D., is a Licensed Psychologist and a Professional Clinical Counselor with a background in community mental health, community and intercultural activism, women's empowerment, and transpersonal psychology. She has been in private practice for fifteen years, opening in 1999 at the Nakaia Wellness and Whole Life Center, Inc. She trained in Gestalt therapy with the master Gestalt therapist, Ansel Woldt, Ed.D. Email contact: holly999@raey.com

Geoff Warburton, M.Sc., is a private psychotherapist and Director of SBC in London, a bereavement support agency. He specializes in spiritual growth through the integration of psychotherapy with the wisdom traditions. His work has been profoundly influenced by the techniques of A. H. Almaas, the founder of the Ridhwan School and Bert Hellinger, the founder of Constellation work.
Email Contact: g.warburton@btinternet.com

Gordon Wheeler, Ph.D, teaches the Gestalt model widely around the world, with emphasis on use of the model to shift and deepen our understanding of self, relationship, development, evolutionary psychology, and the co-construction of experience. The author of numerous articles and over a dozen books in the field, he is the Series Director of Gestalt Press (published by Analytic Press), and President of Esalen Institute in Big Sur, California. In clinical practice for over 30 years, he divides his time between California and Cambridge, Massachusetts.
Email Contact: gordon.wheeler@esalen.org

GESTALT INSTITUTE PRESS

The Relationship Bookstore
1537 Metairie Road, Metairie, Louisiana USA 70005

To Order More Copies of this book...

the Bridge: Dialogues Across Cultures

Edited by Talia Levine Bar-Yoseph

$40 USD
add $4 Shipping & Handling inside USA
or $8 additional outside USA
VISA/MC/AMEX or Checks accepted

Place your order by calling us at
(504) 828-2267 or FAX (504) 837-2796
1 800 GESTALT

Email: gestaltinstpress@aol.com
www.gestaltinstitutepress.com
(504) 828-2267 or 1 800 Gestalt

OTHER BOOKS IN ENGLISH

Published by Gestalt Institute Press

The Relationship Bookstore

WHY WE PICK THE MATES WE DO   **$20**
By Anne Teachworth
Foreword by Anne Ancelin Schutzenberger

A FUNNY THING HAPPENED   **$20**
ON THE WAY TO ENLIGHTENMENT
By Lenny Ravich
Foreword by Anne Teachworth

THOSE WHO COME AFTER   **$30**
By Renate Perls with Eileen Ain
Foreword by Richard Kitzler

SUFFERING IN SILENCE: **$20**
The Legacy of Unresolved Sexual Abuse
By Anne Ancelin Schutzenberger and
Ghislain Devroede
Foreword by Anne Teachworth

Also available through The Relationship Bookstore...

THE ANCESTOR SYNDROME   **$35**
By Anne Ancelin Schutzenberger
Published by Routledge, UK

Email: gestaltinstpress@aol.com
www.gestaltinstitutepress.com
(504) 828-2267   1 800 GESTALT